# James Beard's Theory & Practice of Good Cooking

# Other books by James Beard

*Hors d'Oeuvre and Canapés*

*Cook It Outdoors*

*Fowl and Game Cookery*
(Beard on Birds)

*The Fireside Cookbook*

*Paris Cuisine*
(with Alexander Watt)

*James Beard's New Fish Cookery*

*How to Eat Better for Less Money*
(with Sam Aaron)

*The Complete Book of Outdoor Cookery*
(with Helen Evans Brown)

*The James Beard Cookbook*

*James Beard's Treasury of Outdoor Cooking*

*Delights and Prejudices*

*James Beard's Menus for Entertaining*

*How to Eat (& Drink) Your Way Through
a French (or Italian) Menu*

*James Beard's American Cookery*

*Beard on Bread*

*Beard on Food*

*The New James Beard*

*Beard on Pasta*

*James Beard's Simple Foods*

*Love and Kisses and a Halo of Truffles:*
Letters to Helen Evans Brown

*The Armchair James Beard*

# James Beard's Theory & Practice of Good Cooking

By James Beard

*In collaboration with José Wilson*

*Illustrations by Karl Stuecklen*

## RUNNING PRESS
PHILADELPHIA · LONDON

© 1977 by James Beard
Introductory Note © 1999 by Julia Child
Foreword © 1999 by Barbara Kafka
All rights reserved under the Pan-American and International
Copyright Conventions
Printed in the United States of America

9   8   7   6   5   4   3   2   1
Digit on the right indicates the number of this printing

Library of Congress Cataloging-in-Publication Number 98-68481

ISBN 0-7624-0613-5

Editorial consultant: John Ferrone
Cover illustration by Peter Fiore
Cover design by Toby Schmidt
Interior design by Bill Jones
Typography: Goudy Oldstyle

This book may be ordered by mail from the publisher.
Please include $2.50 for postage and handling.
**But try your bookstore first!**

Running Press Book Publishers
125 South Twenty-second Street
Philadelphia, Pennsylvania 19103-4399

Visit us on the web!
www.runningpress.com

# Contents

❧

# Introductory Note

&

*I*t is wonderful for all of us who treasure James Beard to know that his works are being kept alive for everyone to enjoy. What a pleasure for those of us who knew Jim to read him again, and what a treasure and happy discovery for new generations who will now know him. He reads just as he talked, and to read him is like being with him, with all his warmth, humor, and wisdom.

Beard appeared on the American culinary scene in 1940, with his first book, *Hors d'Oeuvre and Canapés*, which is still in print more than fifty years later. Born in Portland, Oregon at the beginning of this century, he came from a food-loving background and started his own catering business after moving to New York in 1938. He soon began teaching, lecturing, giving culinary demonstrations, writing articles and more books (eventually twenty in all). Through the years he gradually became not only the leading culinary figure in the country, but "The Dean of American Cuisine." He remains with us as a treasured authority, and the James Beard Foundation, housed in his own home on West 12th Street in New York, keeps his image and his love of good food very much alive.

Beard was the quintessential American cook. Well-educated and well-traveled during his eighty-two years, he was familiar with many cuisines but he remained fundamentally American. He was a big man, over six feet tall, with a big belly, and huge hands. An endearing and always lively teacher, he loved people, loved his work, loved gossip, loved to eat, loved a good time.

I always remember him for his generosity toward others in the profession.

For instance, when my French colleague, Simone Beck, came to New York for the publication of our first book, my husband and I knew no one at all in the food business, since we had been living abroad for fifteen years. Nobody had ever heard of us, but our book fortunately got a most complimentary review from Craig Claiborne in the *New York Times*. Although we had never met him before, it was Jim who greeted us warmly and introduced us to the New York food scene and its personalities. He wanted friends to meet friends, and he literally knew "everyone who was anyone" in the business. He was not only generous in bringing them together, but eager that they know each other. It was he who introduced us to the late Joe Baum of the then-famous Restaurant Associates and The Four Seasons, among other famous restaurants. He presented us to Jacques Pépin, at that time a young chef from France who was just making his way in New York, and to Elizabeth David, England's doyenne of food writers, as well as to many others.

It was not only that he knew everyone, he was also a living encyclopedia of culinary lore and history, and generous about sharing his knowledge. So often when I needed to know something about grains, for instance, I would call him and if the information was not right in his head, he would call back in a few minutes either with the answer or a source. This capability and memory served him well in his books and articles, as well as in conversation and in public interviews.

James A. Beard was an American treasure, and his books remain the American classics that deserve an honored place on the shelves of everyone who loves food.

—*Julia Child*
*April 1, 1999*

# Foreword

※

*I* miss James Beard. I miss the many classes that we taught together in San Francisco and New York. In San Francisco, we taught for weeks at a time in a temporary kitchen set up by Chuck Williams of Williams-Sonoma in a dining room of the Stanford Court. In New York, we taught at Peter Kump's first temporary cooking school and, of course, in Jim's own kitchen—the ceiling, covered in brilliant blue maps; the walls, decorated with copper pots and molds and choice samples of majolica.

My first class in Jim's kitchen verged on disaster. He had left me on my own with a group of professionals—and only electric burners (which he preferred) to cook on. I was making bouillabaisse, which requires very high heat to force an amalgamation of the olive oil, the gelatin in the fish stock, and the acid of the tomatoes and white wine. I had had the wit to try the burners to see if they forced a rollicking boil. What I didn't realize was that the burners had heat sensors and would only maintain enough heat to keep the bottom layer of liquid at a boil. The bouillabaisse took forever. In addition, I broke the rouille. The students sneered. By the next day, when I was teaching a class of non-professionals, avid readers of Jim's weekly column, I had worked out the worst glitches. The sauce broke again; but I corrected it and the students were pleased. This variation of students was typical of the classes that were a mixed bag of professionals—writers and chefs—and would-be professionals. Jim thought everyone could turn a love of food into a profession. He encouraged many to do so.

Even more than the classes I miss sharing good and ample meals with Jim like the ritual first night in San Francisco blood sausage at Le Central, the crack-of-dawn breakfast in his room, and lunches at the old Coach House. However, as I re-read *Theory & Practice*, I realize that what I miss most are our endless conversations about the history and procedures of cooking.

I admire anew Jim's vast knowledge, comprehension, common sense and the conciseness that gives his work its distinctive tone and order. This book was written with José Wilson before Jim and I came into each other's lives; but many of the subjects formed the leitmotif of our planning for classes—what we wanted to teach whether organized by technique or ingredient or both—or our agreements and disagreements. The re-issuing of this book can only add to the enormous number of fans and students who made up and still make up his audience. It is a book to treasure and constantly refer to.

The very first time Jim and I met, I was a terrified younger person being interviewed for a job editing a book with which we would both be involved. He was a senior, important person, the general consultant to the book. We had a fight—ferocious on his part, stubborn on mine—about the way a pâté mold should be lined. Fortunately, none of our other disagreements became so heated. This one was resolved the way most of them were with tolerance, affection and neither side changing opinion. I wish I could still chew over with him the way to roast—quickly at high heat (my preference) or at lower heat, turning and basting (his method)—or whether peppercorns should *really* be boiled for hours.

Mostly we agreed; but I think it was the passion expressed in our disagreements that brought us so close. We also loved the history of food and could lose ourselves for hours doing research in the books that littered each of our houses.

Teaching was what Jim loved best. He had an extraordinary rapport with students. I never knew him to come away from a class without declaring that it was the best class he ever taught. It is that love of teaching, all the passion, knowledge, and the orderliness of his mind that makes this book so invigorating and useful.

As with *The Fireside Cookbook*, his first major book, *Theory & Practice* is arranged as a theme with variations. Here the themes are the great basic techniques of western cooking. After introducing the tools used, the whole field is succinctly reduced to ten chapters such as "Frying" and "Baking," each with excellent and illustrative recipes. It is a bold plan and in his own mode with additional sections containing terms and methods, a concordance of ingredients and instruction on carving—an activity he always did with assurance and flair.

I am grateful to Jim as generations of cooks have been and as future generations will be. I will certainly turn to this book whenever I am thinking about culinary matters. I will think we are talking and will continue the discussion.

"No, I don't add sugar to bread dough to feed the yeast. Yes, you are so right about most things." Yes, yes, yes to your brilliant *James Beard's Theory & Practice of Good Cooking!*

—*Barbara Kafka*
*May 6, 1999*

# Preface

⁊

*I*n my twenty-five years of teaching I have tried to make people realize that cooking is primarily fun and that the more they know about what they are doing, the more fun it is. I love having them ask questions because that's the only way they are going to understand a term or a technique. When I spot a student who is hungry to know all the whys and hows and wherefores, I try to encourage his or her inquisitiveness, knowing that this is the first sign of a creative cook. What is the difference between braising and roasting? Why must you roast a certain cut and braise another? Why do you bake a loaf of bread at a certain temperature and a cake at a different heat? What does it mean to "proof" yeast? Why is pastry precooked for some tarts, fully cooked for others, and not precooked at all when you bake a pie? Then there are the questions that come up about flavoring and seasoning. Why is it that a touch of nutmeg improves the flavor of a béchamel sauce or a soufflé base? Can you really cook chicken with 40 cloves of garlic without the garlic being overpowering? Why are freshly ground black peppercorns preferable to white? Why is it essential to cook shrimp in a well-seasoned liquid?

As a student absorbs the answers to all these continual questions, his understanding deepens and is reflected in the more experienced way he uses his cooking hands, can tell by touch when something is done to perfection, can identify flavors and compare dishes, knows exactly what to do at the market. At that point the student is on his own. He no longer needs to follow slavishly a set recipe; he can rely on his own skills—his taste memory, the understanding he has gained of techniques, flavorings, and food combinations—and build on his knowledge.

When you cook, you never stop learning. That's the fascination of it. Within the last year I have been put on a no-salt, low-calorie diet and I'm discovering all kinds of things about flavoring I never knew before. It is possible to cook without salt, or without butter and flour, if you understand the principles of seasoning, reducing, and liaisons. I challenge anyone who thinks differently to spot the absence of salt in a dish skillfully seasoned with garlic and herbs. I have not had to give up the principles of good cooking—and neither would you. Don't look on your diet as a deprivation and turn to dreary diet cookbooks, which are generally so depressing. Good food and good cooking will be even more important to you when you have to follow a limited regime, so follow the principles of cooking herein included—eliminating simply what the doctor orders—and the adventure of discovering a new palette of flavors will be a refreshing challenge.

This book, which José Wilson has helped me put together, is designed to bring every one of you to that stage of being a creative, intuitive cook. Over the years, José has worked with me at my cooking school and she knows well our students' needs. We have tried to present the theory and practice of cooking so that you will understand them just as they learned them. We discuss each technique in considerable detail as we would in our classes, anticipating the variety of questions all of you might ask if we were there at your side. Then we show how that technique works, demonstrating in very explicit recipes the way it is applied to the various kinds of meat, to fish, to vegetables, to fruits. We compare the different leavening powers of eggs, yeast, baking powders, and we explore the mysteries of thickeners and emulsions. Always there is a recipe to learn by, usually a simple master recipe followed by ones that are a little more complex and demanding. In other words, the recipes are designed to help you build such a solid grounding in every possible area of cooking that you'll be able to tackle anything.

But because the secret to really good cooking starts in the market, we have included a Concordance in this book. It is the Concordance that finally makes everything work because the materials you buy must always concord with the techniques you apply to them. You have to know not only what to look for in order to select good produce, but also how best to cook what you buy. So in the Concordance we have put down everything we think you ought to know about apples and meat cuts and fish and spices and herbs and grains and dairy products, with dozens of different suggestions as to how to use each product. We hope you'll find there the answers to all your questions about food so that you can shop confidently, imaginatively, and constructively, building your menu in your head as you select what tempts you that day and what is a good bargain. With the aid of the Concordance, you'll be able to determine how best to cook what you bring home. By checking out that particular food, you will be directed to the right technique, then back to the basic recipes of this book to select the appropriate one on which you can, of course, work out your own variations. For, once you have made the lessons in the chapters a part of your cooking knowledge, and with the Concordance to guide you in shopping, you'll be ready to improvise, invent, experiment, and, finally, find your own cooking style.

*Note:* The very explicit, simple master recipes are all marked ❧.

# James Beard's Theory & Practice of Good Cooking

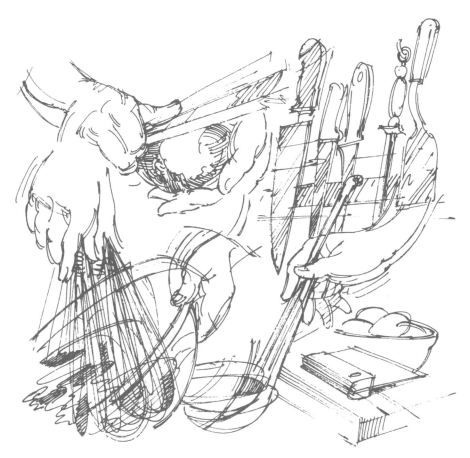

# Good Cooking
# Needs Good Tools

Cooking starts with your hands, the most important and basic of all implements. They were the earliest tools for the preparation of food, and they have remained one of the most efficient, sensitive, and versatile. Hands can beat, cream, fold, knead, pat, press, form, toss, tear, and pound. They are so sensitive that the instant your fingers touch or feel something, they transmit messages to your brain about texture and temperature. Just by touching a broiled steak or a roast, you can learn to tell when the meat is done to your liking. To test the temperature of a sauce, a soup, a stew, or a vegetable purée, just dip your finger in. Then touch your finger to your tongue, and you'll know whether the seasoning and flavoring are right or need some adjustment. There are prissy people who think sticking fingers in food is dirty, but there's nothing disgraceful about touching food if your hands are clean, and don't let anyone tell you there is. After all, we eat lots of foods with our fingers. Isn't one of the best-known products advertised as being "finger lickin' good"? I can think of no more rewarding and sensuous a pleasure than plunging one's hands into a batter or dough and mixing or kneading away.

I learned to cook with my hands at a very early age, long before I ever held a spoon or a beater. I can remember making a cake—a quick, simple coffee-cake—by first opening my hand like a big fork to mix and beat the batter and then cupping it like a spoon to scoop the batter from the bowl. It seemed the most natural thing in the world, and it taught me the feel of batters and doughs as nothing else could have done.

In my classes I encourage my students to get their hands into cake batters and soufflé mixtures, for once they get the feel of the texture and consistency this way, they never forget it. I find many people have difficulty learning to fold in egg whites with a spatula and tend to overfold. If you learn to fold them in by using the side of your hand to cut down and the palm to bring the mixture up and over, you soon grasp the technique of quick, light folding that doesn't deflate the egg whites. Later on in this book I'm going to tell you in detail how to mix a cake batter, fold in egg whites and separate eggs with your hands, and how to test a piece of cooked meat for doneness by pressing it with your fingertip. That's also a good way to judge whether a cake is baked. The light pressure of a finger will tell if the surface is firm and the cake underneath resilient. There are innumerable occasions in cooking when you can rely on your hands and your brain to give you these quick, accurate messages. Try mixing a salad with your fingers to learn how much dressing is needed to coat the greens—not drown them.

Next to hands, the most important tools are good knives. A knife can do practically everything in the way of cutting, slicing, mincing, chopping, even scraping and pounding. If you don't own a meat pounder, you can use the flat of a big heavy knife, such as a Chinese cleaver, to pound and flatten. Then there's a little trick I always show my students for peeling garlic—a pesky job. If you crush the garlic clove lightly with the flat of a heavy knife blade, the skin will split and come off in one piece.

Knives are the best friends a cook can have, to be treasured along with the family silver. They are just as valuable and will last equally long if properly treated—and by that I mean they should be sharpened regularly, never allowed to soak in a bath of detergent or to go in the dishwasher. Instead merely wipe your knives clean with a damp cloth after you've used them and store them in a proper knife rack where the blades won't bang against each other or anything else.

*T*o begin with, there are just three knives you really should have. First, and most important, comes what is variously known as a French knife or a French chef's or cook's knife, a knife with a wide, tapering, triangular blade. Formerly all the best French chef's knives were made from carbon steel, which was soft enough to sharpen properly, but now the good quality high-carbon stainless-steel knives are by far the best. The two brands I recommend are Zanger and Henckels. Both are expensive, but there is no economy in buying cheap knives. They just don't perform properly. A good knife will be perfectly weighted, with a blade that is wide and rather heavy at the butt near the handle, tapering to a triangle and a more pronounced thinness at the point. The reason for this shape and weight is that a chef's knife is designed to cut, slice, and chop.

TO CUT: *Use the thinner, pointed end of the knife to pierce the skin and to make the initial cut. Then lower the blade.*

TO SLICE: *Hold what you are cutting firmly, bending your fingers so that the tips of the nails rest on the surface of the object and the bent fingers serve as a guide to the knife blade that will come down parallel to them, almost touching. After you slice, move your fingers back just the width of the next slice. Repeat. I prefer to keep a grasp on the handle of the knife with my thumb pressing the top to help guide the knife. If you are slicing something round, first cut a slice from the bottom so that the object will lie flat instead of rolling.*

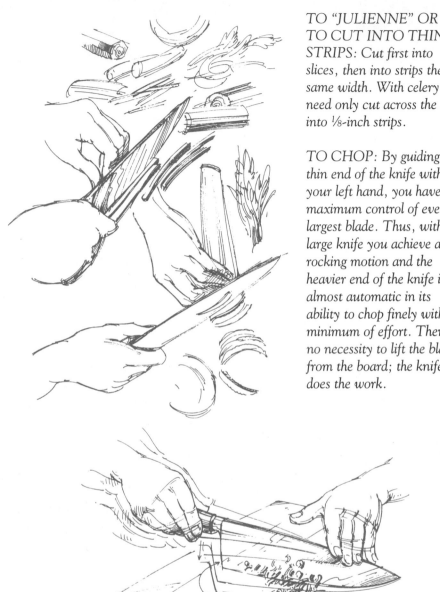

TO "JULIENNE" OR TO CUT INTO THIN STRIPS: *Cut first into slices, then into strips the same width. With celery you need only cut across the stalk into ⅛-inch strips.*

TO CHOP: *By guiding the thin end of the knife with your left hand, you have maximum control of even the largest blade. Thus, with a large knife you achieve a rocking motion and the heavier end of the knife is almost automatic in its ability to chop finely with a minimum of effort. There is no necessity to lift the blade from the board; the knife does the work.*

The second important knife is a slicing knife, which has a fairly thin, supple blade with a rounded or pointed end and is designed for slicing roast meats, turkey, pot roast, or corned beef brisket from paper-thin to medium-thick or very thick. This knife takes the place of the one in old-fashioned carving sets and is something no one can really get along without.

Last, but by no means least, there is the little paring knife, which may either have a triangular blade and look like a miniature chef's knife, or a small, curved scimitar-like blade and is excellent for mincing or cutting into small dice.

TO MINCE: *To cut a single clove of garlic or a shallot, hold the bud the same way you would a larger object, with your fingers bent, and cut with the point of a well-sharpened paring knife in fine strokes, first making thin, horizontal slices almost to the end of the bud but not slicing completely through, then turning your knife again and cutting down in slices of the same thinness to achieve minuscule dice. Actually the same procedure is used with a medium-sized or a large knife to chop an onion, an apple, a potato, etc., into uniform dice.*

There are many other knives that can be added to these basics. You may want to have two or three sizes of chef's knife, which comes in different blade sizes from 6 inches up to a giant of 14 inches—the most useful are the 8-, 10-, and 12-inch sizes, for a large blade will, naturally, chop a greater quantity than a small one. Then you might add a boning knife, which has a thin flexible blade about 6 inches long (see illustration, page 164); a smaller, triangular-bladed boning knife for chicken breasts and small birds; a bread knife with a serrated blade (also good for cutting crumbly cakes); a very long, thin, flexible ham slicer; and a Chinese cleaver. To keep your knives sharp, you should also have either the traditional long sharpening steel or an inexpensive little gadget made by Zanger called a Zip-Zap that looks like a miniature sharpening steel but is made of a special ceramic that is even harder than steel.

TO SHARPEN A
KNIFE, *hold it at a
20-degree angle to the
sharpener and, with a
quick swinging motion of
your wrist and forearm,
slide the blade across it.
Don't lay the blade flat
and scrape, just bring the
edge down and across,
maintaining the 20-degree
angle, until the tip touches
the bottom of the
sharpener. Then repeat in
an upward direction with
the opposite side of the
blade. Do this half a*

*dozen times whenever you use a knife and it will keep the edge keen and aligned.
When the edge wears down, as it will with constant use, you can have it
professionally sharpened and ground. Look in the yellow pages for the names of
knife grinders, or ask your butcher where he has his knives ground. Knives with
serrated edges do not need sharpening, of course.*

The following list gives my recommendations for the equipment you should
have in your kitchen. It isn't necessary to rush out and buy everything at once.
Start with the equipment you really need and add to it as you go along. Get
the best pots and pans you can afford. Cheap, flimsy pieces are false economy.
Thin pans will not distribute heat evenly and tend to burn and scorch food.
Heavy-duty pans and skillets, like good knives, are a long-term investment,
and it's better to buy one decent pan than a whole set of useless ones. Sets of
pans are rather pointless, anyway. There always seem to be one or two you
never use. You are much better off buying pans for individual purposes, such as
sauces, braising, and sautéing, plus at least one big pot of 8-quart capacity that
you can use for pot roasts and pasta and soup. When it comes to materials, I
happen to prefer stainless steel with an aluminum inlay between the steel layers in the bottom, or heavy-duty copper lined with stainless steel or tin, or
heavy cast aluminum, with an occasional piece of enameled iron for sauces and
custards and suchlike things, but the choice is really up to you. Just be sure the
pans are really heavy-duty and have tight-fitting covers. For baking, stainless-
steel pans, while more expensive than tin or aluminum, are preferable because

they won't warp and are easier to clean. For bread, I like the loaf pans of sheet iron, which conduct heat well and give a good brown crust. For broiling, I find the aluminum foil pans with ridged bottoms a boon because they are easy to clean and can be used over and over.

I'm all for anything that saves time and work in the kitchen and that goes for electrical appliances. There are two labor-saving devices which I think should be part of any well equipped kitchen, because they do a better, more professional job of beating, mixing, whipping, chopping, grinding, and mincing than any but the most skilled cook could accomplish—and in a fraction of the time. One is the heavy-duty KitchenAid electric mixer, a formidable machine of many uses. It has a whisk for beating light things such as eggs, egg whites, batters, cream, and mayonnaise and a paddle for heavier mixtures like mashed potatoes and pastry doughs. There's an optional dough-hook attachment for kneading bread and other yeast doughs and a positive battery of optional attachments such as a meat grinder and a sausage stuffer, a vegetable shredder, a jacket to hold ice or hot water when beating mixtures that must be kept cold or warm, and a highly efficient ice-cream freezer.

The other device, a comparatively recent and quite invaluable piece of equipment, is the Cuisinart Food Processor. Having a food processor in the kitchen is the equivalent of having an extra pair of hands. While it does many of the same jobs as the KitchenAid, it does them in a different way, for this machine operates on the principle of centrifugal force and combines many of the attributes of

the mixer and a blender. I use the food processor for all kinds of things—chopping meat; slicing, chopping, shredding, and puréeing vegetables; making pastry, brioche, cake, and crêpe batters as well as mayonnaise. Although I find that I use my blender less now that I have a food processor, it is still an extremely useful piece of equipment for liquefying ingredients, making soups, crêpe batter, purées, bread crumbs, and grated cheese, and definitely earns its kitchen space. Throughout this book I have indicated where the mixer, food processor, or blender can take over in a recipe. These pieces of equipment are expensive, but they are incredibly versatile and save an enormous amount of labor, which in my book means they are worth every penny. I'm constantly amazed at people who, while they think nothing of spending a couple of hundred dollars for clothes or sports equipment for a vacation trip, hesitate about buying something that will save them hundreds of hours of arduous dog work—and enable them to turn out better meals with greater ease.

# Kitchen Equipment Check List

## KNIVES
♦ 1 8-inch chef's knife
♦ 1 10-inch or 12-inch chef's knife
♦ 2 paring knives
♦ 1 slicing knife
♦ 1 serrated-edge bread knife
♦ 1 boning knife with 6-inch blade
♦ 1 sharpening steel or "Zip-Zap" sharpener

### OPTIONAL ADDITIONS
♦ Ham slicer
♦ Small boning knife
♦ Chinese cleaver

## POTS AND PANS
♦ 2 1-quart sauce pans, with covers
♦ 2 2-quart saucepans, with covers
♦ 1 4-quart pan, with cover
♦ 1 8-quart braising pan or large round or oval pot, with tight-fitting cover
♦ 1 10-inch straight-sided, flat-bottomed sauté pan, with cover
♦ 1 12-inch sauté pan, with cover

- 1 10-inch skillet of heavy metal (such as iron) with metal handle (so it can go in the oven)
- 1 iron crêpe pan, with 6-inch bottom diameter
- 1 cast-aluminum omelet pan, with 6-inch bottom diameter, or 1 Teflon-lined cast-aluminum omelet pan, to double for crêpe
- 1 fish poacher with rack, 18 or 22 inches long
- 1 open roasting pan of heavy-gauge stainless steel, about 18 x 12 inches and 2½ inches deep
- 1 stainless-steel, adjustable V-shaped rack, to fit in the roasting pan
- Aluminum foil broiling pans, assorted sizes

## OPTIONAL ADDITIONS
- Deep fryer with basket, regular or electric
- 10-quart stock pot
- Double boiler, preferably heatproof glass

# BAKING EQUIPMENT

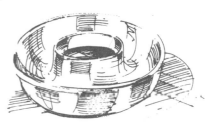

- 3 or 4 heavy-duty cookie and baking sheets
- 2 11 x 15-inch heavy-duty jelly roll pans
- 3 9-inch round cake pans
- 1 9-inch square cake pan
- 1 8-inch to 9-inch tube cake pan
- 2 9 x 5 x 3-inch bread pans
- 2 8-inch pie pans
- 2 9-inch pie pans
- 1 9-inch tart pan with removable bottom
- 1 9-inch flan ring
- 1 muffin pan
- 2 or 3 wire cake racks
- 1 oval gratin dish, lined copper or other metal
- 2 ovenproof gratin or baking dishes, porcelain or pottery, medium and large
- 1½-quart terrine, with cover, ovenproof porcelain or earthenware, for pâtés
- 2 or 3 casseroles, with covers, ovenproof porcelain, earthenware, or enameled iron, in assorted sizes
- 1-, 1½-, and 2-quart soufflé dishes, porcelain, earthenware, or Corning glass
- 1- and 2-quart lacquered tin charlotte molds (may double for soufflés, mousses)
- 1 6-cup ring mold (may double for cold mousses, gelatin molds)

◆ 1 decorative pudding mold, about 6 cups (such as a melon mold, may double for cold mousses, ice cream)

## MEASURING AND MIXING EQUIPMENT
◆ Glass liquid measuring cups in 1-, 2-, 4-, and 6-cup sizes
◆ 2 sets metal dry measuring cups
◆ 2 sets measuring spoons
◆ 2-cup flour sifter
◆ Mixing bowls, glass or earthenware, assorted sizes

## STANDARD KITCHEN EQUIP]
◆ Apple corer
◆ Potato peeler
◆ Poultry shears
◆ Melon-ball scoop
◆ Biscuit, cookie, and pastry cutters
◆ Dough scraper (can double as an all-purpose scraper)
◆ Ice-cream scoop
◆ Small vegetable slicer with adjustable blade, such as Feemster model
◆ Mandoline vegetable slicer (for julienne vegetables, plain and waffle-cut potatoes)
◆ Mouli-julienne (French disk-type vegetable grater, slicer, and shredder)
◆ Cheese grater, stainless-steel, four-sided box type
◆ Nutmeg grater
◆ Mortar and pestle, ceramic or marble
◆ Pepper mill
◆ Salt mill
◆ Food mill, for puréeing
◆ Strainers and sieves, assorted sizes and meshes
◆ Colander
◆ Funnel
◆ Can opener
◆ Corkscrew
◆ Bottle opener
◆ Screw-top-jar opener
◆ Wooden spoons and spatulas, assorted sizes
◆ 2 wooden kitchen forks
◆ 2 metal kitchen forks
◆ 2 slotted or perforated metal kitchen spoons

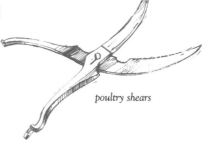

poultry shears

- 1 solid metal kitchen spoon
- 3 or 4 wire whisks, assorted sizes
- 2 or 3 rubber spatulas, wide and narrow blades
- 2 or 3 metal spatulas, wide and narrow blades
- 1 broad-bladed pancake turner
- 2 skimmers, open wire and fine mesh
- 1 large soup ladle
- 1 2-ounce ladle, for measuring crêpe batter
- Meat thermometer, type that registers from 0° to 220° F., such as Taylor Bi-Therm model
- Candy thermometer
- Deep-fat thermometer
- Pastry board
- 2 pastry brushes
- Rolling pin, ball-bearing or heavy French type
- Plastic-lined pastry bag and sets of round, star, and ribbon piping tubes
- Metal scoops for flour and sugar
- Storage jars and canisters
- Lemon squeezer
- Large earthenware bowl or crock for marinating meats
- Meat pounder
- Larding needle, long wood-handled type
- Trussing needles and fine string
- Cheesecloth
- Skewers, short for closing vent of poultry, long for kebabs
- Metal kitchen tongs
- Wood chopping block (if there is no wood countertop)

# PAPER, PLASTIC, AND CLEANING PRODUCTS
- Aluminum foil, light and heavy-duty, short and long rolls
- Cooking parchment
- Paper towels
- Plastic wrap, short and long rolls
- Plastic food bags, several sizes

- ◆ Plastic freezer-storage containers
- ◆ Waxed paper
- ◆ Scotch cleaning pads
- ◆ Vegetable brush

## ELECTRIC APPLIANCES
- ◆ Blender
- ◆ Can opener
- ◆ Cuisinart Food Processor
- ◆ Hand beater
- ◆ Heavy-duty mixer, preferably KitchenAid (K5A model), optional attachments
- ◆ Small coffee mill (to grind coffee beans or whole spices)

## OPTIONAL EQUIPMENT
- ◆ Kitchen scales, graduated in ounces and grams
- ◆ Salad dryer
- ◆ Ice-cream freezer, manual or electric
- ◆ Unlined copper beating bowl and balloon whisk (for egg whites)
- ◆ 6-cup pudding basin (for steamed puddings)
- ◆ Deep pie dish (can double as vegetable dish or baking dish)
- ◆ Brioche, tartlet, and barquette pans
- ◆ Stripper
- ◆ Zester

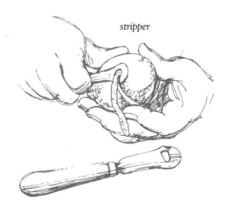

*stripper*

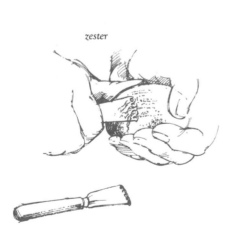

*zester*

# Boiling

$D$id you ever stop to think, when you boil an egg, poach a chicken, simmer a soup, or blanch a cauliflower, that they are all part of one basic cooking process—boiling? In one form or another it enters into many of the recipes we prepare, whether we are making a base for a soufflé or a stock for a stew. Essentially, boiling is the action of liquid, at various temperatures, on food. Meat is brought to a full boil in order to cook the surface rapidly and sear in the juices and flavors, the same thing that happens when it is seared in fat over heat, or browned under the broiler. When you bring meat or poultry to a boil, the chemical reaction between the food and the liquid brings forth a frothy scum, which must be skimmed off. The scum may continue to form for as long as 5 or 10 minutes and, if you want a good finished dish, you must skim and keep on skimming to remove those undesirable elements. After this initial boiling, the heat should be turned down so the liquid merely simmers, a process that tenderizes the meat.

Vegetables, on the other hand, are boiled or blanched in order to tenderize them and to break down and expand the tissues, which brings out a well-defined, characteristic flavor. If you taste certain vegetables when they are raw, when they are partially cooked, and when they are fully cooked, you'll learn a very interesting lesson. Take a green bean, for instance. Taste it raw, taste it halfway through the cooking, and then when it is done as you like it and you'll notice the difference in flavor between the various stages.

Pasta is always immersed in rapidly boiling water and boiled very fast in order to expand the starch granules and make them tender to the bite—*al dente*, as the Italians say. There is also a school of rice cookery, to which I happen to belong, where the rice is tossed by small handfuls into a big pot of rapidly boiling water, so that the water never ceases to seethe and boil. This produces a less starchy rice than when it is cooked in only a little water, and each grain is separate rather than sticking together.

Water and other liquids boil when brought to a temperature of 212° F. (or 100° C.) at sea level and the temperature reduces one degree for every 500 feet of altitude. In high-altitude cities, such as Denver, there is a different set of rules for boiling.

If you want to check on the various stages of boiling, it is a simple enough matter. Half fill a large saucepan or pot with water and place it on a large burner over high heat. Watch carefully as it begins to heat and tiny bubbles form on the bottom of the pan. Then the steam will start to rise and when the liquid has reached ebullition, or the boiling point, it will seethe and surge and bubble, and the bubbles will rise to the surface and break more and more rapidly. In this fast or rolling boil, the kind used to reduce stock by evaporation and intensify its flavor, or to cook pasta, the liquid moves fiercely and rapidly, rolling, rising, and vaporizing like lava in the crater of a volcano. When you are making preserves, you will notice the recipes often call for a rolling boil. Because of the density of the syrup, the boil is much more vigorous and surging and the cooking takes place in a large kettle that allows plenty of room for expansion. This is also true with certain thick mixtures, such as a tomato sauce or polenta (cooked cornmeal); when they come to a boil, they puff up from the bottom of the pan rather than seething on top.

Now reverse the boiling process by turning the heat down under the pot of liquid and observe how long it takes to subside from this violent motion through the various boiling stages before the liquid reaches the faint ebullition that marks the simmering point, the gentlest form of boiling. Simmering, as used in cookbooks, is a word with a double meaning. You can refer to simmering or to poaching, which are virtually the same process. Poaching, in which something is brought to a slow simmer and kept there, is known professionally as a feeble ebullition. This is exactly what it sounds like—a boil that is hardly a boil at all, just a faint, lazy bubble that rises to the surface and slowly pops, like a carefully blown soap bubble. We talk about poaching a fish, poaching eggs, or poaching fruit in syrup. Simmering is maybe one degree less active than poaching—the feeble, steady ebullition you need when you are making a stew or a pot-au-feu. If you look in the pot, you will see the almost unbelievably slow bubbling, the surface of the liquid barely moving (in more poetic cookbook writing, the liquid is said to "smile"), that helps to mingle the seasonings with the other ingredients and to relax and tenderize the flesh of the meat or poultry.

It's interesting to consider that after you have simmered a stew or a stock, sometimes for hours, either to imbue the flesh with flavor or to extract the flavor from the meat, fowl, and bones for your stock, you go to the other extreme for reducing. After straining the stock, you turn the heat very high and let it seethe, bubble, and boil away until the vaporization reduces the volume by one-half to two-thirds, intensifying the flavor and slightly thickening the liquid. The final extension of this process is the making of a *glace de viande*, or meat glaze, in which the stock is clarified and then reduced by slow steady boiling over a period of hours or days until it is no more than a thick jelly or glaze.

Blanching is another boiling technique. Again, you are using the action of boiling liquid to achieve certain results. In blanching (synonymous with parboiling, a word which has been in our cooking terminology for years), food is immersed in boiling water and allowed to steep or to cook slightly, hence, parboil. Blanching might be called a method of searing with water preparatory to further cooking.

There are all kinds of reasons for blanching. Certain vegetables are blanched to soften them slightly, or to remove their strong flavor—cabbage, for example. Peppers are blanched to cook them partially before they are stuffed and baked. Lettuce is blanched before being braised. Some vegetables are blanched, or parboiled, to shorten their cooking time, like the potatoes, carrots, or onions you want to roast in the pan with the meat.

It's not uncommon to blanch julienne strips of hard or watery vegetables, like turnips and zucchini, prior to sautéing them quickly in butter, or to blanch green beans that are then dressed in a vinaigrette sauce. In each instance, it is essential, after blanching, to plunge the vegetables immediately into ice-cold water to stop them from becoming overcooked. To prepare vegetables for freezing, you usually blanch and cool them in the same manner. Or, if you are making a pale, creamy dish like a *blanquette de veau*, you might blanch mushrooms for just a minute in water acidulated with lemon juice or vinegar to keep them white, so they look more attractive in the finished dish.

Other foods are blanched, like tomatoes, to make it easy to remove the skins. Peaches are blanched before peeling and almonds are blanched and soaked to soften the tough little skins, enabling you to rub them off easily between your thumb and finger. Salty meats, such as ham, salt pork, or bacon with a very smoky quality, may be blanched, or parboiled, to draw off the excess salt and strong odors or flavors before being added to a dish.

Yet another of the many facets of boiling is steeping—the hydrating process for making tea or extracting flavor from a dried herb or root.

Each of these related processes of boiling is extremely important to the everyday round of cooking, no matter how familiar and simple it may sound. For instance, we boil eggs. Don't let anyone tell you that an egg is "soft cooked" or "hard cooked." It is *boiled*, no matter what some of the rather precious folk in the food world may say who insist on changing the terminology. "Boiled" is a much more honest term, because we do bring eggs to the boiling point and keep them at a boil for a certain length of time. If you are making a soft-boiled egg for breakfast, you boil it for 3 minutes on the dot. Hard-boiled eggs are boiled rapidly for 2 or 3 minutes and then left to rest in the hot water, with the heat turned off, for another 8 or 9 minutes. If you are making an egg mollet, you bring it to a boil; boil 5½ minutes, then remove it; put it in cold water at once, shell it whole, and use it as you would a poached egg.

So let's examine the whole world of boiling and learn how to apply the right technique to what we are cooking.

## ☙ Boiled Corned Beef and Cabbage

*This might qualify as a New England boiled dinner. It's a good, hearty, basic dish that will serve 6, with some meat left over for cold corned beef sandwiches or 4 to 6 servings of corned beef hash.*

*When we talk about "boiled beef" or a "boiled dinner" we don't really mean boiled; we mean simmered. Naturally, to create a simmer you first have to bring liquid to a boil and you do have to let the liquid boil for a little at the start of the cooking, to draw off certain elements in the beef that would cloud the broth. These form a grayish-brown scum on the surface and should be skimmed off with a skimmer or spoon.*

*Corned beef is beef that has been cured in a pickling solution, which used to be the way beef, pork, and sometimes lamb were preserved for the winter. It's very traditional and one of the most delicious American beef dishes. There are different kinds of corned beef. There's a very spicy kosher corned beef, the plain corned beef, and some simulated corned beef that is not nearly as good as the old-fashioned, pure kind we are so used to. Corned beef brisket is the choicest cut because it has some fat and good marbling and makes a flavorful, tender finished product that slices well and looks good on the plate.*

*To cook the corned beef you will need a good big pot, an 8- to 10-quart size, which can be aluminum, Magnalite, Corning Ware, anything of that sort. The size is more important than the material.*

Makes 6 servings, with leftovers

6 pounds corned beef brisket
1 onion, peeled and stuck with
   3 cloves
10 large garlic cloves, peeled
1 tablespoon freshly ground
   black pepper

## THE ACCOMPANYING VEGETABLES

6 medium onions, peeled
6 good-sized carrots, scraped
6 to 10 medium potatoes
6 turnips, peeled
1 medium cabbage

Wipe the corned beef well with a damp cloth. Put it in the pot and cover with cold water. Bring to a boil over rather high heat, and boil for 5 to 6 minutes, skimming off the grey foamy scum that rises to the surface with a wire skimmer or large spoon. This will give you a clearer, purer broth. It's very important, with any boiled meat, to skim off this scum drawn from the meat.

Add the onion stuck with cloves, the garlic cloves, and the pepper and boil another 10 minutes, skimming. Then reduce the heat to a simmer (250° on a burner with a thermostat), cover the pot, and let it simmer at a faint, gentle ebullition for 2 hours. At this point, test the meat for tenderness with a large fork. As this is not a very tender piece of meat, it will offer some resistance, but it should just yield to the fork. You must be careful not to overcook corned beef or the meat will become dry and stringy. It's very important to maintain some moisture in the meat. If you are not sure about the tenderness, remove the meat to a plate and cut off a tiny piece from the edge to taste. If you have a meat thermometer, check the internal temperature, which should be 145° to 150°.

If the meat seems tender, turn off the heat and let it rest in the liquid. If it does not test tender, either continue cooking or, if you have started it in the morning and are ahead of serving time, leave it in the liquid and finish the cooking later.

## COOKING THE VEGETABLES (*1 hour before serving*)

Traditionally, all the vegetables for a corned beef dinner are cooked in the pot with the meat. I have long since decided that the vegetables look and taste better if they are cooked separately in plain salted water, instead of in the briny, fatty broth. If you have sufficient pots and burners, I recommend that you follow this procedure—each vegetable will then retain its own character and flavor. However, it is perfectly acceptable to cook the potatoes with the beef, provided you scrub them and leave them in their skins so they don't absorb the fat, and to use only one extra pot, first putting in the longest-cooking vegetables, the onions and carrots, then the turnips, and finally the cabbage. Or, if you have a large pot and a steamer, put the onions and carrots in the water and steam the turnips over them. Cook the cabbage separately.

Here is a timetable for the vegetables:

ONIONS. Put in a pot with water to cover, seasoned with 1 tablespoon salt. Bring to a boil, cover, and simmer 1 hour or until crisply tender when tested with the point of a knife.

CARROTS. Follow the same procedure, seasoning the water with 2 teaspoons salt and ½ teaspoon marjoram. Simmer 30 minutes, or until tender when tested.

POTATOES. Scrub but do not peel. Follow the same procedure, seasoning the water with 1 tablespoon salt, or simmer with the corned beef, for 30 minutes or until tender. If you are planning to make corned beef hash, cook the 4 extra potatoes, otherwise allow 1 per person.

TURNIPS. Leave whole if small; halve or quarter if large. Follow the same procedure, seasoning the water with 2 teaspoons salt. Simmer for 20 minutes or until tender when tested.

CABBAGE. Remove coarse or discolored outer leaves and cut in sixths. Put in a pot with water to cover, seasoned with 2 teaspoons salt. Bring to a boil and boil rapidly, covered, for 10 to 12 minutes, or until just tender but not over-cooked or soggy.

I am not an advocate of using pressure cookers for vegetables. I realize that many people consider them one of the greatest kitchen aids, but I think they rob vegetables of all flavor. However, if you are a pressure cooker addict, by all means use it for the vegetables for this dish, following your rule chart for timing, for it will certainly speed up the process.

When you are ready to serve, remove the beef from the broth (discard the broth; it cannot be saved for any other use) and let it stand on a hot platter in a warm place for 10 minutes, to firm and settle the meat. This makes it easier to carve. Surround it with the drained vegetables, the potatoes still in their jackets. Do not add butter—the vegetables are better plain. Slice only as much meat as you need, keeping the rest in one piece for future use. Serve with the vegetables, with a variety of mustards, horseradish, and, if you have any, good homemade pickles.

# Stock

It is a great aid and comfort always to have on hand good homemade beef, chicken, and veal stock, but you have to be realistic about it. You must gauge your stock-making by the space you have to keep it. One of the greatest of all wastes is to make a big pot of stock and then have to leave most of it in the refrigerator until it has gone sour, as so often happens. Two or three days is about as long as you should keep stock in the refrigerator; if you keep it longer you should remove it and boil it up again before using. If you are keeping stock for any length of time you really have to freeze it, in which case you can safely keep it up to three months. So before you start making stock, see how much space you can spare in your freezer for long-term use and in your refrigerator for short-term cooking.

I have somewhat limited storage space, so if I want to make a small pot-au-feu—the French boiled dinner—for myself and have bought a piece of beef shin and a bone, I remove the meat when it's tender and make a meal of it, then keep on cooking the bone and stock until I have about 2 quarts of good strong stock, which I cool. I then skim off the fat that rises to the top, put the stock in half-pint and pint containers, and keep them in the freezer, so that I can take out just enough for a sauce or a soup, rather than having to thaw the contents of a big container and refreeze what I don't need.

For chicken stock, I cook a batch of backs, necks, and gizzards until I have a good strong broth, then I eat the gizzards. I may later poach a chicken or two in the stock for *poule au pot* or a chicken salad or hash. After they have cooked, I have a much richer, double-strength stock which, when strained, degreased, and cooked down until it has reduced by one-third or one-half, gives me an elegant concentrated stock for sauces, or to clarify and use as chicken consommé. I let it stand in the refrigerator until the fat rises to the top, remove the fat, and divide the stock among small plastic containers for freezing.

If you don't have a freezer, or don't want to keep a large supply of stock on hand, you can always make a quick batch with a few gizzards, or some beef and a chicken, if you're making a pot-au-feu.

Veal being as expensive as it is, even for the knuckles and lesser, bony cuts, it's awfully hard to part with $12 to $14 to make veal stock, but sometimes it's a necessity. Get a knuckle of veal, a piece of neck, and the less desirable parts of the shoulder and cook them, leaving the meat in only until tender, then strip the meat from the bones and make jellied veal from it; after that put the bones back in the liquid and cook them down until you have a strong veal stock. That's the economical and intelligent thing to do.

If you really can't make and store stock, canned beef bouillon or canned chicken broth are perfectly adequate, but for the most part canned stocks are not as delicate and honest in flavor and therefore not as good for cooking, although they do serve their purpose. Don't, however, use the canned consommé, which is too highly spiced and pronounced in flavor to make good stock.

Vegetable stocks—the water in which onions, carrots, and other aromatic vegetables have been cooked—can be saved, combined, cooked down and used for braised dishes or those that need to be cooked with a good deal of liquid, like boiled beef. They add flavor, but unless you have an immediate use for them I think it's rather silly to fill up your freezer or refrigerator with cooked-down vegetable juices. Any space you can spare is better used for chicken, beef, or veal stock, which are real necessities.

# ❧ Chicken Stock or Broth

2 pounds chicken gizzards
2 pounds chicken necks and
   backs
1 onion, peeled and stuck with
   3 cloves
1 leek, well washed and
   trimmed (see page 378)
1 carrot, scraped
2 garlic cloves, peeled
1 bay leaf
1 sprig of parsley
1 teaspoon dried thyme
6 peppercorns
3 quarts water
1 tablespoon salt

Put the chicken pieces, vegetables, garlic, herbs, peppercorns, and water in a deep 8-quart pot or a stockpot and bring to a boil. After 5 minutes, skim of the scum that forms on the surface with a wire skimmer or a large spoon. Continue to boil rapidly for 15 minutes, skimming, then reduce the heat; cover the pot and simmer for 2 to 2½ hours. Season with salt to taste—about 1 tablespoon. Strain the broth through a sieve lined with several thicknesses of cheesecloth into a large bowl and cool thoroughly in the refrigerator. Save the gizzards (they are good eating) and discard the other chicken parts and vegetables. When the stock is cold, remove the layer of fat that has formed on the surface. You will have about 2½ quarts of stock.

## Double Chicken Broth

Put the cold, fat-free stock in an 8-quart pan with a whole stewing fowl or roasting chicken weighing 4 to 5 pounds. Bring slowly to a boil, skim off any scum that forms on the surface; reduce the heat; cover and simmer gently until the chicken is very tender, about 1 hour for a young chicken, 2 to 2½ hours for a fowl. Remove the chicken and either serve it as poached chicken or remove the skin, take the meat from the bones, and use it for chicken dishes—salad, hash, chicken pie, or creamed chicken. Strain the broth through cheesecloth into a bowl, cool, and skim off the fat. You now have about 2 quarts of beautifully rich, strong broth to use for cooking. Should you want to reduce it even more and clarify it, for consommé, here's how to do it.

## Chicken Consommé

For chicken consommé, the broth must be absolutely fat-free and clear. Put the broth back in a pan and boil slowly until it has reduced to one-half or one-third of its original volume. To remove any lingering traces of fat, strain into a 2½-quart pan through a sieve lined with cheesecloth or a linen towel. To clarify the stock, add 1 egg white, beaten to a froth, and 1 crushed eggshell. Over medium heat, beat well with a rotary beater or a wire whisk until the stock comes to a boil and the egg white rises to the surface (it will have gathered together any impurities in the soup that would cloud it). Stop stirring, remove pan from the heat, and let it stand for 5 minutes, to settle. Then, without agitating the stock, strain it through a sieve or colander lined with several thicknesses of cheesecloth or a linen towel that you have wrung out in cold water (this traps the impurities in the egg white and any vestige of fat that might remain is chilled by the damp cloth). The liquid should just drip through into the bowl beneath; don't attempt to hurry the process or you won't get a perfectly clear consommé. When it has all dripped through, pour into plastic containers, cool, and freeze.

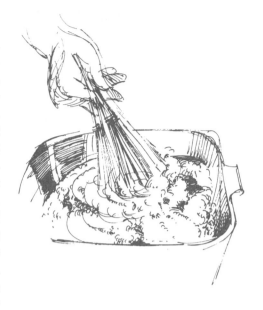

# ❧ Veal Stock or Broth

4 pounds neck of veal
  Or neck plus bony parts
  of the shoulder
1 veal knuckle
1 calf's foot, if available
1 onion, peeled and stuck with
  2 cloves
1 teaspoon dried tarragon
1 bay leaf
3 or 4 celery leaves
1 sprig of parsley
3 quarts cold water
1 tablespoon or more salt

Put all ingredients except the salt in a deep 8-quart pot or stockpot. Bring slowly to a boil and skim off all the scum that forms on the surface. Reduce the heat, cover the pot, and simmer for 2½ hours. Add salt to taste, 1 tablespoon or more, and skim off any scum on the surface. (Test the meat. If it is tender, you can strip it from the bones to use for jellied veal, returning the bones to the stock. If not, return and continue cooking until it is.) Continue to simmer, covered, for 1 to 1½ hours more.

Remove the stock from the heat and strain through a sieve lined with several thicknesses of cheesecloth into a bowl. Cool until the fat rises to the top and then skim it off. You will have about 2½ quarts of stock. Refrigerate or freeze.

JELLIED VEAL. Pour over the meat taken from the bones just enough fat-free stock to cover, and allow to set. The chilled veal stock should make a strong jelly, because of the gelatin content of the bones, but if it doesn't set firmly, you can stiffen it by adding up to 1 tablespoon unflavored gelatin for each pint of stock. To do so, return the stock to a saucepan and heat. Soften the gelatin in ¼ cup cold water, then stir into the hot stock until dissolved.

VEAL ASPIC. If you further reduce and clarify the veal stock, as you did for the chicken consommé, you will have a delicious, sparkling clear aspic to coat a cold dish.

# ❧ Pot-au-Feu and Beef Stock

While there are many versions of the classic pot-au-feu, I have evolved one that I find very useful because it gives me the initial makings of a good flavorful beef stock which can be cooked down until very strong and concentrated, and then frozen. Reduced even further and clarified, it can be boiled down, down, down, very slowly, until it forms *glace de viande*, a highly concentrated meat glaze or essence.

In addition to the beef and chicken you will need plenty of bones—and you can throw in a few chicken necks and backs, too, which make the stock richer. This can't all be made in one pot—it would have to be fantastically large—but if you have two 8- to 10-quart pots, you can divide the ingredients between them. If you have only one big pot, cook the basic pot-au-feu one day, cool and degrease the leftover stock, and the next day boil this with bones, chicken necks and backs, vegetables, and seasonings.

## Pot-au-Feu

**Makes 8 servings, plus leftover beef**

FOR POT-AU-FEU

2 to 3 pounds bones (beef,
  beef marrow, veal)
5-pound piece shin of beef
1 large onion, peeled and stuck
  with 2 cloves
1 carrot, scraped
1 leek, well washed and
  trimmed
1 white turnip, peeled
2 garlic cloves, peeled
1 bay leaf
1 sprig of parsley
1 teaspoon dried thyme
1 tablespoon salt
4- to 5-pound roasting chicken,
  trussed (see page 73)

POT #2

5 to 6 pounds bones
2 pounds chicken necks
  and backs
Repeat the vegetables and
  seasonings above

ACCOMPANYING
VEGETABLES FOR
THE POT-AU-FEU

Medium potatoes, scrubbed,
  skins left on (1 or 2
  per serving)
Leeks, well washed and
  trimmed (1 per serving)
Carrots, scraped (2 per serving)
Other accompaniments:
  Crisp slices of toasted
  French bread, coarse salt,
  cornichons (tiny French
  pickled gherkins), French
  mustards

Put all the pot-au-feu ingredients except the chicken in the first pot with water to cover. Put all the ingredients in pot #2 with water to cover. Bring the water in both pots to a boil over high heat and boil for 5 minutes, skimming off the scum that rises to the surface. Reduce heat until water just simmers; cover the pots and cook for 3 hours. Check now and then to see that the water is simmering, not boiling. After 2½ hours, test the meat on the beef shin with the point of a knife. If it seems to be getting near the point of tenderness (there will be some resistance; the knife will not go in easily), add the chicken, which will take 45 minutes to 1 hour to cook. If necessary, add more water to barely cover the chicken. Continue to simmer until the chicken and beef are tender, removing the chicken if it is done before the beef, covering it with foil and keeping it warm. Let the bones in the second pot continue to cook up to 4 hours.

About 30 minutes before the end of the cooking time, put the potatoes to boil in salted water to cover, first cutting a small strip from around the center, a little belly band, which will prevent them from bursting. Add the other accompanying vegetables —leeks and carrots—to the pot-au-feu.

When the chicken and beef are tender, remove them to a large platter; scoop out the leeks and carrots, and arrange with the potatoes around the meats. Strain the broth from the pot-au-feu and bring it to a boil, carefully skimming off as much as possible of the fat that rises and forms a skin on the surface (have the pot half on, half off the heat, and boil slowly; in this way the fat will form to the side away from the heat and is more easily skimmed). Serve some of this broth in bowls, accompanied by ¾-inch-thick slices of French bread, crisped in a 250° oven. Carve the beef and chicken and serve with the vegetables and dishes of coarse salt, sour pickles, and horseradish. Leftover beef may be used for beef salad or other cold beef dishes.

## Beef Stock

Strain the broth from the pot-au-feu into a large bowl through a sieve lined with several thicknesses of cheesecloth and chill overnight. The next day, remove the layer of fat on the top; put the broth in a large pot, uncovered, and simmer very slowly for 3 to 4 hours to concentrate and reduce the stock. Strain again; refrigerate or freeze. At this point the stock may be clarified in the same way as the chicken stock, using 1 egg white, beaten until frothy, and 1 eggshell for each quart of stock.

GLACE DE VIANDE. After clarifying the stock, boil it down, very, very slowly in an open pan, at the faintest ebullition, until it has reduced to a thick syrup or glaze, being careful that it does not stick or burn. This can take from 24 to 48 hours, depending on how much stock you start with. The syrup should be thick enough to coat a spoon. Strain this into a jar; cool, then cover and refrigerate or freeze.

COLORING BEEF STOCK. There are two ways to give beef stock a deep, rich brown color. One way is to put the bones in a shallow pan, such as the broiler pan, before boiling them, and bake in a 450° oven for 30 to 40 minutes until nicely colored, or to brown them under the broiler about 6 inches from the heat, turning once. Then cook as before, for 4 hours.

The other way, if you are making a brown sauce and want it to be glossy and richly colored, is to make a caramel coloring and add a few drops when you make the sauce. This method is described in the chapter Thickeners and Liaisons, page 275.

# Poule au Pot (Chicken in the Pot)

*I believe it was Henri IV who first advocated a chicken in every pot and poule au pot has passed down through the years as his memorial. It is a perfect dish for Sunday lunch. You might wish to double the recipe, for the cold edition is almost better than the hot.*

**Makes 4 servings**

4- to 5-pound roasting chicken
1 beef marrow bone
4 to 6 leeks, well washed and
   trimmed
4 medium onions, peeled
4 carrots, scraped
2 medium turnips, peeled
1 rib of celery
1 teaspoon thyme
2 or 3 sprigs of parsley
1½ tablespoons salt

## THE STUFFED CABBAGE LEAVES

1 good-sized head of cabbage
2 medium onions, peeled and
   finely chopped
1 garlic clove, peeled and
   finely chopped
4 tablespoons (½ stick) butter
1½ pounds ground pork
½ pound mushrooms,
   finely chopped
3 or 4 chicken livers, chopped
2 teaspoons salt
1 teaspoon thyme
½ cup freshly made bread
   crumbs
¼ cup cognac
2 eggs, lightly beaten
Cabbage liquid or chicken
   broth for poaching
12 small new potatoes

Truss the chicken (see page 73) and put it in an 8-quart pot with the marrow bone, vegetables, thyme, parsley, salt, and enough water to cover the chicken. Bring to a boil, skim off the scum that rises to the surface; reduce the heat; cover the pan and simmer the chicken for 50 minutes to 1¼ hours, or until it is just tender (the leg will move easily). Be careful not to overcook it. Should the chicken be done before the vegetables, remove it to a hot platter and cover with foil to keep warm.

While the chicken is poaching, blanch the cabbage by boiling it in salted water to cover for 15 to 18 minutes, or until the leaves separate easily from the head. Remove and drain, reserving liquid.

To make a stuffing for the leaves, sauté the onions and garlic in the butter in a heavy skillet over medium heat until they are barely wilted, then, with a fork, blend in the ground pork, chopped mushrooms, chicken livers, salt, and thyme. Return the skillet to heat and cook for 10 minutes, tossing from time to time; then add the bread crumbs, cognac, and eggs and cook the mixture over low heat until thickened. If it seems too liquid (it should be firm but moist), carefully drain off excess fat.

Gently remove the leaves from the cabbage and spread them flat on a board. Cut out a V-shaped piece from the bottom of the coarse rib in the center of each leaf, so it will roll easily. Put some of the stuffing on each leaf. Then roll it up carefully, tucking in the sides as you do so to make a neat package. Arrange the stuffed leaves, seam side down, side by side

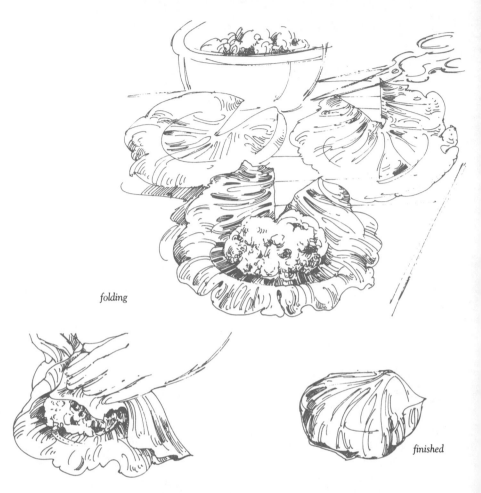

*folding*

*finished*

in a skillet, putting them close together so they don't unroll. Pour in enough of the reserved cabbage liquid (or chicken broth, if you prefer) to cover and simmer them gently for 30 minutes.

Twenty minutes before serving, peel a band of skin from around each potato to stop it from bursting. Put the potatoes in a pan with cold water to cover and 1 tablespoon salt, bring to a boil, then boil until just pierceable with the point of a knife. Drain and return to the pan over low heat to remove any remaining moisture.

Taste the chicken broth for seasoning, and adjust if necessary. Serve the chicken on a hot platter surrounded with the stuffed cabbage leaves, the potatoes, and the vegetables from the pot. Serve each person some of the broth separately. Carve the chicken and serve. This dish is usually accompanied by small bowls of coarse salt, cornichons, and grated Gruyère cheese. A Beaujolais—a Moulin-à-Vent or a Fleurie—is the best wine to serve.

# Steaming

## 🍃 Beefsteak and Kidney Pudding

*Steaming in simmering water is the method used to cook the British steak and kidney pudding, a very old form of cookery which survives here mainly in steamed puddings, such as Christmas pudding. The pastry for this is quite different from regular pie pastry—it is lubricated by finely chopped suet. I well remember, as a young man when I was first in England, eating at a small bistro near the office of some friends. Although the proprietor was a Belgian, there was always a magnificent steak and kidney pudding on Wednesdays to which he gave a rather Continental touch by using wine instead of the customary water or stock.*

**Makes 4 servings**

### SUET PASTRY
½ pound cold beef suet
4 cups all-purpose flour
1½ teaspoons salt
6 to 8 tablespoons ice water

### FILLING
2 pounds top round of beef
　or beef chuck, cut into
　2½ inch cubes
Flour
1 or 2 veal kidneys
　Or 6 to 8 lamb kidneys
2 large onions, peeled and
　finely chopped
1 cup finely sliced mushrooms
3 tablespoons chopped parsley
1 tablespoon salt
1 teaspoon thyme
1 teaspoon freshly ground
　black pepper
1½ cups boiling water or
　beef stock

To make the pastry, chop the suet very, very fine by hand. Combine with the flour and salt and rub together until the mixture resembles coarse meal. Add the ice water (don't add it all at once; you may not need 8 tablespoons) and pull the pastry together by rolling it into a ball and kneading it very well until it is smooth and well blended. Sprinkle it with a little flour and chill for 30 to 40 minutes.

Divide the pastry into two pieces, one twice as large as the other. Roll the larger piece into a circle about ¼ inch thick, roll it over the rolling pin, and unroll it over a 6-cup pudding basin, letting it slip into the basin and easing it into the bottom of the bowl and around the sides, leaving an overlap around the top. Roll out the smaller piece and cut from it a   strip an inch wide and long enough to go around the circumference of the basin. Dampen the edge of the pastry lining the basin and fit the strip around it.

Toss the beef cubes lightly in flour and put in the pastry. Trim the covering membrane and fat from the veal kidneys. Cut them into 1-inch cubes; sprinkle them lightly with flour and mix with the beef. (If you can't find veal kidneys and use lamb kidneys, they should be soaked in milk for 1 hour to take away some of their strong flavor, then dried and cut in cubes.) Add the onions, mushrooms, parsley, and seasonings. Mix all the filling ingredients together well with your hands and then pour in the water or stock.

Roll the remaining piece of pastry again into a circle large enough to fit the top of the basin. Dampen the edge of the pastry strip with cold water and put on the top crust. Pinch and crimp the two edges together to seal them well. Cover the top of the pudding with a piece of foil, tucking it over the sides of the basin and tying it with string, then put the basin on a clean dish towel that has been wrung out in hot water, sprinkled well with flour, and shaken to get rid of the excess.

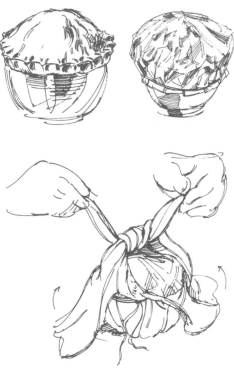

Tie the towel securely under the rim of the basin with string; bring up the diagonally opposite corners of the towel, two at a time, and knot them over the top of the basin to provide a handle

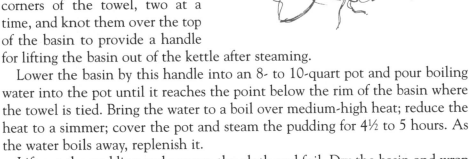

for lifting the basin out of the kettle after steaming.

Lower the basin by this handle into an 8- to 10-quart pot and pour boiling water into the pot until it reaches the point below the rim of the basin where the towel is tied. Bring the water to a boil over medium-high heat; reduce the heat to a simmer; cover the pot and steam the pudding for 4½ to 5 hours. As the water boils away, replenish it.

Lift out the pudding and remove the cloth and foil. Dry the basin and wrap it in a linen napkin. Serve the pudding from the basin and accompany with boiled potatoes and a red wine.

# Poached Sausages

Link sausages are usually poached in about ½ inch of water for 4 to 10 minutes, according to size, after which they can be sautéed, broiled, or baked. The initial poaching precooks the sausages and draws off some of the fat. Large, meaty sausages such as Polish *kielbasa*, Italian *cotechino*, and French garlic sausage are best poached. Prick the sausages well on both sides with a fork before poaching to prevent the skins from bursting as they cook and allow the fat to drain.

# Sausages with Sauerkraut

*Sausages and sauerkraut are a time-honored and excellent combination. You need not use all the sausages specified—two types would be sufficient, one large (kielbasa, cotechino, or garlic sausage) and 12 small sausages (bratwurst, weisswurst, or knockwurst).*

**Makes 8 servings**

2 pounds fresh sauerkraut
4 strips ½-inch-thick bacon or salt pork
1 medium onion, peeled and sliced
About 2 to 2½ cups chicken or beef broth
1 kielbasa, cotechino, or garlic sausage
12 shallots or green onions, peeled and chopped
Red wine to cover the sausage
4 bratwurst
4 weisswurst
4 knockwurst
2 tablespoons butter

Wash the sauerkraut well in a colander under cold running water, lifting it up with your hands to let the water run through it. Drain well. Arrange the bacon or salt pork in the bottom of a saucepan; add the sauerkraut and then the onion. Pour on enough broth barely to cover. Bring to a boil; cover; reduce the heat and simmer for 40 minutes.

Meanwhile, put the *kielbasa* or other sausage in a deep skillet with the shallots or green onions and add red wine barely to cover. Bring to a boil; reduce heat to a simmer and poach, turning the sausage several times, for 35 to 40 minutes.

At the same time, put the bratwurst, weisswurst, and knockwurst in another skillet, with water barely to cover, and poach for 10 minutes. Remove and drain the bratwurst; now melt the butter in that same skillet and sauté the bratwurst over medium heat until lightly browned.

To serve, arrange the sauerkraut on a platter and surround it with the various sausages. Halve the smaller sausages and thickly slice the large one. Serve with boiled potatoes, a choice of mustards, and either an Alsatian Riesling or beer.

# Poached Fish and Shellfish

Although fish is sometimes poached in salted water or milk, or water and white wine, the more usual way to cook it is in a court bouillon, which gives it additional flavor.

A court bouillon (the term originally meant a short sauce or small flavoring agent) is the aromatic seasoned liquid used to cook certain foods—fish, galantines (boned, stuffed, and poached poultry or meat), birds, pigs' or calves' feet, and various poached or boiled dishes. The ingredients of a court bouillon vary according to the food being cooked, but they usually include, in addition to the water, vinegar and herbs; or herbs and spices; or red or white wine (depending on the dish), seasonings, herbs, and spices. A court bouillon is made by a process of boiling, reducing, simmering, and, if the liquid is to be used for a sauce after the food has been cooked, a second fast reduction by means of rapid boiling. A court bouillon may be as simple or as elaborate as you wish. Here are recipes for both types.

## Court Bouillon I

1 cup white wine vinegar
1½ tablespoons salt
1 onion, stuck with 2 cloves
1 rib of celery or a few leafy
   celery tops
4 or 5 slices of carrot
½ teaspoon thyme
6 peppercorns
1 bay leaf
2 or 3 sprigs of parsley
6 cups water

Put the ingredients in a pot large enough to hold whatever fish you are going to cook, and bring to a boil over high heat. Continue to cook at a fast boil for 5 minutes, or until the liquid is slightly reduced and the flavors concentrated. Turn the heat down so that the liquid is just simmering before lowering the fish (steaks, fillets, or whole fish) into it.

# Court Bouillon II

*This version includes wine and fish heads and bones, which give it a more intense flavor. If you can't get heads and bones, buy a largish, bony fish that can be discarded afterward—a fish that is not for eating.*

4 cups white wine
½ cup white wine vinegar
1 large onion, peeled and
    stuck with 2 cloves
2 carrots, scraped and thinly
    sliced
2 garlic cloves, peeled and
    crushed
1 teaspoon dried thyme
1 teaspoon dried tarragon
1 rib of celery
12 peppercorns
1 bay leaf
6 sprigs of parsley
2 tablespoons salt
2 to 3 pounds fish heads
    and bones
8 cups water

Bring all the ingredients to a full, rolling boil in a large pot and boil for 5 minutes. Reduce the heat until the liquid is simmering, cover the pan, and simmer for 1 hour. Remove and discard the fish bones and heads, or the whole fish, before adding the fish to be poached.

# Fish Poached in Court Bouillon

Measure the depth of the fish at its thickest point to determine the cooking time (see page 113). Wrap the fish in cheesecloth or place it on a double thickness of heavy aluminum foil large enough to extend above the rim of the fish cooker or cooking pot. Lower the fish into the simmering court bouillon and simmer it 10 minutes per measured inch. Carefully remove it from the court bouillon by lifting the ends of the foil or cheesecloth, and transfer it to a heated platter.

If you are making a sauce from the court bouillon, keep the fish warm. Reduce the bouillon by rapid boiling to about 2½ cups and strain it through a linen towel or napkin. You can make a sauce using ¾ cup of this reduced liquid, adding ¼ cup dry white wine, and enriching it with cream and egg (see white wine sauce for fish, page 274).

Use the white wine court bouillon II to poach large fish such as striped bass, salmon, and red snapper.

# Poached Fillets of Fish with White Wine Sauce

*In this case, the fish is not poached in a court bouillon, but in equal parts of water and white wine, and the reduced poaching stock is used to make and flavor the sauce.*

**Makes 4 servings**

4 large or 8 small fish fillets
White wine and water
¼ teaspoon salt
1 sprig of parsley
1 slice of onion
3 tablespoons butter
3 tablespoons flour
½ cup heavy cream
2 tablespoons finely chopped
　parsley
½ teaspoon dried tarragon
Salt, freshly ground black
　pepper, nutmeg
2 tablespoons grated
　Parmesan cheese

Measure the fillets, which will be poached according to the general rule of thumb for all fish—10 minutes per measured inch of thickness (see page 113). Lay them flat in one layer in a large skillet and barely cover with equal quantities of white wine and water. Add ¼ teaspoon salt, parsley sprig, and slice of onion. Bring the liquid to the boiling point, then reduce the heat and simmer gently for the required cooking time. Test for doneness with a fork or toothpick—if the fish flakes easily, it is done. Slide a long metal spatula under each fillet and carefully remove, without breaking, to a hot baking dish. Keep the fish warm while you make the sauce.

Strain the poaching liquid and measure. Reduce to 1 cup by boiling rapidly over high heat. Melt the butter in a saucepan; blend in the flour and cook over medium heat for a minute or two, stirring with a wooden spatula, until the roux is golden and bubbling. Then mix in the reduced fish stock and stir over medium heat until the sauce is smooth and thickened. Mix in the cream, parsley, and tarragon and stir until heated through. Taste for seasoning, adding salt if necessary, a little freshly ground pepper, and a little grated nutmeg. Pour over the fish, sprinkle with grated Parmesan cheese, and put under a preheated broiler until the surface of the sauce is lightly browned. Serve with tiny boiled potatoes and a purée of spinach, and drink a dry white wine—an Alsatian Riesling or a Mountain White from California.

# Shellfish à la Nage

One of the best ways I know to cook shellfish is à la nage, the French term for a style of preparation in which shellfish are both cooked and served "swimming" in a white wine court bouillon and eaten hot, tepid, or cold. If you live in a part of the country where you can get fresh-water crayfish, try this recipe with them; otherwise use large raw shrimp, or small lobsters (use the timing for boiled lobsters in the following recipe).

**Makes 4 to 6 servings**

COURT BOUILLON

2 or 3 carrots, scraped

2 medium onions, very thinly
  sliced

½ cup parsley sprigs

1 teaspoon thyme

1 bay leaf

1 tablespoon salt

4 peppercorns

4 cups dry white wine

1 or 2 cups water

THE SHELLFISH

4 dozen crayfish or
  large shrimp
  Or 4 to 6 small lobsters

With the tines of a fork or a stripper, the little gadget that cuts thin strips from lemon rind, score the outside of the carrot and then slice it very thin—the idea is that the slices will look like flowers and be more attractive in the plate than plain old carrot rounds. Put all the court bouillon ingredients in a deep pot and bring to a rolling boil over high heat. Then drop in the crayfish and cook for 10 minutes at the boiling point—not a rolling boil. If using shrimp, cook for 3 minutes. Remove at once and arrange in deep serving bowls or soup plates and ladle some of the aromatic court bouillon around them, with little bits of the carrots and onions. Sip the bouillon as you eat the shellfish. It's a good idea to have some melted butter and lemon wedges to enhance the delicate flesh of the shellfish, which are shelled at the table by the diners.

# Boiled Lobsters

Once an East Coast delicacy, lobsters are now shipped all over the country. Most lobsters sold in markets weigh a pound to a pound and a half, but it is definitely worth buying larger lobsters if you can find them. Always look for lobsters that are active and lively, for these give the best eating. If your fish market can pick out the females, they are preferable for they have the coral, or roe. Ask to have the claws tied, if that has not been done already, so you will have no trouble with the beast. Count on one lobster per person.

You will need a large pot—an 8-quart size, or larger if you are cooking more than a couple of lobsters. Fill it about half full of water, season with 3 tablespoons salt, and bring to a boil. Grasp the lobsters firmly behind the head and sink them, head first, into the boiling water. This assures a sudden death. After the water returns to a boil, boil the lobsters 5 minutes for the first pound and 3 minutes more for each additional pound.

Don't cool the lobsters in the water or they will be overcooked. Remove them immediately and serve hot or, if you are serving cold lobster, let cool.

If you are serving them hot, cut off a little piece of the shell at the head and drain the liquid from inside. Then split the lobsters in half lengthwise with a heavy chef's knife, remove the dark intestinal vein that runs down the center of the body, and crack the claws with lobster or nut crackers. Leave the toma-lley (the greenish liver) and any coral (the bright red roe) in the shell.

Serve the lobsters with melted butter, wedges of lemon, good bread, and chilled white wine. Provide lobster crackers and picks for winkling the meat from the claws.

If you are serving them cold, split and crack the lobsters and serve with may-onnaise.

# Soups

*Onion soup is surely one of the world's most comforting dishes. This version, slightly different from the usual, comes from Alsace, and one of the secrets of its richness is the beef stock with which it is made.*

## Onion Soup au Gratin                                        Makes 4 servings

2 medium-large onions, peeled
   and coarsely chopped
6 tablespoons butter
1 tablespoon flour
1 cup dry white wine
2 cups beef stock
Salt, freshly ground black
   pepper
Pinch of nutmeg
10 tablespoons grated
   Gruyère cheese
8 to 12 small slices of French
   bread
   Or small squares of bread

Sauté the onions in 3 tablespoons butter in a heavy saucepan over medium heat until they are limp and golden brown, shaking the pan well as they cook so they don't stick or burn. Stir in the flour, then mix in the wine and the beef stock. Season with salt and pepper to taste, and add the nutmeg. Cover and simmer over very low heat for 1 hour, then add 2 tablespoons of the cheese.

While the soup simmers, melt the re-maining 3 tablespoons butter in a skillet and sauté the bread over medium-high heat until crisply brown on both sides. Ladle the soup into ovenproof bowls; arrange two or three of the fried bread croutons on top and sprinkle with about 2 tablespoons cheese. Put in a 450° oven or under a hot broiler until the cheese melts and forms a thick browned crust.

# Four-Day Vegetable Soup

I happen to think that vegetable soups made without meat stock are infinitely more intriguing. The results are often so delicate and unexpected that one is inspired to improvise constantly and find new and even more delicious combinations, for to my mind, success with vegetable soups is entirely a matter of inspiration, taste, and inventiveness.

I remember going through the refrigerator and the vegetable basket one winter day while living in France and coming up with a considerable array of bits and pieces, which I turned into a thoroughly good soup. This continued with a series of variations for four days (hence the name of the soup), resulting in three hot soups and one cold. Each time I had a totally different and distinctive product. This recipe, then, is not to be slavishly followed, but to serve as a starting point for your own ideas.

**Makes 8 cups**

THE BASIC SOUP

1 large onion, peeled and
  finely chopped
3 garlic cloves, peeled and
  finely chopped
2 cups finely chopped cooked
  cabbage
2 carrots, peeled and shredded
1 small turnip, peeled and
  finely diced
4 whole mushrooms, chopped
4 leaves and stems of Swiss
  chard
2 small zucchini, finely diced
1 tomato, peeled, seeded,
  and chopped
3 or 4 leaves fresh rosemary
  Or 1 teaspoon dried
  rosemary, crushed
Salt, freshly ground black
  pepper

Put all the vegetables and the rosemary in a deep pan with water to cover and salt and pepper to taste—about 1 tablespoon salt and 1 teaspoon pepper. Bring to a boil gradually over low heat. Cover and simmer the soup gently for 1½ to 2 hours, or until all the flavors are well blended. Taste and correct the seasoning.

Four of us ate the soup that night, and the next day I added to the remainder another couple of peeled and chopped tomatoes, a few leaves of finely chopped spinach, another zucchini, and a few leftover cooked chickpeas. I added a bit of grated lemon rind and a touch of onion about 10 minutes before serving.

For lunch on the following day I had the soup cold with a dollop of *crème fraîche* and finally, on the fourth day, I added 2 or 3 peeled and diced beets, another cup of cabbage, 3 or 4 more mushrooms, and a little vegetable broth from vegetables I had cooked for lunch.

Of course, if you have some chicken or vegetable broth you can add it to your soup. The secret is to have variations of color and texture and flavor.

# Mussel Soup

*Mussels make one of the most delicious of all soups. Cooking them in a tightly covered pot causes the shells to open and the shellfish to yield up their delicious liquid for the broth.*

**Makes 6 servings**

2 quarts mussels
12 shallots, peeled and left
　whole
2 or 3 sprigs of parsley
1 teaspoon dried thyme or
　tarragon
6 tablespoons butter
1 cup dry white wine
Heavy cream to taste
Garnish: Whipped cream,
　lightly salted; finely
　chopped parsley

Clean the mussels. With a scouring pad and a knife scrub and scrape off the encrustations on the shells; wash them well and pull or snip off the beards, the stringy black thread protruding from the shell. Put them in an 8-quart pot of heavy aluminum, enameled iron, or stainless steel with the shallots, parsley, thyme or tarragon, butter, and wine. Cover the pan tightly; bring to a boil, then reduce the heat to medium and cook the mussels for about 12 to 15 minutes. Remove the opened mussels and cook any with shells that remain shut for another 5 minutes. If they still do not open, discard them, for they are dead.

Remove the opened mussels from the shells and put them in the container of a blender or food processor. Strain the broth through a triple thickness of cheesecloth (this will trap any sand that came out of the mussel shells), then put the shallots from the mussel broth and about 1 cup of the broth in the blender or food processor with the mussels and blend or process until smooth. Stir this purée into the remaining strained broth, reheat, then stir in heavy cream to taste. Serve the soup in cups, topped with a spoonful of salted whipped cream and a sprinkling of chopped parsley.

# Pasta

Pasta is so good, and so easy to cook if you know how. The main thing to remember is that it must have a really big pot and plenty of water, which gives it room to expand and to move around, so that the pieces don't stick together. The water should be well salted, for nothing tastes worse than bland pasta. If you like, you can add a little oil to the water, which helps to prevent the strands from sticking together.

Pasta is the comprehensive Italian name for dried starch products (such as spaghetti, noodles, macaroni) that we usually call by name. The shape and size are unimportant, for the taste and method of preparation are the same.

In some cities you may find shops where pasta is freshly made. Because it is not dried until hard, like the commercial packaged products, it cooks in a very short time, a matter of 2 or 3 minutes, but it will not stay fresh too long. For best results it should be bought and cooked at once. Only the ribbony types of pasta such as fettuccine, tagliatelle, and lasagne can be bought fresh. The tubular pastas are put through a machine that shapes them into cylinders and they are practically always bought dry.

When it comes to the commercial, packaged pastas, you'll find there is a tremendous difference among those of the various manufacturers. It's a good idea to try different imported and domestic pastas until you find the one that best suits your palate and bite.

How much pasta does one cook? This depends entirely on whether you are serving it as a first or a main course—and also on who is going to eat it. As the late Alice B. Toklas was wont to say, "How do I know what appetites they will have?" How true. I know people who will cook a half pound of pasta for two, and others who will stretch it to serve three or four. I feel that a pound is about right for 4 servings, but this is a place where you should make your own decision.

## ❧ To Cook Pasta

For 1 pound of pasta, put 4 quarts of water in an 8-quart pot (you need a large pot because the water is kept at a rolling boil) and season it with 3 tablespoons of coarse salt—that's kosher salt. Cover the pan and bring the water to a full, rolling boil over high heat. Remove the cover; add 1 or 2 teaspoons of oil and the pasta of your choice. If you are cooking long thin strands of spaghetti or linguine, push them in the middle with a wooden spoon as the strands begin to soften so they are submerged. If the water drops below a boil, cover the pan briefly until it is back at the boil, then remove the lid.

Cook the pasta rapidly, at a seething, rolling boil. If you are cooking commercial pasta, start testing after 6 minutes. Fish out a strand with a long-handled fork or tongs and bite into it. Different pastas have different cooking times. The only way to know when it is done to your liking is to keep testing and tasting until it has reached the degree of doneness and firmness you like—but don't, please, overcook it until it is limp, soft, and mushy. It should be cooked but firm to the bite—al dente.

The minute the pasta is cooked, drain it in a colander (with small holes) or a large sieve, then return it to the pot and toss it with your hot sauce.

While in Italy I learned a trick that I think improves pasta immensely. Instead of just adding the sauce and tossing it with the pasta, stir them together gently with two forks and then let the sauce and pasta cook over low heat for 2 to 3 minutes, so the pasta becomes imbued with the flavor of the sauce.

## Pasta with Butter and Cheese (Pasta al Burro)

*Certainly the simplest and in many ways one of the most satisfying preparations of pasta is just to give it some melted butter and cheese.*

**Makes 4 servings**

1 pound spaghettini or
    fettuccine or macaroni
8 tablespoons (1 stick) butter,
    melted or softened
1 to 1½ cups freshly grated
    cheese (Parmesan,
    Romano, or Pecorino)
Freshly ground black pepper

Cook the pasta in boiling salted water, testing after 6 minutes, until it is done to your taste. Drain well in a sieve or colander; return to the cooking pot and add the butter. Toss well with two forks, then add ½ to ¾ cup of the grated cheese and a few grinds of pepper and toss well again, until the pasta is coated. Serve in heated deep plates, such as soup plates, pass the rest of the cheese in a bowl and the pepper mill, for seasoning to taste.

### Variations

♦ Use half shredded Gruyère and half Parmesan or Romano.

♦ After adding the cheese, add ½ cup slightly warmed heavy cream and toss until well mixed. Freshly ground pepper is needed here as well.

## Spaghetti with Garlic and Oil (Spaghetti Aglio e Olio)

*Equally simple, this pungent mixture will please garlic lovers.*

**Makes 4 servings**

1 pound spaghetti
1 cup good olive oil
5 or 6 garlic cloves, peeled
    and finely chopped
Freshly ground black pepper
1 to 2 tablespoons chopped
    parsley, preferably Italian
    Or 1 to 2 tablespoons
    chopped fresh basil

Cook the pasta in boiling salted water until done to your taste. While it is cooking, heat the oil until barely warm, add the garlic, and let it soak in the oil for 2 or 3 minutes. The amount of garlic depends on your tolerance—I usually gauge 1 clove per person and 1 or 2 extra. Drain the pasta and toss it with the oil and garlic, and freshly ground pepper. If you prefer, you may strain the garlic from the oil, but in doing so you lose the whole point of this dish. Cheese is superfluous with this, but chopped parsley or basil are wonderful.

### Variations

♦ Coarsely chop 4 or 5 garlic cloves and sauté them in ¼ cup olive oil until just lightly colored. Do not allow to darken or burn or the flavor will be bitter. Combine with ½ teaspoon crushed, dried hot red pepper and ¾ cup heated olive oil. Toss the pasta with the mixture as above.

♦ Add 8 to 10 anchovy fillets, coarsely chopped, to either of the oil and garlic mixtures. Toss the pasta with the sauce and garnish with chopped flat-leafed Italian parsley.


## Spaghetti with Clam Sauce

**Makes 4 servings**

1 pound spaghetti
⅓ cup olive oil
3 garlic cloves, peeled and
   finely chopped
2 7-ounce cans minced clams
½ cup chopped parsley,
   preferably Italian

Cook the pasta in boiling salted water until done to your taste. While it is cooking, heat ¼ cup of the oil in a skillet, add the garlic, and sauté until just lightly colored, not brown. Add the rest of the oil. Drain the clams and add the liquid from them, and ¼ cup parsley, and heat to the boiling point. Then add the drained clams and heat through thoroughly. Drain the spaghetti, cook it briefly with the clam sauce, and sprinkle with the rest of the parsley.

### Variation

♦ Chop about 1 dozen fresh or canned oysters for the sauce in place of clams.


## Tomato Sauce for Pasta

If you can't get really ripe tomatoes, canned Italian plum tomatoes make an excellent sauce.

**Makes about 3 cups**

¼ cup olive oil
1 large onion, peeled and
   finely chopped
3 garlic cloves, peeled and
   finely chopped

Heat the oil in a heavy, deep saucepan, add the onion and garlic, and sauté over medium heat for a few minutes, until golden. Do not brown. If you are using fresh tomatoes, peel, seed, coarsely chop them and add. Or add the

2 pounds ripe tomatoes
  Or 4 cups canned Italian
  plum tomatoes with their
  liquid
1½ teaspoons salt
½ teaspoon freshly ground
  black pepper
2 leaves fresh basil
  Or 1 teaspoon dried basil
3 tablespoons tomato paste

canned tomatoes with their liquid and cook over medium-high heat for 10 minutes, or until the liquid is reduced by a third. Add the salt, pepper, basil, and tomato paste and let the sauce cook at medium-high heat for 5 minutes more.

## Variations

♦ Sauté ½ pound thinly sliced mushrooms in 4 tablespoons hot butter for 3 minutes, tossing well. Add the tomato sauce and simmer for 2 to 3 minutes.

♦ Add to the sauce ½ pound Italian sausages, cut into thin slices and cooked for 4 to 5 minutes in a heavy skillet over medium heat until the fat has drained out and they are cooked through. Drain all but about 4 tablespoons of fat, and cook 2 to 3 minutes more. Add the tomato sauce and simmer for 2 to 3 minutes.

# Rice and Other Grains

There are many varieties of packaged rice on the market today, but the most popular and common are Carolina rice, a plump, creamy, long-grain rice, and converted long-grain rice. Oddly enough, converted rice, which has been parboiled, steamed, and dried, takes longer to cook than Carolina rice. Brown rice, much favored by health-food fans, is a natural, unpolished rice with only the husk removed (milling and polishing make the rice white) that requires a much longer cooking time. Arborio rice from Piedmont, a very starchy Italian rice with a round, short grain, is considered by many people to be the only rice to use for a risotto, but I've made risotto for years with long-grain Carolina and converted rice with very good results.

Cooking rice presents a problem to many people, and there are innumerable theories about how it should be done. For Carolina rice, I have found that the old Oriental cooking method I have known all my life works the best.

# ❧ Old-Fashioned Boiled Rice

**Makes 4½ cups rice, 4 to 6 servings**

Bring 4 quarts of water and 2 tablespoons of salt to a rapid boil in a 6- to 8-quart pot. Throw in 1½ cups of rice in small handfuls, making sure that the water continues to boil throughout. Boil the rice rapidly for 15 minutes, uncovered, then drain through a sieve. Do not overcook. This will give you fluffy rice with well-separated grains, slightly firm to the bite.

If the rice seems a little moist and not fluffy, after draining return it to the pan and dry out over very low heat for 2 or 3 minutes, stirring it occasionally with a fork to fluff it up. Always stir cooked rice with a fork, or toss it with two forks. Using a spoon bruises the grains and makes them sticky.

This method also works well with the Italian short-grain rice.

# Steamed Converted Rice

*For converted rice, I prefer to steam it covered. When you steam rice, remember that it will expand to three times its original volume (1 cup raw rice makes 3 cups cooked).*

**Makes 4 servings**

2½ cups water
1 teaspoon salt
1 tablespoon butter or oil
  (optional)
1 cup converted rice
1 or 2 tablespoons soft butter
  or oil (optional)

Put the water, salt, and butter or oil, if desired (this is not necessary if you are going to add butter or oil to the cooked rice), in a pan and bring it to a rapid boil. Add the rice, and when the water returns to the boil, cover the pan tightly, turn down the heat, and cook the rice over very low heat, without lifting the lid, for 20 to 25 minutes, until the water is completely absorbed. You may, for richer rice, substitute chicken stock for the water. The simplest addition is butter or oil. Add soft butter or oil to the rice. Toss with a fork until the grains are well coated.

## Variations

♦ HERBED RICE. With the oil or butter add 2 to 3 tablespoons finely chopped parsley and 1 to 2 tablespoons finely cut chives. Other herbs that might be added with the parsley and chives are chopped fresh tarragon and chervil.

♦ RICE WITH PINE NUTS. After adding the butter or oil, toss the rice with ½ cup pine nuts, which give a pleasant crunchiness.

♦ PUNGENT PARSLEYED RICE. Add to the cooked rice 6 to 8 chopped shallots that have been lightly sautéed in 2 tablespoons olive oil or butter until just limp and golden, and 2 to 3 tablespoons chopped parsley.

♦ SAFFRON RICE. Crush ¼ teaspoon saffron threads in a mortar and pestle, then add to the cooking water. (Saffron is very expensive but also highly concentrated.)

# Risotto

*I like to use a heavy skillet of cast aluminum, plain or enameled cast iron, or copper and stainless steel for risotto—the Italian rice dish in which the grains, though firm, become creamy like a pudding. A pan that will distribute heat and hold it well aids the bubbling activity and gradual absorption of liquid that a risotto requires.*

*The next important thing is to have good stock or broth. If making seafood risotto, clam juice may be used, but it is best to use homemade chicken, beef, veal, or fish stock if possible. These stocks keep well in the freezer. There are so many variations of risotto that it is always a pleasure to have the wherewithal on hand to make it at the last minute. I am particularly partial to chicken and fish stock for risottos because I like to use seafood and various meats and vegetables that blend well with those flavors.*

*The simplest risotto is made with rice, butter or oil, onion, stock, and Parmesan cheese.*

**Makes 4 servings**

6 tablespoons butter
1 small onion, peeled and
very finely chopped
1½ cups rice (long- or
short-grain)
3 to 4 cups homemade chicken
or beef stock, heated
½ cup freshly grated
Parmesan cheese

Melt 4 tablespoons butter in a heavy skillet; add the onion and cook over medium heat, stirring, until light golden. Add the remaining butter and, when it has melted, the rice. Stir the rice around in the butter with a fork until the grains have become coated and almost translucent.

Keep the stock hot in a pan on another burner. When making risotto, the stock is added by degrees, not all at once, so it must be kept at a simmer or the rice will not cook properly. When the rice is coated with butter, pour 1 cup of the stock into a measuring cup and add to the rice. Stir vigorously for a minute with a fork, then let the rice cook over medium-high heat until the liquid is almost absorbed, stirring it now and then so it does not stick to the pan. Add another cup of stock and continue to cook and stir until the liquid is almost absorbed. The rice should bubble and gradually soften and become creamy—at this point, add the stock more cautiously, ½ cup at a time, stirring until it is absorbed. You don't want to drown the rice with liquid, only add as much as it can absorb. You may find you need less, or possibly more, than the amount specified. As it cooks, taste a grain now and then.

When the risotto is done, after 25 to 30 minutes, the rice will be creamy and tender, but still *al dente* in the center, just firm to the bite, with all the liquid absorbed. Keep stirring well in the final cooking to prevent the rice from sticking to the pan. When done, sprinkle with the Parmesan cheese and stir it in with the fork. Serve at once, on hot plates.

## Variation

♦ RISOTTO VILLA D'ESTE (Risotto with Smoked Salmon). Cook the risotto as before, but substitute simmering fish stock for the chicken stock. When the risotto is almost done, stir in ½ cup heavy cream and let it cook down for 1 minute. Then stir in ⅔ cup finely shredded smoked salmon, distributing it evenly throughout the rice, 2 to 3 tablespoons finely chopped parsley, and 3 tablespoons freshly grated Parmesan cheese. Serve at once. A tablespoon or two of finely chopped fresh dill may be mixed in for an unorthodox but delicious touch.

# Rice Salad

*The secret of a good rice salad is to use freshly cooked rice and toss it with oil while it is hot. This coats the cooling grains and keeps them separate and fluffy.*

**Makes 6 servings**

4½ cups freshly cooked long-grain rice (*see page 41*)
3 tablespoons olive oil
¾ cup finely chopped green onions
Or red Italian onion
½ cup peeled, seeded, and diced cucumber
½ cup seeded and diced green or red pepper
½ cup peeled, seeded, and chopped tomato
¼ cup chopped parsley
2 tablespoons chopped fresh basil, if available
½ to ¾ cup vinaigrette sauce (*see page 290*)

The minute the rice is drained, put it in a bowl; add the oil and toss well with two forks until the grains are completely coated. Cool the rice at room temperature.

Mix in the chopped vegetables and herbs; add vinaigrette sauce to taste, according to how moist you like your rice salad—it should be well coated but not soggy. Toss lightly with two forks and serve in a salad bowl, which may be lined with greens, if you wish. This is a good summer accompaniment to broiled or grilled meat and poultry.

# Bulghur (Cracked Wheat) Pilaf

*Bulghur, or cracked wheat, a staple of Middle Eastern cooking, is light golden brown in color, with a nutty taste and texture. It is very good with meat kebabs or broiled chicken; as an alternate to rice; and may be used, like cooked rice, for stuffings.*

**Makes 4 servings**

2 tablespoons butter
1 tablespoon finely chopped
   onion
1 cup medium- or coarse-
   grind cracked wheat
½ teaspoon salt
¼ teaspoon freshly ground
   black pepper
2 cups chicken stock

Melt the butter in a skillet; add the onion and sauté over medium heat for 2 or 3 minutes, stirring, until limp and golden. Add the cracked wheat and stir until the grains are well coated with butter. Add the salt, pepper, and stock and bring to a boil. Lower the heat; cover the pan tightly and simmer gently for 15 minutes, or until liquid is absorbed and wheat tender.

## Variations

♦ Add toasted sliced almonds to the cooked pilaf.

♦ Sauté ½ cup sliced mushrooms in 2 tablespoons butter and add to the cooked pilaf.

# Cornmeal Mush (Polenta)

*American cornmeal mush, which is basically the same as Italian polenta, is a good and somewhat different accompaniment to meats, especially pork, game, chicken, sausages, chili and spicy Mexican dishes, or with salt cod, spinach, or just tomato sauce. Mixing the cornmeal with cold water first makes the texture less grainy.*

**Makes 4 to 6 servings**

1½ cups cornmeal
4½ cups cold water
1 teaspoon salt
4 tablespoons (½ stick)
   unsalted butter
½ cup grated Parmesan cheese

Put the cornmeal in the top of a double boiler and stir in 1 cup of the water. Mix well. Bring the rest of the water to a boil in another pan. When the cornmeal is well mixed, stir in the boiling water and cook over very low heat, stirring constantly, until the mixture comes to a boil. Stir in the salt. Put enough water in the bottom of the double boiler to come just below the top section. Bring it to a simmer. Put on the top of the double boiler with the cornmeal mush, cover, and steam over the simmering water for 1 hour. Stir in the butter and cheese and serve.

## Variation

♦ FRIED CORNMEAL MUSH. Pour the cooked cornmeal into a loaf pan and chill thoroughly until firm and set. Remove from the pan; cut into slices and sauté in butter until crisp and brown on both sides. Or, if you prefer, brush the slices well with melted butter on one side, sprinkle with grated Parmesan cheese, and brown under a hot broiler.

# Dumplings and Gnocchi

Chicken with dumplings is one of those simple but good American dishes we inherited from our European ancestors. Gnocchi, the Italian name for very small dumplings, are made of different starchy mixtures—potatoes, cream-puff paste, semolina, cottage cheese stiffened with flour. After poaching, they are usually served sprinkled with butter and grated cheese and heated through in the oven, or covered with a sauce. They make a pleasant change from other starches, as an accompaniment to sautéed dishes such as chicken livers or veal, or can be eaten like pasta, as a light luncheon dish, with a cheese or tomato sauce.

One advantage of gnocchi is that they can be made in advance and either chilled and reheated in the oven, or left in the cold poaching water, with a paper towel laid on the surface of the liquid to prevent the gnocchi from drying out, then gently reheated in the water. While dumplings are usually simmered in a covered pot to expand the starch granules in the flour, gnocchi are poached uncovered. Do not let the water boil, or the vigorous action may cause the dumplings or gnocchi to disintegrate.

## Old-Fashioned Chicken and Dumplings

*Follow the recipe for poached chicken in double chicken broth (page 20). While the chicken is cooking, make up the dumplings, which will be added for the last 15 minutes of cooking time.*

**Makes 4 to 8 servings**

DUMPLINGS
2 cups sifted all-purpose flour
3 teaspoons baking powder
1 teaspoon salt
2 eggs
⅔ cup milk

Sift the dry ingredients together. Beat the eggs and milk together lightly and blend with the flour mixture to make a fairly stiff dough. About 15 minutes before the end of the cooking time, remove the lid from the pot in which the chicken is cooking and drop rounded tablespoons of the dumpling dough over the surface of the liquid, spacing them a few inches apart as dumplings puff up. Cover the pan, keeping the liquid at a simmer, and cook the dumplings for 15 minutes, until light and cooked through. Do not remove lid while dumplings are cooking. Serve with the poached chicken.

# Potato and Semolina Gnocchi

*Semolina, also called farina, is a granular starch derived from the durum wheat used to make pasta. The quick-cooking farina breakfast cereal sold in supermarkets can be used for this recipe.*

**Makes 4 to 8 servings**

1½ pounds mealy potatoes, Idaho or Maine type
1 teaspoon salt
½ teaspoon freshly ground black pepper
Pinch of mace
1½ cups milk
1 cup farina breakfast cereal
½ cup grated Gruyère cheese
2 eggs, beaten
¼ cup melted butter
2 to 3 tablespoons grated Parmesan cheese

Peel and quarter the potatoes, put in salted water to cover; bring to a boil and boil until tender when pierced with a fork or knife point. Drain; put back over low heat to dry out, shaking the pan, then mash with a fork. Season with the salt, pepper, and mace and gradually beat in the milk, using a wooden spatula or an electric mixer. Place over medium heat in a 2½-quart saucepan and slowly mix in the farina until the mixture is very stiff. Mix in the grated cheese, then remove from the heat and mix in the eggs. Put the mixture in a flat buttered baking pan and refrigerate for 3 hours, or until firm enough to roll.

Have ready a large pot three-quarters full of simmering salted water. Take up tablespoons of the mixture and roll into balls between the palms of your hands. Drop the gnocchi into the water, about 8 at a time, and cook them for 4 minutes at a simmer, or until they rise to the surface, which means they are cooked. Remove with a slotted spoon as they cook and arrange in a well-buttered gratin dish. When all are cooked, drizzle melted butter over the top, sprinkle with the Parmesan cheese, and heat through in a 375° oven for 10 to 15 minutes. These will serve 4 as a light luncheon dish, or 8 as an accompaniment.

The gnocchi may also be served with a tomato sauce (see page 39).

# Eggs

The egg is a perfect object lesson in the techniques of boiling and poaching. To watch a poached egg form is to see a vivid example of the firming action of the cooking process. Eggs for poaching or soft-boiling should be the freshest possible. The fresher the egg, the firmer and more shapely the white of a poached egg will be.

## Poached Eggs

There are many different theories about poaching eggs, but this is the method I have found works best.

Use a skillet or a flat-surfaced pan that is not too deep—this enables you to slip the eggs in easily. Add water to a depth of 2 to 3 inches, 1 teaspoon salt, and ½ teaspoon vinegar, which helps the whites coagulate. Bring the water to a slow boil in which the bubbles just break the surface, not a fast, rolling boil which would whip the whites away before they could set, giving you a ragged-looking result. Have beside you paper towels or a linen cloth on which to drain the eggs, a slotted spoon or a flat, perforated skimmer for removing them from the water (I find the round, flat, well-perforated skimmer sold in Japanese stores that carry kitchen utensils ideal), and a large spoon for basting.

Break each egg into a tiny cup (such as a Japanese tea cup or a half-cup-size metal measuring cup with a handle), lower the cup into the water, and very quickly tip out the egg, holding the inverted cup there for a second or two to keep the white from spreading. Don't try to do too many eggs at one time—two or three, according to the size of your skillet, are about as many as can be handled easily. As soon as all the eggs are in the water, remove the pan from the heat and let the eggs poach very gently in the hot water for 3 to 4 minutes, basting the tops with spoonfuls of hot water if necessary. When the whites are firm and set, and the yolks just filmed with white, remove the eggs with the perforated skimmer and place them on the towels to absorb the excess water.

If you aren't going to use the eggs right away, lower them gently into a dish of cold water to stop the cooking, then remove, dry on towels, and put on a plate, covered with plastic wrap, until required. If the white is at all ragged, you can trim it with scissors.

## Soft-Boiled Eggs

Plunge the eggs into a pan of boiling water and boil for 3 minutes after the water returns to the boil. Give very large eggs 30 seconds more. Then remove from the water and serve. If the eggs are very cold, take the precaution of pricking the end of the shell with a needle before putting them in the water, which will prevent them from cracking. There's a little egg-pricking gadget on the market now, but a needle works just as well.

## Eggs Mollet

This type of boiled egg, which is used for eggs in aspic and similar dishes, both hot and cold, has a soft, runny yolk, but a white firm enough to stand up to handling—rather like an egg poached in its shell. Boil it like a soft-boiled egg, but give it 5½ to 6 minutes, then remove it from the hot water and immediately plunge it into very cold water to stop the cooking. As soon as the shell is cool enough to handle, shell it and either use it immediately or cover it with plastic wrap until needed.

## Hard-Boiled Eggs

Put the eggs in boiling water (if they are cold, prick them first) and boil for 3 minutes, then leave them in the water, with the heat turned off, for 9 minutes. Remove and run cold water over them, or plunge them into cold water. Let them cool completely before refrigerating or shelling.

# Dried Beans

The dried beans sold in supermarkets are washed and sorted before packaging and, unlike those sold loose, do not need to be picked over and washed before cooking. The recommended method of cooking is first to bring them to a boil in water to cover, boil them for 2 minutes, remove them from the heat, and let them soak, covered, in the cooking water for 1 hour. Then add extra water to cover, if necessary, and any seasonings and flavorings required in the recipe; bring to a boil, reduce the heat, and simmer, covered, until tender. Salt is added not during the initial cooking, but with the other seasonings, after the beans have softened in the water. There are also packaged, quick-cooking beans, peas, and lentils that have been specially processed and do not need presoaking. They usually take about 30 minutes to become tender. This type is labeled "quick-cooking" or "no soaking needed."

# Breton Beans

*This is the classic accompaniment to roast gigot, or leg of lamb, prepared in the Breton style. One pound of dried beans equals 6 cups cooked.*

**Makes 6 to 8 servings**

1 pound (2 cups) white
 beans, preferably Great
 Northern
1 onion, stuck with 2 cloves
2 garlic cloves, peeled
1 bay leaf
Salt, freshly ground black
 pepper
¼ cup tomato purée

Put the beans in a deep saucepan and add water to cover. Bring to a boil; boil 2 minutes, then remove the pan from the heat and let the beans cool, covered, in the cooking water for 1 hour. Don't let the beans sit in the liquid for longer than 1 hour or they will become too soft. Cook them soon after they have cooled.

After 1 hour, if needed, add more cold water to cover, the onion, garlic, bay leaf, and 2 teaspoons salt. Bring to a boil, then reduce the heat until the liquid is simmering; cover the pan and simmer for 45 minutes. Then add the tomato purée (don't add it until the beans have had this cooking time, as the acidity of the tomato may harden them). Continue to cook until just tender, about another 20 to 30 minutes, checking for tenderness now and then. The beans should be tender when bitten, but not soft, mushy, or broken. During the cooking, check the pan to see that the liquid is simmering, not boiling, as this would break up the beans. If they seem to be getting too dry, add a little more water.

When the beans are cooked, taste them, add more salt if needed, and pepper to taste. Drain the beans and discard the onion and bay leaf. When serving the beans with roast lamb, you may, if you like, stir 1 or 2 tablespoons of the pan juices from the roast into them, just before serving, and garnish them with a sprinkling of chopped parsley.

## Variation

♦ WHITE BEAN SALAD. Follow the directions for cooking the beans, but do not add the tomato purée. Drain and cool. Put the beans in a bowl with 1 cup finely chopped green onion and 4 tablespoons chopped parsley. Add 1 cup vinaigrette sauce (see page 290) and toss well. Allow to stand 1 to 2 hours before serving to mellow the flavors. If desired, the salad may be garnished with rings of thinly sliced red onion and 1 tablespoon chopped parsley.

# Vegetables

Many people believe in cooking vegetables by plunging them into quantities of boiling water and then boiling them rapidly until they are tender. It does no harm, especially if you are cooking root vegetables or green beans. However, I have experimented considerably with vegetable cookery and I find that I get extremely good results simply by putting vegetables in a pan, barely covering them with cold salted water (about 1 teaspoon salt per cup of water), putting on the lid, and bringing them to a boil over low heat and then simmering them very gently until they are tender. I have had splendid results with new potatoes, young carrots, green peas, and other tender things. Somehow gentle cooking in a minimum of water for the minimum time seems to give them a fresher taste.

When I cook corn on the cob, I put it in cold water and just bring it to a boil, without cooking further. It is done perfectly, without that starchy "cooked" taste I dislike in most corn on the cob.

There are other vegetables, notably asparagus and green beans, that I like to cook rapidly in water to cover in an open pan. Asparagus I lay flat in a skillet, cover with cold salted water, bring to a boil, and then cook very fast until it is barely tender, removing the stalks to a paper-towel-lined dish as they are ready. Depending on the thickness of the stalks, and there is always some variation, asparagus will take from 7 to 12 minutes to cook. You can't leave it—you must watch and test carefully until it is done to your personal taste and bite. You can tell when the spears are done by picking one out with tongs and gently shaking it—if the stalk bends slightly and the tip droops over and bobs back and forth, it is done: it should be crisply tender and a brilliant green. I cook green beans in the same way, picking one out and biting into it after 5 or 6 minutes' fast boiling, at which point it is easy to determine how near it is to being done.

If you try this minimum-water method, you'll find that it works pretty well for most vegetables. There are, of course, exceptions. Spinach should be put in the pan with only the water that clings to the leaves after washing, covered, and wilted down very rapidly over high heat. Other fast-cooking leafy greens, such as chard leaves, mustard greens, beet greens, and turnip greens, need very little water, just enough to keep them from sticking to the pan, and only a light sprinkling of salt. I cook artichokes in plenty of rapidly boiling salted water, with a lemon slice and clove of garlic, in a covered pot large enough to allow the water to circulate around them.

When it comes to cooking, it is impossible to give hard-and-fast cooking times. The only way to know if a vegetable is done is to test it with a fork or the point of a small sharp knife or to take one piece out and bite into it. The timing depends on so many things—the age, the size, the natural degree of tenderness (snow peas, for instance, need hardly any cooking, nor do very young green peas), and whether the vegetable in question is whole or cut up. Most green vegetables will cook in 15 minutes or less—be sure not to overcook them; root vegetables will take longer.

# ～ Basic Vegetable Purée

Many vegetables, after being boiled, can be turned into the soft, smooth mixture we call a purée by being put through a sieve or food mill and whipped with butter and seasonings. A blender or food processor does a speedy and smooth job of puréeing and mixing.

Firm vegetables are best suited to purées. Some good candidates are potatoes, parsnips, carrots, celery root, rutabagas, white turnips, salsify, Jerusalem artichokes, kohlrabies, cauliflower, broccoli, green beans, green peas, spinach, cooked dried beans, lentils, and chickpeas (or canned chickpeas). Certain purées go well together in combination, such as potato with celery root, or carrot, or rutabaga.

For 2 pounds sieved vegetable, use from 4 to 6 tablespoons butter, depending on the consistency of the vegetable. If the mixture is on the dry side, beat in a few tablespoons of heavy cream or sour cream. Potatoes, which need plenty of moisture, are usually beaten with boiling milk as well as butter. Here are some simple variations on the purée:

## Puréed Potatoes

*Mashed or whipped potatoes, more elegantly known as* purée de pommes de terre, *ideally should be light, fluffy, and creamy and they must be made at the last minute so they won't sit and become soggy. Opinions differ as to whether the potatoes should be cooked in their jackets or not. I believe that if they are floury and mealy they should be peeled.*

**Makes 6 servings**

Peel 2 pounds potatoes and cook them in salted water to cover until they are tender. Drain them, return them to the pan, and let them dry over medium heat for a few minutes. Mash the potatoes with a wooden or wire masher or put them through a food mill or potato ricer into a bowl. Add ½ to ¾ cup boiling milk and about 5 tablespoons softened butter and whip the potatoes with a whisk or wooden spatula or in the bowl of an electric mixer, using the whisk attachment. The potatoes must be smooth, very hot, and rather loose in texture. Do not let them get too thick and pasty or they will lose their delicacy. Season them with freshly ground pepper to taste and transfer them to a heated serving dish. Add a dot of butter and serve them very hot. To keep the potatoes hot, put them in a well-buttered pan set over hot water and cover them with buttered waxed paper.

## Purée of Celery Root
Makes 6 servings

Simmer 2 to 2½ pounds celery root in salted water to cover until it is just tender. Peel it, cut off the little root ends, and cut the bulbs in quarters. Put the bulbs through a food mill. Whip the purée with 6 tablespoons butter, 1 teaspoon freshly ground pepper, and additional salt, if needed. Spoon it into a heated vegetable dish, sink a large piece of butter in the center, and serve it at once.

Or you may combine the celery root purée with an equal quantity of puréed potatoes and whip them together with 1 stick butter and 3 to 4 tablespoons heavy cream. Spoon the purée into a heated vegetable dish and top it with a square of butter and some chopped parsley.

## Carrot Purée
Makes 6 servings

Scrape 2 pounds carrots and cut them into two or three pieces. Simmer them in salted water to cover until they are tender, drain them well, and put them through a food mill. Finish the purée in any of the following ways:

♦ Blend the carrots with 6 tablespoons butter, ⅛ teaspoon nutmeg, and additional salt, if needed. Spoon the purée into a heated serving dish and top it with bits of butter and some chopped parsley.

♦ Mix the carrots with 4 tablespoons butter and ¼ cup heavy cream. Blend the purée well with a spatula, spoon it into a serving dish, and top it with chopped parsley.

♦ Combine the carrots with an equal quantity of puréed potatoes. Add 6 tablespoons butter and 6 tablespoons heavy cream, and whip the purée with a wooden spatula or a heavy whisk until it is smooth and creamy.

## Puréed Parsnips with Madeira
Makes 6 servings

Wash and trim 5 to 6 pounds parsnips and put them in a 6- to 8-quart pan with salted water to cover. Simmer the parsnips until they can be pierced, drain them, and let them cool until they can be handled. Peel them and cut them into pieces 3 to 4 inches long. Put the pieces through a food mill and combine the purée with ½ cup melted butter, ½ cup Madeira, ¼ cup heavy cream, ¼ teaspoon nutmeg, and salt to taste. Beat the purée well, adding more butter or cream if it seems too dry. Spoon it into a 6-cup baking dish, sprinkle it with finely chopped walnuts, and top it with pieces of butter. Heat the purée in a 375° oven for about 20 minutes, or until it is heated through. Serve it very hot with game or roast fowl or pork.

# Vegetables à la Grecque

*Although this style of poaching tender young vegetables in a flavorful court bouillon, known as à la Grecque, did originate in Greece, it has now become completely iden-tified with the French cuisine. As the vegetables are eaten cold, rather than hot, they can be made in quantity and kept in the refrigerator in containers, to be brought out when you want a simple first course or cold vegetables for a summer buffet. Serve the different vegetables in the small serving dishes called raviers, or in flat pottery or glass dishes. A sprinkling of chopped fresh parsley or, if you like the flavor, chopped fresh coriander, makes a pleasant garnish.*

COURT BOUILLON
½ cup oil (olive, peanut,
   or corn)
⅓ cup white wine vinegar
⅓ cup dry white wine or
   vermouth
1 teaspoon salt
½ teaspoon freshly ground
   black pepper
1 bay leaf
1 or 2 garlic cloves, peeled
Dash of Tabasco
1 teaspoon dried thyme,
   tarragon, oregano, or basil
   Or, even better,
   1 tablespoon chopped
   fresh herb

SELECT FROM THE
FOLLOWING VEGETABLES
*Young tender green beans*
*Wax beans*
*Whole green onions or tiny white onions*
*Small, firm mushroom caps*
*Leeks, whole or halved*
*Fennel bulbs, halved or quartered*
*Fingers or cubes of eggplant*
*Small, firm zucchini, halved or thickly sliced*
*Celery hearts (tight white cores), halved*
*Flower buds of broccoli or cauliflower*
*Tiny young carrots*
*Tiny cymling or pattypan squash*
*Artichoke bottoms or quartered artichokes,*
   *trimmed and choke removed*

Do not simmer vegetables together, as they will have different cooking times. Cook your selection separately.

   Put the court bouillon ingredients in a large shallow pan or deep skillet, then add the cleaned, trimmed vegetable and just enough water barely to cover. The court bouillon is sufficient for 1 pound of green beans or carrots, or 1 large eggplant, cubed, or 8 artichoke bottoms, or a dozen mushroom caps.

Bring the liquid to a boil very slowly over medium heat, then reduce the heat and poach until the vegetable is just crisply tender when pierced with a fork or the point of a small sharp knife. Do not overcook. Remove from the heat, taste the liquid for seasoning, and add salt, if needed; then let the vegetable cool in the liquid. When cool, transfer to a refrigerator container or serving dish. Strain the poaching liquid and use again for other vegetables. If necessary, add more water.

# Fruit

Poaching in a simple syrup of sugar and water or wine is a classic method of preparing fruit for dessert. As the syrup is merely the cooking agent, it should not be overly sweet. Firm-fleshed large fruits, such as peaches, pears, apricots, or pineapples, are best for this process. You can also poach cherries and softer fruits, such as plums, gooseberries, and rhubarb, but they won't be as firm or as attractive as the larger fruits.

## ᴥ Poached Peaches

**Makes 4 servings**

1 cup sugar
1 cup water
1-inch piece of vanilla bean
   Or ½ teaspoon vanilla
   extract
4 ripe but firm, unblemished
   peaches

Combine the sugar, water, and vanilla bean in a heavy saucepan large enough to hold the peaches. Bring to a boil, and boil slowly for 8 minutes to make a simple syrup.

Meanwhile, put the peaches in a deep pan, pour over them enough boiling water to cover, bring it to a boil again, reduce the heat, and simmer the peaches for 3 minutes. This parboiling helps the skins to slip off easily and slightly softens the fruit. Remove the peaches from the water and peel them. Drop them into the syrup, reduce the heat, and poach them at a feeble simmer until just tender when pierced with a fork, from 4 to 12 minutes. Do not overcook. The time depends on the ripeness of the peaches. Remove the peaches to a serving dish, bring the syrup to a rolling boil, and reduce by boiling fast for 4 to 5 minutes, watching carefully to see that it does not turn dark and caramelize. Let it cool slightly, then pour over the peaches and chill before serving.

# Pears Poached in Red Wine

**Makes 6 servings**

2½ cups red wine
1½ cups sugar
1 lemon slice
2 cloves
6 firm and slightly underripe
    pears

Combine the wine, sugar, lemon, and cloves in a large flat-bottomed pan, such as a sauté pan. Bring to a boil over high heat, stirring until the sugar dissolves. Peel, core, and halve the pears, dropping each peeled half into a bowl of water acidulated with 1 tablespoon lemon juice to prevent discoloring. Reduce the heat so the syrup is simmering, drain and add the pears, and poach until tender, turning them once, for 10 minutes, or until just tender when pierced with a fork, but not overdone (the time depends on the size and firmness of the pears). They should still hold their shape and not be mushy. Serve hot, with a little of the syrup, or cool in the syrup and serve cold, again with a spoonful or two of syrup.

# Applesauce

**Makes 4 servings**

When making applesauce, you need just enough water to create the steam necessary to soften the apples, as they themselves contain a lot of liquid. Apples also vary so much in tartness that it is folly to sweeten them before cooking.

Peel 3 pounds of cooking apples, such as greenings or pippins, cut them into sixths, and cut out the cores with a small sharp knife. As you peel them, drop them into a bowl of cold water acidulated with 1 tablespoon lemon juice, to prevent them from turning brown. Place apples in a heavy saucepan and add ½ cup water. Cover and cook over medium heat at a gentle simmer until they are almost soft. Taste and add sugar, a little at a time, then taste again. When the apples are sweetened to your taste, continue simmering uncovered for 2 or 3 minutes to melt the sugar and cook down the sauce. If you like your applesauce spiced, add ¼ teaspoon of your favorite spice (such as ground cinnamon, nutmeg, mace, or cloves) when adding the sugar. For a smoother applesauce, put the cooked apples through a food mill to make a purée.

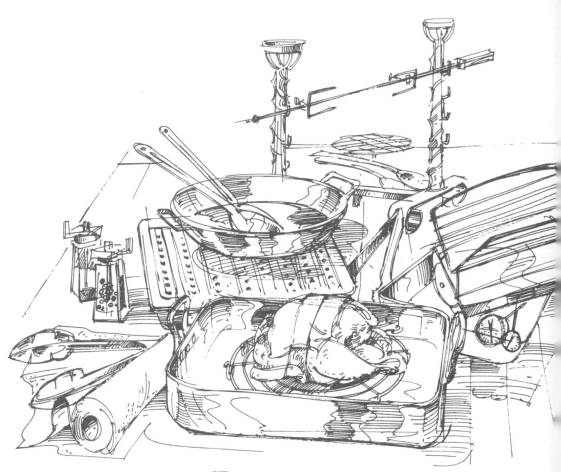

# Roasting

Whenever I think of roasting, my mind returns to our big family kitchen, which was equipped with a very large wood-burning stove. When we had guests for dinner, my mother or Let, who was our sometime-chef after my mother gave up her hotel business, prepared a glorious standing rib roast. First, she would go to her butcher, who obeyed her every wish and command, pick out the roast at least 2½ weeks ahead of time, and ask that it be hung an additional time, until the day she wished to roast it. She felt, and rightly, that well-aged beef had better flavor and better texture, as well as greater tenderness. Sometimes it would arrive covered with green mold, which was trimmed off before cooking, and I learned that this made the roast taste better.

My mother would buy quite a lot of extra suet and render it in the huge professional roasting pan that had been used in the hotel kitchen. It was a big, oblong black pan with rather shallow sides and in it was a rack with very short legs, just enough to elevate the meat from the pan bottom. On the day of the party, the suet was rendered in this pan until it was bubbling hot, wafting a lovely beef-scented air through the house. The roast, rubbed with flour, salt, and pepper, was put with this bubbling fat into a very hot oven and that first enticing sizzle as the meat hit the rack gave a wonderful preview of what was to come. The meat was basted regularly with the fat, then taken from the oven when it had just about reached its peak of perfection and placed on a hot platter on the back of the stove. The rack was removed and a good deal of the fat poured off—a ticklish business—and the pan returned to the oven to bake the Yorkshire pudding while the roast rested. The pudding batter, poured into the hot fat and popped into a 450° oven, rose to the most glorious golden-brown crispness and puffiness and took on a marvelous beef flavor. There was never any Yorkshire pudding left over. With the roast beef and Yorkshire pudding we had pan gravy and sometimes potatoes roasted in the fat to a crisp, well-done brownness, a most glorious combination. That was my introduction to roasting, and it created in me a passionate love for properly roasted meat that has lasted all my life.

Roasting is one of the oldest and most spectacular forms of cooking. Originally, roasting was done on a spit in front of the fire. What we call roasting, meat cooked by dry heat in the oven, was known until the end of the nineteenth century as baking. Spit-roasting was the popular way of cooking a piece of meat, while baking had a rather plebeian implication, as if you couldn't afford a spit for your fireplace.

Years ago, in the great houses, the spits were operated by dogs or by the scullery maids. I remember seeing in a house in France, between Cognac and Angoulême, traces of the sixteenth- and seventeenth-century kitchen which the owners had left for their own and their friends' enjoyment, while creating a modern kitchen in another part of the house. In the old fireplace was a treadmill spit that had been worked by dog power—or by manpower, which must have been a most exhausting job. A more civilized and later form of spit was operated by counterweights, and there was also a rather primitive form of tin oven that stood in front of the fire, with a curved reflector back to intensify the heat and a pan underneath to catch the drippings.

Anyone who has a spit on his outdoor grill or in his fireplace can testify to the delicacy and deliciousness of meat roasted in this way. A side of beef, a baron or leg of lamb, even a tiny rack of lamb will all come forth with great flavor and perfect texture. Some years ago, when I visited André Surmain in Majorca, he cooked a suckling pig on an electrically driven spit in front of a fire, and it was one of the most delicious pigs I have ever eaten.

Unfortunately, few of us these days can have a large fireplace with a revolving spit, and apartment-dwellers can't even have a charcoal barbecue with a rotisserie, so our roasting is done in the oven. Modern ovens are ideal for roasting—efficient, foolproof, and accurate because they are well calibrated, which means they are tested for calibration, or the accuracy of the thermostatic control. Occasionally, if you have an oven tested, you may find it will be 25 to 50 degrees off one way or the other, something that can easily be adjusted then and there.

There is a great deal of controversy about temperatures for oven roasting. Some contend that low-temperature roasting, at 325°, results in juicier meat and less shrinkage. Another school believes that the most effective method is to sear the meat at 450° or even 500° for 45 minutes to an hour; searing means sealing the surface by exposing it to high heat. Then reduce the heat to 350° or 325° for the remainder of the cooking period. There's a lot to be said for this method. It seems to me that, in most cases, high-temperature roasting gives a crustier exterior and juicier interior. However, there is always the chance—and this is the result of a great deal of testing on my part—that roasting too long at a high temperature gives you a well-done streak around the meat, while the inner part is pink or rare, as the case may be. In some ways you get a more even flavor and perhaps a more delicate texture from roasting throughout at a low temperature. I'm not going to take sides on this, because I roast both ways, and there are even some things, a fillet of beef or a chicken, indeed most birds, that I roast completely at a high temperature. I find that if chicken is roasted at 425° or even 450° for the entire cooking time, the result is crisper and better than if it is seared and cooked at a lower temperature, or cooked the whole time at 325°.

Roasting is a dry-heat process in which the meat or bird is cooked on all sides by even heat circulation. (For this reason, microwave ovens are not satisfactory for roasting, as the interior of the meat cooks first.) The roast should always be placed on a rack in a shallow roasting pan—either one of the adjustable V-shaped racks or a flat rack—or on the broiler rack and pan. Look at the display of roasting pans on page 56 and you'll realize how easily you can improvise. The important thing is never to put the meat directly in the pan or use one of those deep, high-sided pans incorrectly sold as a "roaster." Contact with the fat and juices in the pan will give the underside of the roast a soggy, stewed quality, no matter how carefully you roast it. With a rack and shallow pan the heat penetrates all sides evenly and the bottom will have the same crusty finish as the top.

I believe, as my mother did, that basting is an important part of roasting. A well-basted roast of beef has a character all its own. I don't think rack or leg of lamb needs basting, but a shoulder can benefit. Certainly veal is improved by regular basting—in fact, I prefer to braise veal so that it gets more moisture and flavor—and even pork can take some basting. Turkey and most game birds are all the better for basting. If you want my honest opinion, a big spoon is better to use for basting than those bulb basters, which I don't think do an efficient job. A big basting spoon holds plenty of pan juices and should be used frequently during roasting.

*P*robably one of the greatest aids to roasting ever invented is the meat thermometer, and by this I do not mean the old-fashioned meat thermometer with a dial listing recommended temperatures for different meats, from rare to well done. I remember when meat thermometers like this first came on the market, recommending internal temperatures that were quite ridiculous: 140° for rare beef, 170° for pink lamb, and 185° for turkey. Well, that may have been to the taste of the people who made up the meat charts these thermometers were based on but not to those of us who like our meat rare and our birds succulent. At 140° you get beef that is medium- or medium-to-well-done, lamb roasted to 170° is grey and tasteless, and at 185° the breast of the turkey is dried out.

Neither did these recommendations take into account the all-important factor that the internal temperature of meat or poultry continues to increase for 10 to 15 minutes after it comes out of the oven. It cooks, so to speak, by its own stored-up heat, so the temperature goes up another 10 to 15 degrees. If you roast beef to 125° or 130° and let it rest for 15 or 20 minutes, it will be the perfect temperature and the juices will have had time to settle and the connective tissues to become firm, so that the meat carves more easily and is tender to the knife and to the bite. If you cook lamb to 130° or 135°, no more, and then let it rest, you'll have delicious French-style pink, rarish lamb, rather than a stringy, gray-brown horror.

For years we were warned that pork had to be roasted to 180° to 185° to kill any possible trichinosis parasites. Well, now that they have found the bacteria are killed at 150° to 155°, we cook pork to no more than 165°, which gives a much better, juicier result. The same goes for veal. If veal, a rather dry meat, is cooked to 160° or 165°, preferably with some liquid (the process is actually nearer braising than roasting), it comes out juicy and perfectly done. Always remember that meat absolutely must have that 15-minute rest period (the exception would be a tiny rack of lamb, which shouldn't rest quite as long, as it would cool off too much).

If you are buying a meat thermometer, the most accurate available is the type that registers from 0° to 220° and comes with either a large or a small dial. These thermometers, which are based on the type used in laboratories, are so sensitive that they test temperature in just about a minute. Unlike most you'll still find on the market, these delicate thermometers must never be left in the meat while it is roasting; the high oven heat would ruin them. Instead, they should be inserted in the thickest part of the meat during the latter part of the estimated roasting time. Don't let the thermometer touch the bone as bones conduct heat, and that could throw your reading off. (You'll probably notice that roasts with the bone in cook somewhat faster than boneless ones—for that very reason.) Leave the thermometer in only until the needle settles.

Because these sensitive thermometers register from 0°, you can also use them to test the temperature of the meat before it goes into the oven. It's useful to make a note of this, because you can learn by experience how long it takes for a roast to reach the required internal temperature, depending on whether it has been frozen and thawed, left in the refrigerator, or allowed to warm up to room temperature.

I believe, incidentally, that meat should be left at room temperature before roasting, not taken straight from the refrigerator. There is a lot of controversy about this. The late Michael Field and I had a constant battle about it, because he insisted that it made absolutely no difference and I insisted that it did. I have always felt that meat left for 1 or 2 hours at room temperature cooks faster. If my roast is really big, I may leave it out for 3 to 4 hours. If you test the meat with your thermometer after taking it from the refrigerator and after letting it warm up, you'll see the difference it makes.

Testing with a meat thermometer is a much more accurate way of roasting meat than following the old so-many-minutes-per-pound method that the meat charts in many books give you, which never allows for the fact that two roasts of exactly the same weight may be of different shapes and thicknesses, a factor that will definitely affect the cooking time. To prove my point, recently I cooked two legs of lamb of almost identical weight but different thicknesses. One was rather flat, the other fully cushioned, compact, and rounded. The flatter leg, tested with the meat thermometer, took 40 minutes less cooking time than the plump, cushiony one. These are the little differences that one has to take into account when roasting in the oven. The variation in time can be just as great if you are roasting on a spit outdoors, even more so, for here the wind and the temperature of the air can noticeably affect the cooking time.

Roasting is a tricky and fascinating process. Even a meat thermometer is not always an infallible guide. I find it is chiefly my fingers that, through experience, can tell me by the way the meat feels whether or not it is done. The surface should feel firm to the touch, neither soft and yielding nor hard and resistant, with a springy resilience underneath. As you become a more experienced roast cook, you will learn to trust your hands, your sense of timing, and your accumulated knowledge. If you roast a great deal, on the spit and in the oven, you will find it an enormous benefit to make your own meat chart, with a schedule of the temperatures and times you have found to be perfect for your own taste. Yours may well differ from mine, or from those given in other cookbooks, but only you know what your preferences are.

I'm often asked whether I find any difference between fresh and frozen meat after it has been cooked. I have done many blindfold tests with students and with friends, and I can honestly say that I don't. Provided the meat is of top quality and has been commercially flash-frozen, the flavor and texture are just as good, sometimes even better. I'm not talking, of course, about the special you bring home from the butcher and throw into the freezer, because that will never be very satisfactory. Unless meat is professionally frozen, ice crystals will form inside.

Frozen roasts should be thawed, or they take too long to cook, although I find that small cuts such as steaks and chops are better cooked from the frozen stage and the regular cooking time doubled. If it's an emergency and you haven't time to thaw the roast, put the meat in the oven at 325° and roast it slowly.

While roasting may be one of the more demanding of the kitchen arts, requiring care, thought, and accuracy, it is also one of the most worthwhile. A fine roast, or a roast bird, is a magnificent sight when it is finished, arranged on a platter or carving board with some appropriate garnish, and brought to the table or the buffet for the carving ceremony.

Carving used to be one of the necessary skills of any host. Well, I'm afraid that most people today would not qualify as good carvers. I do know a few who are, including some women, but the art of carving in public, which used to be considered one of the delightful happenings at dinner with good friends, seems to have gone by the board. If you are proud of the meat you have roasted, you should be even prouder of it after you have carved it, so I suggest you study the carving drawings on pages 399–403 and practice a bit. Then, don't hide your talents in the kitchen, but let your guests have the pleasure of watching you carve a standing rib roast, a rack of lamb, or a turkey at table.

# Lamb

## ᭦ Roast Leg of Lamb

*At one time, lamb was very unpopular in this country—all because it was usually overcooked. I don't blame anyone turning against lamb that has been roasted until it is gray—brown, stringy, and unpalatable. Fortunately, I grew up in a home where lamb was treated properly.*

*Lamb is perfect when it is from rare to pink. The French like it very rare. Most Americans prefer it pink. I'm on the side of the very rare, but I will settle for pink. I suggest you try it pink first and see how juicy and delicious it can be when it is not overcooked, and then gradually you may find you want it rare. I can assure you that once you have had properly cooked lamb, you'll never again roast it to death.*

*A leg of lamb is covered with a tight, papery tissue called the fell, which should be removed before cooking. If the butcher has not already removed it, take a very sharp, pointed paring knife and loosen the fell from the fat and flesh, then cut or tear it off in chunks. It usually comes off easily. At the same time, remove a good deal of the fat from the lamb—this will improve the flavor considerably. Now you are ready to prepare the lamb for roasting.*

**Makes 8 to 10 servings**

*5- to 8-pound leg of lamb, fell and most fat removed*
*6 to 8 garlic cloves*
*2 to 3 tablespoons cooking oil*
*1 teaspoon dried rosemary*
*Salt, freshly ground black pepper*

Make 10 or 12 small incisions all over the top of the lamb with a small sharp paring knife, pushing the point in about 1 inch deep. Lightly crush the garlic cloves with the side of a heavy knife or cleaver, or with a meat pounder, to break the skins so they peel easily. Peel the garlic and cut the cloves into thin slivers. With your finger, push the slivers of garlic into the incisions in the lamb. Then rub the roast all over with a little of the oil, massaging it in with your hands.

Crush the rosemary in the palm of one hand, pressing it down with your other thumb to break up the spiky little leaves. (Rosemary is an easy herb to grow in the garden or in a pot, and you'll save money by drying your own.) Rub the crushed rosemary onto the lamb and then sprinkle it with freshly ground black pepper. Preheat the oven to 350°.

I find a broiling pan is perfect for roasting a leg of lamb. It allows the heat to circulate all around the meat so that it cooks more evenly and doesn't need basting. Oil the rack of the pan lightly and put the roast on it. Just before you put the roast in the oven, sprinkle it with salt. Many people will tell you that this will draw out the juices, but it is my feeling that when meat is salted just before roasting, the seasoning penetrates better and aids the flavor, while the oven heat helps to seal the surface.

Put the roast in the oven and forget it for 1 hour. After an hour, test the internal temperature with a meat thermometer to see how it is progressing. Insert the thermometer into the meatiest part of the leg, being careful not to let it touch the bone. The desirable finished temperature for the lamb, rare, is 135°. At the end of the first hour, the temperature should be between 90° and 100°, depending on the thickness of the meat. At this point, if you wish to serve the lamb with Bordelaise (see page 276) or mint sauce (see opposite page), prepare the sauce and set aside.

When the thermometer registers around 100°, you know that you have perhaps 25 to 30 minutes to go. If it is only 90°, you may need 35 to 40 minutes more. Return the roast to the oven, let it cook 15 to 20 minutes, then retest. When it has reached 135° remove the lamb to a carving board or a hot platter and let it rest for 10 to 15 minutes in a warm place before carving. Lamb fat congeals at a low temperature, so be sure always to serve the lamb on hot plates and a hot platter. For carving technique, see the drawing on page 402.

Roast leg of lamb is delicious served with just the pan juices. Sautéed potatoes are very good with it, and so is ratatouille, a Provençal vegetable stew with great affinity for lamb, or white beans mixed with a little cooked tomato, Breton style (see page 49). The English like mint sauce with lamb. To make it: wash, dry, and finely chop enough fresh mint leaves to make ¼ cup. Dissolve 2 teaspoons superfine sugar in 2 tablespoons boiling water and add to the mint leaves with ⅛ teaspoon salt and 3 tablespoons cider vinegar or wine vinegar. Taste, and add more sugar or vinegar as needed. The sauce should be thick. Let stand 30 minutes before serving for the flavors to mellow. Makes about ½ cup.

## Alternative Method for Roasting

Preheat the oven to 450°. Roast the lamb at that temperature for 25 to 30 minutes to sear, then reduce the heat to 325° and continue roasting as before. You may want to try both this and the preceding method to find out which you prefer. Both have virtues. Roasting part of the time at a high temperature gives you a crustier surface, but I find that it makes the outside of the meat slightly overdone. Roasting at one temperature for the entire time causes less shrinkage and more evenly colored slices when the lamb is carved. Take your pick.

## Roast Leg of Lamb, Baker's Style

This differs from the basic roast leg of lamb only in the garnishing. However, as potatoes are roasted with the lamb, use a rack and a shallow roasting pan instead of the broiler pan and rack.

Prepare the lamb as directed in the master recipe, putting it on a rack in a shallow roasting pan in a 350° oven.

Peel 2 pounds of small new potatoes, put them in salted water to cover, bring to a boil, and boil, covered, for 10 minutes. Drain the parboiled potatoes. After the lamb has roasted for 30 minutes, arrange the potatoes in the roasting pan. Melt 6 tablespoons unsalted butter in a small pan and, as the lamb and potatoes roast, baste potatoes well every 10 to 15 minutes, with the pan juices and butter. When the lamb has about 15 minutes' roasting time left, sprinkle both lamb and potatoes with salt and freshly ground black pepper. When the meat thermometer registers 135°, transfer the lamb from the roasting rack to a carving board and let it rest for 10 to 15 minutes in a warm place, keeping the potatoes warm in the turned-off oven. Carve, arrange the slices on a hot platter, and pour the pan juices over them. Arrange the roast potatoes around the meat and garnish them with a sprinkling of chopped parsley. A purée of green beans is a good accompaniment. Drink a good red Bordeaux or a light red Burgundy.

# Beef

You'll hear a lot of different advice about the proper roasting temperature for beef. Some people believe in searing the meat first at a high temperature, then reducing the temperature for the rest of the cooking time. Others prefer to roast the beef throughout at one temperature—high, medium, or low. I'm going to give you two methods for a rib roast of beef. In one the beef is seared first at a high temperature and then cooked until done at a low temperature. In the other method, it is cooked throughout at very low heat. Choose the method you prefer according to the way you like your beef. The seared roast will be crisp on the outside with a well-done streak near the surface and a rare eye of the rib. The slow-roasted beef will be perfectly cooked throughout and an even pink from the fat to the bone. Both are excellent eating and both are excellent methods of roasting beef. Carve both roasts thin for the best flavor, appearance, and eating. Thick slices lack the delicacy fine beef should have. Do not trim off all the fat when carving. I am among those who feel that the true flavor of the meat lurks in the fine crisp fat—and anyone who really doesn't care for the fat can always cut it off at the table.

## ~ Presearing Method for Rib Roast of Beef

Choose preferably a 4- or 5-rib roast cut from the first or prime ribs, to serve 6 people, with some leftovers; if you are having a large dinner party you may need a 7- or 8-rib roast. Have the roast "cut short"—with the short ribs removed, sometimes referred to as a 7-inch cut. The chine bone should be removed by the butcher, the ribs left intact, and the roast well trimmed of any connective tissue and gristle and the excess fat. A properly prepared rib roast should be well balanced—even in size and compact. Rub the meat well with ½ teaspoon freshly ground black pepper and ½ teaspoon of thyme if you wish. For added zest, you can also rub the fat and bone with a crushed garlic clove, but this is a matter of taste. Preheat the oven to 500°.

Place the roast on a rack in a shallow roasting pan and roast bone side down at 500° for 35 to 40 minutes, basting twice with 2 to 3 tablespoons melted butter or beef fat. Reduce the heat to 325° and continue to roast the beef for 30 minutes longer. Test the internal temperature by thrusting the meat thermometer into the thickest part of the eye of the rib, being careful not to touch the bone at any point. Remove the thermometer and continue roasting, basting every 20 minutes with the pan juices or melted beef fat. You may salt the roast after any of the bastings. Test again for temperature after 30 minutes and make a final test within 20 minutes after that. Estimate about 12 to 14 minutes of cooking time per pound of roast. When the roast reaches 120° to 125°, depending on how you like your meat, remove it to a hot platter or carving board and let it rest in a warm place for 15 to 20 minutes. Turn up the oven to 450°. Bake the Yorkshire pudding (see below) while the beef is resting and being carved. To carve, turn the roast on the side that gives it the best balance for carving and hold it in place with the back of a heavy fork while carving with a good sharp knife (for carving, see page 399). Serve it with the pan juices and Yorkshire pudding, or with a Bordelaise or Béarnaise sauce. If you like roast potatoes with your roast beef, place peeled, parboiled pieces of potato in the pan juices after the searing period and cook them with the meat, turning once during the cooking time and basting along with the beef. Salt and pepper them and arrange them around the carved roast, or serve them in a separate dish with a sprinkling of chopped parsley.

## Yorkshire Pudding

Makes 8 servings

2 eggs
1 cup milk
1 cup sifted all-purpose flour
½ teaspoon salt
½ teaspoon freshly ground
  black pepper
¼ cup beef drippings (melted
  beef fat), heated

Beat the eggs with a whisk or electric hand beater until quite light, then gradually beat in the milk and flour. Or you can put those ingredients in an electric blender or electric mixer and blend or beat just until the batter is smooth. Season with the salt and pepper. Preheat the oven to 450°. Put a baking pan measuring 11 x 14 x 2½ in the oven and let it get very hot. Remove and pour in the hot drippings and then the batter. Put on the center shelf of the oven and bake for 10 minutes, then reduce the heat to 375° and continue to bake for 15 to 20 minutes, or until the pudding has risen and is puffed and brown. Do not open the oven door during the first 20 minutes of baking. Cut in squares and serve immediately with roast beef.

## ❧ Low-Temperature Method for Rib Roast of Beef

Use the same cut as for the preceding technique. Leave the meat at room temperature for several hours, then rub it well with ½ teaspoon freshly ground black pepper and ½ teaspoon rosemary. Place it on a rack in a shallow roasting pan and take the internal temperature of the meat.

Preheat the oven to 250°. Roast at 250° without basting for approximately 20 minutes per pound. After 2 hours, take the internal temperature, salt the roast well, and add another grind or two of black pepper. Continue to roast the meat for 1 hour more. Again take the temperature and calculate the approximate time it will take for the roast to reach 120° to 125°. If you want to accompany the roast with Yorkshire pudding, see preceding recipe for preparation. When the meat is done, remove it to a hot platter or carving board and let it rest for 15 to 20 minutes before carving. For a change serve the roast with a Bordelaise sauce, parsnip purée flavored with Madeira (see page 52), and watercress.

## COLD ROAST BEEF

Served cold or allowed to cool out of the refrigerator until it is almost at room temperature, roast beef makes a delicious, tempting offering for a buffet. For a cold buffet serve it sliced paper thin with a selection of mustards and breads. For a cocktail buffet cut it into strips, place it on fingers of bread cut to the same size, and spread with mustard or horseradish butter.

# ～ *Roast Fillet of Beef*

*To my thinking, a beef fillet, an expensive but meltingly tender boneless piece of meat which should always be served very rare, is best roasted quickly at a high temperature with several bastings. Now that so many ranges are equipped with self-cleaning ovens, high-temperature roasting, an inevitably messy business, presents few problems and seems to be increasingly popular.*

*When you buy the fillet, have the filet mignon (the thin tapering piece at one end of the fillet) removed, as it is too thin for roasting. Use it for another recipe—beef scallops or brochette of beef. Ask the butcher to bard the fillet, that is, to wrap it with thin sheets of pork fat or flattened beef suet and tie it well (see illustration on next page).*

**Makes 8 to 10 servings**

4- to 5-pound fillet of beef, well trimmed, with all fat and tendon removed, then barded with fat
6 tablespoons butter, melted Or 3 tablespoons butter and
3 tablespoons olive oil Or ⅓ cup rendered beef suet (see note on next page)

Preheat the oven to 500°. Place the barded fillet on a rack in a shallow roasting pan and roast at 500° for 25 minutes, basting it well every 8 minutes with melted butter, butter and oil, or rendered suet. Suet gives a lovely flavor. Remove the barding fat after the fillet has roasted for 20 minutes to allow the surface to brown. After 25 minutes, test the internal temperature of the beef by inserting a meat thermometer—for rare fillet, it should register 120°. When the meat reaches that temperature, remove it to a hot platter or a carving board and let it rest for 5 minutes

before carving. Unlike other beef roasts, a delicate rare fillet is always carved into slices ½ inch thick. Serve it with a Béarnaise sauce (see page 280).

Potatoes Anna and a purée of broccoli go well with this. Drink a fine red Burgundy.

*Note.* To render any suet, cut into small pieces and cook in a heavy skillet over medium-low heat until the fat is liquefied. Strain before using.

# Pork

Pork is probably the most delicious—and the most misunderstood—of all meats. Served hot in winter it is a hearty, warming dish, and in summer, served cold, it attains the utmost in delicacy and flavor. If I had to narrow my choice of meats down to one for the rest of my life, I am quite certain that meat would be pork.

In recent years there has been a tendency in pig breeders to cut down the fat content of pork—like almost everyone else, the pig has been placed on a reducing diet. As a result, there is a trend to meat that is not quite so lavishly fat-streaked and marbled as formerly, and this sometimes has the effect of toughening the fiber.

American pork cuts are quite different from those in France, Italy, and England. If you have an Italian or other European pork store in your neighborhood, you will find that you can get some variations from the usual cuts if you speak to your butcher in advance. There are a great number of pork butchers throughout the country. They may take a bit of finding, but they are there if you look. Italian and German neighborhoods in New York and other cities with a large and varied ethnic population usually have excellent pork butchers and *charcutiers*. In the German, Polish, and Hungarian sections you are likely to find not only all kinds of pork cuts, but also sausages, cured meats, and other types of pork products. If you are interested in good food, do avail yourself of the opportunities to investigate ethnic markets in your area.

# ❧ Roast Pork Loin

*Probably the most commonly used cut of pork is the loin. In United States parlance the loin is the stretch from the shoulder to the leg (see page 370) that takes in the ribs and the loin chops with the tenderloin. It is usually sold divided into the rib end, the center cut, which includes a small portion of the loin, and the loin end. Or you can buy the entire loin. The roast may be bought boned and tied, or left with the bones intact. In this case, the chine bone that runs the length of the loin should be removed or cut through to facilitate carving, and the roast should be trimmed of excess fat and securely tied.*

**Makes 6 servings**

5-pound pork loin, trimmed
  and tied
2 to 3 garlic cloves, peeled and
  cut into thin slivers
1 teaspoon dried thyme or
  summer savory
Coarse (kosher) salt, freshly
  ground black pepper
12 small new potatoes,
  scraped or peeled
6 small carrots, scraped and
  whole
  Or 3 large carrots, scraped
  and quartered
12 small white onions,
  peeled*
Watercress for garnish

*If onions are dropped into
boiling water for 20 seconds,
their skins will slip off easily.*

About 1 hour before roasting the pork, pierce the fat all over with the point of a small sharp knife and insert slivers of garlic into the holes. Rub the loin lightly with thyme or summer savory and then with coarse salt. Preheat the oven to 325°.

Put the loin, fat side up, on a rack in a shallow roasting pan and roast at 325° for 25 to 30 minutes per pound, about 2¼ to 2½ hours.

Parboil the potatoes, carrots, and onions for 5 minutes in salted water to cover (this softens them slightly, so they cook faster) and arrange them around the meat in the roasting pan for the last hour of roasting time. When you add the vegetables, baste them with the pan juices and sprinkle the loin with a little salt and pepper. Continue to roast the meat until the internal temperature reaches 165°. Check 30 to 40 minutes after adding the vegetables to find how near the meat is to that mark, inserting the thermometer at the thickest part, but not touching the bone.

When the meat is done, transfer it to a hot platter and let it rest in a warm place for 10 to 15 minutes before carving. Arrange the roasted vegetables around it and garnish with watercress.

Carve the roast downward, cutting between the bones. If the meat has been boned, cut in slices about ⅜ inch thick. Skim the fat from the pan juices and serve them with the pork. A dish of sautéed, glazed apple rings (see page 192) is a perfect accompaniment. Wine for such a dish might be a chilled Alsatian Riesling.

# Marbelized Fresh Ham

*The fresh ham or leg of pork is a most satisfactory roast for a large number of people, and equally good hot or cold. I find that my Italian pork store in New York always handles fresh hams, and is well acquainted with boning and stuffing them with herbed and other mixtures that make them particularly succulent. The English and sometimes the Italians leave the scored skin on and roast it to a crisp, chewy perfection. I find this delicious, but most people prefer to have the skin removed.*

*This rather elaborate dish is best served cold. Roast it early in the morning and let it cool until evening, without refrigerating, if possible. If you must refrigerate, leave it out of the refrigerator for at least several hours before serving. This is a good choice for a buffet party.*

**Makes 16 to 20 servings**

¾ cup white raisins
⅓ to ½ cup dry sherry
8 garlic cloves
½ cup chopped Italian (flat-leaf) parsley, packed
1 cup shelled pistachio nuts
12- to 15-pound fresh ham, boned, rolled, and well tied
1 teaspoon crushed dried sage
Coarse (kosher) salt, freshly ground black pepper
6 tablespoons unsalted butter
⅓ cup apple jelly
1 teaspoon crushed aniseed (optional)

Soak the raisins in sherry to cover until puffed, then drain. Reserve sherry.

Chop 5 garlic cloves and the parsley rather coarsely, and chop ¾ cup pistachio nuts very coarsely. Make deep incisions in the ham with a long, heavy, wooden-handled larding needle, turning the needle before removing it so that it makes small cavities in the meat—these need not be done in any pattern. Combine raisins, chopped garlic, parsley, and chopped pistachios and stuff the mixture into the cavities with your fingers, packing it in as tightly as possible—a wooden chopstick is a good aid. Push in the remaining whole pistachios here and there.

Mince the remaining garlic and blend with the crushed sage. Rub the outside fat with the mixture, then sprinkle with salt and pepper. Put the ham on a rack in a roasting pan and roast in a 325° oven for 25 to 30 minutes per pound. Combine the sherry drained from the raisins, the butter, and the apple jelly in a small saucepan and heat gently until butter and jelly are melted. If you like the flavor of anise, add the crushed aniseed to the mixture—this will result in a more highly perfumed ham. Baste the ham every half hour with the mixture as it roasts. Keep the basting mixture warm while using it.

When the ham reaches an internal temperature of 165° (insert meat thermometer in the thickest part) remove it from the oven and let it cool. If you are going to chill the ham, brush it well with the pan juices, wrap in plastic wrap, and refrigerate until ready to serve.

Carve the ham into thin slices. They will be beautifully marbled with the mixture of raisins, nuts, and herbs. Serve the ham with a Cumberland (see page 71) or a rémoulade sauce and white beans vinaigrette (see page 49) sprinkled with chopped fresh basil and parsley and garnished with tomato sections. Crisp Italian bread goes well with this meal, as does a fine sparkling wine—a good American or French champagne of a pleasant vintage. The famous mustard fruits of Cremona (available in specialty food shops) are admirable with this ham.

Note. If the ham is much larger, increase the stuffing ingredients proportionately.

# Glazed Ham

*The smoked hams sold in supermarkets are usually labeled "cook before eating," "fully cooked," or "ready-to-eat"—the last two mean the same thing. According to USDA inspection regulations, hams must be heated to a certain internal temperature during the smoking process. The "ready-to-eat" have been heated to a higher temperature (around 160°) than the "cook before eating" and are perfectly safe to eat cold, but I find that in order to be really palatable they need a certain amount of cooking and flavoring and are much tastier if basted with sherry, Madeira, dry cider, wine, or ginger ale during baking. Ready-to-eat or fully cooked hams need only to be baked until they reach an internal temperature of 130°, just sufficient to heat them through, but a cook-before-eating ham should be boiled or baked to an internal temperature of 160° to 165°.*

*Country hams, which are prepared and sold directly or by mail order by small smokehouses across the country, are vastly superior to the bland and tasteless supermarket hams. Generally, they are well and slowly cured (with salt) and heavily smoked, which gives them a more pronounced flavor and a better texture. Some are the cook-before-eating type and need to be simmered in water before baking; others are ready-to-eat. When you buy these hams, follow the directions given on the wrapper for the length of cooking time. Occasionally the ham may be very salty and need some soaking in cold water for a few hours to remove the excess salt. To check, cut off a bit of the ham and, if it is not fully cooked, sauté it in a little fat until thoroughly cooked and then taste it.*

*A whole ham can weigh from 10 to 20 pounds, but if that is just too much meat for you, you can buy half of a ham, either the meatier butt end or the less expensive but equally tasty shank end. Allow about ½ pound of ham per person, or ¾ to 1 pound for a shank end with a lot of bone. If you want an even smaller ham, buy the smoked butt or smoked picnic shoulder—these come from the foreleg and are fattier but less expensive than hams from the hind legs.*

1 ready-to-eat (fully cooked)
ham, about 10 to 12
pounds
Or half of a ham, weighing
about 6 to 8 pounds
2 cups dry sherry, Madeira,
or white wine
1 to 1½ cups dry bread
crumbs
1 tablespoon dry mustard
½ cup brown sugar
2 tablespoons Dijon mustard

Preheat the oven to 350°. Put the ham, skin and fat side down, in a large, deep roasting pan with the wine and bake approximately 10 to 15 minutes a pound for a whole ham, 15 to 18 minutes for a half ham, basting from time to time with the liquid. When tested with a meat thermometer, inserted in the thickest part but not touching the bone, the internal temperature should be 130°.

Remove the ham from the oven and trim off the skin or rind and all but about ¼ inch of the fat. Mix together the bread crumbs and dry mustard and rub the mixture into the fat with your hand. Press brown sugar into the crumbs and dot all over with Dijon mustard. To glaze the ham (that is, to melt the sugar and give the fat a glossy brown finish), put the ham under the broiler, if it is deep enough, about 10 inches from the heat, and watch carefully to see that the mixture does not scorch—the sugar should melt into the crumbs and leave a nice glaze. Otherwise turn up the oven heat to 450° and bake the ham 15 to 20 minutes more, or until nicely glazed.

With hot ham, serve potato and semolina gnocchi (see page 46), a purée of spinach, and a mustard hollandaise or Cumberland sauce.

With cold ham, serve a salad of white beans and tiny bits of chopped tomato, cucumber, and green pepper, tossed with a well-flavored vinaigrette sauce and garnished with thinly sliced red Italian onions. A hot corn or spinach soufflé is also a nice accompaniment to a cold ham, with a selection of French and German mustards. Champagne or a very fruity Alsatian white wine or a rosé wine goes well with either hot or cold ham.

## CUMBERLAND SAUCE

Remove the zest (the orange part of the rind) from 1 orange with a potato peeler and chop it very fine. Put in a small pan with 1 cup of Port wine or Madeira and cook over medium-high heat until the liquid is reduced to ⅓ cup. Add the juice of the orange, 1 tablespoon lemon juice, 1 cup currant jelly, and a pinch of cayenne pepper or ground ginger. Stir until the jelly is melted, then serve the sauce. Makes about 1 cup.

# Roasted Spareribs

*Finally, an excellent cut of pork to consider for roasting—the spareribs. Succulent and versatile as they are, in the last few years good spareribs have been ruined by too many sweet and sour sauces intended to make them taste glamorous or Oriental or some such thing. To be quite frank, I think there is nothing as good as simple roasted spareribs seasoned merely with salt and pepper.*

**Makes 4 servings**

*2 sides spareribs, about
  4 pounds, heavy bone or
  gristle section removed
Coarse (kosher) salt, freshly
  ground black pepper*

Put the ribs on a rack in a shallow roasting pan and roast them in a 350° oven for 30 minutes, then season the ribs well with salt and pepper, turn, season the other side, and continue roasting them for another 30 minutes. At the end of an hour they should be nicely browned and fairly crisp on the outside. Roast them another 10 to 15 minutes if you like them very well done.

Remove the ribs to a carving board and cut between the ribs into smallish sections. Heap them on a hot platter and serve with sauerkraut cooked in chicken broth with a few juniper berries. Add perfectly boiled potatoes in their jackets and you will have a delightful feast. Drink the beer of your choice.

# Chicken

Perhaps my predilection for good chicken is something I was born with because both my parents were ardent chickenphiles. More likely it is due to the fact that nothing is better than a well-cooked, well-presented roast chicken. Game, turkey, and goose all have their charms and their advantages, but it is incontrovertible that a perfect roast chicken is one of the world's superb dishes.

Not that chickens don't vary. Seldom can we get the fine chickens that are raised by interested poultry farmers on organic food and with plenty of room to scratch around. These chickens, which used to be common in our markets, have all but disappeared. Instead, the majority of the chickens we buy are raised behind wire and very quickly, which results in a beautiful clean carcass with plenty of meat, but little of the flavor of the old-time birds. I wish that some public-spirited person would start a chain of farms around our larger cities from which we could order the old-fashioned, well-fed, hand-plucked chickens of perfect size. Such a product could command a premium price from restaurants and all of us who pine for a really flavorful bird.

There is another stumbling block to achieving a perfectly roasted chicken. That is the matter of how long the bird should be cooked. If it is roasted until the white meat attains the exact point of juiciness, there is bound to be a touch of pink in the joints of the dark meat. This repulses many people who shun the thought of underdone chicken (which happens to be very good). If the chicken is cooked until the juices at the thigh joint run clear, the white meat will be dry and, to my taste, totally uninteresting. Perhaps the answer is always to roast two chickens, one perfectly cooked, the other overcooked. One can, of course, carve the chicken in the kitchen and put the pink-juiced dark meat under the broiler for a minute or two to satisfy those who cannot reconcile themselves to that pinkness, but it is my feeling that if they once tried the white meat at its proper stage, they would overcome their prejudice.

A roasting chicken of 4 to 5 pounds is the right size for 4 people. Because of modern methods of preparing and plucking chickens, there is no need to pluck the bird. I find, though, that with these new methods the chickens are plucked too well, for the process also removes most of the tiny oil sacs that used to help give color to the skin during cooking. It is well-nigh impossible to get a brilliantly brown skin on a roast chicken now without cheating a bit. That is one of the prices paid for a labor-saving device.

## ❧ *Perfect Roast Chicken*    Makes 4 servings

4- to 5-pound roasting chicken
½ lemon
½ pound (2 sticks) unsalted butter, softened
Salt, freshly ground black pepper
3 tablespoons flour
1 cup chicken or veal stock, heated
1 tablespoon chopped fresh tarragon
   Or 1 teaspoon dried tarragon, crushed
¾ cup heavy cream
1 tablespoon chopped parsley
Watercress

Preheat the oven to 425°. Wipe the chicken with a damp cloth. Rub the inside with the cut lemon, squeezing the juice onto the bone structure as you rub. Cream together 4 tablespoons butter, 1 teaspoon salt, and ½ teaspoon pepper and put the mixture into the cavity. Truss the bird as follows. Thread a long trussing needle with twine and push the legs and thighs back with your hands. Run the needle through the thigh joints and across the bird and pull through. Then cross the pieces of twine, bring them up to the legs, and wrap them around the legs, tying them close together. Bring the twine down and under the tail and then bring it up to the legs again and tie it securely. Turn the bird over. Take the two ends of the twine and bring them down, running the twine back and around the wings. Tie the ends securely. This method will truss the bird tightly and well.

Rub one side with butter. Put the chicken

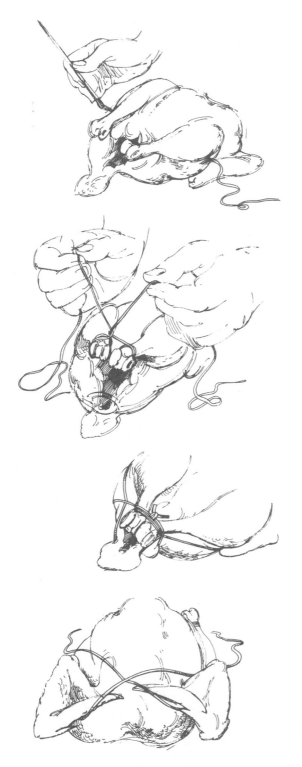

on its side, buttered side up, on a rack in a shallow roasting pan. Roast the chicken in a 425° oven for 20 minutes. Protecting your hands with a wad of paper towels, turn the chicken on its other side, and brush the upper side lavishly with melted butter. Roast it for 20 minutes longer; turn it on its back and baste it well with the pan juices. Sprinkle the bird with about 1½ teaspoons salt and 1 teaspoon pepper. Roast it breast side up for 20 minutes, then baste with pan juices.

After the bird has cooked almost an hour, siphon off about 3 tablespoons of the fat from the roasting pan and transfer it to a heavy saucepan. Blend in 3 tablespoons flour to make a smooth roux (see directions on page 272–273). Simmer the roux over low heat for several minutes, increase the heat, and gradually stir in the hot chicken or veal stock. Stir the sauce with a whisk until it is thickened and simmer it over low heat for 4 to 5 minutes. Season the sauce with the tarragon and salt to taste. Remove the pan from the heat and stir in the heavy cream. Cook the sauce over low heat, stirring, until it is thick and smooth. Correct seasoning if necessary, then stir in parsley. Keep hot until ready to serve. Or, if you prefer, just remove the excess fat from pan juices, mix in a little hot stock, and serve with the bird.

Test the bird for doneness: if the leg and thigh move easily, it is done—sometimes overdone for my taste. Puncture the skin at the thigh joint. If the juices that run out are still a bit pink, it is very close to being done. If they run clear it is definitely done—or overdone. Another way to test for doneness is to insert a meat thermometer into the fleshiest part of the thigh (do not touch the bone). It should register 165° for a perfectly cooked chicken. A 4-pound chicken should not take more than 1 hour to 1 hour and 15 minutes to roast, but you cannot be exact about timing because the bone structure and the amount of flesh and fat on the bones all affect the cooking time.

When the bird is done, remove it to a hot platter and garnish it with watercress. Surround the chicken with sautéed potatoes. For the best serving and eating, carve the chicken into quarters (poultry shears are a great help here). I find that the sliced breast of a roast chicken makes a pretty dull-looking plate, but a juicy, delicious quarter is something else entirely. Serve the sauce in a sauceboat.

Traditionally, potatoes, a salad, and a pleasing red wine are the perfect companions for roast chicken. You might try a California Zinfandel, a Moulin-à-Vent, or even a Côte Rotie with it.

If you wish to serve the chicken cold, do not refrigerate it, or let it get completely cold. When you remove the bird from the oven, let it cool at room temperature and serve it when there is just a suspicion of warmth left—the flavor is much better and the bird juicier.

# Old-Fashioned Sunday Roast Chicken with Stuffing

*Stuffed roast chicken has traditionally figured—and still does—on many families' Sunday dinner menus throughout the country. Usually the bird is overcooked, and the stuffing is often the best part. However, if you use a stuffing that is light, not dense and pasty, and roast the bird for the correct length of time, it can be a delicious dish.*

**Makes 6 servings**

¼ pound (1 stick) unsalted butter

1 large or 2 medium onions, finely chopped

1 garlic clove, finely chopped

20 soft black Italian or Greek olives, pitted and coarsely chopped

1 teaspoon grated lemon zest (see page 363)

1 teaspoon rosemary, crushed in a mortar

½ cup finely diced ham

3 cups fine fresh bread crumbs*

½ cup plus 1 tablespoon chopped parsley

Salt, freshly ground black pepper

5-pound roasting chicken, giblets reserved

8 to 10 thick slices of good smoked bacon

1 sprig of parsley

¼ cup cognac

*Use bread crumbs made from a nonsweetened bread such as French or Italian.

First make the stuffing: melt 6 tablespoons butter in a heavy skillet with a cover. Add the onions and sauté for 2 to 3 minutes. Cover the skillet and steam the onions over very low heat until they are soft and pale gold, about 7 to 8 minutes. Add the garlic, olives, lemon zest, rosemary, and ham. Toss the mixture lightly with the bread crumbs and ½ cup chopped parsley until well blended. Season to taste with salt and pepper. Preheat the oven to 400°.

Wipe the chicken inside and out with a damp cloth, stuff with the stuffing, and close the vent with tiny clamps or with tiny skewers laced with twine. Truss the chicken (see preceding recipe) and rub it lightly with butter. Put it on its side on a rack in a shallow roasting pan. Cover with 4 or 5 bacon slices. Roast for 35 minutes, then turn it onto its other side. Cover the upper side with bacon slices, baste with the pan juices, and roast 35 minutes longer. Turn the chicken breast side up and remove the bacon. Sprinkle it with salt and pepper, brush with 2 tablespoons melted butter, and roast it for 30 minutes more, basting once or twice with the pan juices. Test for doneness as described in the recipe for perfect roast chicken.

While the chicken is cooking, simmer the giblets, including the liver, in 1 cup water with ½ teaspoon salt, 2 or 3 grinds of black pepper, and a parsley sprig for 15 to 20 minutes. Strain the broth and reserve it. Chop the giblets and reserve them. When the chicken is done, transfer it to a hot platter and remove all but 3 tablespoons of the fat from the pan. Add the reserved broth and giblets to the pan, bring the mixture to a boil, and simmer for several minutes, stirring to scrape up the brown bits from the bottom of the pan. Add the remaining chopped parsley and the cognac and reduce the sauce a little by boiling over high heat for 1 or 2 minutes. Pour into a sauceboat and serve with the chicken and stuffing. Braised celery or endive and a bowl of fresh watercress go exceedingly well with the chicken. Drink a California Cabernet Sauvignon or a Moulin-à-Vent.

# Squab Chickens

Tiny squab chickens of about 1 pound make a delicious entrée for a dinner party or, when allowed to cool, a wonderful cold food for picnics or a late supper. They are often difficult to find, but you can usually get them from your market if you order ahead of time. Allow 1 per person. The smaller Rock Cornish hens may be substituted for the squab chickens. Roast them for just 45 minutes.

## Stuffed Squab Chickens

**Makes 6 servings**

¾ cup finely chopped shallots
¼ pound or more unsalted butter
Giblets and livers from the squab chickens
1 tablespoon chopped fresh tarragon
Or 1½ teaspoons dried tarragon, crushed
2 cups cooked rice
Salt, freshly ground black pepper
3 tablespoons chopped parsley
¼ cup chopped pistachio nuts
6 squab chickens
1 lemon, halved
Watercress for garnish

Prepare the stuffing: sauté the shallots in 6 tablespoons butter until they are just limp. Chop the giblets (including the liver) rather fine, and toss them in the butter with the shallots. Add the tarragon, rice, 1 teaspoon salt, ½ teaspoon pepper, parsley, and pistachios. Toss lightly to blend well. If the mixture seems dry, melt 3 to 4 tablespoons of butter and blend in lightly to moisten.

Wipe the squab chickens inside and out with a damp cloth. Rub the cavities with the cut lemon. Stuff the birds lightly, skewer the vents, and truss the squabs. Arrange them on their sides on a rack in a very shallow roasting pan and rub the top sides well with butter. Roast in a 400° oven for 20 to 25 minutes, then turn them onto the other side. Rub the top side well with butter and roast 20 minutes more. Turn breast side up, baste with pan juices, sprinkle with salt and pepper, and roast for 10 to 12 minutes. Be careful not to overcook them. Test the legs for doneness by wiggling the legs and puncturing the joints, as described in the recipe for perfect roast chicken.

Transfer the birds to a hot platter, remove and discard the strings, and garnish with watercress. Serve the squab chickens with tiny green peas, the pan juices, and a good salad. Drink Fleurie.

If you wish to serve the squab chickens cold, do not stuff them unless you like cold stuffing—it is actually quite good. Baste the birds well and be sure to undercook them slightly, as they will continue cooking for a few minutes as they cool.

# Turkey

Turkey, which was once the holiday *pièce de résistance*, has become an all-year, all-purpose bird. One finds all kinds of turkeys in the markets now—frozen birds, broad-breasted birds, butter-filled birds, small birds, birds in parts or sections, and all sorts of boned and rolled birds. There is something for everyone and every occasion.

With all these improvements, there have been some losses. It is very hard to buy a hand-plucked, fresh-killed turkey, but if you can find a market that sells them, they are definitely worth buying.

With turkeys coming in so many sizes, shapes, and conditions, there are really no hard-and-fast rules for roasting and cooking times. It all depends on the shape of the bird, the amount of fat, the way the flesh is distributed, and the internal temperature when it goes into the oven. I am always horrified when newspapers at Thanksgiving time give supposedly infallible timetables for roasting. Nothing could be more designed to produce badly cooked birds— perhaps one reason that turkey is so unpopular with a great many people. Certainly there are few things worse than an overcooked turkey, except perhaps an undercooked one. It must be at the point of perfection to be right. Cooking a turkey perfectly depends on one's attention to the work at hand and sense of the moment when it is done. A perfectly cooked turkey is one of the major achievements of a cook.

## ❧ Roast Turkey with Two Stuffings

*Stuffings for turkey vary a great deal. Some are made with corn bread, nuts, and various additions, but a simple bread stuffing is my favorite, perhaps with a separate meat stuffing, of well-seasoned sausage meat and ground veal, for the neck cavity. After many years, it is my considered opinion that stuffing tastes much better when cooked in a baking dish than inside the bird—it gets nice and crispy, not soggy, and is altogether much more satisfactory and easier to serve. Baste it, as it bakes, with juices from the roasting pan and it will be delicious. So, if you are a traditionalist, roast your turkey with the stuffing inside, but bake some of the bread stuffing separately and you will see what I mean. Leftover stuffing is no problem. Just sauté it in butter.*

Makes 16 or more servings

## BREAD STUFFING FOR THE BODY CAVITY

*1½ cups very thinly sliced green onions*
*½ to ¾ pound unsalted butter*
*2 tablespoons finely chopped fresh tarragon*
*Or 1 tablespoon dried tarragon, crushed*
*1 tablespoon salt*
*1½ teaspoons freshly ground black pepper*
*1 cup finely chopped parsley*
*About 12 cups freshly made soft bread crumbs\**
*½ cup pine nuts*

*\*Use crumbs made from an unsweetened bread such as French or Italian.*

## STUFFING FOR THE NECK CAVITY

*2 pounds good sausage meat (made without filler to extend the meat)*
*Or 2 pounds ground pork with about 30 percent fat*
*1½ teaspoons salt*
*1 teaspoon dried thyme*
*1 teaspoon Tabasco*
*1 teaspoon ground coriander*
*1 teaspoon freshly ground black pepper*
*1 pound ground veal or ham*
*¾ cup pine nuts*
*½ cup finely chopped parsley*

Prepare the stuffing for the body cavity: sauté the green onions in ½ pound butter over medium heat until they are just limp. Add the tarragon, salt, pepper, parsley, and bread crumbs. Toss to blend. Mix in pine nuts and moisten with as much additional melted butter as needed to make a light, not soggy, mixture. Taste and correct seasoning.

Then prepare the stuffing for the neck cavity: combine the sausage meat or ground pork with the salt, thyme, Tabasco sauce, ground coriander, pepper, ground veal or ham, pine nuts, and parsley. Mix the stuffing well. Sauté 1 or 2 teaspoons in a small skillet in 1 tablespoon butter until brown and cooked through (never taste uncooked pork) and taste to check seasoning; correct if necessary.

Wash the turkey well inside and out, or wipe with a damp cloth, and rub the cavity with lemon juice. Stand the bird on its tail and stuff the neck cavity with the meat mixture, taking care not to stuff it too tight. Pull the flap of the neck skin over the stuffing and attach it to the skin on the back of the bird, either by securing it with small skewers or clamps or sewing it with a large needle and fine twine.

Turn the bird breast side up and stuff the cavity lightly with the bread mixture. Do not force stuffing into the cavity or you will not only have soggy, messy stuffing, but run the risk of the bird's splitting during roasting as the steam from the stuffing inflates it slightly. Stuff a piece of crumbled foil into the opening of the vent to prevent the stuffing from oozing out during roasting and close the vent with clamps or skewers or sew it together with

## THE TURKEY AND SAUCE

20-pound turkey, preferably
  one that is fresh-killed,
  hand-plucked, and
  unfrozen; neck, gizzard,
  heart, and liver reserved
Juice of 1 to 2 lemons
About ½ pound (2 sticks)
  unsalted butter
Salt, freshly ground black
  pepper
Whole piece of bacon or salt
  pork rind, big enough to fit
  on the roasting rack
  Or large sheet of well-
  greased heavy-duty
  aluminum foil
1 onion, stuck with 2 cloves
1 garlic clove
1 teaspoon dried tarragon
1 sprig of parsley
1 cup brown sauce (see
  page 275)
¼ cup Madeira or cognac

fine twine. Truss (following the directions for chicken on page 73) and rub the turkey well with butter and a small amount of salt and pepper. Put an adjustable rack in a large shallow roasting pan and put the bacon or salt pork rind or well-greased aluminum foil on the rack where the turkey breast will be. Put the turkey on the rind or foil, breast side down, and cover the top loosely with a piece of foil. Roast in a 325° oven for 1 hour. Remove the bird from the oven; baste it well and turn it onto one side. Roast it for 45 minutes; baste and turn it onto the other side. Roast for 45 minutes, then turn it breast side up. Baste it, rub it with soft butter, and roast for 1 hour more. At this point start the broth: put the reserved neck, gizzard, heart, and liver in a saucepan with the onion, garlic, tarragon, 1½ teaspoons salt, and 3 cups water. Bring the mixture to a boil, skim off any scum that rises to the surface, and add the sprig of parsley. Reduce the heat and simmer the mixture for 35 to 40 minutes. Strain and reserve broth. Chop the giblets and liver very fine and set aside.

Test the turkey for doneness by inserting a meat thermometer into the thickest part of the thigh, but not touching the bone. It should register 170° to 175°. Or test the leg to see if it moves easily and puncture the thigh joint; the juices should be pinkish-red. Be sure not to over- or undercook it.

When the turkey is done, remove it to a hot platter or carving board and let it rest in a warm place for 15 to 20 minutes before carving.

Remove all but 3 tablespoons fat from the pan and pour in the broth. Stir to scrape up all the brown bits from the bottom. Pour the liquid into a saucepan and reduce it by half over rather high heat. Add brown sauce, chopped giblets, and Madeira or cognac. Bring the sauce to a boil; reduce heat and simmer for several minutes. Taste sauce and correct seasoning. Serve it in a sauceboat.

Puréed potatoes (see page 51) with plenty of butter and cream and sautéed Brussels sprouts or turnips sautéed with mushrooms are fine accompaniments. Drink a fine red Burgundy.

# Roast Turkey Without Stuffing

*For cold turkey and various dishes made with cold or cooked turkey, the bird is best roasted unstuffed.*

**Makes 8 to 10 servings**

12- to 14-pound turkey*
Juice of 1 to 2 lemons
¼ pound or more unsalted
   butter
Salt, freshly ground black
   pepper

*Your turkey should
preferably be hand-plucked,
fresh-killed, and unfrozen.

Wash the interior of the turkey or wipe it out with a damp cloth. Rub cavity well with lemon juice. Blend 4 tablespoons butter with 1 teaspoon salt and ½ teaspoon pepper and put it in the cavity. Close the vent and truss the turkey carefully (the same as for chicken; see page 73). Rub one side well with butter and put the bird, buttered side up, on a rack in a shallow roasting pan. Roast it in a 325° oven for 1 hour. Turn it onto the other side, protecting your hands with a wad of paper towels, rub it with butter, and season with 2 teaspoons salt and 1 teaspoon pepper. Roast the turkey for 1 hour more, turn it breast side up, and baste well with the pan juices. Roast it for another 25 minutes and baste it again. If the bird is browning too much, put a piece of foil loosely across the top. Roast it for 30 minutes more, then test for doneness by wiggling the legs to see if they move easily or by piercing the thigh joint with a carving fork. If the juices run pale pink, remove the turkey from the oven. It will continue to cook as it cools. You can also test for doneness by inserting a meat thermometer into the thickest part of the thigh, not touching the bone. It should register between 170° and 175°.

Turkey roasted without stuffing may be eaten hot with a sauce suprême (see page 274), or with a simple bread sauce, but it is at its best cooled, sliced, and served with a tart homemade mayonnaise flavored with lemon juice, a rice salad (see page 43), crisp vegetables, and perhaps hot corn bread and butter with good preserves. Drink a full-bodied white Burgundy with it.

# Goose

Goose is one of the most flavorful and juicy birds we have, with rich, dark, succulent flesh. Although it is extremely difficult to get freshly killed geese, there are excellent frozen geese on the market, available in sizes from 6 to 14 pounds, which make very tasty and tender eating. Frozen geese should be thawed before roasting, from 1½ to 2 days in the refrigerator or 6 to 10 hours at room temperature (for the medium size) or 4 to 5 hours in cool water. Leave the goose in its wrapping to thaw and when thoroughly thawed, refrigerate until you are ready to stuff and cook the bird. Goose needs to be roasted with a fruity stuffing to flavor the bird.

# ✒ Roast Goose with Prune and Apple Stuffing

**Makes 8 servings**

An 8- to 10-pound goose, fresh or frozen and thawed

STUFFING
6 tablespoons butter
½ cup finely chopped onion
5 to 6 cups fresh bread crumbs
2 teaspoons salt
1 cup cooked peeled chestnuts or canned chestnuts
2 cups peeled and chopped apples
1 cup pitted prunes, soaked for 2 days in Madeira to cover
1 teaspoon thyme
½ teaspoon nutmeg

GRAVY
Giblets and neck from goose, liver reserved
⅓ cup white wine
1 teaspoon salt
3 or 4 peppercorns
1 sprig of parsley
1 small onion, stuck with 1 clove
1 small carrot, scraped and halved
The goose liver
1 small onion, peeled and chopped
2 tablespoons goose fat (from the roasting pan)
Beurre manié (see page 270)

Remove the giblets and neck from the cavity and reserve for the stock. Remove excess fat from the body cavity. You can render this fat slowly in a heavy skillet and keep it for cooking—goose fat is pure, full of flavor, and marvelous for sautéing potatoes, meats, and poultry.

To make the stuffing, melt the butter in a large skillet; add the onion and sauté over medium heat until limp and golden. Remove from the heat and mix in the bread crumbs, moistening them well with the butter. Then add the remaining stuffing ingredients and mix them well together with your hands or a wooden spatula. Stuff the goose about two-thirds or three-quarters full (the fruit and crumbs will expand during the roasting). There will be some leftover stuffing, which can be put in a baking dish and baked in the 350° oven alongside the goose the second half of its roasting time. It never matters if you overestimate on stuffing; in fact it is better to do so as everyone always wants more than the cavity will accommodate. You usually calculate ¾ to 1 cup of stuffing per pound of bird, though a bird with a small cavity may take no more than ½ cup per pound.

After stuffing the goose, truss it, and sew up or skewer the vent (see sketches on page 74). Rub the skin with salt, which helps to crisp it. Place the goose breast side up on a rack in a roasting pan—a goose has so much natural fat there is no need to baste it or to protect the breast from overcooking. Preheat the oven to 400°.

Roast for 1 hour at 400° to start rendering fat from the bird. Then prick the skin all over with a fork, to let the fat escape; reduce the temperature to 350° and roast for another hour. As the fat renders from the goose, remove it to a large jar, using a large spoon or bulb baster, and keep it for cooking. Leave some fat in the pan each time.

While the goose is roasting, put the neck and giblets (but not the liver) in a pan with 2 cups water, the wine, seasonings, parsley, clove-stuck onion, and carrot. Bring to a boil; boil 1 minute, skimming off the scum, then reduce the heat; cover and simmer slowly for 1 hour, adding a little more water if the stock reduces too much; it should cover the giblets. Strain the stock, chop the giblets fine and reserve for the sauce. Quickly sauté the goose liver and the chopped onion in 2 tablespoons of the fat rendered from the goose. As soon as liver is firm, remove and chop fine.

An 8- to 10-pound goose will take 2 to 2¾ hours to cook. After the second hour, test to see how near done it is by pressing the leg meat with your fingers (protected with paper towels). When done, the meat should feel soft and the juices from the thickest part of the thigh, when it is pricked with a fork, should run yellowish, with a little pink but not red tinge. If the goose needs more cooking, reduce the oven heat to 325° for the rest of the roasting time.

Bake the excess stuffing in the oven during the last 1¼ hours of cooking, basting it two or three times with a tablespoon or two of the goose fat to keep it moist. If it gets too brown on top, cover the dish lightly with aluminum foil.

When the goose is done, remove it to a hot platter and allow it to rest for 15 minutes while you make the sauce. Skim the fat from the pan juices; add the giblet stock to the pan and bring to a boil by setting the pan on a burner over medium-high heat, scraping with a wooden spatula to lift the brown glaze from the pan. Thicken to taste by stirring in *beurre manié* and simmering until the sauce thickens. Stir in the chopped giblets and liver.

Good accompaniments for this rich, fruit-stuffed bird would be a purée of potatoes (see page 51) or a purée of parsnips (see page 52) and a green vegetable such as broccoli or spinach. Serve extra stuffing and sauce separately.

For carving directions, see page 400.

# Duck

Most of the ducks we buy are Long Island ducks, a strain developed in this country that has a thick layer of fat under the skin and not very much meat. The fat acts as insulation for the meat, so rather than cooking these ducks at a high temperature, they are best roasted in a moderate 350° oven to allow time for the fat to render from the duck, otherwise the meat would be over-cooked before the fat was drawn off. To get a lovely crispy brown skin on duck, raise the heat to 500° for the last 15 minutes of roasting time. One school of thought holds that if you leave all the accumulated fat in the pan and keep basting the duck with it, the skin will be crisper. You might try that method sometime and see how you like it. However, if you're going to raise the temperature at the end, there shouldn't be more than a cup of fat in the pan, or you'll have a very smoky, grease-splashed oven.

Ducks marketed for roasting usually weigh from 4½ to 5 pounds, but because of the fat, you don't get many servings from them. One duck will serve 2 amply, 4 at a pinch, depending on the rest of the menu. Like geese, most ducks, except on the West Coast, are sold frozen. They can be left wrapped and thawed in the refrigerator for 1 to 1½ days, at room temperature for 4 to 5 hours, or in cool water for 2 to 3 hours. After thawing, roast at once, or refrigerate.

## ❧ Roast Duck with Peaches          Makes 4 to 8 servings

2 4- to 5-pound ducks, fresh
    or frozen and thawed
½ lemon
Coarse (kosher) salt
⅓ cup Port or Madeira
1½ cups brown sauce (see
    page 275)
4 tablespoons brown sugar
8 peach halves (fresh, peeled
    peaches or firm canned
    peaches)
1½ tablespoons unsalted
    butter
⅓ cup bourbon

Wipe the ducks, remove the giblets and neck (they can be saved for making stock) and the loose fat from the cavity and around the neck. Rub the ducks well, inside and out, with the lemon. Rub salt inside the ducks and all over the skin, which helps to crisp it. Truss the ducks and arrange them on a rack in a shallow roasting pan. Preheat the oven to 350°.

Roast the ducks at 350° for 1 or 1½ to 2 hours, according to how well-done you like your ducks. At 1 hour, duck will be rare (I happen to like it that way); at 1½ hours, medium rare.

When the ducks have been in the oven for 30 minutes, prick the skin all over with a fork. This lets the fat drain out as it melts and keeps the skin crisp. During the roasting, prick once or twice more. As the fat accumulates in the pan, remove any excess with a spoon or bulb baster and put in a jar for future use. Leave about a cup of the fat in the pan each time to prevent the juices from burning and scorching. If you like a really crispy brown skin, about 20 minutes before the ducks are done, increase the heat to 500° and roast for 15 minutes longer. (Reduce the cooking time by 5 minutes to allow for the higher temperature.)

To test duck for doneness, press the flesh of the thigh with protected fingers and wiggle the leg. The flesh should feel soft and the leg move easily. Prick the thigh with a fork. For medium-rare duck, the juices should be slightly rosy, not bloody, but not yellow and clear, a sign that the duck is well done. Well-done duck will have overcooked, dry, and tasteless meat.

When the ducks are done, remove them to a hot heatproof platter and let stand for 10 minutes to allow the juices to settle before carving. Meanwhile, make the sauce and broil the peaches. Skim off the fat from the roasting pan; add the wine and bring the wine and pan juices to a boil over medium-high heat, scraping up the brown glaze from the pan with a wooden spatula. Add this liquid to the brown sauce, bring it to a boil in a saucepan, reduce the heat, and simmer for 2 to 3 minutes to reduce it slightly.

Spread the sugar on the cut sides of the peaches; cut up the butter and dot it over the sugar; put the peaches in a baking dish or on a baking sheet and broil until the sugar and butter are melted and bubbly and the peaches heated through. Arrange the peaches around the ducks; heat the bourbon in a small pan; ignite it; pour the flaming bourbon over the peaches and serve. The flaming may be done at the table if you like.

Duck does not slice well, as the breast has so little meat. The best way to carve duck is to cut it into halves or quarters with poultry shears (see page 105) and serve each person a half or a quarter. To go with the duck, you might have fried cornmeal squares or a purée of potatoes and celery root (see page 52) and either a braised vegetable or a salad of endive and julienne strips of beet. Drink a red wine—a Bordeaux, a California Cabernet Sauvignon, or a Côtes du Rhône.

# Game Birds

Most roast game is delicious in itself and gains nothing from being smothered with other flavors. The most agreeable complements to game birds are juniper berries, tarragon, onion, leeks, cabbage, and sauerkraut. These do not all go with all birds, but they are fairly interchangeable.

The currant-jelly school of thought, like the cranberry school, is to my mind to be avoided. If one has regard for fine wine, which goes so magnificently with game, there is certainly no reason to attempt to mask the flavor of the bird with sharp sweets.

One of the most pleasing foundations or accompaniments for game is a very American food—corn—in the form of either cornmeal mush or hominy grits, cut into squares or oblongs and sautéed in butter until brown and crisp. The texture and taste blend well with the wild, gamy flavor and give a definite quality to certain dishes. I much prefer corn to wild rice, which most people feel is the answer to what to serve with all game.

Another delicious accompaniment I like is the giblets of the game birds chopped and sautéed in plenty of butter with salt, freshly ground pepper, and perhaps a touch of cognac or wine, and spread on toast fried in butter or on the sautéed cornmeal mush or hominy grits previously mentioned.

## Roast Pheasant

*Although wild pheasant is still fairly plentiful in some parts of the country, compared to past times it is exceedingly rare. However, it is easy enough to buy pheasants raised in captivity. These are the next best thing to the wild birds and sometimes a better bet, as they are usually sold when they are the right age for the oven. They generally weigh about 2½ to 3 pounds, and one pheasant will serve 2 or 3.*

**Makes 2 to 3 servings**

2½- to 3-pound pheasant
¼ pound or more unsalted
　butter
4 sprigs of parsley
4 sprigs of fresh tarragon
　Or 2 teaspoons dried
　tarragon
Sheet of fresh fat
　Or salt pork barding fat*

*Pound it thin, to fit over the breast of the bird.*

Because pheasant is rather dry, wipe the pheasant inside and out with a damp cloth. Put a lump of butter (2 or 3 tablespoons) in the cavity with the parsley and tarragon. Butter the skin of the bird well and bard the breast with the sheet of fat, tying it on securely (see illustration on following page). Put the pheasant on its side on a rack in a shallow roasting pan and roast it in a 375° oven for 15 minutes, basting every few minutes with the pan juices and melted butter. Turn it on its other side and roast it for another 15 minutes, basting again. Turn the bird breast side up; cut the string that secures the barding fat so that the fat just lies loosely on the breast and roast it for 10 to 15 minutes, basting frequently. Test the pheasant for doneness by piercing the meat near the thigh and leg joint. If the juices run pale pink, the bird is juicily done. If the juices run clear, the bird is thoroughly done and the breast meat will be fairly dry. If the pheasant needs additional cooking, remove the barding pork; baste the bird well and continue to cook for about 15 minutes or until it is done to taste. The average time for roasting pheasant is about 45 minutes, although many people prefer it roasted a full hour or even more.

Serve the pheasant with crisply sautéed cornmeal mush squares, bread crumbs sautéed in butter, and, if you wish, a velouté sauce made with chicken broth and cream and seasoned with chopped tarragon. To my taste, a good red Burgundy of a recent vintage or a fine full-bodied white Burgundy go equally well with roast pheasant.

# Roast Wild Duck

*The cooking of duck is a highly individual matter. There are those who cannot stand the sight of blood running in a roasted bird. Then there are others to whom a well-done duck is absolutely unthinkable. Something can be said for both attitudes. I adore rather underdone duck, but I have a friend who roasts hers, stuffed, for over an hour, and when I eat them I am convinced that they are far and away the finest ducks I have ever tasted.*

*Some cooks feel that wild duck should be marinated in wine or brandy, or a combination of the two, with herbs and seasonings. It is my belief that something as precious as a good duck needs very little to improve its superb flavor save the good butter, wine, brandy, and simple seasonings used during its roasting. Duck does not need a marinade unless it is a pretty fishy-tasting and -smelling bird—and then it won't be improved much whatever is done to it. However, if you do have to cope with this kind of bird, an onion stuck with a few cloves and some red wine will help to make it more palatable. Rub the interior well with a cut lemon or lime before popping the onion into the cavity and let the bird marinate in wine for some time before roasting.*

*I have also found that wild duck benefits from being rubbed with butter or olive oil and then basted with butter during the cooking period. Sometimes I vary the process and baste during roasting with a blend of red wine and melted butter. Wild ducks are also enhanced if they are flambéed after they issue from the oven. A good cognac, Armagnac, or gin are the most acceptable spirits. The gin, heavy with juniper, is a very satisfactory flavor for finishing off the duck.*

*The length of time you roast wild duck depends on your taste and that of your guests. One duck, unless it is large, will serve only 1 person, so if you wish to go to the trouble you may time each bird separately.*

FOR EACH SERVING
1 *wild duck*
3 or 4 *juniper berries*
  Or ½ *teaspoon dried thyme*
4 to 5 *tablespoons unsalted*
  *butter*
2 to 3 *tablespoons red wine,*
  *Port, or Madeira*
*Salt, freshly ground black*
  *pepper*
2 *tablespoons cognac*
  (*optional*)

Be sure the birds are well cleaned; wipe outside and cavity with a damp cloth. Put juniper berries or thyme and 1 tablespoon butter in the cavity of each bird. Rub the skin with 1 tablespoon butter (or use olive oil) and put the duck on a rack in a shallow roasting pan. Melt 2 to 3 tablespoons butter per bird and combine with an equal amount of red wine, Port, or Madeira. Roast ducks in a 450° oven for 17 to 18 minutes, basting them once or twice with the wine mixture. Season the cooked ducks with salt and pepper and flambé them with cognac if you wish (see page 85). For convenience, split the ducks in half with shears before serving. Serve some of the pan juices with the ducks.

If you like your ducks better done, roast them in a 450° oven for 20 minutes, then reduce heat to 350° and continue to roast 25 to 30 minutes longer, or to your preferred degree of doneness, basting frequently. Remember, though, that wild duck should not be roasted for more than 45 minutes in all, unless it has a stuffing.

To vary the flavor for the duck cavity, try a stalk of celery, a quarter of an onion, 1 or 2 crushed garlic cloves or a sprig of thyme or parsley or a combination of these. You may also put a sheet of barding pork fat over the breast of the bird, although this is not necessary if it is to be cooked quickly.

With the duck, serve squares of sautéed hominy grits or a barley casserole (especially good when cooked with the duck giblets) or wild rice, and cabbage, kale, Brussels sprouts, or glazed turnips—there are many contrasting vegetables that go well with duck. An orange and onion salad with watercress, chicory, or romaine with a rosemary vinaigrette is also a pleasing contrast. However, eschew the salad if you are going to give the duck the great wine it deserves. Duck can take a fine aged Burgundy—a Clos de Vougeot, an Echézeaux, or a Clos de Bèze—or one of your best Bordeaux. Other than that, a good Rhône, such as a red Hermitage, is excellent and if you wish to serve a California wine, a choice Cabernet Sauvignon from the Napa Valley or a Pinot Noir would be the thing.

# Venison

Of all the furred game, venison is the most generally available, both to the hunter and to the nonhunter. Good venison can be found in markets in the larger cities where fine meats and poultry are sold, or it may be ordered by mail and shipped, in which case the meat will have been frozen.

Hunters and their friends, who usually have a great deal of venison on hand in their lockers or freezers, are lucky in that there are good butchers in many sections of the country who will take over the carcass and skin it, hang it, cut it up to order, and either hold or freeze the meat. An experienced butcher can also judge the age of the venison and advise as to the best treatment for the meat and what may be expected from it. If the animal is old and the meat less than tender, it is best to relegate it to a ragout or have it minced for hamburgers. The most desirable cuts for roasts are, of course, the saddle, the rack, and the haunch or leg. According to your preference, you should decide if you want the meat hung for a long time until it develops a really "gamy" flavor or if you would rather have it hung only for several days and eaten fresh or after marination. This is a question you have to answer for yourself, although my feeling is that a fine young deer is delicious roasted without having been marinated.

## Marinade for Venison

1 carrot, peeled and cut into julienne strips
1 onion, peeled and thinly sliced
1 rib of celery, cut into small pieces
1 garlic clove, peeled
Several sprigs of parsley
1½ teaspoons dried thyme
1 bay leaf
1 teaspoon dried summer savory
1 teaspoon freshly ground black pepper
½ cup olive or peanut oil
½ cup red wine vinegar
1 bottle of dry red wine

Combine all ingredients. Marinate any cut of venison for roasting in the mixture for 2 to 5 days, turning it once or twice a day.

# Roast Rack of Venison

*A rack of venison, which is not very large and will serve only 2, may be roasted on the spit or in the oven and it is best when roasted quickly and basted well. Marinate the meat first for 3 to 5 days.*

**Makes 2 servings**

1 rack of young, tender venison

2 tablespoons olive or peanut oil

1 teaspoon dried thyme or rosemary

½ teaspoon freshly ground black pepper

4 tablespoons unsalted butter, melted

¼ cup dry white wine

½ cup freshly made bread crumbs

2 tablespoons butter

¼ cup chopped parsley

Prepare the rack by trimming the ribs well and scraping the ends of the rib bones to remove meat and fat, the way a butcher prepares a rack of lamb (this, in butcher's terms, is known as "Frenched"). Wrap exposed bones with pieces of foil to prevent them charring. Preheat the oven to 450°. Rub the meat and bone well with the oil, thyme or rosemary, and pepper. Put the meat on a rack in a shallow roasting pan and roast at 450° for 15 minutes. Combine the melted butter and white wine and baste the meat well with it. Continue to roast for 5 minutes, then reduce the temperature to 400° and roast 5 minutes longer. Test the internal temperature with a meat thermometer by inserting it lengthwise into the thickest part of the meat, but not touching the bone. It should register 130°. Remove the rack from the oven; turn off the oven and preheat the broiler. Sauté the bread crumbs in 2 tablespoons butter until lightly browned, then combine with the parsley, mixing well, and press them into the meaty part of the venison with your hand until they adhere well. Put the rack under the hot broiler, about 4 inches from the heat, and leave it just long enough for the surface of the crumbs to brown. Transfer the rack to a hot platter and let it rest for 5 minutes before carving it into chops. Serve with crisp sautéed potatoes and a green vegetable such as broccoli. Drink a Juliénas from Beaujolais.

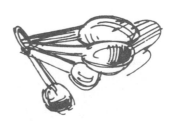

# Roast Haunch of Venison

*The haunch is the leg and part of the loin. If it is from a fine young animal have the meat hung for 10 days to 2 weeks.*

**Makes 8 servings**

1 large or 2 small garlic
  cloves, peeled and chopped
Freshly ground black pepper
1 teaspoon dried thyme
1 venison haunch, weighing
  8 to 12 pounds
¼ pound (1 stick) unsalted
  butter, softened
Salt
2 cups dry red wine
1 cup strong veal or chicken
  broth
2 teaspoons tomato paste
Beurre manié (*see page 270*)
3 tablespoons Madeira
Watercress or parsley

Combine the garlic, 1 teaspoon pepper, and the thyme. Blend the mixture well with your hands and rub it vigorously into the meat. Let it stand for 1 hour.

Preheat the oven to 450°. Spread the roast with 2 to 3 tablespoons softened butter and put it on a rack in a shallow roasting pan. Roast at 450°, basting it once with the rest of the butter, for 30 minutes. Reduce heat to 350° and continue to roast for 1 to 1½ hours for an 8-pound haunch or proportionately longer for a larger one, allowing 12 to 15 minutes per pound. After roasting for 1 hour, test with a meat thermometer, inserting it in the thickest part of the meat but not touching the bone. When the venison is done, the internal temperature will be 130°. If it is anywhere near that, continue to test at 10-minute intervals. About 15 minutes before you estimate the meat will be done, sprinkle it with salt.

While the meat is roasting, put the red wine in a pan. Bring to a boil, then reduce the heat and simmer until the wine is reduced to 1 cup.

Remove the cooked venison to a hot platter and let it rest for 10 to 15 minutes before carving. Skim the fat from the juices in the pan and combine the pan juices with the broth and red wine, scraping well to incorporate the brown glaze in the pan. Pour the liquids into a saucepan and mix in the tomato paste, 1 teaspoon pepper, and salt to taste. Bring the liquid to a boil; reduce the heat and drop in small balls of *beurre manié*, stirring the sauce and simmering it until thickened to your taste. Add the Madeira and simmer the sauce a little longer to eliminate the alcohol—about 5 minutes.

Garnish the roast with watercress or parsley and serve polenta (cooked cornmeal) with it. Serve the sauce separately and drink a good red Bordeaux.

If you prefer to marinate the haunch before roasting, put it in a large nonmetallic bowl, pour the marinade over it, and leave for 5 days, turning the meat over at least once a day. When ready to roast, remove it; dry well on paper towels and roast as above, using ½ cup of the strained marinade in place of ½ cup of the wine.

# Vegetables

Certain root vegetables, notably onions, potatoes, carrots, and parsnips, are delicious when roasted, either in the pan with the roasting meat or separately in a pan of rendered beef fat or suet, which gives them the same lovely flavor they get from the meat drippings.

You'll have noticed that a couple of the meat recipes had pan-roasted vegetables as an accompaniment. I've found by experience that they cook better, especially if the meat is being roasted at a medium temperature, if they are first parboiled for 5 minutes, to soften them slightly. Small new potatoes may be roasted whole, either peeled or in their thin skins, with a little belly band of skin cut from around the center to prevent them from bursting. Larger potatoes should be peeled and halved or quartered, according to size. Small carrots or parsnips may be left whole, larger ones halved or quartered. The small white onions are better for roasting than the large yellow ones. Prepare the vegetables; parboil them, bringing them to a boil in water to cover with 1 teaspoon salt; drain and then arrange them in the pan, around the roast, for the last hour of cooking time. Or put them in a roasting pan containing about ½ inch of hot rendered beef fat or suet and roast in a 425° oven for 40 minutes, or until just tender when pierced with a fork or the point of a small sharp knife.

# Broiling and Grilling

*B*roiling and grilling, the application of intense direct heat to meat and other foodstuffs, is probably the oldest, most basic, and most functional of all the cooking processes. It can be done over an outdoor fire, a charcoal, gas, or electric grill, or under the oven broiler. I remember, as a child, our grills at the beach over fires of the driftwood we gathered. Our fuel was mainly the bark from fir and spruce trees, which was very plentiful along the beach because of the Oregon lumber industry. Believe me, nothing was better for grilling than that wonderful aromatic bark when it had burned down to glowing, white-encrusted coals. Our primitive little grill stuck over the fire did noble work with hamburgers, frankfurters, marshmallows speared on sticks, and all those other things that children love to eat outdoors. Sometimes we would nail a split salmon to a plank and grill it alongside the fire, as the Indians used to do.

The words "grilling" and "broiling" are practically synonymous. One grills or broils on a grill, originally known as a gridiron. According to my infallible authority, the Oxford English Dictionary, grilling was "the process of broiling on a gridiron or similar apparatus over or before a fire" and a grill was a piece of meat or fish broiled on a gridiron. Hence the adoption of the term "grill room" for restaurants or hotel dining rooms where grilled foods are prepared and served. In French, the verb to broil is *griller* and broiled fish is a *grillade*.

The first gridirons, of which you see drawings in old English and American cookbooks, were little four-footed iron grills that were placed over coals in the fireplace. This could be a very messy way of cooking. The fat dripped onto the coals, sending forth smoke and odors, although fortunately, to a great extent these dissipated up the chimney. When I was a child, the only way we could broil in the kitchen was to remove the lid from the wood stove and put a grill over the open flame. Although this chancy process managed somehow to bring forth some delicious morsels, our grilling had to be performed with the windows open to let out the smoke, and the fat that dripped into the fire caused quite a mess. Thank goodness, the advent of gas and electric ranges changed all that.

Today, most of our broiling is done with gas or electricity. It is my personal feeling that electric broilers do a more efficient job than gas ones. As it takes time to become accustomed to the performance of any broiling unit, whether it is the newest type or an older one, it is always a good idea to try it out with various pieces of meat and poultry to establish the correct timings and distances from the heat for your particular unit. You also have to learn how to adjust the flame for best results if you are using one of the older gas broilers.

It's fun to play around with broiling, to experiment with the basic rules of distance and timing and then set up your own chart. The timing will vary according to the unit and to how you like your meat cooked. Broiling or grilling is not just a matter of throwing a piece of meat under the broiler or over a charcoal fire, it is a pretty scientific process you should master, for in these days of quick meals and diets, broiling has become one of the most popular forms of cooking. Not only is it functional and fast, but the direct heat cooks out a great deal of the fat in meat or poultry and chars the surface, giving great flavor. The main difference between grilling over charcoal and broiling under a broiler is the distance from the heat, as the heat of charcoal is much more intense.

There are, of course, some drawbacks to broiling. It will not tenderize meat, so you should only broil the more tender cuts and those that are best suited to the process, like beef and lamb. I refrain most of the time from broiling pork, including pork chops, because the intense heat tends to dry out and harden the flesh. I find braising or sautéing gives the meat more succulence. The same is true of most cuts of veal, except perhaps for a *paillard* of veal, a very thin slice from the leg which is pounded until it is even thinner, then brushed with oil or butter and broiled for less than a minute very close to the heat. Veal chops or veal steaks, on the other hand, need the moist heat of braising and sautéing.

Fish lends itself well to broiling, provided you baste it well and don't overcook it. Shrimp and scallops, either the large sea scallops or the tiny bay scallops, are delicious broiled, and so are soft-shelled crabs, but I don't recommend it for larger shellfish, such as lobster. To me, a broiled lobster is a dried-out, tasteless disaster. Among the organ meats, liver and kidneys respond well to fast broiling, and so do little chicken hearts and livers cooked on skewers. This method of stringing pieces of meat, fish, and vegetables on sticks or skewers, known in France as *en brochette* and in other parts of the world as kebabs or kabobs, is as old as time. It may well have been one of the first ways anyone ever grilled over an open fire.

When you come to think about it, there are comparatively few foods that don't lend themselves to broiling. You could cook a whole breakfast under the broiler, if you wanted to—broiling your grapefruit, your bacon, and your toast. Although it may not have occurred to you, toasting is really broiling bread. In France, as a matter of fact, toast is *pain grillé*, grilled bread. Maybe you are old enough to remember how bread used to be toasted before we had electric toasters—on a long-handled wire toasting fork in front of the fire, first on one side, then on the other.

There's another aspect of broiling that dates back to the old days when a piece of solid metal called a salamander was heated in the fire until it was red hot and then passed over the surface of a finished dish to give it a lovely brown glaze. One of the most famous of all the traditional English and American desserts, crème brûlée—a baked custard sprinkled with a thin layer of sugar which is then exposed to intense heat until it caramelizes and forms a thin, brittle crust—used to be finished this way. Now we caramelize the sugar under the broiler. Then there are all the dishes which we serve gratinéed—spread with crumbs, dotted with butter or sprinkled with cheese, and put under a hot broiler for a few minutes until the top is delicately browned and takes on a deliciously toasty quality. Or the broiler may be used to glaze a dish covered with a mornay or hollandaise sauce—perhaps poached fish fillets, or vegetables, or sauced oysters, or clams on the half shell.

Broiling is a fascinating cooking technique and probably the one requiring the most active participation on the part of the cook.

## GENERAL RULES AND RECOMMENDATIONS FOR BROILING

♦ If you are going to be completely scientific about broiling, use a meat thermometer, the kind that registers from 0° to 220°, to test the internal temperature during broiling of very thick cuts of meat, such as a 3-inch steak or a boned butterflied leg of lamb.

♦ Generally speaking, your meat will cook better and faster if you remove it from the refrigerator and let it warm up at room temperature for 1½ to 2 hours. Refrigeration cools meat considerably and it takes time for the heat to overcome this interior chill. While frozen meats may be broiled without defrosting, you will have to allow twice as long a broiling time as for a fresh cut. Sear them about 2 inches from the heat on both sides, to seal the surface, then lower and broil 4 inches from the heat, rather than the usual 3 inches, for the rest of the cooking time. Fish can also be broiled from the frozen state, at the normal distance but for double the cooking time. Chicken, duck, and other poultry or game birds should be thawed before broiling.

♦ Whatever type of broiler you have, it should always be preheated at the highest setting until good and hot. With an electric broiler, the "broil" light will go off when the oven has preheated to the correct temperature. When broiling with electricity, leave the oven door ajar, or the thermostat will switch the broiler off.

Do not preheat the broiler pan and rack, unless you are cooking an extremely thin piece of meat, such as a *paillard* of veal, that broils very fast and is not turned, and therefore needs heat on both sides. Just lubricate the broiler rack well by rubbing it with oil or butter or beef fat so the meat doesn't stick to it and, if you wish, line the broiler pan with foil, which will help to reflect heat upward and make clean-up simpler. Thin fish fillets are best broiled on oiled foil, which you can put over the rack or in the pan itself. I also like to use aluminum foil broiling pans, the type with a corrugated bottom, for broiling a single steak, or chicken, or a couple of chops. They come in various sizes, don't need lubricating, and are easy to clean. However, take the precaution of putting foil pans on a firm metal sheet, such as a cookie sheet or baking sheet. Foil bends easily and you could have a nasty accident with the hot fat.

One great advantage of this type of pan is that while the ridges drain off fat, the pan itself is much flatter and shallower than the broiler rack and pan, which is about 1½ inches deep. With a regular broiling pan and rack, it is almost impossible to use the top oven rack, unless you are broiling a very flat piece of meat like a flank steak, for it brings the surface of the meat too close to the heat. However, you can use a foil pan on the top rack if you want to bring your steak or chop close to the heat to char the surface. As to distances from the heat, you will have to figure out for yourself, according to the type of unit you have, how to increase and decrease the distance. Aluminum foil pans, which can be placed on top of broiler pans and racks to elevate them, are one solution. If your broiler has a grid positioner, so much the better. Mainly you will just have to figure out how to move the oven racks and pans around or, if you have one of the older gas units, how to regulate the heat by increasing or decreasing the flame. As a general rule, a distance of about 3 inches from the heat to the surface of the meat is the best level for cuts of normal thickness (about 1½ inches) and for thin fish fillets. Chicken, poultry, and foods that easily get overcooked, like scallops, shrimp, and whole fish, are better at a distance of 4 inches. A very thick cut like a 3-inch steak or a boned butterflied leg of lamb should be even farther from the heat—from 5 to 8 inches, to allow time for the heat to penetrate. Steaks or lamb chops can be brought closer to the heat toward the end of the cooking time, if you wish, for that last touch of charring. Very thin cuts, say a flank steak, on the other hand, should be no more than 1½ to 2 inches from the heat, as they must cook very rapidly indeed.

◆ Always trim excess fat from meat before broiling, to prevent flare-ups. As to seasoning, there are great differences of opinion about whether you should salt and pepper meat before, during, or after broiling. Personally, I like to season meat before I broil it, but I really don't think it makes one bit of difference. If you feel like experimenting, as I have done in the past, take three pieces of the same meat cut and season one before, one during, and one after and you'll find there is practically no difference in texture and flavor. You don't have to worry about the salt drawing out the meat juices, because the intense heat will seal the surface almost immediately.

◆ While tender cuts need no marinating and seldom, if ever, any basting, fish, shellfish, chicken, game birds, and organ meats like kidneys and liver that have no natural fat do need to be basted or brushed with butter or oil to keep them from drying out.

I am of the opinion that marinating does little or nothing to render tough cuts of meat broilable. They are better braised. However, there are times when you might want to marinate a flank steak, meat kebabs, poultry and game, or fish and shellfish to give added and enhancing flavor. A teriyaki marinade of soy sauce, oil, sherry, and flavorings can be used for many different foods such as broiled chicken, wild duck, flank steak, shrimp, or strips of meat or chicken wound on skewers and broiled in the Japanese style. You can make a very simple marinade for game, poultry, or meat with equal parts of dry vermouth and olive oil flavored with dried or chopped fresh herbs—tarragon or rosemary for chicken, thyme for beef or lamb, thyme and rosemary for most game. Wine and oil marinades, like the one given for beef shashlik (page 112), are also good for game birds, kebabs, and thick cuts of lamb. No marinade should ever be without oil. Unless there is some lubrication, the meat may dry out. What is the difference between a marinade and a basting liquid? Technically, a marinade is a thin sauce in which food is soaked before it cooks and a basting liquid is a thin sauce that is brushed on or spooned over the food as it cooks, but as you can also baste with a marinade, sometimes they are one and the same.

# Beef

## ❧ Broiled Steak

Steaks are bought by thickness, not by weight. Because of the variance in size and shape between the different cuts, it is very difficult to gauge how much a steak is going to weigh. It's my feeling that a 1- to 1½-inch steak is the minimum thickness for broiling; anything thinner is better sautéed. Then, of course, there are times when you splurge and get a very thick steak of 2½ or 3 inches. However, for now, let us take a 1½-inch steak as our example.

When you buy a steak, you must consider the grade. The better the grade, the tenderer the cut. Prime is the top grade, but most of this goes to restaurants. Choice is the grade you are likely to find in your meat market and it is the best buy. When picking out steak, look for meat that is deep red in color and well marbled with creamy-colored fat. If you can, have the steaks specially cut for you rather than picking up a ready-packaged steak in the supermarket. The butcher will weigh the steak after cutting it to the thickness you want.

Allow roughly 6 to 8 ounces of boneless meat per serving. If you are not buying a boneless cut like the eye of the rib or eye of the sirloin but rather a larger bone-in steak such as a sirloin or porterhouse, estimate ¾ to 1 pound meat per serving to compensate for the weight and waste of the bone. You'll find a description of steaks for broiling on page 365.

You don't have to buy individual steaks for everyone. A large bone-in sirloin steak of 4 pounds will feed 4 people nicely if you carve it at table, first cutting around the bone and then slicing it diagonally into ½-inch strips. If you're just cooking steak for yourself, however, you are better off with a small club steak, a rib or eye of the rib, or a strip steak from the loin. If it is rather more than you want to eat, don't worry. Cold steak makes great sandwiches.

BROILING METHOD FOR ANY 1½-INCH STEAK
Preheat the broiler. Trim excess fat from the steak, leaving a rim about ½ inch thick. Slash the rim to keep it from curling.

Brush the broiler rack with oil or rub it with some of the fat trimmed from the steak. Salt and pepper one side of the meat and arrange it, seasoned side up, on the rack of the broiler pan. Before putting the steak under the broiler, press it with your finger. It will feel very soft. Remember this later when you test the cooked steak.

Put the broiler pan under the broiler with the surface of the steak 3 inches from the heat, or as close to 3 inches as possible.

For a very rare steak, broil for 8 to 12 minutes, 4 to 6 minutes a side. For a rare steak, broil for 10 to 14 minutes, 5 to 7 minutes a side. When I'm broiling a steak, I sometimes give it an extra half-minute on the first side, because it doesn't really begin to sear until it has been in the oven for a half-minute. Halfway through the cooking time turn the steak with metal tongs, not with a fork, which would pierce the flesh and let the juices escape, and season the second side before broiling it.

There are two schools of thought about how often to turn a steak during cooking. Some people like to sear one side, turn and sear the second side, turn it back again and cook on each side for the rest of the cooking time. Frankly, I don't think it does anything for a steak to keep on turning it back and forth. Once is enough.

About 2 minutes before the end of the cooking time, test the steak to see if it is done to your liking. There are three ways you can determine this. One is to remove the pan from the broiler and insert your meat thermometer horizontally through the side (not in the top) of the steak to the center, but not touching the bone, if there is one. The internal temperature for a very rare steak is 120° to 125° and for a rare steak 130° to 135°. (Medium, if you must, would be 140° to 145°.) The second way is to make a little cut in the meat near the bone or the rim of fat with a small sharp knife and check the inside of the meat. If it is done the way you like it, that's fine. If not, return the pan to the broiler and continue to cook the steak for a minute or so longer. The third test, which is the one professionals use and you will gradually learn to rely on, is to press the center of the steak lightly with your finger (it won't burn you), remembering how it felt when raw. A rare steak will feel firm on the surface but soft within. Were it to be medium, the steak would feel slightly resistant and a well-done one, perish the thought, would be quite firm. Practice touching steak broiled to the stage you prefer and you'll soon become accustomed to testing this way.

When your steaks are broiled, put them on hot plates or a hot platter. Or, if you are going to carve a large steak at table, on a carving board. I like to put a pat of butter on a steak the minute it comes out of the oven, either plain unsalted butter or butter mixed with an herb such as crushed rosemary or thyme (use a ratio of about ½ teaspoon dried herb to 2 tablespoons butter). The butter melts and runs over the meat, mingling with the juices when you cut into or carve the meat and making a little sauce. If you are carving the steak into slices, spoon some of the luscious mingled juices and butter over each serving.

A good steak needs little or no embellishment. You can sit down and eat it just as it is, or you can have broiled tomatoes or broiled mushrooms with it, or a green salad, or you can shoot the works and have potatoes or French fries, a green vegetable, and a salad. That's up to you. If you wish to be really elegant, you might have a Béarnaise sauce, sautéed potatoes, and a vegetable or salad.

## TIMINGS FOR STEAKS OF OTHER THICKNESSES

+ For a steak 1 inch thick, broil 2 inches from the flame; 3 minutes a side for very rare, 4 to 5 minutes a side for rare.
+ For a steak 2 inches thick, allow the longer broiling time given for a 1½-inch steak, broiling at 3 inches from the heat.
+ For a steak 2½ to 3 inches thick, broil with the surface of the steak 5 to 6 inches from the heat and allow from 20 to 35 minutes total broiling time for very rare, 30 to 40 minutes for rare. With an extremely thick steak you must allow time for the heat to penetrate and warm the interior, even though it does not actually cook it. You'll have a fairly charred surface and a rare interior. The lowering of the rack compensates for the longer broiling time.

# Charcoal-Broiled Steak

*The main difference between oven broiling and charcoal broiling is the distance from the heat, as the heat of charcoal is more intense. Otherwise the timing is much the same.*

Start broiling when the coals have burned down until they have a white feathery covering of ash. The heat at grill level, which should be from 5 to 7 inches above the coals, will be between 325° and 375°, ample for broiling almost any steak or poultry, chops, or fish. If you are grilling a steak, start at a temperature of about 350° at grill level, which you can easily check with a special flat grill thermometer. To sear the steak first, raise the firebox or move the grill closer to the coals, and sear quickly on both sides, close to the coals, then move the steak farther from the heat to finish the cooking. Or if you would rather char the meat at the end of the cooking time instead, follow the same procedure of raising the firebox or lowering the grill. Steaks should be seared, charred, and cooked for equal time on each side.

# London Broil (Broiled Flank Steak)

*Although this thin fibrous steak, the triangular piece on the underside, below the loin, is not a tender cut, it is delicious if broiled very fast and sliced very thin. If you can, get a prime flank steak, which will be a tenderer, better quality. If not, buy the choice grade.*

**Makes 4 servings**

Remove the tough membrane on the outside of the meat with a sharp knife. Rub the steak well on both sides with coarse (kosher) salt, freshly ground black pepper, and a little Tabasco.

Preheat the broiler. Rub the broiling rack with oil; arrange the flank steak on the rack and put the broiler pan and rack on the top oven shelf, so that the surface of the steak is 1½ to 2 inches from the heat. Broil for 3 to 4 minutes on each side for rare meat—which this has to be.

Carve into very thin slices on the diagonal, slicing across the fibers, which will give you tender, edible pieces of meat. Serve with sauce diable (see page 277) and sliced French bread. Flank steak also makes great sandwiches.

## Variation

♦ TERIYAKI FLANK STEAK. Trim but do not season the meat. Put the steak in a dish or deep platter in which it can lie flat and pour teriyaki marinade (see page 103) over it. Marinate for 2 to 3 hours, turning the steak occasionally. Broil as before, 1½ to 2 inches from the heat, for 3 to 4 minutes a side. When you turn the meat, brush the upturned side with the marinade.


# Broiled Hamburgers

*It is difficult to broil hamburgers well, as they are likely to dry out, though a chip of ice in the center of each patty helps. I prefer to sauté hamburgers (see page 161), but if you wish to broil your hamburgers, they should always be cooked to the rare stage.* Allow 8 ounces hamburger for a main-dish serving. Form the meat into 1-inch-thick patties, putting a chip of ice in the center of each, and season the outside with salt and freshly ground black pepper. Preheat the broiler and grease the broiling rack. Arrange the patties on the rack and brush the tops with melted butter or beef fat, or a mixture of oil and butter. Broil 4 inches from the heat for 3 minutes, then turn with a broad-bladed turner and brush the second side with butter. Broil 3 minutes on the second side. This will give you a rare hamburger. Serve with French fried potatoes and sliced beefsteak tomato or sliced onion.

Editor's note: *Because of the risk of foodborne illness associated with raw and undercooked meat, the USDA recommends cooking ground beef to an internal temperature of 160°F.*

# Deviled Beef Bones

When you carve a standing rib roast, leave some meat on the rib bones and you can turn them into crunchy deviled beef bones. If you freeze the bones from 2 or 3 roasts, you should have enough for a meal—3 or 4 ribs a serving.

When you are ready to cook them, thaw them until they have reached room temperature, then cut the ribs apart, leaving some meat between them.

**Makes 2 to 3 servings**

8 to 10 beef ribs from rib roasts

¼ pound (1 stick) butter, melted

2 tablespoons tarragon vinegar

2 to 2½ cups very fine fresh bread crumbs

Have the ribs at room temperature. Preheat the broiler.

Combine the melted butter and vinegar in a deep soup or pie plate and put the crumbs in another pie plate. First dip the ribs in the butter and then roll them in the crumbs, pressing the bones in so the crumbs adhere. Arrange them in a large aluminum foil broiling pan, leaving space between, and broil about 6 to 7 inches from the heat so they cook very slowly and the crumbs don't burn. Keep turning the bones with tongs until you get a good crisp brown coating on all sides. The cooking time will be 15 to 20 minutes. Serve with sauce diable (see page 277).

# Poultry

## ❧ Broiled or Grilled Chicken

Young broiling chickens run from 1½ to 3 pounds in weight. Birds of 2½ pounds are preferable as there is more meat on them than on the small ones. Half a chicken per serving is usual. If you feel this is too much chicken for one person, you can carve the chickens into quarters after they are broiled. Have broiling chickens split lengthwise and the necks and backbones removed.

**Makes 4 servings**

2 2½-pound broiling chickens, split, backbone and neck removed

½ cup melted butter

Oil

Salt, freshly ground black pepper

Preheat the broiler. Rub the rack of the broiler pan with melted butter or oil. Rub salt and freshly ground pepper into both the skin and bone sides of the chickens and then rub them well with butter or oil. Arrange the chickens, bone side up, on the broiler rack. Broil 4 inches from the heat for 12 to 14 minutes, basting once or twice with the butter, then turn with tongs; brush the skin side with butter and continue to broil, skin side up, brushing once or twice more with butter, for 12 to 14 minutes. If necessary, move the chickens closer to the heat for the last 2 or 3 minutes to brown and crisp the skin, but be careful it doesn't burn.

Test for doneness by piercing the joint between thigh and body with the point of a knife. If the juices are slightly tinged with pink, but not red, the chickens are cooked. If red, cook a minute or two longer. Serve with a green vegetable or a green salad.

## Teriyaki Broiled Chicken

**Makes 2 servings**

A 2½-pound broiling chicken, split

TERIYAKI MARINADE
½ cup soy sauce (preferably Japanese or Chinese)
½ cup oil (olive oil, peanut oil, or corn oil)
¼ cup dry sherry
2 garlic cloves, peeled and finely chopped or crushed
2 tablespoons grated fresh ginger root
Or finely chopped candied ginger with the sugar washed off
1 tablespoon grated tangerine or orange rind

Arrange the chicken in a shallow dish or pan. Combine the marinade ingredients and pour over the chicken. Marinate from 1 to 3 hours, turning the chicken frequently to make sure it is well soaked with the marinade. You can leave it in the marinade, refrigerated, for up to 24 hours if you wish. Otherwise marinate for 1 hour at room temperature or 3 hours in the refrigerator.

Preheat the broiler. Grease the broiler rack with oil and arrange the chicken on it, bone side up. To prevent the soy marinade from caramelizing and burning, place the chicken under the broiler about 5 inches from the heat, farther away than it would normally be. Broil bone side up for 12 to 14 minutes, depending on thickness, brushing once or twice with the marinade from the dish. Turn the chicken over with tongs, brush the skin side

with the marinade, and continue broiling for another 12 to 14 minutes, brushing or basting twice with the marinade. If the skin of the chicken seems to be blistering or burning, lower the broiling pan another inch. To test for doneness, pierce the joint between the body and the thigh with a small sharp knife. The juice that trickles out should be faintly tinged with pink. If it is red-tinged, broil a minute or two longer, but do not overcook or the chicken will be dry. Serve on hot plates, with rice and sautéed snow peas or a green salad.

## Broiled Squab

These baby chickens weigh only 1 pound. Have them split, and broil and baste them as for broiled chicken, but give them only 8 to 10 minutes a side. Serve 1 squab per person.

## Broiled Chicken with Flavored Butter

*One of the easiest and best ways to prepare broiled chicken is to make a flavorful mixture of butter creamed with herbs or garlic or shallots, rub some of it on the bone side, and stuff some under the skin so that the flavor penetrates and the butter lubricates the flesh. Tarragon-flavored butter is especially good.*

**Makes 4 servings**

FLAVORED BUTTER
FOR 2 2½-POUND
BROILERS, SPLIT
6 *tablespoons unsalted butter*
1 *teaspoon salt*
½ *teaspoon freshly ground
    black pepper*

CHOOSE ANY OF
THE FOLLOWING
4 *large garlic cloves, very
    finely chopped*
⅔ *cup finely chopped shallots*
⅓ *cup finely chopped parsley
    Or half parsley and half
    chopped chives*
2 *tablespoons chopped fresh
    tarragon
    Or 1½ teaspoons crushed
    dried tarragon*
2 *teaspoons finely chopped
    fresh rosemary
    Or 1 teaspoon well-crushed
    dried rosemary*

Mix the butter, salt, pepper, and chosen flavoring in a bowl, mashing them well together with a wooden spoon or working them with your hands, until thoroughly mixed (or prepare the butter by mixing the ingredients in a blender or food processor).

Lift up the skin of the chicken at the top of the breast and slip your hand under it. Push your hand down between the skin and breast—the membrane connecting skin to flesh will rupture easily as you do so—and then between the skin and flesh of the leg and thigh. Take some of the flavored butter in your hand and rub it over the leg and thigh meat under the skin and then pat a thin layer over the breast meat.

Turn the chickens over and rub the bone side with a little of the butter. Melt the remaining butter in a small pan and reserve for brushing the chickens. Broil the chickens as for broiled chicken, brush melted butter once on the bone side; turn, brush twice on the breast side.

Serve the chickens with sautéed potatoes and a green salad.

# Broiled Duckling

*Duckling, especially the Long Island variety, is more interesting broiled than roasted. The duckling should be cut in half lengthwise with poultry shears, from the vent at the tail, along the side of the breastbone, and then down the center of the back. Allow half a 4- to 5-pound duckling per serving, as there is little meat on the carcass. You may, if you prefer, cut each half in two after broiling and serve it to 4 people.*

**Makes 2 to 4 servings**

*4- to 5-pound duckling, split*
*½ lemon*
*Salt, freshly ground black pepper*

Remove as much fat as possible from the carcass of the duck, then rub the bone side with the cut lemon. Rub both bone and skin side with salt and pepper.

Preheat the broiler. Put the duck halves, bone side up, on the broiler rack and pan (as the duck is so fatty, there is no need to grease the rack). Arrange the pan so the duck is 4 to 5 inches from the heat and broil on the bone side for 20 minutes. Remove the pan from the oven and pour off the fat; turn the duck pieces with tongs and prick the skin all over with a fork to release the fat. Return to the oven and continue broiling for a further 20 to 30 minutes on the skin side, or until the skin is crisp and well browned. If at any time the duck seems to be browning too fast or the skin is in danger of burning, move the pan farther away from the heat.

Test the duck for doneness by piercing the joint between thigh and body, as for broiled chicken. If the juices are faintly tinged

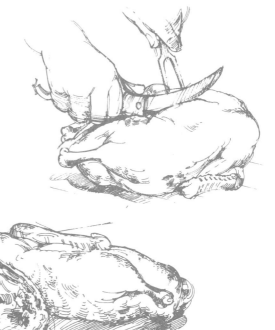

with pink, the duck is done. If red, broil a minute or two longer. Remove the duck to a heated platter or a carving board, if you wish to cut it into quarters. Serve with glazed turnips or tiny green peas. A salad of sliced oranges and onions is also good with broiled duck.

## Variation

♦ BROILED PEPPERED DUCKLING. Omit the pepper when seasoning. After the duck has broiled on the second, skin side for 10 minutes, remove it from the oven. Prick the skin again. Holding each half with several thicknesses of paper towels, press the skin into 2 tablespoons coarsely crushed black peppercorns on a plate until well coated. Lower the broiling pan and rack so the skin of the duckling will be 6 inches from the heat (to prevent the peppercorns from burning) and broil for 10 to 20 minutes. For the last 2 or 3 minutes raise the pan until the duck is about 2 inches from the heat, so the pepper forms a brown, crunchy coating.

# Lamb

## ～ Broiled Lamb Chops

Thick loin or rib chops are the best for broiling. As they have a good deal of fat and most people like their lamb chops broiled rare or pink (medium rare), you should move the chops nearer to the heat, about 2 inches away, 2 minutes before the end of the broiling time in order to char the fat. Thin chops (1 inch thick) are best broiled fast and close to the heat or the meat will be overcooked before the fat is brown.

Ideally, lamb chops should be at least 1½ to 2 inches thick. Even 2½ or 3 inches is not too much, if your chops are to be deliciously rare. As the single lamb chops sold in markets are usually cut 1 inch thick and the double lamb chops 2 inches thick, you will have to ask your butcher to cut them specially if you want other than the standard size. Allow 1 large or thick, or 2 small or thinner lamb chops per serving.

Broiling time depends not only on the thickness of the chops but also on the intensity of heat put out by your broiler. The following chart gives approximate times and distances for chops of different thicknesses. The time given is total broiling time. Allow half the time per side.

| THICKNESS | DISTANCE FROM HEAT | BROILING TIME |
|-----------|--------------------|--------------|
| 1 inch | 2 inches | 5 to 6 minutes for rare |
| | | 6 to 8 minutes for medium rare |
| 1½ inches | 4 inches | 6 to 8 minutes for rare |
| | | 8 to 10 minutes for medium rare |
| 2 inches | 4 inches | 9 to 12 minutes for rare |
| | | 12 to 14 minutes for medium rare |

For 3-inch chops, first give them 3 minutes a side at 4 inches from the heat, then lower to 5 inches from the heat and continue to broil for a further 9 to 12 minutes for rare, 12 to 15 minutes for medium rare.

## BROILING METHOD

Preheat the broiler. Rub the broiler rack with oil. (If you are broiling 1-inch chops, broil them in an aluminum broiling pan which can be put nearer the heat. Be sure to put the pan on a cookie or baking sheet first.)

Season the chops on one side with salt and pepper and arrange on the broiler rack or in the foil pan. Broil according to the chart, turning the chops with tongs midway through the broiling time and seasoning the second side with salt and pepper when turned.

If necessary, raise the chops to within 2 inches of the heat for the last 2 minutes of broiling to brown the fat.

To check for doneness, make a tiny slit in the meat, near the bone. Or, if the chops are very thick, insert a meat thermometer horizontally into the thickest part of the meat, not touching the bone. The internal temperature should be 135° for rare, 140° for medium rare.

Serve broiled lamb chops on very hot plates, as the fat congeals quickly. Crisp fried potatoes or broiled tomatoes and watercress are good accompaniments.

# Broiled or Grilled Butterflied Leg of Lamb

*This unusual way of cooking leg of lamb gives you absolutely delicious, juicy meat. Ask your butcher to trim the fell and most of the fat from the leg and to bone and butterfly it—cut it open and spread it flat—so that the meat is approximately the same thickness all across, about 2½ to 3 inches. It will resemble a thick steak with some fat on one side.*

**Makes 6 to 8 servings**

6- to 7-pound leg of lamb, trimmed, boned, and butterflied (about 5 pounds of boneless meat)

2 to 4 garlic cloves, peeled and cut into small slivers

Salt, freshly ground black pepper

½ teaspoon rosemary or summer savory (optional)

2 tablespoons melted butter

Spread out the lamb, fat side down. Make tiny incisions in the meat with the point of a small sharp knife and insert the slivers of garlic. Season the meat well with salt and pepper and, if you wish, rub it with the rosemary or savory crushed in a mortar and pestle or in the palm of your hand with your thumb.

Preheat the broiler. Lay the lamb on the oiled broiler rack with the fleshy side up, fat side down. Broil 6 inches from the heat for approximately 15 to 18 minutes, depending on thickness (if some parts of the lamb are thicker than others, determine cooking time by the thicker portions). Brush the surface with melted butter, turn the lamb with tongs, and broil fat side up for 16 minutes for rare or 20 minutes for medium-rare meat. Test about 5 minutes before the end of the cooking time by removing the lamb from the broiler and inserting a meat thermometer in the thickest part—it should register 135° for rare, 140° for medium rare.

Continue cooking until the meat reaches the desired temperature, then remove it to a hot platter or carving board, fat side down, and allow to stand for 5 minutes before carving. Carve slices crosswise on the diagonal, from ¼ to ½ inch thick. Serve with a hollandaise sauce (see page 279) into which you have mixed finely chopped fresh mint or finely chopped anchovies to taste. Sautéed potatoes and a purée of green beans are good with this.

# Other Meats

## Broiled Liver Steaks

Allow ⅓ to ½ pound liver per serving. Have calf's liver sliced in steaks 1½ inches thick.

Preheat the broiler and brush the broiler rack with oil or melted butter. Arrange the liver steaks on the rack and brush them well with melted butter. Broil 4 inches from the heat for 4 minutes a side, turning with tongs. Brush the liver well with butter as it cooks. The liver should be lightly browned on the outside and pink on the inside. Do not overcook. Remove from the broiler to a hot platter and sprinkle with salt and pepper. Serve with Béarnaise sauce and sautéed or boiled potatoes.

## Broiled Ham Steaks

The ready-to-eat ham steaks sold in supermarkets require minimum broiling, otherwise they dry out. Buy ham steaks 1 to 1½ inches thick. Slash the fat around the edge to prevent it from curling.

Preheat the broiler and grease the broiling rack. Arrange the steaks on the rack and broil 2 to 3 inches from the heat for 2½ minutes a side, until just lightly browned. Do not overcook. If you wish to glaze the ham slice, brush it with equal quantities of honey and Dijon mustard.

A steak from a country ham, which is precooked but not ready-to-eat, will take longer, about 10 minutes a side, and should be broiled 5 inches from the heat. If you wish, brush the steak with honey or honey and mustard, or baste it with a mixture of equal quantities of melted butter and white wine.

## Broiled Sausages

You can broil either pork sausages or the Italian sweet or hot sausages. Prick them well with a fork and cook them in boiling water for 3 to 4 minutes to blanch and precook them and to draw out some of the fat. Drain, dry, and arrange on a greased broiler rack or aluminum foil pan. Broil 3 inches from the heat, turning once, for about 9 to 10 minutes, or until nicely browned on all sides.

# Broiled Veal Kidneys

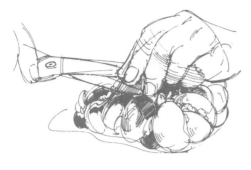

Allow 1 kidney per serving. Remove the skin and any fat from the kidneys, split them in half lengthwise, and cut out the hard core of tubes and fat with a scissors or a small sharp knife.

Preheat the broiler and brush the broiler rack with melted butter or oil. Arrange the kidneys, cut side up, on the rack and brush them well with melted butter or oil. Broil 3 inches from the heat for 5 minutes, turning halfway through the cooking time. Brush the kidneys well during the cooking with butter or oil. When properly broiled, kidneys should be delicately browned on the outside and juicily rare inside. Transfer to hot plates, sprinkle with salt and pepper, and spoon a little melted butter over each serving. Sprinkle each kidney with 1 teaspoon chopped parsley, if you wish. Serve with French fried potatoes, watercress, and English mustard.

## Variation

♦ DEVILED KIDNEYS. Broil the kidneys for 4 minutes, then dip them in a mixture of melted butter, lemon juice, and Tabasco (1 tablespoon lemon juice and ½ teaspoon Tabasco to ⅓ cup melted butter). Roll them in fresh bread crumbs, return to the broiler, and broil quickly on both sides just until the crumbs are browned. Serve with mustard sauce (see page 274).

# Kebabs

This oldest method of grilling (antedating the gridiron), which consists of simply stringing pieces of meat on a twig or sharpened stick and holding them over the fire, is now known as kebab cookery. With the advent of metal, the stick was discarded in favor of the sturdier, reusable skewer or brochette, an implement that has survived virtually unchanged for centuries.

While almost anything in the meat, poultry, game, and seafood line can be strung on skewers and broiled, broiled lamb and beef, in the form of shish kebab and shashlik, are undoubtedly the most popular. They are virtually the same. Shish kebab is the Turkish name and shashlik the Russian for this style of meat cookery.

Lean, tender cuts of meat are best for kebabs: lamb shoulder or leg; pork loin or leg (the fresh ham); the sirloin, top sirloin, and rib cuts of beef. Veal tenderloin or shoulder, while also excellent, needs plenty of lubrication. For each serving, allow ½ to ¾ pound meat. For shish kebab and shashlik, the meat is usually marinated, to add flavor.

# Shish Kebab

Makes 4 to 6 servings

*3 pounds lean lamb, either leg
or shoulder, with most of
the fat removed, cut in
1½- to 2-inch cubes*

MARINADE
*1 cup olive oil
⅓ cup lemon juice
2 garlic cloves, peeled and
crushed
1 teaspoon salt
1 teaspoon freshly ground
black pepper*

OPTIONAL
VEGETABLES
*Whole cherry or plum
tomatoes
Green pepper, cut in
1½-inch cubes
Mushroom caps
Eggplant, unpeeled,
cut in 1½-inch cubes
Small white onions, parboiled
for 5 to 10 minutes,
according to size
¼ cup olive oil
Or melted butter*

There should be practically no fat on the meat. Trim off as much as possible. Combine the marinade ingredients in a glass, stainless-steel, or pottery bowl, add the meat, and marinate for 2 to 48 hours, turning frequently.

Remove the meat cubes from the marinade (there is no need to dry them) and string them on steel or iron skewers, about 14 inches long, leaving about 2 inches of space at the handle and tip of the skewers. Push the pieces close together. This gives a juicier, rarer result than spacing out the meat, as it protects the inner surfaces from the heat. If you like to cook vegetables on the same skewer as the meat, alternate the meat cubes with any or all of the optional vegetables. Or you may string the vegetables on separate skewers and cook them alone.

Preheat the broiler. Remove the rack from the broiler pan. Arrange the skewers across the pan, handles resting on one side, tips on the other (you should be able to get about six skewers on the pan). Or use aluminum foil broiling pans to support the skewers. Brush kebabs and vegetables with oil. Broil with the surface of the meat approximately 3 inches from the heat, turning the skewers often and brushing with the marinade, for about 9 minutes for rare, 12 minutes for medium rare. Test by making a small cut in one of the cubes to see if it is done to your taste. Do not overcook. Serve with rice or bulghur pilaf (see page 44).

If you are broiling the vegetables separately, after putting them on skewers brush them liberally with olive oil or melted butter and sprinkle lightly with salt and pepper. Keep brushing them with oil or butter as you turn the skewers—mushrooms are especially likely to dry out if not well lubricated.

## Beef Shashlik

Makes 4 to 6 servings

3 pounds lean beef sirloin, cut
  in 2-inch cubes

RED WINE MARINADE
²⁄₃ cup dry red wine
½ cup olive oil
2 tablespoons lemon juice
3 garlic cloves, finely chopped
1 teaspoon salt
1 teaspoon freshly ground
  black pepper
1 tablespoon chopped fresh dill
  Or 1 teaspoon dried
  dill weed

OPTIONAL
VEGETABLES
Whole cherry or
  plum tomatoes
Mushroom caps
Squares of green pepper
2 tablespoons oil

Combine the marinade ingredients in a glass or pottery bowl; add the beef cubes and marinate from 4 to 48 hours, turning frequently.

When ready to cook, thread the beef on skewers, as for shish kebab, alternating the cubes, if you wish, with the optional vegetables. Arrange the skewers on the broiler pan and brush with oil, lubricating the vegetables well.

Preheat the broiler. Broil the shashlik 3 inches from the heat, turning and brushing with the marinade, until the meat is crusty on the outside and rare within, about 8 to 9 minutes for rare and 9 to 10 minutes for medium rare. Test by making a small cut with a knife in one of the cubes. Serve the shashlik with rice, bulghur pilaf (see page 44), or potatoes Anna.

# Fish and Shellfish

## ❧ Broiled Fish Fillets

Fresh or frozen fillets are the most universally available form of fish. You can buy fillets of cod, haddock, flounder, sole, sand dabs, salmon (usually the thinner part, from the tail), rockfish, whiting, bluefish, plaice, striped bass, sea bass, and shad. Or you can buy something anonymous, just called "fillets," which can mean any variety of fish.

Broiling fish fillets is tricky. They must be watched carefully and, as they are usually very tender when broiled and break easily, great care should be taken when removing them from the broiler pan. A firm, long-bladed metal spatula or long-bladed professional turner which can be slid under the entire length of the fish is best for this purpose. You can also use a hinged grill with two mesh sides and a handle, the kind in which shrimp and small fish are broiled over charcoal. There are different types available. The smaller the mesh, the easier it is to handle delicate fish. Another good way to cook fillets, especially the very thin ones that are best broiled on one side only and not turned, is to place a long piece of foil on the broiling rack, leaving two overlapping ends to serve as handles. Lightly oil the foil and arrange the fillets on it. Then all you have to do to remove them is to grasp the foil handles firmly and carefully slide the fillets onto a hot platter. If you are broiling fillets on one side only and not turning them, it is also a good idea to preheat the broiler pan first in the oven, so the heat will help to cook the underside of the fish.

Frozen fillets are best broiled without thawing and may be turned easily up to the point at which they have thoroughly thawed. Broil them as you would fresh fillets, but double the cooking time.

**Makes 4 servings**

2 pounds fish fillets

BASIC BASTING
MIXTURE
½ cup melted unsalted butter
   or vegetable oil
   Or a mixture of butter
   and oil
1 teaspoon salt
¼ teaspoon freshly ground
   black pepper
2 tablespoons lemon juice

Combine the basting ingredients in a small pan. Measure the fish at the thickest point. According to the thickness of the fillets, either line the broiler pan with foil or arrange a piece of foil over the broiler rack (place very thin fillets on the rack to bring them nearer the heat, thicker ones in the pan). In either case, leave an overhang of foil to help in removal. If the fillets are thin, heat the pan and rack while preheating the broiler.

When ready to cook, remove the broiler pan and rack. Brush the foil well with oil or melted butter, which will prevent the fish from sticking to the foil. Arrange the fillets on the foil in a single layer and brush them well with the basting mixture. Broil with the surface of the fish 3 inches from the preheated unit, estimating 10 minutes per inch of maximum thickness (very thin fillets may take only about 3 minutes). If the fillets are thinner at the ends than in the center, it is best to underestimate a little or the ends will be overcooked. If the fillets are thick enough to turn (¾ to 1 inch), broil for half the estimated time on one side, then turn, using a spatula or turner; brush well with basting mixture and broil for the remainder of the time on the second side. If too thin to turn, baste during the cooking. The fish is done if the flesh flakes easily when tested with a toothpick or fork.

Transfer the cooked fillets to hot plates or a heated platter and pour over them any of the basting mixture left on the foil.

Sprinkle broiled fish fillets with chopped parsley. Serve with wedges of lemon or lime and, if you wish, with boiled potatoes dressed with melted butter and chopped parsley and a green vegetable or a green salad. Herbed butter, lemon butter, or mustard sauce (see page 274) are also good with broiled fillets.

# Broiled or Grilled Fish Steaks

Fish steaks can be broiled and basted in the same manner as fish fillets, but the surface of the fish should be 4 inches from the heat, 5 to 6 inches if the steaks are frozen. Estimate 10 minutes of cooking time per measured inch of maximum thickness and twice as long for frozen fish. Thin fish steaks will need no turning, but if they are an inch or more thick, they should be turned with a broad-bladed turner after half the cooking time. When done, slide a spatula or turner under the steaks and transfer to hot plates or a heated platter. Serve with wedges of lemon or lime and garnish with parsley or watercress sprigs. Allow 1 small steak or half a large steak (about ½ pound of fish) per serving.

## Broiled Marinated Halibut Steaks

*Thick steaks of firm-fleshed fish such as halibut or swordfish can be marinated before cooking, which gives them flavor and prevents them from drying out.*

**Makes 2 to 4 servings**

*2 halibut steaks, 1 inch thick*

MARINADE
*6 tablespoons olive oil*
*2 small garlic cloves, finely chopped*
*1 teaspoon dried basil*
*1½ teaspoons salt*
*1 teaspoon freshly ground black pepper*
*1 tablespoon lemon or lime juice*

Combine the marinade ingredients in a glass or pottery dish large enough to hold the halibut steaks in one layer. Add the steaks and marinate for 2 hours, turning them two or three times in the marinade.

Line a broiler pan or rack with foil; oil or butter the foil; put the steaks on the foil and broil 4 inches from the heat for 5 minutes a side, brushing with the marinade. Serve on hot plates with fried zucchini (see page 196) and boiled potatoes. Garnish with chopped parsley.

# ✽ Whole Broiled Fish

Whole fish, either small ones or those of fairly good size, are delicious broiled. Have the fish scaled and gutted and the head and tail left on (unless this would make it too large for your broiling facilities).

Rub the skin with oil on both sides and then with coarse (kosher) salt and freshly ground black pepper. Slash the skin in two or three places with a sharp knife, to prevent its splitting when broiled. You can also salt and pepper the inside of the fish and put a slice or two of lemon inside, or, if you wish, stuff a few sprigs of fresh herbs or a sprinkling of dried herbs inside. Crushed or chopped herbs may be rubbed on the skin with the seasonings. Thyme, rosemary, and summer savory are good herbs for fish.

Measure the fish at the thickest point to estimate the cooking time—the rule for any type of fish cookery is to allow 10 minutes per inch of measured thickness. Place a strip of foil on the broiler rack or in the broiler pan; brush it with oil and arrange the fish on it to allow for easy turning. Or, if the fish is not too large, arrange in an aluminum foil broiler pan with a corrugated surface.

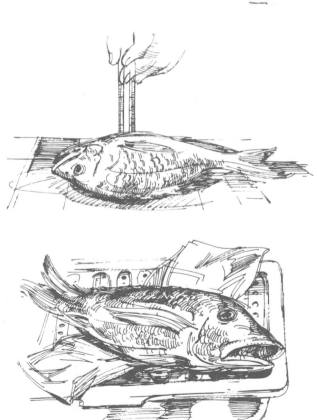

Broil the fish approximately 4 inches from the preheated broiler, according to size (large fish 4 to 6 inches from the heat; smaller fish 2 to 4 inches away), allowing 10 minutes per measured inch of thickness for total cooking time. Halfway through the cooking turn the fish with a large spatula using the foil to help. Be careful not to overcook or let the skin char too much. If the heat seems too intense, lower the pan an inch or two. Test the flesh with a toothpick or a fork 3 or 4 minutes before the end of the estimated time. If it flakes, it is done.

When done, transfer

to a heated platter and serve at once with an appropriate sauce, such as mustard sauce, hollandaise, Béarnaise sauce, or caper sauce.

You may also split the whole fish and broil it, removing the head but leaving the backbone in (which seems to keep the juiciness and flavor). Lay the split fish skin side down on the oiled foil, brush the flesh well with melted butter, and broil 3 inches from the heat, allowing 10 minutes per measured inch. Do not turn the fish but baste it several times during the cooking with melted butter. Season with salt and pepper.

Estimate about ¾ pound whole or split fish per serving, to allow for the inedible parts.

## Broiled Scallops
Makes 4 servings

1½ pounds bay scallops
  (the small ones)
½ cup milk or beer
1 to 1½ cups freshly made
  bread crumbs, from
  unsweetened white bread
Salt, freshly ground black
  pepper
¼ pound (1 stick) unsalted
  butter, melted
1 tablespoon finely chopped
  parsley

Rinse the scallops under cold running water. Drain and dry thoroughly on paper towels. Dip the scallops in the milk or beer and then roll them lightly in the crumbs. Arrange in a shallow foil pan and put the pan on top of the broiling pan and rack. Sprinkle with salt and freshly ground pepper to taste and spoon 4 tablespoons of the melted butter over them. Broil 4 inches from the heat just until the crumbs are lightly browned. Do not overcook, or the scallops will be tough. Transfer to a serving dish and sprinkle with the rest of the melted butter and the chopped parsley.

## Broiled or Grilled Shrimp
Makes 4 to 6 servings

2 pounds large raw shrimp in
  the shell

With kitchen scissors, slit the shell of each shrimp down the back and remove the black intestinal vein. Break off the shell, leaving the tail shell on.

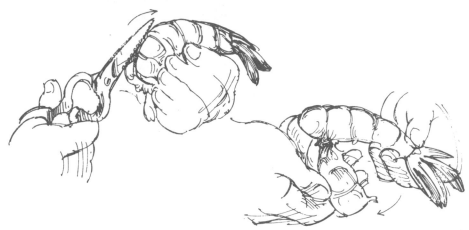

**MARINADE**

*1 cup olive oil*
*2 garlic cloves, very finely*
*chopped*
*1 cup dry white wine*
*1 teaspoon salt*
*1 teaspoon freshly ground*
*black pepper*
*¼ cup finely chopped parsley*

Combine the remaining ingredients in a bowl. Add the shrimp to this marinade and let them soak, turning frequently, for 2 to 3 hours.

Preheat the broiler. Arrange the shrimp in a large aluminum foil pan or on the broiler rack and pan, and broil about 4 inches from the heat for 5 to 7 minutes, according to the thickness of the shrimp, turning them halfway through the cooking time and brushing with the marinade as you turn them. If you have a hinged grill (the type used for broiling shrimp or small fish over charcoal), you can arrange the shrimp in this before putting them on the broiler rack; they will be easier to turn.

# Vegetables

The vegetables best for broiling are those with plenty of natural moisture, such as mushrooms, tomatoes, and eggplant, which is better broiled than sautéed, for in sautéing it tends to soak up too much oil.

## Broiled Mushrooms

Use large flat caps for broiling. Break off the stems and reserve them for some other use. Brush the caps well with melted butter or oil and arrange them on a well-oiled broiler rack, cap side up. Broil 4 inches from the broiling unit for 2 to 2½ minutes, then remove the pan from the broiler. Turn the mushrooms over and in each cap put either ¼ teaspoon butter, a tiny piece of partially cooked bacon, or 1 or 2 drops of olive oil. Sprinkle each one with salt, a grind of pepper, and a tiny dash of Tabasco. Return to the broiler and cook another 2½ minutes. Transfer carefully to a serving plate or to slices of toast, so as not to lose the liquid in the caps. These are good with broiled steak, chicken, or liver.

# Broiled Tomatoes

**Makes 6 servings**

6 large, ripe tomatoes
Salt, freshly ground black
 pepper
2 slices day-old bread
1 garlic clove, peeled
2 tablespoons olive oil
2 tablespoons chopped parsley

Slice about ¼ inch off the top, stem end of the tomatoes, then give each one a slight squeeze to loosen some of the seeds; sprinkle the top with salt and turn the tomatoes upside down on paper towels to drain. Preheat the broiler.

Rub both sides of the bread well with the garlic clove, to impart some garlic flavor to it, then break the bread into small pieces and reduce to fine crumbs in the blender or food processor. Blend the crumbs with the olive oil. When excess liquid has drained from the tomatoes, after about 10 minutes, turn them over and spread the crumb mixture on the tops, then sprinkle the crumbs with a little salt and a grind or two of black pepper.

Arrange the tomatoes in an aluminum foil broiling pan and broil them about 4 to 5 inches from the heat (if necessary to elevate the pan, put the broiler rack and pan on the second shelf of the oven and put the foil pan on top). Broil until the tomatoes are heated through and the crumbs nicely browned, about 10 minutes. Do not let the crumbs burn. Remove from the oven; sprinkle the tops with chopped parsley and serve with broiled meats.

# Broiled Eggplant Slices

Soak 2 or 3 finely chopped or crushed garlic cloves in ½ cup olive oil for 1 hour.

Wash 1 large or 2 small eggplants; trim off the stem end and about ¼ inch of the rounded end and cut them into ½-inch-thick slices, leaving the peel on. Allow 1 or 2 slices of eggplant per serving, according to size.

Preheat the broiler and put the oven rack on the second shelf. Oil or butter a baking sheet large enough to hold the eggplant slices in one layer (or do them in batches, according to how many slices you are broiling). Brush the eggplant slices lavishly on one side with the garlic-flavored oil and sprinkle them with a little salt and freshly ground pepper. Arrange them on the baking sheet and put them under the broiler, with the surfaces about 5 inches from the heat. Broil until lightly browned, about 5 minutes, brushing with a little more oil if they seem to be getting dry. When browned, turn them over with a metal spatula; oil, salt, and pepper the second side and broil again until browned, about another 5 minutes. They should be just cooked through. Remove them; sprinkle with a little chopped fresh parsley, if desired, and serve with broiled steak or hamburgers. Or sprinkle with chopped fresh mint and serve with broiled lamb. You can also serve hamburgers or thin slices of broiled steak or of butterflied leg of lamb on top of the eggplant slices, omitting the herb. Serve this combination with spicy tomato sauce, if you like.

## Variation

♦ About 2 minutes before the eggplant slices are cooked on the second side, sprinkle them lightly with grated Parmesan cheese and replace under the broiler until the cheese melts and browns.

# Broiled Peppers

*Unless you are eating green or red peppers raw in a salad, broiling is the best way to deal with them. Broiling chars the thin, papery skin so that you can easily scrape it off with the back of a knife and slightly cooks the flesh to a flavorful juiciness. You can also char the skin of peppers by impaling them on a fork and turning them over a gas flame, but the broiling method is really easier. Allow 1 to 2 peppers per serving, according to size.*

Wash and dry the peppers, leaving them whole, and place them on the rack of the broiler pan. Broil under a preheated broiler, about 1½ to 2 inches from the heat, until the skin scorches and blackens, turning them from side to side until the entire surface is blistered and charred. This may take as many as 25 minutes. Remove from the broiler and when just cool enough to handle, scrape the charred skin from the flesh with the back of a silver or stainless-steel knife—don't tear the flesh. Then remove the stems and seeds. Halve, quarter, or cut into slices. Heat a little finely chopped garlic in olive oil (1 garlic clove to ¼ cup oil), and toss—or dress—the hot peppers with the garlic-flavored oil, salt, freshly ground black pepper to taste, and a few drops of lemon juice. Serve with broiled meats and chicken. Or let the peppers cool after skinning and seeding them; cut into strips; marinate in vinaigrette dressing and serve as for vegetables vinaigrette (see page 293), as a first course or part of an hors d'oeuvre selection.

# Fruit

Certain fruits can be sprinkled with sugar, dotted with butter, and broiled, to make a fast, light, and delicious dessert.

## Broiled Grapefruit

For each serving, allow half a grapefruit. Remove the seeds with the point of a knife or spoon. Cut around the membranes and between the outer peel and the pulp with a grapefruit knife to loosen the sections. Arrange the halves on a baking sheet and sprinkle them lightly with about 2 teaspoons brown sugar. Add about ½ teaspoon Grand Marnier to each one. Dot with 1 teaspoon butter cut into small pieces. Preheat the broiler. Broil the grapefruit with the surface 5 inches from the heat until the topping is brown and bubbly—about 5 minutes. If you serve these for breakfast, omit the Grand Marnier.

## Broiled Peaches

Allow 1 peach per serving. They should be ripe but firm. Put the peaches in a bowl, pour boiling water over them to loosen the skins, and leave for 1 to 2 minutes. Peel off the skins, halve the peaches, and remove the pits. Arrange them on a buttered or oiled baking sheet, cut surface up. Sprinkle the cut surfaces lightly with brown sugar and dot with 1 teaspoon butter cut into small pieces. Preheat the broiler. Broil the peaches 4 to 5 inches from the heat until the sugar and butter are brown and bubbling—about 5 minutes—and the peaches soft but not mushy.

## Broiled Pineapple

Cut the leafy top and the bottom from a whole, ripe pineapple. Slice, skin and all, ½ inch thick crosswise. Cut the rind and the eyes from the pineapple slices. Arrange the slices on a buttered baking sheet. Sprinkle each slice with 1 teaspoon brown sugar and dot with 1 teaspoon butter cut into smaller pieces.

Preheat the broiler. Broil the slices 4 to 5 inches from the heat until the sugar and butter are brown and bubbling—about 5 minutes. Serve 2 or 3 slices per person, according to size.

### Variation

♦ FLAMED PINEAPPLE. Arrange the broiled slices on a heatproof serving dish. Heat 6 tablespoons light or dark rum in a small pan; ignite with a match and pour flaming over the hot pineapple.

# Broiled Bananas

Butter a baking sheet and arrange whole, peeled ripe bananas on it. Allow 1 per person. Spread each banana with 2 teaspoons soft butter; sprinkle it with 1 teaspoon brown sugar and squeeze 2 or 3 drops of lime juice over it.

Preheat the broiler. Broil the bananas 4 to 5 inches from the heat, about 5 minutes, until the fruit is soft and the butter and sugar browned and bubbly.

# Gratinéed Dishes

## Oysters or Clams Casino

*About the only time oysters or clams are broiled is when they are served on the half shell as a hot appetizer, with a topping of herbed butter or buttered bread crumbs. Usually they are broiled and served on beds of rock salt, which prevents the shells from tipping over and keeps them hot.*

**Makes 4 servings**

6 slices bacon
24 oysters or clams on the
    half shell
Rock salt
½ pound (2 sticks) unsalted
    butter, at room temperature
⅓ cup finely chopped shallots
    or green onions
½ cup finely chopped parsley
½ cup finely chopped green
    pepper
2 tablespoons lemon juice
1 teaspoon salt
½ teaspoon freshly ground
    black pepper

Arrange the bacon strips on the broiler rack and broil about 2 inches from the heat until half cooked. Remove; drain on paper towels and cut each piece of bacon into 4 pieces.

Arrange the oysters or clams on beds of rock salt in 4 aluminum foil pie plates. Blend the butter, shallots, parsley, green pepper, lemon juice, salt, and pepper well by beating them together with a wooden spatula or blending them in a blender or food processor. Put the herbed butter on top of the oysters or clams and cover with a piece of bacon. Put the pie plates on cookie sheets or baking sheets and slide them under the hot broiler with the oysters or clams about 2 inches from the heat. Broil just long enough to brown the bacon and heat the oysters through. Put the pie plates on serving plates and serve as a first course.

# Stuffed Clams

*As this dish is made with steamed clams, it is advisable to buy a dozen more than you will need. If some prove moribund, they will have to be thrown out.*

**Makes 4 servings**

24 clams in their shells
4 to 5 tablespoons unsalted
   butter
1 cup fresh bread crumbs
1 tablespoon finely chopped
   onion
1 tablespoon finely chopped
   parsley
1 tablespoon finely chopped
   fresh tarragon
   Or 1 teaspoon dried
   tarragon
½ cup thick béchamel sauce
   (page 303), made with
   broth from the clams
1 tablespoon dry sherry
Salt, freshly ground black
   pepper
Cayenne pepper
Rock salt

Scrub the clams thoroughly with a brush under cold running water and rinse several times, to get rid of the sand. Discard any clams with gaping shells, which means they are dead. Place the clams in a large pot with ½ inch of water, bring to a boil; cover the pot and steam just until the shells open, about 6 to 10 minutes. Discard any with unopened shells—after cooking, the muscle holding the two halves of the shell together will relax and the shell will open. If the shell does not open, the clam is not safe to eat.

Strain the broth through cheesecloth, to remove any sand from the opened shells, and use to make the béchamel sauce. Discard the top shell of each clam, saving the flatter bottom one. Take the steamed clams from the shell and chop very fine.

Melt 3 tablespoons of the butter in a skillet. When hot, add the bread crumbs and sauté over medium heat, tossing them with a wooden spatula, until golden brown. Mix ½ cup of the buttered crumbs with the minced clams, onion, parsley, tarragon, béchamel sauce, and sherry. Taste, and add salt, black pepper, and cayenne pepper to taste. The mixture should be fairly spicy, not bland. Fill the reserved half shells with the mixture, mounding it with a teaspoon, sprinkle with the remaining buttered crumbs, and top with the remaining butter cut into tiny pieces.

Arrange the shells on aluminum foil pie plates filled with rock salt, and set the plates on cookie sheets or baking sheets. Preheat the broiler. When ready to serve, put the stuffed clams under the broiler, 2 inches from the heat, and broil just until the crumbs are browned and the clams heated through. Put the pie plates on serving plates and serve as a first course.

# Lobster au Gratin

Makes 4 servings

6 tablespoons unsalted butter
3 cups bite-sized chunks of
 cooked lobster meat
¼ cup cognac
¼ cup dry white wine
½ cup heavy cream
1½ cups hollandaise sauce
 (see page 279)

Melt the butter in a skillet; add the lobster and sauté briefly over medium heat, tossing and turning it with a wooden spatula, until just heated through. Add the cognac to the pan; light with a match and shake the pan until the flames die. Stir in the white wine and the cream and cook for 5 minutes. Do not boil. Pour the lobster mixture into a 2-quart baking dish or casserole and cover it with the hollandaise sauce. Put under a hot broiler, 4 to 5 inches from the heat, just long enough for the sauce to brown and glaze. Do not over-cook or the hollandaise will separate. Serve immediately, with rice.

# Crème Brûlée

Contrary to popular belief and despite the name, this is not a French dish, but an English one. It first appeared in a seventeenth-century English cookbook of Dorset recipes as "burnt cream." Then it became one of the great specialties of Corpus Christi college at Cambridge, where, I think, it probably acquired the more elegant name. There are many recipes for this dessert and many ways of preparing it. The baked custard part is easy to make, but the topping of caramelized sugar (that is, sugar melted until it is brown and bubbly) which gives the dessert its name is a tricky process—you must have a good hot broiler and watch the sugar carefully to make sure it doesn't burn, moving the dish farther from the heat if it seems about to. If you don't get a completely caramelized topping the first time you make this, don't worry. It takes time and practice.

Makes 8 servings

9 egg yolks
6 tablespoons sugar
Pinch of salt
2¾ cups heavy cream
1-inch piece of vanilla bean
½ cup granulated sugar

Beat the egg yolks in a bowl with a rotary beater, whisk, or electric hand mixer until thick, then add the sugar and salt and con-tinue beating until thick, creamy, and light yellow. Meanwhile, heat the cream with the vanilla bean in a heavy saucepan over medium heat, stirring occasionally to prevent the cream from sticking to the pan and scorching, until it comes to the boiling point (tiny bubbles will appear around the edges and the surface will start to move). Remove from the heat and drizzle the cream slowly into the egg mixture, stirring vigorously with a whisk or a wooden spatula, until thoroughly mixed. Remove and discard the vanilla bean. Put the mixture in a heavy enameled-iron or stainless-steel pan and cook over medium heat, stirring constantly, for 3 minutes. Do not let the custard get near the simmering point or it will curdle. Strain the custard into a 1-quart heat-proof baking dish of enameled metal, heatproof glass, or porcelain. Preheat the oven to 325°.

Place the baking dish in a roasting pan and set it in the center of the middle rack of the oven. Pour hot water into the roasting pan to reach to two-thirds the depth of the dish (baking the custard in this hot-water bath prevents it from overcooking or curdling). Bake the custard for 45 to 50 minutes, or until it is set but not overcooked. Cooking time depends on the thickening power of the yolks. Insert a skewer or thin-bladed knife into the custard. It should come out clean. Watch carefully while the custard cooks to see that the water does not boil; if it is getting too hot, add some cold water to the pan.

When the custard is baked, carefully remove the pan from the oven and the dish from the pan. Let the custard cool thoroughly, then cover the top of the dish with plastic wrap and refrigerate until firm and cold (the recipe can be prepared to this point in advance, as much as a day ahead).

A few hours before serving, preheat the broiler to its hottest temperature. Set the chilled custard on a large piece of waxed paper and, using a fine sieve, carefully sift ½ cup sugar evenly over the surface of the custard, making a layer about ¼ inch thick. The waxed paper will catch any sugar that spills over and this can be resifted.

Place the dish on the top broiler rack, so that the sugar is about 1 inch from the heat, and broil until the sugar melts, caramelizes, and forms a crust. Watch carefully to see that the sugar does not burn, moving it farther from the heat if it starts to scorch, and turning the dish around, if necessary, so the sugar melts evenly. When the sugar has caramelized, immediately remove it from the oven and chill in the refrigerator for about 2 hours. The caramelized top should be hard and brittle, and sound hollow when tapped with a finger. Crack the crust as you serve the dessert and give each person a bit of crust along with the custard.

# Braising

"Braising" is a term that is far too seldom used in our gastronomic vocabulary. You'll hear people say, "I'm making a pot roast," or "I'm going to make a stew of this meat," or "I think I'll simmer this in wine," and what it all comes down to, whether they know it or not, is braising, or cooking with moist heat, probably one of the earliest and certainly one of the most effective ways to tenderize tough cuts of meat, game, or mature birds, wild or domestic.

Incidentally, that phrase "pot roast" didn't come into our everyday kitchen lexicon until quite late. Many of the early cookbooks, including those of New England and Michigan, referred to the dish we know as Yankee pot roast as "beef à la mode," and it's quite likely this was one of the dishes that came across the border into New England, Pennsylvania, and Michigan with the French Canadians and even traveled as far as the South. And beef à la mode is just another form of braised beef.

Braising has always been extremely popular in Europe, for good reasons: first, because there used to be fewer tender cuts; second, because using less tender cuts was a thrifty way to eat; and third, because Europeans, in the last 75 or 80 years, anyway, have eaten more game, per capita, than we in the United States, so they have devised ways of braising game birds and furred game that make them more toothsome, tender, and flavorful.

Braising differs from boiling and poaching in one important respect: it is standard practice, in most cases, to brown the meat well before adding the liquid that forms the essential vapors. These aromatic vapors provide the long, moist, tenderizing treatment that produces a well-flavored and delicious piece of meat. Aiding the liquid are the additions—herbs, vegetables, sometimes calves' or pigs' feet or a piece of pork rind—that give the dish a distinctive taste. Sometimes these are part of a marinade in which the meat is bathed for several hours or days before being cooked until it is thoroughly imbued with the various flavors. Certain braised meats, notably the *daubes* of the south of France, are marinated and then cooked in the marinade without browning, but this is not the general rule.

The choice of liquids for braising is wide, and the results are surprisingly and delightfully diverse. Water, naturally, is one, but it needs excellent seasoning and some enriching and thickening ingredient such as a veal knuckle or calves' or pigs' feet, which add natural gelatin. Stock or broth provides its own flavor, enhancing both taste and texture. Wine or beer may be combined with stock or used alone. Cider, other juices, and tomato purée are occasionally combined with the flavorings to give a different character to the dish.

*B*raising can range from a simple matter of browning a piece of meat, adding liquid and flavorings, and simmering it in a covered pot, to a more complex and interesting process based on what is known as a mirepoix, a mixture of finely cut flavoring vegetables that form a bed on which meat, birds, or occasionally whole fish are braised. The mirepoix usually consists of three or more vegetables cut in very fine matchstick strips, or julienne, cooked together in a little fat until just wilted and then arranged on the bottom of the pan in which the braised meat or bird will cook. These vegetables usually include the two great flavoring root vegetables, carrot and onion; in addition, leek, turnip, celery, fennel, or even parsnip might also be tossed in, and they are all wilted down into a lovely soft bed which exudes a delicious aroma and juice that gives great flavor to the meat. Sometimes a little stock, white wine, sherry, or a touch of wine vinegar is added before the meat or bird is braised.

After braising, the mirepoix may be puréed to make a sauce for the dish (if it is cooked a long time, it almost becomes a purée automatically) or it may be served around the meat or bird as an accompaniment.

The mirepoix is not only used with less tender cuts. Sweetbreads, as tender a morsel as you are likely to find, are often cooked on a mirepoix in order to transfer the lovely mixed vegetable flavors to them and to form the basis for a sauce.

Traditionally, the first step in braising is to brown the meat in fat over fairly high heat on top of the stove. It may be dipped in flour, and sometimes in seasonings, before browning, or sprinkled with flour after the initial browning. The flour, which browns too, thickens the liquid and gives a rich deep color. However, I'm a firm believer in browning meat under the broiler. It's just as efficient, really easier, and I happen to prefer the result. Not only does it draw out fat, rather than adding it, but it gives the crusty exterior and flavor conveyed by a word sometimes used in the past for braised dishes—*carbonnade* or *carbonadoes*. Say it, and you get the feeling of meat browned almost to the point of being charred or carbonized. I'm pretty sure that in the old days when meats were spitted and roasted in front of a fire, they were browned this way before being put into a pot and simmered over the coals.

Braising can be applied just as well to small pieces of meat as to large cuts. A beef stew, a navarin of lamb, veal Marengo, all of the many and varied stews and *daubes* and goulashes and ragouts, including *carbonnade Flamande*, that succulent dish of beef and onions simmered in beer, are braised dishes. Even a simple little Irish stew, although the meat isn't browned first but merely cooked with liquid and vegetables, qualifies as braised lamb. Think about it, and you'll see how they all fit the pattern.

I am also of the opinion that any braised dish is best when allowed to cool completely after cooking (which makes it easier to remove the excess fat) and reheated before serving. This somehow seems to mellow the flavors and give the dish a better finish.

The French, the English, and, to a certain extent, the Italians have come up with some extraordinarily fine braised game dishes. The French, with their supreme regard for the beauty of a finished product, make a dish of game birds and vegetables called a *chartreuse* (the name, like that of the liqueur, comes from La Grande Chartreuse monastery near Grenoble, where the dish was invented centuries ago by the Carthusian monks, originally as a molded composition of vegetables alone). The vegetables are precisely cut and arranged in a pattern around the container so that when the dish is unmolded it is revealed as an exquisite *pièce montée*, a delicate shell of rows of carrots, turnips, green beans, green peas, sometimes truffles, enclosing the game filling. A *chartreuse* is a magnificent example of the chef's art, as beautiful to look upon as to eat.

In a homelier vein, one finds such delicious combinations as the great Alsatian dish of pheasant with sauerkraut, an ideal way to use mature birds, as the sharpness of the sauerkraut, the flavor of the wine and seasonings, and the pungency of the sausage merge into a bouquet of mouthwatering tastes that do something sensational to that tough old bird. In that respect we might define braising as the art of making the tough not only tender but infinitely more desirable and tasty.

It's a delight to discover the miracle of braising. When you wander through the supermarket and go through the meats, especially those less tender cuts that look so good but may taste worse than they look, a picture of the mirepoix will come into your mind and you'll know how to transform them into thoroughly delicious and lip-smacking dishes. I'm a great believer in having an idea in my head when I go marketing and then embroidering on that idea as I go through the market and see what looks good that day. This is intelligent shopping. Instead of making up your mind before you shop what you are going to have for dinner, you wait until you get to the market and have the fun of making out your menu there, based on that idea lurking at the back of your mind.

Of course, as I mentioned before, it's not only tough cuts that benefit from braising, so don't limit yourself to the meat counter. Chicken can be braised. So can delicate foods like sweetbreads, fish, even vegetables. However, one must be extremely careful when braising fish not to overcook it, but just to give it that benediction of the mirepoix and the wine or other liquid that supplies the necessary moisture, for here the cooking is done more by flavored steam than by simmering liquid.

If you have never tasted a braised vegetable, you'll find it is a revelation, completely different from one that is eaten raw, plainly cooked, boiled, sautéed, or fried. Root vegetables like fennel and onions are superb when braised. So are leafy greens like lettuce and endive, or red cabbage. Once you have learned how to braise one vegetable, you can move on to a ragout of different kinds of vegetables, first giving the longer-cooking vegetables time to become tender, then adding to the aromatic, steaming mélange those that are quicker-cooking. You might start with artichoke bottoms, small white onions, and carrots and then add blanched green beans, asparagus, fresh peas. One has to have a good sense of texture and timing but the resulting combination, in which the taste and texture of one vegetable favors another in a most exciting and unusual way, is well worth the care you put into it. This is just one example of how, having learned the basic principles of braising, you can come up with new ideas and combinations of tastes in your own fashion.

# ❧ Swiss Steak

Swiss steak is a dependable, economical, easily prepared braised beef dish that has been an American favorite for a long time. How, I wonder, did it ever get that name? It's not Swiss, and it's not really steak, in our accepted usage of that word. Be that as it may, it's delicious, simple, and enables you to make a good meal from an inexpensive and less tender cut of meat that needs long, slow cooking to make it tender. The best cuts for this are a piece of chuck steak from the shoulder or a bottom round of beef. If you are shopping in the supermarket, where meats are precut and packaged, look at the chuck steak carefully. If it has part of the blade bone in it and a lot of fat, don't buy it. You are better off paying a little more and buying a piece of bottom round, which is all meat, rather than a piece of chuck with a lot of waste. The meat should be cut like a steak, from 2 to 2½ inches thick, weighing about 2 to 2½ pounds, which will serve 4 persons of good appetite. If you find a chuck steak without too much fat and just a tiny bit of bone, buy it. You can cut around the bone. Meat that has the least bone is the best buy, even though you may pay 2 or 3 cents a pound more for it.

To cook the Swiss steak you'll need a very heavy skillet or sauté pan with a tight-fitting cover, about 2½ to 3 inches deep, made of iron, cast aluminum, stainless steel, enameled cast iron, or pottery. You'll also need kitchen tongs and an old dinner plate or a cleaver or meat pounder, to pound the flour into the steak.

**Makes 4 servings**

2 to 2½ pounds chuck steak
  or bottom round, cut 2 to
  2½ inches thick
½ cup or more of flour
1 teaspoon freshly ground
  black pepper
2 onions, peeled and sliced
2 garlic cloves, peeled and
  chopped
3 to 4 tablespoons butter,
  butter and oil, bacon fat,
  or beef drippings
1½ teaspoons salt
1 to 1½ cups red wine
½ cup water, beef stock,
  canned beef broth, or
  beef bouillon

Put the meat on a cutting board and sprinkle the top quite heavily with flour—at least 2 or 3 tablespoons. Then grind ½ teaspoon pepper over it. Using the edge of the dinner plate like the edge of your hand, the back of a cleaver, or a meat pounder, pound the flour into the meat until a good deal of the flour is absorbed, working first along the width of the meat and then the length. Keep pounding so that the plate makes pressure marks in the meat and the flour holds in there. When you have done one side, dust off the excess flour and repeat the flour-and-pepper process on the other side. The steak should absorb 4 to 5 tablespoons of flour, which will give body to the sauce as it cooks and thicken it—this is the technique that makes it Swiss steak.

After the flour is pounded in, let the meat rest for 10 minutes. Slice the onions and chop the garlic during this time.

Melt the fat in the skillet or pan over medium-high heat (375°, if you have a burner with a thermostat) until it is bubbling and sizzling, but not smoking. Dip the meat in the remaining flour and place it in the hot fat. Let it bubble and sizzle over medium-high heat for 4 to 5 minutes, until deliciously brown on the underside, being careful not to let the flour burn. Just as you are about to turn the steak, add the onions and garlic to the pan. Turn the steak, brown it on the other side, and let the onions and garlic take on color. Sprinkle with the salt, remove the pan from the heat, and add the red wine and water, stock, or bouillon—or use ¼ cup water and ¼ cup stock. The wine will give the sauce a good color and richness, and when blended with the broth and water the flavor is not too intense. You should add just enough liquid to come halfway up the steak—you don't want to inundate it, as you will get some liquid from the onions as they cook down.

Return pan to the heat, reduce to a simmer, cover tightly, and simmer for 1½ hours. Test for doneness with a fork or the point of a sharp knife and turn the steak. If it is tender enough (the fork or knife should penetrate the meat easily), taste the sauce to see if it needs more salt and pepper or more chopped garlic. If it still needs cooking, cover again and continue simmering until tender. You don't want the meat to be so tender that it loses all its texture, but it should be tender enough to cut easily.

When done, transfer the steak to a hot platter and, using a slotted spoon to drain off the liquid, spoon the onions over it. Then see if there is a lot of fat on the top of the sauce—there shouldn't be, unless your beef was too fat. To remove excess fat, let the sauce boil up for a minute, then remove it from the heat and skim off the fat on the surface.

Pour the sauce over the steak, putting any surplus in a small bowl or gravy boat to be served separately, and sprinkle with some chopped parsley. Plain boiled potatoes or boiled buttered noodles go well with this, and a salad. Drink the same kind of red wine you used in cooking and follow with cheese and fruit.

# Veal

Veal, a rather dry meat, benefits immeasurably from the slow, moist braising process and the flavorings that enhance and accentuate its delicate taste and texture. The quality of veal varies so greatly around the country that it is next to impossible to be sure of a continuing supply of good meat, and if we must depend on veal that is less than perfect, braising is probably the best way to deal with it.

## ❧ Braised Shoulder (or Leg) of Veal

*This is a classic and more complex form of braising than that used for Swiss steak. First you make a mirepoix, which acts as a bed for the meat and adds flavor, and a veal stock for the sauce (if you have veal stock in the freezer, you can use that), so there are several steps in the preparation.*

*For our meat we have chosen a boned, rolled, and tied shoulder of veal. You may use either the boned shoulder or the more expensive boned leg, and have it rolled and tied for you by the butcher who does the boning.*

*The first step is to make the veal stock. This can be done the morning of the day you cook the veal, or the day before and refrigerated, or weeks before and stored in the freezer. Veal stock is always good to have on hand, so even though this is not the more elaborate stock you would make for soup, just a liquid for the sauce, it pays to make a larger quantity than you need and freeze what is left.*

*The actual braising may be done, for the most part, in the morning and finished later in the day, which enables you to cool the broth and skim off all the fat before finishing the dish. It's a time-consuming process, but worth it because the results are satisfactory in every way.*

*For cooking, you will need a deep 6-quart pot to make the stock and a large, heavy 6- or 8-quart braising pan for cooking the mirepoix and the veal. Any suitably heavy material such as cast aluminum, enameled cast iron, stainless steel, or lined copper will do. It should have a tight-fitting cover and be large enough to hold the meat comfortably.*

**Makes 6 to 8 servings**

### THE VEAL BROTH

2 to 2½ pounds bones from
   the veal, plus 1 veal knuckle
2 quarts water
1 onion, stuck with 2 cloves
1 rib of celery
1 sprig of parsley
Salt

Put the veal bones, knuckle, and water in the pot and add the onion, celery, and parsley. Bring to a boil. Skim off any scum that rises to the surface. Reduce the heat to low, cover, and cook at a faint boil for 1½ hours. Taste the stock and add as much salt as you feel it needs. Cook for a further 45 to 60 minutes, then strain the stock through a wire sieve into a large bowl and allow to cool. When cool, remove the fat from the top. If done ahead, store the stock in a screw-top jar or a covered bowl and refrigerate or freeze, depending on when you are going to use it. You will have about 1½ quarts, of which you will need 1½ cups for the sauce.

## THE MIREPOIX

2 large onions, peeled
2 large carrots, peeled
1 small white turnip, peeled
2 or 3 ribs of celery
Several sprigs of parsley
3 large or 6 small garlic
   cloves, peeled
4 tablespoons peanut oil
   Or 2 tablespoons peanut oil
   and 2 tablespoons butter
2 tablespoons wine vinegar
1 tablespoon salt

Slice the onions and cut the slices in half or thirds. The other vegetables should be cut into thin julienne, or pieces of about matchstick size. Slice the carrots and cut into small strips, then cut the strips in half. Slice the turnip and cut into small strips. Cut the celery into small strips and then into shorter pieces. Leave the parsley sprigs and garlic whole.

Heat the oil, or oil and butter, in the braising pan, add the vegetables, and let them wilt down in the fat. Add the wine vinegar—this gives a slight acidity that offsets the sweetness of the onions, carrots, and turnip. Add the salt. Cover the pan and simmer for about 30 minutes. The vegetables will throw off a good deal of highly flavorful liquid, which will add to the richness of the sauce and the finished dish.

## THE MEAT AND SAUCE

4 pounds of boned, rolled,
   and tied shoulder of veal
Salt, freshly ground black
   pepper
1½ teaspoons thyme
1 bay leaf
3 to 6 tablespoons butter
3 tablespoons flour
1½ cups veal stock
1 tablespoon glace de viande
   (optional; see page 24)

There are two ways to brown meat for braising. One is to brown it carefully on all sides in a pan in a mixture of butter and oil. The other, and to me the more satisfactory, way is to brown it under a preheated broiler, turning it from one side to another as it browns so that it colors evenly. This is a less fatty way of browning meat, especially good if you are watching calories.

Arrange the meat on the broiler rack and place it about 4 inches from the broiling unit. Watch very carefully, turning it as it colors, until it achieves a nice rich brownness. Salt the meat lightly as it browns, using 2 teaspoons of salt—I find that if you add salt at this point it cooks into the meat and seasons it better.

When the meat is browned, you may continue the braising process, or if you wish, you can leave it until the next day. In this case, let the meat cool before wrapping it in foil and refrigerating it.

To continue the braising, preheat the oven to 450°. Draw the chopped cooked vegetables (the mirepoix) together into the center of the braising pan to form a bed for the veal. You want a little liquid so the veal will cook with moist heat, but not too much. If the mirepoix has given off so much liquid that it covers the vegetables, remove some with a spoon and reserve it to use in the sauce.

Sprinkle the vegetables with 1 teaspoon of thyme and add the bay leaf. Put the veal on the bed of vegetables and sprinkle the meat with the remaining thyme.

The veal may be braised in a covered pan on top of the range at a low simmer, or in the oven. I prefer to braise in the oven, where the meat is surrounded by the aromatic steam from the pan. Lay a piece of buttered foil lightly across the top of the braising pan; place the pan in the 450° oven and cook for 30 to 35 minutes. Then reduce the heat to 350° and continue to cook, allowing approximately 20 minutes per pound from the time the meat goes into the oven. The internal temperature of the meat, when tested with a meat thermometer, should be 160° to 165° depending on how pink you like your veal. I feel that if it is slightly pink in the center, it is juicier and more pleasing to the palate than if it is cooked completely all through, but this is a matter of personal taste.

When the veal is cooked, remove it to a warm platter and keep it warm while you make the sauce. Drain the liquid from the braising pan through a sieve into a bowl and skim off any fat. Reserve the mirepoix vegetables and keep them warm.

Melt 3 tablespoons of the butter in a heavy saucepan, add the flour, stirring in well, and cook over medium heat, stirring, until the mixture is golden and bubbling. Add the liquid from the braising pan and the 1½ cups of veal stock and stir constantly until the sauce comes to a boil and thickens. Reduce the heat, season to taste with salt and pepper, and, if you have *glace de viande* (see page 24), add 1 tablespoon to the sauce to give it a beautiful richness and glaze. Otherwise, as the sauce simmers, stir in an additional 2 or 3 tablespoons of butter, 1 tablespoon at a time.

Cut the strings and remove them from the veal. Arrange the veal on a hot serving platter and surround with some of the mirepoix vegetables. You may garnish the platter with watercress or parsley, putting it at one end so it does not interfere with the carving. Serve the sauce separately in a bowl.

Buttered noodles, or new potatoes sprinkled with parsley and chives or chopped fresh mint and butter are excellent with the veal, and you may have cooked green beans, tossed in butter, or a salad.

# Stuffed Breast of Veal

Hot or cold, a stuffed breast of veal is both spectacular and as simple as any dish can be. This is the least expensive cut of veal and the braising process makes it very tender and flavorful. A good butcher who has been trained to bone meat properly will be able to bone the breast and cut a pocket in it for the stuffing, so that when stuffed it may be formed into a good shape that will slice easily. If this is not possible, buy the breast unboned and merely have the pocket cut in it—you can remove the little rib bones after the meat is cooked by breaking them away from the joints and pulling them free from the flesh. In either case, you will need some bones for the braising— either those removed from the breast or a veal knuckle or some veal neck bones.

**Makes 6 servings**

1 6-pound breast of veal
   (unboned weight), boned
   and with a pocket cut in it*

THE STUFFING
3 tablespoons butter
8 tablespoons (½ cup)
   olive oil
3 large onions, peeled and
   finely chopped
¾ pound fairly lean sausage
   meat (if unavailable
   substitute ground pork with
   25 percent fat)
½ pound ham, finely chopped
1 truffle, finely chopped
   (optional)
1 cup freshly made bread
   crumbs
1 teaspoon dried thyme
Salt, freshly ground black
   pepper
⅛ teaspoon ground cloves
¼ teaspoon ground or grated
   nutmeg
2 eggs, slightly beaten

Prepare the stuffing for the breast. Heat the butter and 3 tablespoons of oil in a skillet, add the onions, and sauté over medium heat until just limp. Add the sausage meat or ground

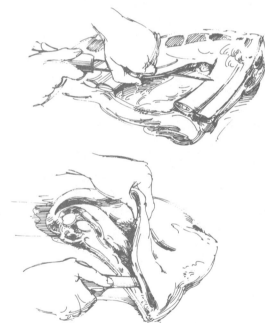

* If the breast of veal you buy has not been boned, cut away the flesh around each rib with a sharp knife, then snap the rib off, leaving the main neck intact. Remove the bone to which the ribs were attached. Cut a deep pocket, almost to the edge of the meat, for the stuffing.

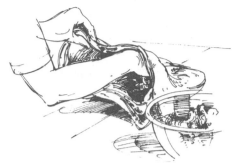

## THE BRAISING MIXTURE AND SAUCE

*Mirepoix of 1 onion, 1 carrot, 2 garlic cloves, 4 sprigs of parsley, all finely cut*

*1 bay leaf*

*Bones from veal breast or 1 veal knuckle*

*1½ cups veal stock, chicken stock, or white wine*

*1½ cups peeled, seeded, and finely chopped tomatoes*

*1 cup pitted, soft black olives*

*½ cup pine nuts*

*¼ cup chopped parsley*

pork, ham, truffle and 1 tablespoon of the liquid from the can, bread crumbs, thyme, 1½ teaspoons salt, 1 teaspoon pepper, cloves, and nutmeg. Blend the stuffing well, remove from the heat, and mix in the eggs. Stuff the pocket in the breast, molding with your hands so that it is fairly even in shape.

Secure the stuffing by sewing up the pocket with a trussing needle and fine string or by closing the opening with skewers or clamps. Heat the remaining 5 tablespoons of oil in a heavy skillet and brown the stuffed breast on both sides over medium-high heat. Butter the bottom of a braising pan large enough to take the breast and arrange in it the mirepoix of cut vegetables, the bay leaf, and the veal bones. Lay the breast on this bed and add the stock or wine and the tomatoes. Cover the pan and braise the meat in a 325° oven for 2 to 3 hours, or until a meat thermometer inserted into the veal registers 170°. If the liquid reduces too much (it should be just sufficient to cover the vegetables), add more stock or wine.

Remove the cooked meat to a hot platter. Purée the pan juices and vegetables by putting them through a food mill or by pushing them through a sieve with a wooden spoon, pressing the vegetables well. Reheat the purée in a saucepan with the olives, pine nuts, and parsley, bringing the sauce to a boil and then simmering it for 5 minutes. Serve the breast of veal, sliced about ¾ inch thick, with the sauce and with tiny new potatoes browned in butter and a purée of green beans. Drink a Beaujolais.

To serve the stuffed breast cold, slice and serve with a spinach salad dressed with olive oil, lemon juice, and a touch of soy sauce, with finely chopped onion, a little chopped garlic, and a handful of pine nuts added just before it is tossed. Or you might vary this and have the cold meat with a dish of hot macaroni and the reheated sauce from the veal, plus a salad of Bibb lettuce and raw mushrooms.

# Veal Chops Niçoise

*Veal chops are extraordinarily good when braised with the proper seasonings. Thickly cut loin chops of the choicest veal are the best to buy.*

**Makes 6 servings**

## THE TOMATO SAUCE

2½ cups canned Italian plum
  tomatoes
3 garlic cloves, peeled
1 small onion, finely chopped
1 teaspoon salt
½ teaspoon freshly ground
  black pepper
3 tablespoons butter
1 or 2 leaves fresh basil
  Or ½ teaspoon dried basil
2 tablespoons tomato paste

## THE BRAISED CHOPS

6 veal loin chops, cut 2 inches
  thick
¼ cup flour
6 tablespoons olive oil
Salt, freshly ground black
  pepper
3 garlic cloves, peeled and
  finely chopped
36 pitted whole, soft black
  olives (preferably French)
2 tablespoons fresh basil
  leaves, cut into strips
  Or 1 teaspoon dried basil,
  ground
1 tablespoon freshly chopped
  parsley (optional)

First make the sauce. Put the tomatoes, garlic, onion, salt, pepper, butter, and basil in a saucepan and cook down over medium heat until the mixture is reduced by one-third. Add the tomato paste and cook for 5 minutes, or until the sauce is reduced to about 1½ cups. Taste, and correct the seasoning.

Sprinkle both sides of the chops lightly with flour, shaking off excess. Heat the oil in a skillet or sauté pan and sear the chops quickly on both sides over medium-high heat, salting and peppering them as they cook, until delicately browned. Add the tomato sauce and garlic, cover, and simmer for about 20 to 40 minutes (depending on the age of the veal) or until tender but not overcooked; the point of a knife should penetrate easily. Add the pitted olives and basil and heat through. Taste, and correct seasoning.

Arrange the chops and sauce on a mound of saffron rice and garnish, if desired, with finely chopped parsley. Drink a brisk white wine from Provence, well chilled.

# Veal Birds Western Style

*Veal birds are another very good way of braising veal. For this you need slices of veal cut from the leg and pounded very thin. If the meat you buy is not thin enough, put it between two pieces of waxed paper and flatten with a meat pounder.*

**Makes 4 to 8 servings**

8 slices of veal cut from the
    leg, about 5 inches square,
    pounded ⅜ inch thick
10 tablespoons butter
1 cup finely chopped onion
½ cup finely chopped
    mushrooms
2 garlic cloves, peeled and
    finely chopped
Salt, freshly ground black
    pepper
1½ cups fresh bread crumbs
1½ tablespoons fresh dill,
    finely cut
    Or 1½ teaspoons dried
    dill weed
½ cup white wine
16 thin strips of dill pickle
Melted butter (about
    3 tablespoons)
2 tablespoons oil
1¾ cups chicken or veal broth
Beurre manié *for thickening*
    (see page 270)
¾ cup sour cream
Chopped fresh dill or dried
    dill weed, chopped parsley

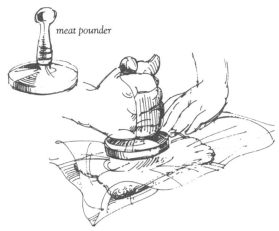

meat pounder

For the stuffing, melt 5 tablespoons butter in a skillet, add the onion, and sauté until just limp. Blend in the mushrooms, garlic, 1 teaspoon salt, ½ teaspoon pepper, bread crumbs, fresh dill or dill weed, and about ½ cup white wine, or just enough to moisten the mixture. Spread some of the filling on each slice of veal and put 2 strips of dill pickle in the center. Sprinkle a little melted butter on the filling and roll the veal slices up. Tie them securely at each end and in the center with fine string.

Heat the remaining 5 tablespoons butter and the oil in a deep, heavy skillet or sauté pan. Lightly brown the veal birds on all sides over medium-high heat, salting and peppering them as you turn them. Add the broth and simmer the birds, covered, for about 1 hour, or until just tender but not overcooked or stringy. Transfer the birds to a hot platter and keep warm while making the sauce.

Thicken the pan juices with small balls of *beurre manié*, following the method given on page 270, simmering the sauce for 3 or 4 minutes. Keeping the heat medium low, mix in the sour cream, adding it in the center and stirring with a wire whisk or wooden spoon to incorporate it into the sauce. Let it just heat through, being careful not to let it boil or the sour cream will separate. Add a little more dill (about 1 tablespoon chopped fresh or 1 teaspoon dried dill weed) and about 2 teaspoons chopped parsley.

To serve, arrange the birds on a platter around a mound of freshly cooked fluffy rice, spoon some of the sauce over them, and serve the rest separately in a bowl. Braised leeks go well with the birds. Drink a brisk white wine such as Pouilly-Fumé or a California Fumé Blanc.

# Beef

The beef cuts generally chosen for braising are the top round, top sirloin, rump, bottom round, brisket, and chuck. Thin slices from the round, cut into squares, are often stuffed, rolled, and braised. Thick or thin round and chuck steaks also benefit from the liquids and additions employed in the braising process. The Swiss steak on page 129 is a perfect example. As all beef cuts vary in texture and degree of tenderness, the cooking times tend to differ. Testing, by inserting the point of a small sharp knife into the meat after it has cooked for a certain amount of time to see how much resistance it encounters, is really the only way to determine when the meat is done. The long cooking once associated with braising seems preposterous now, but meat then was much less tender than it is today. In Europe, where the lesser cuts of meat are generally quite different from ours, a cut equivalent to bottom round or chuck will take twice as long to cook as the American product. We have developed beef in which there is a marbling of fat throughout, so the texture breaks down sooner and the cooking time is cut accordingly.

Brisket is a popular cut for braising. It has a rich, full flavor and, with its even layers of fat and lean, slices well and looks appetizing whether served hot or cold. The famous French dish *boeuf à la mode* can be made with brisket, which in the following recipe is first marinated to give it additional flavor and to tenderize the meat.

## ❧ Boeuf à la Mode (French-Style Pot Roast)

**Makes 6 servings, with leftovers**

6-pound brisket of beef
2 pigs' feet (preferably long cut; see page 371), split lengthwise
Salt, ground nutmeg, freshly ground black pepper

When you buy the beef, have a good deal of the fat cut away, and ask the butcher to split the pigs' feet for you.

Arrange the brisket and pigs' feet in a large earthenware, enameled, or glass bowl (don't use metal containers for a marinade contain-

1 large onion, peeled and
    studded with 3 cloves
1 onion, peeled and sliced
1 large carrot, peeled and
    sliced
3 garlic cloves, peeled
1 teaspoon dried thyme
¼ cup cognac
Red wine to cover
¼ cup rendered beef fat
    (see page 67)
4 tablespoons (½ stick) butter
3 to 4 tablespoons tomato
    paste
1 rib of celery
1 leek, trimmed and well
    washed
2 sprigs of parsley

ACCOMPANIMENTS
12 to 18 small white onions,
    peeled, with a cross cut in
    stem end
2 tablespoons butter
6 leeks, trimmed and well
    washed
6 whole carrots, scraped
12 small potatoes
1 tablespoon chopped parsley

ing wine). Salt the brisket well and sprinkle it lightly with nutmeg and freshly ground black pepper. Add the clove-studded onion and sprinkle the sliced onion and carrot over the meat. Add 2 garlic cloves, the thyme, a heaping teaspoon of freshly ground black pepper, the cognac, and enough red wine to barely cover the meat. Let the meat stand in the marinade for 6 to 12 hours.

When you are ready to cook the meat, heat the beef fat and butter in a heavy braising pan. Remove the brisket from the marinade and dry well with paper towels. Brown the meat on all sides in the hot fat over medium-high heat until it is evenly colored. Remove the sliced carrot and onion from the marinade with a slotted spoon and cook them briefly with the beef. Add the pigs' feet, cover the pan, reduce the heat, and simmer for at least 30 minutes. Strain the marinade and add to the beef with the remaining garlic clove, the tomato paste, celery, leek, and parsley. Bring to a boil, then cover and cook in a preheated 300° oven for 2 hours.

Remove the meat from the pan and add the small onions, which have been briskly cooked and tossed in the butter until lightly browned, the leeks, and the carrots. Return the beef to the pan, cover, and continue to cook in the oven until it is just tender—not grainy and overdone. Transfer the meat to a hot platter and keep warm. If the vegetables are not quite done, continue to cook them in the oven until they are. Meanwhile, boil the potatoes in salted water to cover, either peeled or in their jackets, until done.

Pour off the sauce from the pan, strain it, and skim off the fat. Arrange the vegetables on the platter around the meat. Sprinkle the meat with the chopped parsley. Serve the skimmed sauce separately, in a sauceboat. Serve the dish at once.

Leftover cold beef makes a perfectly splendid salad with the addition of diced onion, celery, boiled potatoes, hard-boiled eggs, strips of green pepper, and a vinaigrette sauce (see page 290).

# Estouffat de Noël (Braised Beef with Wine and Brandy)

One of the most famous dishes of Gascony, in France, is the estouffat, or estouffade, a dish of braised beef cooked in a covered earthenware casserole, always with Armagnac, the brandy of the region. This estouffat de Noël is a traditional Christmas Eve dish, to which the Armagnac and the gelatin content of the pork rind give a special rich, luscious body and taste. If you can't get pork rind (sold by pork stores and butchers), substitute a pig's foot, split.

**Makes 8 to 10 servings**

1-pound piece of pork rind or
   1 pig's foot, split lengthwise
8 shallots, peeled and
   quartered
3 or 4 onions, peeled and
   quartered
1 carrot, peeled and cut into
   long strips
1 garlic clove
1 teaspoon dried thyme
Grated nutmeg
6-pound piece top round of
   beef, neatly tied to keep
   its shape
Salt, freshly ground black
   pepper
1½ cups Armagnac
2 cups good full-bodied red
   wine, such as a Rhône or a
   California Petite Sirah

Preheat the oven to 350°.

Put the pork rind or pig's foot on the bottom of an 8-quart casserole or pot. On this, make a bed of the vegetables, add the garlic, thyme, and a sprinkling of grated nutmeg. Salt the beef lightly. Make an indentation in the center of the vegetables and in it lay the beef. Add the Armagnac and red wine. Cover the pot with a piece of aluminum foil and then the lid.

Put in the oven and cook for 35 minutes, then reduce the heat to 300° and cook for 1 hour. Then reduce the heat to 250° and cook for at least 2, preferably 3, hours or more (long, slow cooking is essential to the success of this dish). Or you may simmer the estouffat on top of the stove for 1½ hours, then finish the cooking in a 250° oven.

Remove the casserole or pot from the oven about an hour before serving to let the fat settle on top. Skim off the fat and reheat the beef in the sauce. Or you can make the estouffat the day before and let it cool overnight, then remove the fat before serving and reheat the meat—to my mind the dish tastes better when made ahead and allowed to cool completely. Before serving, taste the sauce and correct the seasoning. Serve the estouffat with either boiled potatoes or macaroni to soak up the lovely sauce. Cut up the pork rind or the meat from the pig's foot and serve it with the beef. Drink the same kind of red wine you used for cooking.

# Viennese Goulash

The principal flavoring for a Hungarian goulash is paprika, which should also be Hungarian and of the best quality. Hungarian paprika has much more flavor than the standard supermarket type and is well worth buying for any dish requiring paprika. You'll find it in specialty shops that sell spices and herbs. The difference in this recipe, which is a Viennese variation, is the paste of caraway seeds, garlic, and lemon zest stirred in for the final cooking time, which gives a fresh and spicy flavor.

**Makes 6 servings**

4 tablespoons butter
2 tablespoons salad oil
6 medium onions, peeled and thinly sliced
¼ cup Hungarian paprika
¼ cup white wine or cider vinegar
3 pounds beef rump or chuck, cut into 2-inch cubes
Salt, freshly ground black pepper
1 teaspoon thyme
½ cup tomato purée
4 tablespoons flour
2 cups beef broth
1 tablespoon caraway seeds
Zest of 1 lemon, finely chopped
2 garlic cloves, peeled

Heat the butter and oil in a 12-inch sauté pan or a 6-quart braising pan. Add the onions and sauté until golden over medium heat, stirring them so they do not stick to the pan or brown. Mix in the paprika and wine or vinegar. Cook 4 minutes. (Spices such as paprika and curry powder should always be cooked a little in fat, to bring out the flavor and prevent the raw taste that occurs when they are not cooked first.) Push the onions to the side of the pan, add the beef cubes, a few at a time, and sear them on all sides. Don't overcrowd the cubes or they will reduce the heat too much and not brown properly. Remove them to a plate as browned.

When all the beef is browned, replace it in the pan, season to taste with salt and pepper, add the thyme and tomato purée, and simmer over medium-low heat until the liquid is reduced to a glaze. Sprinkle the beef with the flour, and toss with a spatula until the flour is well colored. Add the beef broth (there should be just enough to cover the meat) and simmer, covered, until the beef is tender when pierced with the point of a knife—about 2 hours.

Meanwhile, grind the caraway seeds, the finely chopped lemon zest (the yellow part of the rind, without any pith), and the garlic to a paste with a mortar and pestle. When the beef is cooked, stir this paste into the goulash and cook a further 10 minutes to blend the flavors. Serve with noodles.

# Jeanne Owen's Chili con Carne

*Our southwestern chili con came certainly qualifies as a braised beef dish, for it is, by definition, a stew. This recipe, while not for purists, is rather different and utterly delicious. It improves with aging, so make it the day before you wish to serve it, and reheat.*

**Makes 6 servings**

⅓ cup olive oil
3 pounds lean round steak, cut into 1-inch cubes
2 onions, peeled and finely chopped
3 garlic cloves, peeled and finely chopped
Salt
4 cups boiling water
1 teaspoon caraway seeds
2 teaspoons sesame seeds
½ teaspoon oregano
2 to 4 tablespoons chili powder, or to taste
1 cup pitted green olives
2 1-pound cans kidney beans, drained and well rinsed

Heat the oil in a large sauté pan or 6-quart braising pan, add the beef, a few cubes at a time so the pan is not too crowded, and sauté over brisk heat, turning to brown on all sides. Add the chopped onions and sauté over medium heat for 2 or 3 minutes, then add the garlic. Season with salt to taste, add the boiling water, the caraway and sesame seeds, and the oregano. Reduce heat, cover, and simmer for 1 hour.

Gradually stir in the chili powder, testing frequently until you achieve the degree of flavor and hotness that suits your palate. Then add the olives, cover, and simmer for another hour. Taste, and correct the seasoning, then mix in the kidney beans and heat through. Toasted French bread, tortillas, or corn bread go well with this, and a crisp green salad. Beer is the only drink that can stand up to the spiciness of the chili.


# Oxtail Ragout

*Oxtail is a part of the animal that many people ignore because they don't know how to cook it. Braised oxtails make a delicious and eminently simple meal. This is another dish that tastes better if made a day or two in advance, chilled, the fat completely removed, and then reheated, after the flavors have had a chance to blend and mellow. I also like to brown the oxtails under the broiler, which draws out their excess fat and makes them beautifully brown and crispy.*

**Makes 6 servings**

5 or 6 pounds of oxtails, cut into joints for serving
Salt, freshly ground black pepper
3 tablespoons oil

Put the pieces of oxtail on the broiler rack and pan and broil until nicely colored and crispy around the edges, about 15 minutes, salting and peppering them as they brown, and turning them once.

3 tablespoons unsalted butter
  or beef drippings
3 large onions, peeled and
  thinly sliced
4 carrots, scraped and halved
2 white turnips, peeled and
  sliced
4 whole garlic cloves, peeled
Bouquet garni (see page 360)
4 to 5 cups beef broth
¾ cup Madeira
Beurre manié (see page 270;
  optional)
2 tablespoons chopped parsley

In a skillet, heat the oil and butter or beef drippings left in the broiler pan, add the onions, and sauté over medium heat until golden and limp. With a slotted spoon, transfer the onions to an 8-quart braising pan, add the carrots to the skillet, and sauté them lightly for 3 minutes. Add these, the turnips, and the garlic cloves to the braising pan, lay the oxtails on top, and add the bouquet garni. Add the beef broth (there should be just enough to barely cover the oxtails), bring to a boil over high heat, skim off the scum that rises to the surface, and continue to boil and skim for 5 minutes. Reduce the heat, cover, and simmer for 3 to 3½ hours, adding more liquid if it reduces too much (it should just cover the oxtails). Test the meat for tenderness with the point of a small sharp knife—it should penetrate the meat easily. Add the Madeira and cook, covered, for 10 minutes. Taste the broth for seasoning, adding salt, pepper, and a touch of thyme if it needs more herb flavor. Let the ragout cool and skim off the fat, then reheat before serving. Or chill it in the refrigerator for a day or two before serving.

Reheat the ragout, and when heated through remove the oxtails and vegetables to a hot platter. Discard the bouquet garni and let the broth cook down over high heat for 2 or 3 minutes.

I prefer the broth the way it is, but you can thicken it, if you wish, with small balls of beurre manié (see page 270), dropping them into the broth a few at a time and simmering until the sauce is thickened as you wish. Pour broth or sauce over the meat and sprinkle with the parsley. Serve with boiled potatoes, rice, or buttered noodles. A good green salad is the best accompaniment to this hearty dish, which can take a robust red wine, a Bordeaux or Rhône, or a California Cabernet Sauvignon or Petite Sirah.

# Lamb

The flavor of good lamb comes through the braising process admirably. Just about every part of the animal—leg, shoulder, breast, shanks, and chops—takes well to the various styles of slow cooking that meld meat and seasonings into a savory, succulent dish.

Probably the most basic braised lamb dish, which manages to be both simple and elegant, is Irish stew. Recipes for Irish stew can be found in Escoffier, Montagné, and practically every lexicon of good cooking—and they differ a great deal. Good Irish stew is not a thin soup with meat and vegetables floating in it, but a hearty dish of meat, potatoes, and onions cooked slowly until rather thick in texture. In the purest version, it contains neither carrots nor turnips.

## ❧ Irish Stew

Makes 6 servings

3 pounds lamb rib or
    shoulder chops
Butter (to grease the
    casserole)
5 or 6 medium potatoes,
    peeled and sliced
3 teaspoons chopped parsley,
    mixed with 1½ teaspoons
    dried thyme
3 large onions, peeled and
    sliced
Salt, freshly ground black
    pepper
2 cups water
2 to 3 tablespoons chopped
    parsley

Trim the fat from the chops, leaving the meat on the bones. Butter a 2- to 2½-quart casserole. Preheat the oven to 300°.

Arrange a layer of one-third of the potatoes in the bottom of the casserole and cover with a layer of chops topped with a third of the parsley-thyme mixture. Add a layer of half the onions, then a third more potatoes, the remaining chops, herbs, remaining onions, and finally, the remaining potatoes and herbs. Season well with salt and pepper and add the water. Cover and cook the stew in the preheated oven for 2 to 2½ hours, or until the meat is tender and the potatoes and onions soft. Serve in soup plates with a sprinkling of parsley on top, and drink beer with it.

Irish stew always benefits from being cooked the day before and allowed to cool thoroughly. Skim off any fat and reheat the stew.

# Braised Shoulder of Lamb with Ratatouille

**Makes 6 servings**

4- to 5-pound shoulder of
  lamb, boned and tied
6 garlic cloves, peeled and cut
  into slivers
2 or 3 anchovy fillets, cut into
  small pieces
Salt, freshly ground black
  pepper
Olive oil
2 medium onions, thinly sliced
4 small zucchini, trimmed and
  cut into ½-inch slices
1 green pepper, halved,
  seeded, and cut into thin
  strips
1 medium eggplant, peeled
  and diced
1 teaspoon dried basil
  Or 2 tablespoons chopped
  fresh basil
2½ cups canned Italian plum
  tomatoes
¾ cup pitted, soft black olives
¼ cup plus 2 tablespoons
  chopped parsley

Make small incisions in the meat with the point of a small sharp knife and insert half the slivered garlic (reserve the rest for later) and the anchovy pieces in the incisions. Rub the meat well with salt, pepper, and olive oil and put it on a rack in a roasting pan. Roast for 30 minutes in a 400° oven.

Meanwhile, make the ratatouille. In an 8-quart braising pan heat 5 tablespoons olive oil; add the onions and sauté over medium heat until just wilted and pale gold. Add the reserved garlic, the zucchini, and the green pepper. Sauté over rather brisk heat for 5 minutes, then add the eggplant. Mix the vegetables well with a wooden spatula; season them with 2 teaspoons salt, 1 teaspoon pepper, and the basil.

Remove the lamb from the oven and place it in the middle of the vegetable mixture in the braising pan. Add the tomatoes and bring the mixture to a boil on top of the stove. Reduce the oven heat to 325° and braise the lamb in the oven, covered, for 1½ to 1¾ hours, or until the lamb is tender and the ratatouille cooked down and well blended. Add the olives and ¼ cup chopped parsley and cook 10 minutes longer.

Transfer the lamb to a hot platter and remove the strings. If the ratatouille is too liquid (it should be thick, without visible liquid), reduce it over rather high heat for a few minutes, stirring it well so it doesn't stick. Taste and correct the seasoning. Slice the meat and serve with the ratatouille spooned over and around it. Sprinkle the dish with chopped parsley and serve with crisp hot French bread. Drink a light red wine, such as a Mâcon.

# Pork

## Braised Pork Hocks, Italian Style

*Pork hocks are a good and economical buy. As veal shanks have become expensive and hard to find, I have adapted the classic Italian recipe for* ossi buchi, *or braised veal shanks, to pork hocks.*

**Makes 4 servings**

3 tablespoons butter
3 tablespoons oil
4 meaty pork hocks
1 teaspoon salt
½ teaspoon freshly ground
  black pepper
1 cup dry white wine
½ cup chicken or beef broth
1½ cups canned Italian plum
  tomatoes

GREMOLATA GARNISH
1 large garlic clove, peeled
  and coarsely chopped
Zest of 1 medium lemon,
  removed with a zester or
  grater
⅔ cup chopped parsley

Heat the butter and oil in a deep heavy skillet or sauté pan that has a cover. Add the pork hocks and brown well on all sides over medium-high heat, salting and peppering them as they cook. Add the wine, broth, and tomatoes, cover the pan, and simmer for 2 hours, or until the meat is tender and coming away from the bone.

Meanwhile, prepare the *gremolata*, a garnish that gives a very fresh spicy flavor. Combine the garlic, lemon zest, and parsley. When the pork hocks are cooked, transfer them to a hot platter, spoon the sauce over them, and sprinkle with the *gremolata*.

Serve with rice.

## Braised Pork Chops with Sauerkraut

*Braising is a good way to cook pork chops, which become dry and tough if broiled.*

**Makes 4 servings**

4 slices of thickly cut bacon
3 pounds fresh sauerkraut
1 large onion, sliced
Salt, freshly ground black
  pepper
2 tablespoons rendered pork
  fat or butter
4 pork chops, cut from the
  loin and 1 inch thick

Arrange the bacon strips in the bottom of a heavy braising pan. Rinse the sauerkraut well under cold running water in a colander, then squeeze out as much water as possible with your hands (this gets rid of most of the salt in which it was pickled). Cover the bacon with half the sauerkraut and the sliced onion, then sprinkle it with 1 teaspoon pepper.

Melt the pork fat or butter in a skillet and

1 garlic clove, finely chopped
Beer (about 2½ to 3 cups)

brown the chops quickly on both sides over medium-high heat. When the meat is browned, arrange it on top of the sauerkraut in the pan, season to taste with salt and pepper, sprinkle with garlic, and pour the pan juices over it. Add the rest of the sauerkraut, sprinkle with a little more pepper, and add enough beer to cover. Bring it to a boil, reduce the heat, cover, and simmer for 1 hour.

Serve with sautéed apple rings (see page 192), boiled or mashed potatoes, and beer.

# Poultry and Game

## Coq au Vin (Chicken in Red Wine)

*Probably the most famous and classic example of braised chicken is the French* coq au vin. *This dish is very much akin to beef* bourguignon, *hardly surprising as they both come from Burgundy and share the regional combination of glazed onions, mushrooms, and salt pork.*

**Makes 6 servings**

8 tablespoons butter
4 tablespoons oil
2 medium onions, thinly
  sliced
¾ cup flour
2 3-pound chickens, cut into
  serving pieces
¼ pound salt pork, diced
  small
18 firm white mushroom caps
18 small white onions,
  peeled*
2 teaspoons sugar
Salt, freshly ground black
  pepper
1 bay leaf
4 sprigs of fresh thyme
  Or ½ teaspoon dried thyme
2 tablespoons chopped parsley
Red wine (French Burgundy
  or California Pinot Noir)

Heat 6 tablespoons of the butter and 3 tablespoons of the oil in a heavy skillet and add the sliced onions. Sauté over medium heat until lightly browned. Lightly flour the chicken pieces. Push the onions to one side of the pan and brown the chicken pieces over medium-high heat, a few at a time, removing them to a large casserole as they are browned.

In another skillet, render the salt pork by cooking until the fat has melted and the pieces of pork are brown and crisp, then add the mushroom caps and toss in the fat until lightly browned. Heat the remaining butter and oil in another skillet and sauté the onions until lightly browned, then sprinkle with the sugar and cook, tossing, until caramelized. Transfer all the cooked ingredients to the casserole with the chicken, season

*If the onions are dropped into boiling water for 20 seconds, their skins will slip off easily.*

to taste with salt and pepper, and add the bay leaf, thyme, and parsley.

Rinse the skillet in which the chicken was browned with ½ cup red wine, scraping up the brown glaze from the pan. Pour this into the casserole and add enough additional wine to just cover the chicken and vegetables. Cover the casserole and cook in a 350° oven for 40 minutes, or until the chicken is tender. Serve with small boiled potatoes.

# Chicken Calandria

*This rather unusual, spicy chicken, named for its originator, is like many braised dishes best made a day in advance and reheated.*

**Makes 4 servings**

1 cup white, water-ground
  cornmeal
4½-pound roasting chicken,
  cut into serving pieces
½ cup olive oil
3 medium onions, peeled and
  finely chopped
3 garlic cloves, peeled and
  finely chopped
1 cup dry red wine
1 teaspoon sesame seeds
½ teaspoon caraway seeds
Pinch (⅛ teaspoon) each:
  mace and marjoram
3 cups boiling water
Salt
1 cup whole, blanched
  almonds
1 cup pitted green olives,
  preferably the small
  Spanish olives
4 tablespoons chili powder

Put the cornmeal on waxed paper or a pie plate. Add the chicken pieces, and coat them lightly on all sides. Shake off any excess and reserve the cornmeal. Heat the oil in a 6-quart braising pan. Add the chicken pieces and sauté them lightly on all sides over medium-high heat. Lower the heat to medium, add the onions and garlic and let them just wilt down. Mix well with the chicken. Add the wine, sesame and caraway seeds, mace, marjoram, and boiling water. Season with salt to taste, cover, reduce the heat, and simmer for 10 minutes, until flavors are blended. Then mix in the almonds, olives, and chili powder, cover, and simmer until tender, another 20 to 30 minutes. It can be refrigerated at this point. Before serving, reheat. Mix 3 tablespoons of the leftover cornmeal with ½ cup water and stir it into the pot to thicken the liquid. Stir until the cornmeal expands and thickens, 2 or 3 minutes. Serve at once, with French bread and a green salad. With this spicy chili-flavored dish, beer is the best thing to drink.

# Duck with Beans

Makes 4 servings

2 cups pinto beans
1 onion, stuck with 1 clove
1 teaspoon oregano
1 tablespoon salt
3 slices salt pork, diced
5- to 6-pound duck, cut into
   serving pieces, like a
   chicken
½ cup flour, seasoned with
   1 teaspoon salt
1 medium onion, chopped
1 teaspoon dried basil
Freshly ground black pepper

Soak the beans overnight in water to cover. Next day, drain, put in a saucepan with the clove-stuck onion, oregano, and boiling water to cover. Bring to a boil, reduce the heat, cover, and simmer very, very gently until tender, which can take 3 hours or more as pinto beans are very dry. Do not let the beans boil; it is the gentle simmering that keeps them whole. Add more liquid if it cooks away. When the beans are almost cooked, season them with 1 tablespoon salt—always salt dried beans after they have cooked for a while, not before, or they will toughen. Drain the cooked beans and reserve the liquid.

Cook the diced salt pork in a skillet over medium heat until the fat is rendered and the salt pork crisp. Remove and reserve the crisp pieces. Coat the duck with the seasoned flour, shaking off the excess, and brown it on all sides in the hot fat over medium-high heat.

Mix the beans with the crisp pieces of salt pork, the chopped onion, and the basil. Season to taste with black pepper. Put half the beans in the bottom of a large casserole, arrange the duck pieces on top, and cover with the rest of the beans. Add the reserved bean liquid and enough boiling water to cover the beans. Cover and cook in a 350° oven for 1½ hours, or until beans and duck are cooked. Add more liquid if necessary—the dish should not have too much liquid, but should be just moist.

Serve with crisp French bread, an orange and onion salad, and drink a red Rhône wine or a California Pinot Noir.

# Braised Pheasant

*Wild pheasants are frequently tough, and best when braised with some contrasting flavor. If a good-sized mature bird comes your way (you can tell whether it is mature or not by the size of the spurs on the feet and the feel of the breast bone, which in an older bird is not supple but rigid and hard), this is a good way to cook it.*

**Makes 4 servings**

1 mature pheasant
½ lemon
About 12 tablespoons butter
Salt, freshly ground black
   pepper, grated nutmeg
¼ cup oil
3 or 4 cooking apples (see
   page 340)
3 teaspoons sugar
1 tablespoon lemon juice
⅓ cup calvados or applejack
¾ cup heavy cream

Clean the pheasant well and rub the interior with the cut lemon. Butter the cavity and sprinkle it with nutmeg. Butter the exterior of the bird and rub with salt, pepper, and nutmeg.

Heat the oil and 4 tablespoons butter in a 12-inch skillet until bubbling and brown the bird on all sides over medium-high heat until evenly colored. Liberally butter the inside of a braising pan or earthenware casserole of 6-quart capacity. Core, peel, and slice the apples thick, then spread them over the bottom of the casserole. Sprinkle them with the sugar, ½ teaspoon salt, ¼ teaspoon nutmeg, and dot with butter—about 3 or 4 tablespoons cut into small pieces. Add the lemon juice. Place the pheasant on the apples and cover the pan or casserole tightly—if the lid does not fit tightly, first cover the top with a piece of aluminum foil, tucking it over the sides; this will seal in the steam and juices. Cook in a 350° oven for 1 hour, remove, and test for tenderness by inserting the point of a knife in the thigh; juices should run clear.

If tender, remove to a hot flameproof platter; heat and ignite the calvados and pour it flaming over the bird. Remove the apple mixture to a small pan; mix in the heavy cream and bring to a boil. Simmer for 4 minutes and serve as a sauce with the pheasant.

To serve, carve the pheasant into quarters, arrange on a platter, and top with the sauce. Garnish the platter with mounds of buttered rice tossed with chopped pistachio nuts and chopped parsley.

# Vegetables

## Braised Fennel

*Certain root vegetables braise very successfully. One is fennel, which takes on a completely different character, losing the strong anise taste of its raw state.*

**Makes 4 servings**

2 heads of fennel
5 tablespoons unsalted butter
1 cup chicken or beef broth
Salt, freshly ground black
   pepper
1 tablespoon chopped chives

Fennel has feathery green tops on long white stalks that look rather like dill. These should be trimmed off at the point where the bulbous part of the fennel begins. Also remove any discolored or very tough and stringy outer leaves. Cut the heads into quarters.

Melt the butter in a skillet; add the fennel quarters and brown them lightly over medium heat on all sides. Add the broth, bring the liquid to a boil, then reduce to a simmer, cover the skillet, and let the fennel cook gently (it should not boil) until just tender when pierced with the point of a knife, about 30 to 40 minutes, according to size. Season with salt and pepper to taste, remove the fennel to a hot vegetable dish, turn up the heat, and let the liquid reduce by about half, until it is rather thick. Pour over the fennel and sprinkle with chopped chives.

## Braised Celery

*This is an eternally popular dish, which is best made with celery hearts. Trim off the large, coarse outer ribs, leaving only the tight bunch of tender white ribs and leaves in the center.*

**Makes 4 servings**

4 tablespoons (½ stick)
   unsalted butter
4 celery hearts, split
   lengthwise
1 teaspoon salt
¼ cup strong chicken or beef
   stock
½ teaspoon freshly ground
   black pepper
1 tablespoon chopped parsley

Melt the butter in a heavy skillet or saucepan, add the celery hearts, sprinkle with salt, add the stock, and cook, covered, over medium heat, turning the hearts carefully with two spoons once during the cooking time, until just tender and pierceable, about 30 minutes. Remove the celery to a vegetable dish. Boil pan juices down to ⅓ cup and pour over the celery. Season with pepper, sprinkle with parsley, and serve.

# Braised Lettuce

*This leafy vegetable is extraordinarily good braised and served with lamb, beef, game, and roast or braised chicken. I have found that the old recipes for braised lettuce give too long a cooking time, so I have formulated my own somewhat revolutionary way of preparing it, which, to my palate, produces a pleasanter result.*

**Makes 6 servings**

6 heads of Boston or Bibb
   lettuce
2 leeks
   Or 2 medium onions
2 carrots
½ pound bacon
Chicken, beef, or veal stock
4 tablespoons (½ stick)
   unsalted butter
Salt, freshly ground black
   pepper

Remove the outer leaves from the lettuce, then wash the heads under cold running water, pulling the leaves apart to loosen them and wash away all sand between them (this is especially important with Bibb lettuce, which is usually very sandy). Wrap the heads in paper towels to dry. Trim the root end and all but 1 inch of the green top from the leeks and wash them well under cold running water, separating the leaves to rinse out lurking sand. Dry and cut into fine julienne (matchstick-sized) strips. If leeks are not available, use onions, peeled and thinly sliced. Peel the carrots and also cut into julienne strips.

Arrange the carrots and leeks or onions in a layer in a heavy sauté pan and top them with 2 slices of the bacon, cut into small pieces. Arrange the dried lettuce heads on the bed of vegetables and cover with the remaining bacon slices. Add enough stock to barely cover the lettuce. Bring the liquid to a boil over high heat, then reduce the heat to low, cover the pan, and simmer, covered, for 20 to 30 minutes, or until just tender and pierceable (Bibb lettuce, which is more compact, with heavier leaves, sometimes takes longer to cook than Boston). Carefully remove the lettuce heads with wooden spoons or tongs and drain on paper towels. Strain the stock. It may be saved and used for soups or stews.

Melt the butter in a large skillet, add the drained lettuce, and reheat in the butter. Season with salt and pepper to taste. Transfer the braised lettuce to a heated serving dish and spoon some of the butter over it.

# Red Cabbage with Chestnuts

Red cabbage goes well with game and red meats. The following recipe, which comes from the central part of France, works as a complete vegetable course—the chestnuts supplying the starch.

Makes 6 to 8 servings

4 pounds red cabbage
5 tablespoons unsalted butter
2 pounds peeled chestnuts
1½ teaspoons salt
1 teaspoon freshly ground
    black pepper
Chicken broth

Wash the cabbage, quarter it and cut out the core, then cut it into very thin shreds with a large chef's knife.

Melt the butter in a heavy sauté pan over medium heat. Add the cabbage, chestnuts, salt and pepper, and just enough chicken broth to cover. Bring the liquid to a boil, then reduce the heat to low, cover, and simmer for 40 to 45 minutes.

# Sauerkraut

Sauerkraut is often overlooked as an accompaniment to meat and poultry, yet its tart, fermented flavor is a perfect balance for any form of pork—from roasts and barbecued spareribs to pigs' knuckles and sausages—or to boiled beef, rich and fatty goose and duck, turkey, and many game birds.

The best buy is the fresh sauerkraut packaged in plastic bags and sold in German pork butcher shops and many supermarkets, but canned sauerkraut is also acceptable. Fresh sauerkraut is very salty and should always be rinsed well before using.

Makes 4 to 6 servings

2 1-pound packages of fresh
    sauerkraut
4 to 5 slices salt pork or
    bacon, cut ⅛ inch thick
Freshly ground black pepper
Bouquet garni (see page 360)
2 peeled garlic cloves
10 crushed juniper berries
    Or 2 tablespoons gin
Chicken stock, white wine, or
    beer to cover (about
    4 cups)

Rinse the sauerkraut well in a colander under cold running water, tossing it with your hands. Drain well. Line the bottom of a large heavy pot with the salt pork or bacon (if you use salt pork, soak it in cold water for 30 minutes to remove the excess salt). Put layers of sauerkraut into the pot, grinding black pepper on each layer. Tuck in among the layers the bouquet garni and garlic, then add the juniper berries or gin. Pour on enough liquid (I prefer chicken stock, which gives a more delicate flavor) to cover, bring to a boil, then reduce the heat to a simmer and simmer slowly for 2 to 4 hours. The longer it cooks, the better it tastes.

# Braised Peas with Lettuce

*By cooking tender young green peas this French way, they retain all their flavor and texture because the damp lettuce leaves add moisture to the heat, while the touch of sugar brings out their sweetness.*

**Makes 4 servings**

8 tablespoons (1 stick)
  unsalted butter
1 head Boston lettuce
3 pounds green peas, shelled
1 teaspoon salt
1 teaspoon sugar

Wash but do not dry the lettuce. Melt the butter in a heavy 2½-quart saucepan and cover the bottom of the pan with damp lettuce leaves. Put the peas on top, sprinkle them with the salt and sugar, and cover with more damp lettuce leaves. Cover tightly and cook over low heat for 20 to 25 minutes, or until the peas are just tender. Serve the peas with or without the lettuce.


# Braised Onion Slices

*Braising is an excellent way to cook onions because it gives them a great deal of flavor. The whiskey, though not traditional, makes them extra-special.*

**Makes 6 servings**

2 tablespoons olive oil
2 tablespoons butter
4 large yellow onions, peeled
  and cut into 1-inch-thick
  slices
1 teaspoon salt
½ teaspoon freshly ground
  black pepper
¼ cup chicken or beef broth
¼ cup Scotch whiskey

Melt the oil and butter in a heavy skillet or sauté pan. Add the onions and sauté them over high heat for 2 minutes to brown them slightly. Add the salt, pepper, and broth. Reduce the heat to low, cover, and simmer for 10 minutes, or until just tender when pierced with the point of a sharp paring knife. Add the whiskey and cook for a further 5 minutes, until the alcohol has volatilized and the sauce is slightly reduced. These are delicious with roast or broiled beef, roast lamb, or roast chicken.

# Sautéing

There is a great deal of confusion about what is sautéing and what is frying. To some people, the mere fact that something is cooked in a skillet or flat pan in fat means that it is fried. Well, it's not. Frying is like baptism in certain religious sects—there must be total immersion. Occasionally you'll encounter the term "pan-fried," which is just an American way of saying "sautéed."

What, then, is sautéing? Sautéing is cooking food on top of the stove in a relatively small amount of fat in, preferably, a heavy-duty sauté pan or skillet, and it's a fast, deft procedure. A sauté pan, known in France as a *sautoir* or *sauteuse*, is specially constructed and designed for sautéing. It is a straight-sided, heavy-bottomed pan about 2½ to 3 inches deep that comes in different diameters, usually 10, 12, and 14 inches. The handle is longer than that of most skillets because in sautéing you have to shake the pan and sometimes toss the food in it. It should also have a tight-fitting cover for sautés, such as chicken, that are cooked covered after the initial browning in fat.

You can use other pans for sautéing—a skillet or frying pan, especially one of heavy iron or of cast aluminum, with or without a Teflon lining, or any fairly shallow, flat, long-handled pan large enough to accommodate in one layer the food you are going to sauté, plus that tight-fitting cover. (See the preceding page for an assortment of equipment.) Provided it is not made out of a flimsy material or is difficult to handle, almost any pan of this sort is acceptable. Heavy lined copper, stainless steel with aluminum plate on the bottom, and cast aluminum are good materials for sauté pans and skillets. However, if a sauté includes wine or egg yolks, it is inadvisable to cook it in an unlined aluminum or iron pan, for chemical reaction between the metal and the wine (or other acid foods, such as vinegar or tomatoes) or the egg yolk can discolor your sauce. It doesn't harm the food, it's just a matter of aesthetics.

The simplest and most basic form of sauté, which does not need covering, is the one you'll find on menus all around the world—a sauté meunière, or sauté in the style of the miller's wife (presumably because it implies a light dusting of flour on the food). This is usually applied to fish-sole meunière, trout meunière, sand dabs meunière—the delicate flesh of which needs quick cooking and a little protection from the heat, hence the flour. The fish are first sprinkled with flour and then sautéed quickly in butter, or butter and oil, turned to give a lovely golden color on both sides while the inside stays tender and not dried out or overcooked. This, with a blessing of salt and pepper, a squeeze of lemon, and a sprinkle of parsley, is the sauté meunière, one of the most famous of all ways of preparing fish. Nothing could be simpler or better. It's a triumphant example of a sauté.

A similar sauté, perhaps the best known next to the meunière, applies to thin, thin slices of meat, usually veal scaloppine or scallops, slices cut from the leg and pounded flat. These are sometimes floured, sometimes not, and sautéed very quickly in butter, oil, or a combination of the two. The seasoning may be merely salt and pepper and a little lemon juice, or there may be herbs, or white wine, or Marsala wine, the classic Italian version, to make a little sauce for the meat. This is a quick dish, in and out of the pan before you know it, and seldom, if ever, covered. The other famous meat dish is beef Stroganoff, made with thin slices of tenderloin sautéed very fast in butter and oil, just to sear them so they remain deliciously rare inside. The slices are removed and sour cream and seasonings mixed into the pan juices, then briefly combined with the beef and served in what is really a minute sauté, although too often in this country it is bastardized into a stew, which it was never meant to be. Then, of course, we have offal, the kidneys, liver, sweetbreads, brains, all those delicious little bits that need the fast cooking of a sauté to keep them juicy and tender.

Chops can be sautéed very successfully, though here the thickness of the meat requires that they be cooked further, covered. Pork chops, for instance, are often quickly sautéed, covered, and simmered very slowly with flavorings and a touch of liquid until tender, then served with a sauce made from the pan juices, after the chops are removed. You can also sauté them and then put the pan, covered, in the oven so the chops braise slowly under a moist blanket of vegetables and liquid—or the whole process can be carried out on top of the stove. I once did a year of demonstrations around the country and one of the dishes people loved most was a very interesting sauté of lovely thick pork chops, browned quickly along with 1 or 2 strips of thick bacon, then covered with sauerkraut, a little finely chopped garlic, freshly ground pepper, and beer, and simmered, covered, until the chops were tender and beautifully flavored with the smoky bacon and pungent sauerkraut. It's basically the same recipe as the one on page 146.

Chicken sautés, which are legion in the dictionary of cooking, fall into two categories—the ones that are browned, and the ones that are not. Those that are sautéed a golden brown, perhaps with the aid of a light dusting of flour, are known as a *sauté brun*, a brown sauté. For the other, the white or *sauté blond*, the chicken is merely seared on the surface, but not allowed to color. It's a very minor difference. For a brown sauté the pieces are browned on both sides, for a blond sauté they are cooked just until the outside is firm and the color creamy. The pieces are then seasoned with salt and pepper, covered, and cooked gently for 5 to 8 minutes. The next step in a chicken sauté is to add liquid—a small amount of white or red wine, sherry, Port or Madeira, stock or tomato juice, or tomato purée  and the flavoring additions, which can be herbs, certain spices, chopped garlic, shallot, or onion, tiny bits of ham, tomato, green pepper, mushrooms, or many different ingredients, all of which are put in at a point about midway in the cooking, usually after the sauté has simmered, covered, for about 10 minutes. These additions help to tenderize and flavor the flesh of the chicken and create the infinite variations possible with a basic chicken sauté. Some of them will be added with the liquid before covering and simmering the sauté; others will be added after it has simmered for a while.

Once the chicken has simmered to tenderness, remove it to a hot dish and keep it warm while you cook down the pan juices for a sauce, perhaps adding more wine or more herbs to finish it off. Sometimes a recipe will call for a touch of *glace de viande*, beef stock reduced to a jelly, which gives the finished dish a nice glaze, or a tablespoon or two of butter, which also enriches the sauce and gives a pleasant body and glaze. Or if the recipe were for a creamy sauté, you'd add cream, or egg yolks mixed with cream, or the sauce might be thickened with cornstarch, arrowroot, or *beurre manié*. The sauce would be poured over the chicken or served with it, according to the recipe.

Sautéing is a process with many facets. A surprisingly large number of everyday cooking procedures fall within the realm of sautéing. I can remember one day, years ago, when I was demonstrating omelet-making. As I melted the butter in the pan, added the eggs, shook the pan, and swirled the omelet around I suddenly realized something that I had never considered before—an omelet is a sauté of egg! Scrambled eggs are also a sauté, if you define the process, because again one melts the butter, adds the eggs, and moves them around gently until they have cooked to perfect, creamy delicacy.

Vegetables, another tender and delicate food, sauté very nicely. Depending on their texture they can be sautéed raw, like onions, or after parboiling. Tiny green beans, for instance, are blanched or parboiled in water, drained very well, and then sautéed in plenty of butter with a vigorous shaking of the pan so that the beans don't overcook but just acquire the flavor that comes from that quick, hot kiss of butter. Asparagus can be blanched, drained, and cooked in butter in the same way (but one has to handle them very gently lest the tips break), with a finishing touch of some grated cheese. Onions for a vegetable course, cut in very thin rings, are either sautéed gently in butter to a delicate deep ivory color or more intensely until they turn quite brown and crisp on the edges, then seasoned with salt and pepper. Thicker slices that take longer to cook may be finished off by adding cheese and covering the pan so the onions steam and the cheese melts, or by adding wine such as Madeira or sherry, covering the pan, and letting the onions steam and cook down in the wine.

Apple rings are very often sautéed as an accompaniment to meat, especially pork, or to certain chicken dishes. The apples are cored, cut into slices, and sautéed in butter and oil with a light sprinkling of sugar until they are delicately browned and caramelized. After caramelizing they may be flambéed with a little calvados or cognac. And pears, pineapples, or bananas can be sautéed quickly in butter for an easy dessert.

It's a far cry, in every way, from frying to sautéing. We talk about fried ham. Well, there's no such thing. It is sautéed in butter, maybe after being parboiled in the sauté pan with water to draw out some of the salt and make it tender. The pan is dried, the butter added, and the ham gently sautéed to a delicate brown tenderness, after which the ham is removed and those who like the famous red-eye gravy add some water to the pan to dissolve the glaze.

People who say they can't prepare a meal for company without spending hours over a hot stove are just foolish. In slightly over an hour, they can make a simple *salade composée*, a light soup or seafood first course, and a chicken, veal, or pork sauté with a vegetable, and with cheese and fruit have an excellent meal for 4. Sautéing is an almost foolproof form not only of quick cookery but of good cookery. I love sautés. One of the persons who taught me most about cooking over a period of years, Jeanne Owen, made at least thirty different chicken sautés, all absolutely delicious. She'd do one with white wine, salt, and pepper and then add perhaps a dash of tarragon or a little thyme, or a red wine sauté with shallots and onion and garlic, or a sauté with garlic, tomato, and rosemary, each one taking no more than 25 to 30 minutes and producing a magnificent meal for 2 or 4 with practically no effort. So you see, once you master the sauté you are well on your way to becoming a good cook and a good host or hostess.

# Beef

## ✒ Steak au Poivre

*One of the simplest of all sautés is a steak* au poivre, *which is now popular throughout the world, although I can remember the time when you found it only in France. Gradually, people became so enamored of this delicious combination of pepper-flavored beef and cognac, sometimes a little cream, that you find it served from New York to Seattle.*

*The best cut for individual steaks* au poivre *is the loin strip, otherwise known as a shell steak, a faux filet, a sirloin strip steak, or a New York cut, according to what part of the country you live in. This is the loin steak without the smaller part, the fillet, and usually with the bone trimmed away, although sometimes a little bit of the bone is left on. The steak should be 1½ inches thick.*

*To cook the steaks you will need a heavy-duty skillet or sauté pan, 12 inches in diameter—it must be large enough to accommodate the two steaks, side by side, with some room left over. They must not be squeezed together.*

**Makes 2 servings**

2 sirloin strip steaks, about 1½ inches thick
1½ tablespoons black peppercorns
1 teaspoon or more salt
3 tablespoons unsalted butter
3 tablespoons salad oil
⅓ cup cognac or bourbon

About 2 hours before you plan to cook the steaks, remove them from the refrigerator and leave at room temperature. Before cooking, trim any excess fat from the side of the steak with a small, sharp paring knife, leaving just a thin strip for lubrication—a good piece of sirloin will be well marbled with fat and that will also lubricate the meat as it cooks. Fat is the flavor-giver for meat, and if you cut off all the fat you will take away some of the flavor of the meat, the part that settled in the fat.

Now crush or grind the peppercorns very, very coarse. If your pepper mill doesn't grind coarsely enough, it is advisable to crush them in a mortar and pestle, or to wrap them in a towel and beat them with a mallet, or you may use a blender or food processor, which does the job fast and isn't so arduous.

Sprinkle the top of each steak with 1 to 1½ teaspoons of the ground peppercorns, and with the heel of your hand (which has the most strength in it), press the pepper into the meat. Turn the steaks and repeat on the other side. Let the steaks rest for 15 minutes before sautéing. Just about 2 minutes before you put the steaks on to cook, sprinkle one side with salt, using about ½ teaspoon for each steak. Many people tell you that this will draw out the juices, but I maintain that when meat sears as fast as this does, the salt is absorbed and the surface immediately sealed.

Heat the butter and oil in the skillet or sauté pan over medium-high heat (425° if you have a burner with a thermostat). As oil can be heated to a higher temperature than butter without burning, the oil prevents the butter from burning at the rather high heat one uses to sauté steak. For this reason, you should also use sweet rather than salted butter, which is more inclined to burn. If you prefer, you may omit the butter and use all oil, or you can substitute beef drippings, if you have any, or chop up the fat you trimmed from the steak, throw that into the pan, and let it melt and render into fat.

When the fat is sizzling but not smoking (if it smokes, it is too hot, and you will have to throw it out and start again), place the steaks, salted side down, in the hot fat. The steak will sizzle as it hits the fat and you don't want it to stick, so shake the pan very gently to move the steaks around. Cook for about 3 minutes on that side, shaking the pan back and forth very gently, then salt the uncooked side, turn the steaks with tongs, and cook 3 minutes on that side. Now reduce the heat to medium (350° on a thermostat) or below medium, turn the steaks again, and cook a further 3 minutes on each side—that's 3 minutes a side for searing plus 3 minutes a side for cooking at the lower temperature.

To make sure the steak is done to your taste, remove the pan from the heat, and with a very sharp paring knife and a fork make a small incision in the thickest part of the steak (or, if there is bone, next to the bone) and push the meat apart to see if it is cooked as you like it. If not, you may give the steaks a minute or two more. Six minutes a side should give you a really rare steak. Eight minutes a side will give you medium-rare steak.

Remove the steaks to a hot platter and keep warm. Shake the pan well, remove it from the heat, and pour the cognac or bourbon into the pan. Strike a long kitchen match and very carefully place it at the side of the pan—the fumes of alcohol from the heated cognac will immediately ignite and burn with a great flame, so keep your head and hands well out of range as you do this. Hold the pan by the handle and shake it gently until the flames die down— they will have burned off all the excess fat and lifted the brown glaze from the bottom of the pan, making a little sauce for the steak. Should a tiny bit of flame linger, fan it out quickly with your hand. Pour the sauce over the steak and serve at once.

Contrary to what some people think, the pepper should on no account be scraped off the steak before you eat it, but eaten and enjoyed. It's really like a condiment, and it is that lovely charred peppery taste and crunchy crustiness on the outside that makes steak au poivre the great dish it is. You may serve the steaks as they come, or cut them into thin diagonal slices. Sautéed potatoes, a green salad, and a good red wine are all you'll need with this delicious steak.

## ❧ Sautéed Hamburgers

*A good hamburger is one of the most basic meat dishes you can make, but even here there are one or two tricks you should know. In my opinion, hamburgers are best pan-fried or sautéed in a heavy skillet in oil, a combination of butter and oil, or clarified butter (see page 344), all of which can be heated to a higher temperature without burning than plain butter. I think this gives a juicier, crustier hamburger than broiling, and it is easier to control the degree of doneness. You will need a heavy iron skillet, or whatever you normally use for sautéing (with a Teflon-lined skillet, you won't need much fat, just about 1 tablespoon for flavor), and a large spatula for turning the hamburgers.*

**Makes 4 servings**

2 pounds chopped beef, preferably top round or chuck, with 20 to 25 percent fat

Coarse (kosher) salt, freshly ground black pepper

2 tablespoons peanut oil
  Or equal quantities of oil and butter
  Or clarified butter

Divide the meat into 4 equal portions, seasoning it to taste with salt and pepper, and form it gently and lightly into patties with your hands, almost tossing it back and forth. Be careful not to press or overhandle the meat. Too much handling makes for heavy, solid patties, and that is not what you want at all. The meat should just hold together. You can make your patties round or oval, thick or fairly flat, according to how you like them. For rare hamburgers, make them thick. For medium, make them thinner. They won't be perfectly shaped. They'll be sort of free-form, but that's all right. Taste is more important than appearance.

Heat the oil, or whatever you are using, in a heavy skillet. There should be just a film of fat on the surface. When it is hot, but not smoking, put the patties in the pan and cook briskly on one side for 4 minutes over fairly high heat until good and brown. Turn them carefully with a large spatula and cook 4 minutes on the other side. Press the browned surface gently with your finger. See how much firmer it is than the uncooked meat. Then press the sides.

These will be less firm because the center meat has not cooked as much.

At this point you can almost gauge how near to done the hamburgers are. Reduce the heat slightly and, if you like them rare, give them 2 more minutes on each side. Press them again and you'll find they are slightly resistant to the touch. Transfer them to hot plates and serve at once. When you cut into the hamburger and find it done to your liking, remember the way the patty felt when pressed. This is a very simple test, but it will give you confidence in the message your fingers can send to your brain. A broiled steak can be tested in the same way.

# Beef Liver Bourguignon

*Beef liver, which is not as delicate in flavor as calf's liver, benefits from a flavorful red wine sauce. As with all offal, beef liver should be sautéed quickly and not over-cooked or it will be tough and unpleasant. Speed is essential for this dish, so you should make the croutons first.*

**Makes 4 servings**

2 slices white bread
12 tablespoons (1½ sticks)
   unsalted butter
3 garlic cloves, finely
   chopped
6 slices bacon or salt pork,
   diced
½ cup flour
Salt, freshly ground black
   pepper
4 good-sized slices of young
   beef liver, ⅜ inch thick
4 medium onions, peeled and
   sliced
½ to ¾ cup red wine
1 tablespoon chopped parsley
   and chives

Trim the crusts from the bread, cut each slice in two diagonally and then in two diagonally again, making 8 triangles. Heat 6 tablespoons butter in a heavy skillet and when the butter is hot and sizzling, add the garlic and the bread pieces and sauté them quickly, turning frequently, over medium-high heat, until brown and crisp. Be careful not to let the butter, garlic, or bread burn. Remove to paper towels to drain, and keep warm in a 200° oven.

Wipe out the skillet with paper towels, removing all butter and residue, then add and melt the remaining butter, add the bacon or salt pork dice, and sauté over medium heat until the fat is rendered and the pieces are brown and crisp. Remove to paper towels and drain. Season the flour with 1 teaspoon salt and ¼ teaspoon pepper and coat the beef liver

lightly with the flour, shaking off any excess.

Heat the butter and fat in the pan until hot and sizzling, add the liver slices, and sauté quickly over medium-high heat until browned on each side, about 3 to 4 minutes on one side and 1 minute on the other—the liver should still be rare, pink, and juicy in the center. Remove to a hot platter, cover with foil, and keep warm. Add the onions to the fat in the pan and sauté until limp and golden, then replace the bacon or salt pork dice, add just enough red wine to cover, reduce heat, and simmer gently for 5 minutes.

Add the liver slices to the sauce and let them just heat through, then arrange the liver slices on a hot platter, pour the sauce over them, top with the fried bread triangles, and sprinkle with parsley and chives.

Serve at once. Serve with potatoes Anna and pass the rest of the sauce in the bowl. A red Burgundy or similar full-bodied red wine is best with this.


# Zrazys Nelson

*This Polish recipe involves three different sautés—potatoes, cucumbers with mushrooms, and thin slices of tender fillet of beef.*

**Makes 6 servings**

8 to 10 medium-small
  potatoes, boiled in their
  jackets until done but
  slightly undercooked and
  firm, so they slice easily
½ pound or more unsalted
  butter
Salt, freshly ground black
  pepper
4 cucumbers, peeled and
  thinly sliced
18 firm white mushrooms,
  thinly sliced
4 tablespoons flour
2 cups heavy cream
1 tablespoon tomato purée
12 slices of beef fillet, about
  ½ inch thick
French fried onion rings
  (canned may be used)

Peel the potatoes and slice about ¼ inch thick. Heat 4 tablespoons butter in a heavy skillet and sauté the potatoes in batches over medium-high heat until nicely browned and crisp at the edges. Add more butter as needed. As they are cooked, sprinkle lightly with salt and pepper and transfer them to a large serving platter, making a bed for the beef. Keep warm in a 250° oven.

Rub out the skillet with paper towels, add and heat 4 tablespoons butter and, when bubbling, add the cucumbers and mushrooms and sauté over fairly high heat, tossing and turning, until cucumbers are soft and mushrooms lightly browned. Mix in the flour. Gradually add the cream and cook over medium heat, stirring constantly, until thickened. Mix in the tomato purée and season to taste with salt and pepper. Keep warm while sautéing the beef.

Melt 4 tablespoons butter in another heavy skillet or sauté pan and, when hot and bubbling, sauté the beef slices on both sides very quickly over high heat, a few at a time, for about 2 to 3 minutes a side, or until nicely browned on the outside but still rare inside. Do not over-cook. As they are cooked, sprinkle them lightly with salt and arrange on the bed of potatoes. Cover with the cucumber-mushroom sauce and serve topped with French fried onion rings, which have been heated on a baking sheet in a 350° oven until crisp.

# Poultry and Game

## ❧ Chicken Sauté with White Wine and Tarragon

For sautéing, chicken is cut into serving pieces—either quartered into 2 breast halves with wings attached and 2 legs and thighs, or disjointed into smaller pieces, with the wings separated from the breast, and the legs from the thighs. Although you can buy chicken cut up for frying or sautéing in the supermarket, it has usually been pretty sloppily done. Often the chicken has merely been sawed or hacked into pieces, leaving splintery bits of bone. It is preferable, and also more economical, to buy a whole chicken and cup it up yourself, which not only gives you neat, perfect serving pieces, but also the gizzards, neck, and back to make into stock. The wing tips, which are not very meaty, can be cut off and added to the stock pot.

Take a sharp knife and, using your fingers to locate the joint, cut through the connecting skin and flesh. Bend the leg back, away from the body, until the hip joint appears. Cut through at the connecting joint. Cut skin between leg and thigh, locate joint, and cut through. Next, remove the wings from the breast, (unless you are doing a dish that calls for the wing bone to be attached, such as the recipe that follows or chicken Kiev).

Now grasp the chicken by the back and hold it so that you can cut through the entire length of the bird with a large sharp knife; this means cutting through the ribs and straight down to the wing joint. Bend the back and then with a heavy knife cut through the bones at the shoulder to sever the breast from the carcass. The back may be cut in two crosswise and simply used for stock. Cut the breast in half up the center with your knife, slicing through the wishbone at the top. You will now have 8 serving pieces as illustrated.

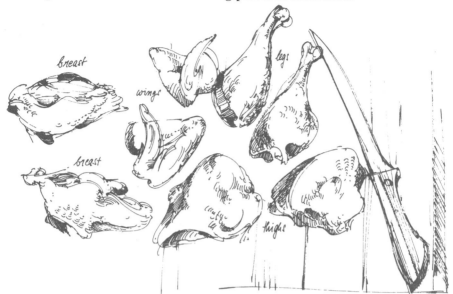

*You can vary this sauté endlessly, by using different herbs, vegetables, stock, sherry, or red wine in place of the white wine, or by blazing the cooked chicken with brandy. The tarragon in this recipe can be replaced with parsley, if you prefer.*

**Makes 4 servings**

6 tablespoons unsalted butter
2 frying chickens, each
   weighing 2 to 2½ pounds
Salt, freshly ground black
   pepper
½ cup dry white wine
2 tablespoons chopped fresh
   tarragon
   Or 2 teaspoons dried
   tarragon

Melt the butter in a large, heavy skillet or sauté pan that has a tight-fitting cover. When it is hot (the slight foaming of the melted butter should subside, but do not let it turn brown), brown the chicken pieces over medium-high heat, turning them as they brown so that all sides are evenly colored. Lower the heat, sprinkle the chicken with salt and pepper to taste, cover the pan, and simmer gently for 5 to 8 minutes. Remove the cover and check the pieces, rearranging them

so they cook evenly. Add ¼ cup of the wine, cover the pan again, and cook for another 10 minutes. If you are using dried tarragon, put it to soak in the remaining wine.

Uncover the pan and move the breast and wing sections to the top, arranging them over the leg and thigh pieces. The dark meat takes longer to cook and during the final cooking should be at the bottom of the pan, closest to the heat. Sprinkle the chicken with the tarragon (if dried, remove it from the wine by straining it through a little sieve—reserve the wine), cover again, and cook the chicken until tender, but still moist and juicy. This will take 5 to 10 minutes, so check after 5 minutes.

Remove the cooked chicken to a hot serving platter. Add the rest of the wine to the pan, turn the heat to high, and stir the juices with a wooden spoon or spatula until they boil and blend, scraping up the brown bits from the bottom of the pan. Boil until reduced by half, then pour the juices over the chicken and serve immediately. With this you might have boiled rice or bulghur pilaf and a green vegetable, such as green peas, braised French style (see page 153), or just French bread and a green salad. Drink the same kind of wine you used for cooking.

## Chicken Sauté with Armagnac

*Only the white meat is used for this delicate and suave sauté.*

**Makes 4 servings**

8 tablespoons (1 stick)
  unsalted butter
4 half chicken breasts, with
  wings attached
Salt, freshly ground black
  pepper
6 shallots, peeled and very
  finely chopped
2 egg yolks
¾ cup heavy cream
⅓ cup Armagnac

Melt the butter in a large, heavy skillet and when the foaming stops add the chicken and sauté over medium-high heat on both sides until golden. Season with salt and pepper to taste, reduce the heat, cover, and cook gently for 15 to 20 minutes, or until the breasts are just cooked through.

Remove the chicken to a hot flameproof serving platter, or put in the top part of a chafing dish, and pour a little (about 2 tablespoons) of the melted butter over it.

Add the shallots to the pan and cook them in the remaining butter until just limp and golden, stirring them so they do not brown. Beat the eggs and cream together lightly in a measuring cup or small bowl and stir into them a couple of tablespoons of the hot pan liquid, which tempers the yolks and prevents them from curdling when added to the pan. Pour the mixture into the pan and stir constantly over low heat until the sauce is well blended and slightly thickened. Do not allow it to get too hot or to boil or the eggs will curdle. Remove from heat and keep warm.

Heat the Armagnac in a small pan, ignite with a match, and pour blazing over the chicken. When the flames die down, spoon the sauce over the chicken and serve immediately. Serve with a potato purée and green beans tossed in butter. Drink a Pinot Chardonnay or Fumé Blanc.

# Chicken Panné

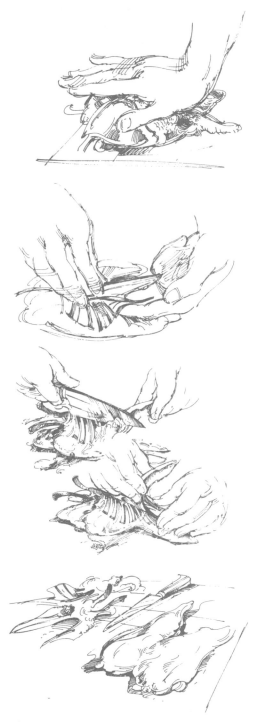

Chicken breasts pounded until very thin, like veal scaloppine, sauté very fast and stay beautifully tender and succulent. It is extremely important not to overcook the breasts, or they will dry out—the chicken is done as soon as the coating is browned. Panné means that the chicken is coated with flour, beaten egg, and crumbs.

You can sometimes find boned chicken breasts in the supermarket, but it is much more economical to do it yourself. If you are working with a whole chicken, follow the procedure for cutting up on page 164, eliminating the last step; in other words, leave the breasts whole —don't split them until you have boned them.

First, break the breastbone by pressing firmly on it with the flat of your hand. Pull the skin from the breast with your fingers.

Turn the chicken breast over and slip your fingers between the flesh and the rib cage. Pull the rib cage away from the flesh.

Then take your small sharp chicken-boning knife and scrape the flesh away from the wishbone and larger bone at the top of the breast, pulling the bone out with your fingers as it is loosened. Should you wish to remove the long stringy white tendon that runs the length of the breast, hold the protruding end of the tendon firmly with your fingers, scrape with the knife to loosen it from the flesh, then give it a firm tug and it will come out easily.

3 whole boned chicken breasts
1 cup flour
3 eggs, beaten
2 to 2½ cups freshly made fine
   bread crumbs
6 tablespoons unsalted butter
   or more
3 tablespoons or more
   peanut oil
Salt, freshly ground black
   pepper
¼ cup cognac
2 egg yolks
1 cup heavy cream

Cut the breasts in half up the center. Put each half breast between two sheets of waxed paper, lay it on a wood counter or chopping block, and pound with a meat pounder until about ⅜ inch thick, as you would for veal scaloppine (see page 137). As you pound, push the pounder outward to flatten and spread the flesh. As each piece is flattened (it will almost double in size), put it between sheets of waxed paper. Put the flour on a large piece of waxed paper, the beaten eggs in a shallow baking dish or pie pan, and the bread crumbs on another large sheet of waxed paper, lining them up in that order. Dip the chicken pieces, one at a time, first in the flour, coating both sides lightly (as you lift the breast out, pat and shake it gently to get rid of excess flour), then lay it in the egg, turning to coat both sides, then lay the breast in the crumbs. Toss the crumbs over the breast, making sure both sides are well coated, then transfer to a cookie sheet lined with waxed paper. Put waxed paper between the breasts so they do not stick together, then refrigerate until ready to cook, to firm and set the coating. This can be done several hours ahead of time.

When you are ready to cook them, remove the breasts from the refrigerator. Heat the butter and oil in a large, heavy skillet (preferably plain iron or Teflon-coated) over high heat until it is hot and bubbling, but not browned or smoking. Put the chicken breasts in the pan in a single layer, no more than 2 at a time. They should not be crowded together or they will steam rather than sauté. As you put the pieces in the pan, turn the heat to medium-high. Brown quickly on both sides, sprinkling the breasts with salt and pepper as they cook. This will take no more than a minute or two a side, just until the coating is lightly browned. Adjust the heat so the crumbs do not burn. Add more butter and oil between batches, if necessary, and each time heat until bubbling.

When the pieces are cooked, transfer them to a hot platter. When they are all cooked, turn off the heat, replace the breasts in the pan, and pour the cognac over them. Ignite the cognac with a match and shake the pan until the flames die down. Remove the chicken pieces to a platter and keep warm in a 250° oven while making the sauce.

Beat the egg yolks in a small bowl and mix with the cream. Heat the juices in the skillet and add a little of the hot pan juices to the egg-cream mixture, to warm the eggs through so they will not curdle when put into the pan. Pour the mixture into the pan and cook over medium heat, stirring, until smooth and lightly thickened. Do not let the sauce get near the simmering point or it will curdle. Taste the sauce and adjust the seasoning. You may need salt and pepper. Serve the chicken pieces on hot plates and spoon sauce over each piece. Puréed broccoli goes well with this, and tiny new potatoes, or rice.

## Sauté of Chicken Livers

*Chicken livers make a very easy, fast sauté. Prepare the toast or noodles before starting the livers.*

**Makes 4 servings**

4 tablespoons (½ stick)
  unsalted butter
4 shallots, finely chopped
1 pound chicken livers,
  trimmed of connecting
  threads and any bitter green
  or blackish discolorations
Salt, freshly ground black
  pepper to taste
2 tablespoons chopped parsley

Melt the butter in a heavy skillet and when hot, add the shallots and sauté over medium heat, stirring, for 3 or 4 minutes until limp and golden. Add the chicken livers, raise the heat to high, and sauté, tossing and turning them, until well browned on all sides and just cooked through, about 5 minutes. Do not overcook or they will toughen; they should still be pink inside. Season with salt and pepper to taste, sprinkle with the parsley, and serve immediately on crisp toast or on a bed of noodles cooked with a garlic clove, drained well, and tossed with butter, salt and pepper, and a little grated nutmeg. The sautéed livers may also be folded into individual omelets, just before they are rolled and turned out.

# Rabbit Sautéed with Tarragon

*If you buy a whole, cleaned and skinned rabbit, weighing 3 to 3½ pounds, it should be cut into serving pieces. The two back legs may be left whole or cut into thighs and drumsticks, the smaller front legs should be left whole, and the saddle, the choicest part, cut in two. Frozen rabbit, which is already cut into serving pieces, need only be thawed and dried well on paper towels before cooking. The giblets may be cooked in the pan with the rabbit to add flavor. Sauté the liver separately in a tablespoon of butter, as it should not be cooked long.*

**Makes 4 servings**

½ cup flour
1 teaspoon salt
½ teaspoon freshly ground
   black pepper
2½ teaspoons dried tarragon
1 young, tender rabbit,
   weighing 3 to 3½ pounds
4 tablespoons unsalted butter
4 tablespoons oil
1 cup dry white wine
¼ cup chopped parsley

Place flour, salt, pepper, 1½ teaspoons tarragon, and rabbit in a plastic bag and shake well, to coat the rabbit. Remove and shake off excess flour.

Heat the butter and oil in a large skillet or sauté pan with a tight-fitting cover. When hot but not brown, add the rabbit and brown the pieces over medium-high heat, turning them carefully with tongs. When they are browned, add ½ cup wine, reduce the heat, cover, and simmer for 15 minutes. Remove the cover, turn the pieces, and rearrange so they cook evenly, then cover and simmer until tender—from 20 to 30 minutes, according to the age and tenderness of the rabbit. There should be no resistance when the flesh is pierced with the point of a small, sharp knife. When tender, remove the pieces of rabbit to a heated platter, add the remaining ½ cup wine, and turn up the heat. Add the remaining tarragon and the parsley; bring the liquid to a boil and boil rapidly until reduced by half, then pour the pan juices over the rabbit and serve. Crisply sautéed potatoes and a celery salad with a mustard vinaigrette dressing go well with this. Serve with the same kind of white wine used for cooking.

# Sautéed Pheasant with Cabbage

*When I was young, we often indulged in sautéed pheasant. Somehow the delicate game flavor was more pronounced than when the pheasant was roasted. For sautéing, the pheasant must be young and tender, and I also feel it should be done in two skillets, one for the dark meat, which takes longer to cook, and one for the white meat. One pheasant will serve 2 to 4, depending on the size of the birds and the size of the appetites.*

**Makes 4 to 8 servings**

2 young pheasants, disjointed
into serving pieces like
chickens
½ cup flour
Salt, freshly ground black
pepper
¼ teaspoon dried thyme
¼ teaspoon paprika
6 to 8 slices of good bacon
6 tablespoons unsalted butter
1 medium head of cabbage
1¼ cups heavy cream

Put the pheasant pieces in a plastic bag with the flour, 1 teaspoon salt, ½ teaspoon pepper, the thyme, and the paprika and shake until the pieces are lightly coated with the seasoned flour. Remove and shake off excess.

Divide the bacon between two heavy 10-inch skillets (one should have a tight-fitting cover). Cook the bacon over medium heat until the fat is rendered and the bacon is just beginning to crisp. Remove it, drain on paper towels, and keep warm in a 250° oven.

Add 3 tablespoons butter to one pan and, when it has melted into the bacon fat and is hot and sizzling, add the dark meat pieces, skin side down, and sauté over medium-high heat until brown on one side, then turn and brown the other side. Five minutes after starting the dark meat, put the remaining butter in the other pan and, when hot and sizzling, add the white meat pieces, skin side down, and brown over medium-high heat. Then turn and brown the second side.

While the pieces are browning, shred the cabbage and parboil it in salted water for 10 minutes. Drain well.

Reduce the heat under both pans and continue to cook the pheasant until just tender, about 15 to 20 minutes, adding the cabbage to the dark meat, and covering the pan so the meat will be tenderized by the steam. Five minutes before the end of the cooking time, uncover, season both white and dark meat with salt and pepper to taste, add the cream to the pheasant and cabbage, and simmer until tender. If the white meat is cooked first, remove it to a hot platter, cover with foil, and keep warm. Combine the pheasant and cabbage on the platter and garnish with the crisp bacon. Serve with small boiled potatoes.

## Variation

♦ If you like a juniper flavor, tuck a few juniper berries in with the cabbage.

# Sautéed Quail

*Tiny quail, with their delicate flesh, are delicious sautéed. Do not overcook these little birds, and serve 1 or 2 per person, depending on size.*

**Makes 3 to 6 servings**

4 tablespoons (½ stick)
   unsalted butter
¼ cup peanut oil
6 quail
1 teaspoon or more salt
Freshly grated nutmeg
¾ cup white wine
½ cup cognac
1 cup seedless or seeded
   white grapes
6 rounds of buttered toast

Heat the butter and oil in a large skillet with a cover until very hot, but not brown. Add the quail and sauté them on all sides until delicately browned, turning frequently. Season with salt to taste and grate a little nutmeg over them. Add the white wine, reduce the heat, and simmer the quail, covered, for about 10 minutes. Turn off the heat, remove the cover, add the cognac to the hot pan, ignite it, and flame the birds, shaking the pan gently until the flames die down. Add the grapes. Cover and simmer for about 8 minutes, or until quail are tender. Serve them on the toast croustades and garnish with the grapes. A purée of parsnips with butter and Madeira and a salad of Belgian endives with a well-flavored vinaigrette sauce goes well with this.

## Variation

♦ Remove the breasts from the quail (use legs and carcasses for stock), and sauté in 3 tablespoons butter and 3 tablespoons oil until delicately browned, season with salt and nutmeg, add ¼ cup white wine, and simmer, covered, until just tender, about 10 minutes. Do not flame or add grapes. Serve on toast croustades.

# Veal

As I've said, the meat that takes best of all to sautéing is veal, the thin slices cut from the leg and pounded until they are paper-thin and flat that are known as scallops, escalopes, or scaloppine. The pounding tenderizes the meat, enabling it to be cooked very quickly, in about 5 to 8 minutes depending on thickness and tenderness. Although pale pink, top-quality veal is expensive, it is a better buy than the darker, pinkish-red veal that comes from an older animal (really, young beef) and therefore is not so tender. Two to three thin scallops, according to size, are enough for a serving, and 1½ pounds of very thin scallops should be enough for 4 to 6 people. The important point is to cook them fast, and not to overcrowd the pan, which reduces the heat and makes them steam rather than sauté. The following is a very simple, basic recipe for sautéed veal scallops.

# ❧ Veal Scallops Fines Herbes

8 large or 12 medium veal
  scallops (about 1½
  pounds), pounded until thin
½ cup flour
6 tablespoons unsalted butter
3 tablespoons olive oil
2 tablespoons finely chopped
  chives
2 tablespoons finely chopped
  parsley
1 tablespoon finely chopped
  tarragon
  Or 1 teaspoon dried
  tarragon
⅔ cup dry white wine
Salt, freshly ground black
  pepper

Coat the scallops lightly with flour, brushing off excess. Heat the butter and oil in a heavy skillet and when hot but not brown (butter should just stop foaming) add the scallops, a few at a time, and sauté them quickly over high heat, about 3 or 4 minutes a side, until delicately browned. Remove and keep warm while you do the rest of the scallops. Add the chopped herbs and wine and cook for 2 minutes at high heat. Season to taste with salt and pepper and serve immediately, with the pan juices poured over the scallops. Serve with sautéed potatoes and julienne strips of blanched, sautéed carrot and zucchini (see page 190).

# Veal Kidneys Flambé

4 veal kidneys
4 tablespoons unsalted butter
3 tablespoons oil
½ cup cognac or Armagnac
Salt, freshly ground black
  pepper
1½ teaspoons Dijon mustard
1 tablespoon Worcestershire
  sauce
¼ teaspoon Tabasco
1½ cups heavy cream
Beurre manié (see page 270)
1 tablespoon chopped parsley

Clean the kidneys, removing the outer membrane and the core of fat and white tubes in the top (see page 110). Cut in medium-thin slices. Combine the butter and oil in a large skillet and heat until hot and bubbling, add the kidneys, and sauté very quickly (about 4 minutes) over high heat, shaking the pan and tossing and turning the kidneys several times until browned. Turn off the heat, add the cognac or Armagnac, and ignite with a long kitchen match, standing well back. Flame the kidneys, shaking the pan until the flames die. Season with salt and pepper to taste, the mustard, Worcestershire sauce, and Tabasco, and

stir in the cream. Add small balls of *beurre manié* and cook over medium heat, stirring, until the sauce is just lightly thickened. Do not overcook or the kidneys will toughen. Taste and correct the seasoning. Sprinkle with chopped parsley and serve with rice and a green salad.

# ❧ Sautéed Sweetbreads with Virginia Ham

*When sweetbreads are sautéed, they should be soaked in ice water, blanched, and weighted to firm the texture before they are trimmed and cooked.*

Makes 6 servings

3 pairs sweetbreads
½ pound or more unsalted
  butter
12 slices bread, trimmed of
  crusts
12 small slices Virginia ham
12 large mushroom caps
⅔ cup plus 2 tablespoons flour
Salt, freshly ground black
  pepper
1 tablespoon lemon juice
¼ teaspoon nutmeg
3 eggs, lightly beaten
1½ to 2 cups fresh bread
  crumbs
½ cup brandy or calvados
1½ to 2 cups heavy cream
¼ teaspoon Tabasco
2 tablespoons chopped parsley

Soak the sweetbreads in ice water for 30 minutes. Put in a deep saucepan with water to cover, 1 teaspoon salt, and 1 tablespoon lemon juice (which helps to keep them white), bring to a boil, reduce the heat, and simmer for 10 minutes. Remove and plunge into ice water to stop their cooking any further. When cool enough to handle, remove the covering membrane, connecting tubes, and particles of fat. Put the sweetbreads on a baking sheet, cover with waxed paper, put another baking sheet or chopping board on top, and weigh down with several cans of food. Leave for 2 hours. This makes the sweetbreads firm and compact enough to slice.

When ready to cook, remove the sweetbreads and halve them lengthwise into 12 even "cutlets."

Heat 6 tablespoons butter in a very heavy skillet and when it is hot and has stopped frothing, add the bread squares, a few at a time, in a single layer and fry just until golden on both sides. Do not allow the butter to get too dark or burn, or the bread to get too dark. Add more butter if necessary. Remove, drain on paper towels, and keep hot in a 250° oven. Heat the ham slices in 2 tablespoons butter, drain, and put on the toast. In another skillet, sauté the mushroom caps over medium-high heat in 3 tablespoons butter, tossing them so they cook on all sides, until lightly browned—about 3 to 4 minutes. Remove and keep warm.

Season ⅔ cup flour with 1 teaspoon salt, ¼ teaspoon pepper, and the nutmeg. Dip the sweetbread "cutlets" into the seasoned flour, then into the beaten eggs, and then into the bread crumbs. Heat 6 tablespoons butter in a large skillet, and when it stops frothing, add the sweetbreads and sauté, a few at a time, over medium-high heat, until delicately browned on all sides. When all are cooked, return to the pan, turn off the heat, pour in the brandy or calvados, ignite it, and flame the sweetbreads, shaking the pan until the flames die. Remove to a platter, cover with aluminum foil, and keep warm while making the sauce.

Blend 2 tablespoons flour with the butter and juices in the skillet, adding a little more butter if the mixture seems too floury, and cook over medium heat, stirring, until it starts to bubble. Gradually stir in the cream and the Tabasco and cook over low heat, stirring, until thickened. Taste and correct the seasoning.

To serve, top each ham slice with one piece of sweetbread. Spoon the sauce over the sweetbreads and top with a mushroom cap. Sprinkle with parsley. Serve 2 per person.

Traditionally, this elegant dish was finished and served *sous cloche*—under a glass bell. The toast, ham, and sweetbreads were put on individual gratin dishes, covered with a heatproof glass bell, and gently reheated in the oven, then covered with the sauce and served under the bell, or *cloche*.

# Pork and Lamb

## Pork Chops Niçoise

*Sautéed pork chops are succulent and delicious. For sautéing, they should be cut 1 to 1½ inches thick, and those from the loin or rib section are preferable. You can trim some of the fat from the chops, render it, and use it for the sautéing.*

**Makes 6 servings**

3 to 4 tablespoons rendered pork fat or olive oil

6 pork loin chops, cut 1 to 1½ inches thick

4 ripe tomatoes, peeled, seeded, and finely chopped
Or 1½ cups canned Italian plum tomatoes

3 garlic cloves, peeled and finely chopped

1 medium green pepper, seeds and ribs removed, finely chopped

1 tablespoon fresh, chopped basil
Or 1 teaspoon dried basil

1½ cups black olives (preferably the Niçoise olives)

Heat the pork fat or oil in a heavy skillet and brown the chops lightly on each side over fairly high heat, allowing about 3 minutes a side. Do only as many chops at one time as will fit into the pan without crowding. Add extra fat or oil if required. Replace the chops in the skillet and add the tomatoes, garlic, green pepper, and basil. Cover the pan and simmer for 25 minutes, turning the chops once during the cooking. Add the olives and continue cooking for another 10 minutes over low heat, or until the chops are tender when tested near the bone with the point of a small sharp knife. Serve with rice mixed with chopped parsley.

# Deviled Breast of Lamb

*One of the most delicious of all ways to cook economical breast of lamb is first to poach it in a court bouillon and then cut it into pieces, crumb, sauté, and serve with a sauce diable.*

**Makes 6 to 8 servings**

2 or 3 3-pound breasts of
  lamb, trimmed of most
  of their fat
2 large onions, peeled and
  each stuck with 2 cloves
12 to 14 garlic cloves, peeled
1 leek, well washed and
  trimmed
1 carrot, peeled
1 bay leaf
2 teaspoons salt
1 teaspoon rosemary
Water or stock to cover
2 eggs, lightly beaten
1 cup flour
2 cups dry bread crumbs
6 tablespoons clarified
  unsalted butter (see
  page 344)
  Or 3 tablespoons unsalted
  butter and 3 tablespoons oil

Put the lamb breasts in a deep pan with the onions, garlic, leek, carrot, bay leaf, salt, rosemary, and enough water or stock to just cover the lamb. Bring to a boil, skim off any scum that forms on the surface, reduce the heat, and simmer the lamb for 1 hour, or until it is quite tender when tested with the point of a small, sharp knife. Remove and drain the breasts, put them in a shallow dish or pan (such as a roasting pan), cover them with aluminum foil, and weigh them down with a board or baking sheet with canned goods on top. Let the meat cool and then chill it.

When ready to prepare, pull the rib bones from the breasts and cut the meat into serving pieces, about 1 to 1½ inches wide. Put the eggs, flour, and bread crumbs in separate pie plates. Dip the lamb pieces in the flour, then into the egg, then roll them in the crumbs.

Heat the butter or butter and oil in a large, heavy skillet. Sauté the lamb in the hot fat, a few pieces at a time (do not crowd too many in the pan), over medium-high heat until delicately brown and crisp on both sides. Serve on a very hot platter with a sauce diable (see page 277). Crisp shoestring potatoes and a large bowl of plain watercress are excellent with this. Drink a Beaujolais, such as a Fleurie.

# Fish

While sautéing, like frying and broiling, ranks among the more common ways of cooking fish, all these processes require care and attention if the delicate flesh is to be perfectly cooked and not overdone.

For a simple sauté, or sauté meunière, the fish is cooked in a small amount of unsalted butter or, better yet, butter and oil (remember, the oil, which can be heated to a higher temperature, keeps the butter from burning), turned once during the cooking process, seasoned with salt and pepper, and sprinkled with chopped parsley.

Sometimes the fish is lightly floured before cooking, and a bit of additional butter may be added at the last minute with a few drops of lemon juice. Clarified butter is excellent for sautéing, as it does not burn as readily as plain butter. If you use clarified butter (see pages 344–345), no oil is necessary.

Sautéing is best done at the very last minute—otherwise the fish will become stale and uninteresting if it stands too long. Small whole fish, split fish, fish fillets, or thin fish steaks may all be sautéed. Frozen fish can be sautéed without thawing, but the cooking time will be almost double, and care must be taken that the skin does not become overcooked. Among fish suitable for sautéing whole are small trout, flounder, lemon sole, rex sole, grey sole, sand dabs, porgies, catfish, butterfish, chub, perch, grunions, and smelts.

## ❧ Sautéed Trout

*Select 4 whole trout of the same size and measure the fish from belly to backbone at the thickest point (see page 113) to estimate the cooking time—the rule for any type of fish cookery is to allow 10 minutes per inch of measured thickness.*

**Makes 4 servings**

4 whole trout
¼ cup flour
7 tablespoons unsalted butter
¼ cup vegetable oil, preferably peanut
Salt, freshly ground black pepper
1 tablespoon chopped parsley

Put the flour on a sheet of waxed paper, add fish and coat lightly with flour on both sides, shaking off excess. Heat 4 tablespoons butter and the oil in a large, heavy skillet and when hot but not smoking, add the fish and cook them for half the estimated cooking time over medium-high heat, then turn and cook for the remainder of the time on the other side. Salt and pepper to taste as they cook. Test the fish for doneness with a fork or toothpick—if they flake easily, they are done—and remove to a hot platter. Add the rest of the butter to the pan, swirl it around until it melts, add the chopped parsley, and pour the sauce over the fish. Serve at once with lemon wedges and plain boiled potatoes. A white wine such as a Muscadet from the Loire or a Pinot Chardonnay is good with sautéed trout.

## Variations

♦ Vary the flavoring by adding chopped dill, chives, or tarragon to the pan.

♦ SAUTEED TROUT AMANDINE. Sauté ½ to ¾ cup thinly sliced almonds (sold packaged) in 4 tablespoons butter in the pan in which the fish were cooked until delicately golden, shaking the pan several times and lightly salting the nuts as they cook. Spoon over the trout and serve immediately.

♦ SAUTEED TROUT WITH BLACK WALNUTS. This is an interesting change of flavor, if you can get these nuts. Add ½ cup coarsely chopped black walnuts to the pan in which the fish are being cooked for the last 3 minutes of cooking time. Remove the fish to a platter and spoon the walnuts, with additional melted butter and chopped parsley, over the trout. Do not have lemon with this version. Steamed buttered rice is a good complement.

# Sautéed Fish Steaks

Swordfish, salmon, and halibut steaks are excellent candidates for sautéing. Have the steaks cut about 1 to 1½ inches thick from the best, center part of the fish (if the fish is very large, divide the steaks in half before or after cooking) and allow one steak or half a steak, according to size, for each serving. Measure the fish at the thickest point and allow 10 minutes cooking time per inch.

For 2 large or 4 medium salmon or halibut steaks, heat 4 tablespoons (1/2 stick) unsalted butter and 1/4 cup oil in a large, heavy skillet until fat is hot but not smoking. Add the steaks and cook over medium-high heat for the allotted time, turning them once halfway during the cooking, until lightly browned on the outside. As for trout, serve with additional melted butter and chopped parsley, lemon wedges, and boiled or sautéed potatoes. If you prefer a sauce with the steaks, skip the melted butter and have a hollandaise or Béarnaise sauce (see pages 279 and 280).

# Fish Steaks Sauté Provençale

*This unusual* sauté provençale, *a variation on the simple sauté, is a good way to prepare almost any fish that can be cut into steaks—cod, swordfish, and snapper, as well as halibut and salmon.*

**Makes 4 servings**

3 tomatoes, peeled, seeded, and chopped
2 tablespoons unsalted butter
2 large or 4 medium halibut or salmon steaks
¼ cup flour
6 tablespoons olive oil
2 large garlic cloves, finely chopped
4 tablespoons chopped parsley
Salt, freshly ground black pepper
¼ cup white wine

Cook the tomatoes slowly in the butter until they are almost a paste, but with enough of the pieces left to give them texture—about 20 minutes.

Measure the fish steaks at the thickest point to estimate the cooking time (see page 128). Spread flour on waxed paper, add fish, and coat lightly on both sides, shaking off excess. Heat the oil in a large, heavy skillet until hot but not smoking, add the fish, and cook for half the estimated time. Turn the fish and add the garlic, shaking the pan gently. Then add 3 tablespoons chopped parsley, shaking the pan once more, and season the steaks with salt and pepper to taste. Cook for the rest of the time, then transfer the fish to a hot platter. Pour the wine into the pan and swirl it around. Pour the pan juices over the fish and garnish with the cooked tomatoes. Sprinkle with the remaining tablespoon of parsley and serve with lemon wedges. Drink a white wine—a Blanc de Blancs is a good choice.

# Sautéed Fish Fillets

In many parts of the country, fresh or frozen fillets are the main form of fish available in the markets. They may be sold under their varietal names, under the vague and all-encompassing term "fillets," or as "fillets of sole," which has come to mean any fish at all related to the flounder family. Sautéed fillets need very careful handling, constant attention, and a minimum of cooking. Some are so thin that they take barely more than 3 minutes. Cooking by measured thickness is vitally important here, for an overcooked fillet resembles nothing so much as well-seasoned cardboard.

If you are cooking frozen fillets from the frozen state, double the cooking time.

Fillets vary so much in size that it is hard to say whether to allot 1 or 2 per person. To be on the safe side, estimate approximately ⅓ to ½ pound of fish per serving. Flour the fillets lightly. In a heavy skillet heat 4 tablespoons (½ stick) unsalted butter and ¼ cup oil until the fat is hot but not smoking. Add the fillets and cook them until they are done, turning them once and taking great care to prevent them from breaking. Serve them with additional melted butter, chopped parsley, and lemon juice.

# Crab

## Soft-Shelled Crab Sauté Meunière

Soft-shelled crabs are delicious when cooked as a simple sauté meunière. These toothsome little morsels may be eaten whole, but first make sure that they have been cleaned by the market where you purchase them, which is usually the case. If you have to do it yourself, fold back the covering at the points of the back with a small, sharp-pointed knife and scrape out the spongy, fingery parts you find there. Then turn the crab over and remove the small apron on front. Allow 2 or 3 soft-shelled crabs per serving, according to size.

Lightly coat the soft-shelled crabs in flour and sauté them on both sides in 1 tablespoon unsalted butter per crab. Season them with salt and pepper as they cook, allowing about 3 to 4 minutes a side. When crisp and done, sprinkle them with chopped parsley and serve with lemon wedges.

## ❧ Sautéed Crabmeat

*Crabmeat, which is bought ready-cooked and needs only heating through, is one of those foods that can be sautéed at the table in a chafing dish or any similar portable cooking unit as easily as in the kitchen, which makes it a good choice for a small party or a tête-à-tête dinner.*

**Makes 4 first-course, 2 main-course servings**

¼ cup clarified butter (see page 344)
4 very thin slices of French bread
4 very thin slices of lemon
1½ cups lump or leg crabmeat
2 tablespoons lemon juice
2 tablespoons cognac
⅓ cup fish stock or bottled clam juice

Heat the clarified butter in a sauté pan, skillet, or blazer pan of a chafing dish, add the slices of French bread, and sauté on both sides until golden and crisp. Transfer them to heated plates.

Put the lemon slices in the pan and heat through in the butter (add more butter if the bread has absorbed it all), then transfer them to the plates with the fried bread croutons.

Add the crabmeat to the pan and toss

⅓ cup white wine
2 tablespoons each: chopped
   parsley and chopped chives
1 teaspoon salt
Freshly ground black pepper
2 tablespoons shredded raw
   carrot
Additional chopped parsley
   (about 1 tablespoon)

lightly in the butter, sprinkle with the lemon juice; heat the cognac in a small pan to release the fumes of alcohol, then touch a match to it and pour flaming over the crab. Shake until the flames die, then pour in the stock and wine and let the mixture simmer gently until the crabmeat is just heated through—do not overcook it. Add the chopped parsley and chives, salt, several grinds of pepper, and a few shreds of carrot. Spoon the mixture onto the croutons and garnish with additional shredded carrot and chopped parsley. Serve with hot French bread and butter, and drink a California Pinot Chardonnay.

# Eggs and Omelets

As I mentioned before, scrambled eggs are really sautéed eggs and as with other delicate sautés, you must take great care not to overcook them—the important thing is knowing the point at which to stop, for the eggs will go on cooking with their own internal heat after they are removed from the stove. People have different ways of making scrambled eggs, but I have gotten the best results by using a small, 9-inch, Teflon-coated omelet pan for from 2 to 4 eggs and a 10-inch skillet for larger quantities. I recommend that you start with the smaller quantity as it is easier to control.

## ❧ Perfect Scrambled Eggs

Makes 1 serving

2 eggs
Salt, freshly ground black
   pepper
1 or 2 dashes of Tabasco
1 teaspoon water (for lighter
   scrambled eggs)
2 tablespoons butter (plus
   extra softened butter for
   richer eggs)

Break the eggs into a bowl, add salt, pepper, and Tabasco, and beat lightly with a fork. For lighter scrambled eggs, also beat in the water. If you like your scrambled eggs thick and eggy, don't use any water.

Melt the butter (a tablespoon for each egg) in a Teflon-coated skillet over medium-high heat and when hot but not sizzling, pour in the eggs. As soon as the eggs begin to coagulate, start making pushing strokes with a rubber or wooden spatula so you get curds.

Lift the pan off the heat from side to side with a circular motion while you push. As the heat in the eggs increases, the curds will form faster and you will have to keep lifting the pan from the heat and pushing faster. When the curds are soft but not too runny, quickly transfer the eggs to a plate. You have to know exactly when to stop applying heat or the eggs will be overcooked, hard little lumps.

If you want very rich eggs, sometimes called "buttered eggs," as you push the curds in the pan add small pieces of softened butter, which will melt in and make the eggs taste even more luscious.

If you are adding chopped herbs, sliced sautéed mushrooms, chopped sautéed scallions, or grated cheese, lace them in as you scramble the eggs.

For finely cut ham or smoked salmon, heat gently in the butter before adding and scrambling the eggs.

# ❧ A Perfect Omelet

Making an omelet requires deftness, speed, plenty of practice, and a pan 9 inches in diameter, with rounded sides and a heavy bottom that will hold the heat. If you use a cast-aluminum or cast-iron pan, it must be used only for omelets and never washed on the inside, merely wiped out with a damp cloth, or the omelet will stick. Should it stick, rub the pan with a sprinkling of coarse (kosher) salt and a paper towel to remove the residue, then rub with a drop or two of oil and a clean paper towel.

However, after many years of omelet-making I have come to the conclusion that the best pan to use is one with a Teflon lining, to which the egg will never stick, no matter how often you wash the pan or use it for other things.

My favorite omelet pan is made of Teflon-lined cast aluminum, 9 inches in diameter, sloping to a heavy bottom 6 inches across. Only the bottom is heavy; the pan itself is light enough to lift and shake with one hand. In this pan it is possible to make an omelet without using any kind of tool—all you need to do is shake the pan vigorously and the eggs will move around and start to set of their own accord.

Don't worry if you can't make a perfect omelet at first. This is a technique you acquire by constant practice and by learning to judge the point when the omelet has set just enough and can be rolled and tipped out. The whole process takes only about 30 seconds, so you can make as many omelets as you need in practically no time. Always make your omelets individually. It's much more difficult, and not very satisfactory, to make a huge one in a big pan and then divide it up.

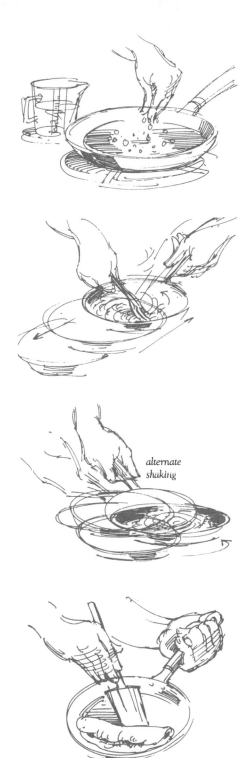

alternate
shaking

*2 very large or 3 small eggs*
*Scant ½ teaspoon salt*
*Pinch of pepper*
    *Or dash of Tabasco*
*1 tablespoon water*
*1 tablespoon butter*

Break the eggs into a bowl, add the seasonings and water, and beat lightly with a fork—don't overbeat, only enough to blend yolks and whites.

Heat your omelet pan over high heat until a drop of water bounces when flicked onto the surface. Add the butter and swirl it around until it melts and foams, which will happen almost immediately if the pan is the right heat. If it browns or burns, the pan is too hot. Remove it from the heat, wipe out the butter with paper towels, swing the pan in the air a little to cool it, and start again.

When the butter stops foaming, quickly pour in the eggs and, shaking the pan with one hand so it moves over the heat, stir the eggs lightly with a fork as if you were making scrambled eggs. (If you use a Teflon-coated pan, use a wooden spatula, not any sort of metal tool, or just shake the pan which will move the eggs around enough.) When the eggs have set to the degree you like (I like mine French style, still creamy in the center, but you may prefer yours a little more set), start rolling the omelet with the fork or spatula, at the end of the pan near the handle. If you are adding a filling, do this before starting to roll. Tip the pan forward so the omelet rolls onto itself.

Now reverse your grip on the handle, holding it from underneath, hold a plate close to the pan with your other hand, and start to invert the pan, which will tip the omelet onto the plate in a neat roll, with the edges underneath and a lovely smooth surface on top. Serve immediately. Omelets can't wait.

If you are making more than one omelet, wipe the pan with paper towels after each one, reheat, and add fresh butter to the pan.

## OMELET FILLINGS

One-third cup of any of the following, freshly cooked or reheated, may be added to the omelet just before it is rolled, and any excess spooned over the top before serving:

- ◆ Sliced mushrooms, sautéed or creamed
- ◆ Creamed chicken or chicken hash
- ◆ Creamed dried beef
- ◆ Buttered green vegetables, such as pieces of asparagus, broccoli, spinach
- ◆ Creamed fish
- ◆ Crumbled crisp bacon
- ◆ Thin strips of ham, frizzled in butter
- ◆ Ripe tomatoes, peeled, seeded, chopped, and sautéed
- ◆ Sautéed lamb kidneys, cut into small pieces
- ◆ Croutons of bread, fried in olive oil, with or without garlic
- ◆ Sautéed sliced onions
- ◆ Or use any other mixture of your choice, provided it is hot. Grated cheese (2 to 3 tablespoons) should be added just before the eggs are set, so it can melt. Herbs, such as finely chopped chives, parsley, and chervil for an omelet fines herbes, or finely chopped watercress should be mixed into the eggs before they are cooked. Use 1 tablespoon fresh herbs.

# Vegetables

If you have never tasted a sautéed vegetable, you're missing something. Like the Chinese stir-frying technique (which it closely resembles), sautéing keeps the crispness and flavor of vegetables intact. Certain vegetables, such as mushrooms, thinly sliced carrots, zucchini, onions, green peppers, and corn kernels, which lend themselves to this fast technique, need no prior cooking. Firmer vegetables, such as turnips, potatoes, cauliflower, Brussels sprouts, green beans, and broccoli, need to be parboiled or blanched first until tender but still crisp.

## Buttered Brussels Sprouts

*Brussels sprouts, members of the cabbage family, are underrated because they are usually very badly cooked to a mushy tastelessness with little or no character. Sautéing keeps them crisp and interesting.*

**Makes 4 servings**

2 pints Brussels sprouts of
   roughly equal size
6 tablespoons butter
½ teaspoon freshly ground
   black pepper
Several drops of lemon juice

Trim the sprouts, being careful not to cut away too much of the stem end. Remove discolored outer leaves. Put them in a 2-quart saucepan with enough boiling, salted water to come one-third of the way up the pan, bring to a boil, and blanch, covered, for 5 minutes, until barely cooked through. Drain well.

Melt the butter in another pan, add the sprouts, and cook, covered, shaking the pan well, for 3 to 4 minutes. Season with the pepper and lemon juice. These are good with broiled or roast meats.

### Variations

♦ Sauté ½ cup thinly sliced almonds in 2 tablespoons butter and add to the sprouts.

♦ Combine sprouts with an equal quantity of whole, cooked, peeled chestnuts, heated in butter and seasoned to taste, and a few pieces of crumbled crisp bacon.

# Carrots Vichy

*I'm sure the reason most of us shun carrots is that they are prepared so indifferently in restaurants—boiled to death and combined with canned peas or dressed with a mere sliver of butter. As a result they have no trace of flavor. This classic way of cooking them is certainly a change for the better.*

**Makes 4 servings**

2 pounds fairly small carrots
1 teaspoon salt
4 tablespoons (½ stick) butter
¼ cup water
½ teaspoon sugar
¼ teaspoon marjoram
1 tablespoon chopped parsley
¼ cup heavy cream (optional)

Scrape the carrots and cut them into very thin rounds. Put them in a saucepan with the salt, butter, and water and cook, covered, over medium heat, shaking the pan from time to time and making sure the carrots do not brown or cook too fast, until they are just tender when pierced with the point of a small, sharp knife. Add the sugar and marjoram and toss well, then sprinkle the carrots with parsley and serve. If you like, add the cream to the carrots just before sprinkling them with parsley.

# Sautéed Cauliflower

*Cauliflower is another vegetable that tends to be rather dull and uninspiring. Sautéed to buttery crispness, cauliflower has a flavor that is so different you'll find it hard to know what you're eating.*

**Makes 6 servings**

1 very large cauliflower
  Or 2 medium cauliflowers
12 tablespoons (1½ sticks)
  butter
Salt, freshly ground black
  pepper
1 teaspoon lemon juice

Parboil the cauliflower in boiling, salted water to cover for 4 to 6 minutes. Drain well and slice very thin or chop rather coarse—the center may not even be warmed through, but don't worry about that. Melt the butter in a large heavy skillet and when foaming, add the cauliflower and toss it well over very, very low heat for a few minutes until it has absorbed almost all the butter. Season to taste with salt, pepper, and lemon juice.

# Celery in Butter

*When celery is boiled and dressed with butter it loses all its lovely flavor and becomes something best forgotten. Perhaps this is the reason that most people eat only raw celery and never know how delightful it can be when quickly sautéed.*

**Makes 4 servings**

1 large head of celery, cleaned
   and trimmed
6 tablespoons butter
1 teaspoon salt
½ teaspoon freshly ground
   black pepper

Cut the celery head into thin slices. Heat the butter in a heavy saucepan, add the celery, season with the salt and pepper, and cook, covered, tossing from time to time with a fork, until just tender, about 5 to 6 minutes. Taste, add more salt and pepper if needed, and serve with roast pork or lamb.


# Sautéed Mushrooms with Turnips

**Makes 6 servings**

½ pound mushrooms
6 medium turnips
8 tablespoons (1 stick) butter
Salt, freshly ground black
   pepper
1 tablespoon chopped parsley

Wipe the mushrooms with a damp cloth and slice them lengthwise, through cap and stem, ¼ inch thick. Peel the turnips and slice ¼ inch thick. Parboil the sliced turnips in boiling salted water to cover for 8 to 12 minutes, watching them carefully to see they do not overcook—they should be tender but still crisp. Drain them well, add 3 tablespoons butter and ¼ teaspoon freshly ground pepper, and keep warm over low heat.

    Melt the remaining butter in a skillet, add the mushrooms, and sauté them quickly over fairly high heat, tossing them in the pan and seasoning them as they cook with ½ teaspoon salt and ¼ teaspoon pepper. Combine the turnips with the mushrooms and cook them together, shaking the skillet gently to mix them, for 2 minutes. Transfer to a heated serving dish and sprinkle with parsley. Serve with roasted, broiled, or braised meats, or with duck or game.

# Sautéed Potatoes

*This version of sautéed potatoes is made with potatoes boiled in their skins, which hold them together.*

**Makes 4 to 6 servings**

2 to 2½ pounds potatoes
6 tablespoons butter
1 teaspoon salt
Freshly ground black pepper
1 tablespoon chopped parsley

Boil the potatoes in their skins in salted water to cover until they are just tender when pierced with a knife, about 20 minutes. Drain, and when cool enough to handle, slice them into rounds about ¼ inch thick.

Heat the butter in a heavy skillet until foaming. Add the potatoes and sauté them over medium-high heat until they begin to brown. Turn them carefully with a spatula and cook until browned on the other side. Season them with salt and a few grinds of pepper, carefully transfer to a heated serving dish, and sprinkle with chopped parsley.

## Variation

◆ LYONNAISE POTATOES. Melt 4 tablespoons (½ stick) butter in a skillet, add 4 medium onions, sliced, and sauté over medium heat, turning them frequently, for 10 minutes. Add 1 teaspoon sugar and salt to taste, cover, and cook for 4 or 5 minutes more, until soft. Add the onions to the sautéed and seasoned potatoes and toss the two vegetables together lightly until well blended. Transfer to a heated serving dish and sprinkle with parsley.

# Sautéed Spinach

**Makes 4 servings**

2 pounds fresh spinach, well washed
4 tablespoons olive or peanut oil
1 garlic clove, finely chopped
2 tablespoons soy sauce
½ teaspoon freshly ground black pepper
¼ teaspoon nutmeg

Remove the heavy stems from the spinach, put it in a heavy pan with just the water clinging to the leaves, cover, and boil over high heat until it is wilted down but not cooked, about 2 minutes. Pour off any liquid.

In a skillet heat the oil with the garlic, add the drained spinach, soy sauce, pepper, and nutmeg, and toss them well for 2 or 3 minutes. Taste and add salt if necessary—it probably won't be, as the soy sauce is salty.

# Sautéed Endives with Brown Butter

*Endive, with its tight white head, is another salad green that is traditionally braised and served as a vegetable with roast meats, poultry, or game. In this recipe, browned butter is used as a sauce.*

**Makes 6 servings**

6 endives
14 tablespoons (1¾ sticks)
   unsalted butter
Juice of ½ lemon
Salt, freshly ground black
   pepper to taste

Because endives are specially blanched and packed, they do not require washing. Just trim off a little of the root end, remove any discolored or broken outer leaves, and wipe with a damp cloth.

Melt 6 tablespoons (¾ stick) of the butter in a skillet or saucepan, add the endives in a single layer, and sauté them on all sides over medium-high heat until lightly colored. Reduce the heat, cover the pan, and cook the endives for about 10 minutes, then turn them over and cook, covered, until just tender and pierceable, about 30 to 40 minutes.

To prepare the brown butter, warm the remaining stick of butter over medium heat in a small, heavy skillet, shaking the skillet from time to time, until the butter turns a deep brown-tinged gold. Do not let it burn and get dark.

Arrange the cooked endives on a hot platter or serving dish and sprinkle them with the lemon juice and salt and pepper to taste. Spoon the brown butter over them and serve at once.

# Glazed Turnips

*These are a classic accompaniment to roast duck. Often they are basted at the last minute with some of the pan juices from the duck.*

**Makes 4 servings**

6 to 8 small white turnips
8 tablespoons (1 stick) butter
1 teaspoon salt
1 teaspoon or more sugar

Peel the turnips and with a very sharp knife shape each into two ovals about the size of a walnut but slightly longer—you should get two or more ovals from each turnip.

Heat the butter in a heavy skillet, until foaming, add the turnips, sprinkle them with salt, and cook very slowly over medium-low heat, shaking the pan and turning them often, for about 10 minutes. Sprinkle with 1 teaspoon sugar, shake the pan, and keep cooking and turning the turnips until they are lightly glazed and tender but still crisp. For a heavier glaze, add a little more sugar. Serve with roast duck, goose, or venison.

# Shredded, Sautéed Zucchini

*Zucchini carry a lot of water, and if you are going to sauté them you have to get rid of some of that water first. A very popular way to cook zucchini now is to shred it, squeeze out the water, and then sauté it quickly in butter.*

**Makes 4 servings**

6 medium zucchini (about
　3 pounds)
4 tablespoons butter
　Or 2 tablespoons butter
　and 2 tablespoons olive oil
2 garlic cloves, peeled and
　chopped
　Or 2 tablespoons finely
　chopped shallots
¼ teaspoon dried basil
　Or 2 teaspoons chopped
　fresh basil (optional)
Salt, freshly ground black
　pepper

Wash the zucchini and slice off the stem end and the brown part of the blossom end. Dry. Shred the zucchini, using the coarse side of a grater, a Mouli-julienne with shredding disk, or a food processor with the larger shredding attachment. Put them in a heavy dish towel and twist the towel to squeeze the excess water from the zucchini.

Melt the butter, or oil and butter, add the zucchini and garlic or shallots, and sauté over moderately high heat, turning with a spatula and shaking and tossing in the pan, until tender but not soft and mushy. Do not allow to brown. While sautéing, season with salt and pepper to taste and, if desired, basil.

# Sautéed Zucchini with Walnuts

**Makes 6 servings**

6 medium-small zucchini
3 tablespoons butter
3 tablespoons olive oil
1 garlic clove, unpeeled
Salt, freshly ground black
　pepper
1 cup coarsely chopped
　walnuts
1 tablespoon chopped parsley

Clean and trim the zucchini as in previous recipe. Cut into ¼-inch slices. Put them in a colander, sprinkle with salt to draw out the water, and leave for an hour to drain. Rinse the slices and dry them.

Heat 2 tablespoons butter and the oil in a heavy skillet or sauté pan and when foaming, add the zucchini and garlic clove and sauté, shaking the pan constantly, until the slices are tender but still crisp. (The unpeeled garlic clove gives a little touch of flavor; discard it after cooking.) While cooking, taste a slice to see if it needs additional salt. If so, salt while tossing and give the slices a few grinds of pepper.

Add ¾ cup of the walnuts to the zucchini, shake the pan to blend them together, and heat the nuts through. Transfer to a heated vegetable dish, add the remaining tablespoon of butter and ¼ cup walnuts, and garnish with parsley. This is excellent with roast lamb or with poultry.

# Three-Vegetable Sauté

*Recently I have been experimenting with vegetable dishes and I've come up with some interesting combinations and techniques. One is a mixture of thin strips of rutabaga (the large yellow turnip), white turnips, and peeled broccoli stalks, a part of the vegetable that has a delicious flavor all its own and is all too often thrown away. The vegetables are blanched and then very quickly sautéed.*

**Makes 4 servings**

1 rutabaga
3 small white turnips
Heavy stems from a bunch of
 broccoli
6 tablespoons butter
Salt, freshly ground black
 pepper

Peel and slice the rutabaga and white turnips and cut them into julienne strips of matchstick thickness about 3 or 4 inches long (yellow turnips are rather hard to slice, so use a heavy chef's knife or a Chinese cleaver). Carefully peel the broccoli stalks, using a vegetable peeler or a small, sharp paring knife, and cut them into julienne strips of the same size and thickness as the turnips. You should have about 1½ cups of each vegetable. Combine the three vegetables and drop them into a pan of boiling, salted water. When the water comes back to the boil, let them blanch for 1 minute only. Then immediately drain them and plunge them into cold water to stop their cooking (you can do this blanching an hour or two ahead of the time you are going to cook the sauté). Drain and dry well.

When you are almost ready to serve, melt the butter in a heavy skillet or sauté pan that has a cover. Just toss the vegetables in the hot butter until heated through, the way you would toss a salad, then cover them and cook for a minute or two—no longer. They should not be cooked until soft and limp; they must retain their color and be just crisply tender. Season with salt and pepper to taste and, if you feel they need it, melt a little more butter in the pan and pour it over them.

## Variation

♦ Instead of using turnips and broccoli stems, cut carrots and zucchini into strips of the same size and thickness, blanch them in the same way, and then toss in the butter and cook until just crisp and tender.

# Fruit

Sautéing is an easy and delicious way to prepare firm fruits, such as apples, pears, and pineapples.

♦ SAUTEED APPLE RINGS. Wash and core but do not peel apples and cut crosswise in ½-inch slices. Sauté in hot unsalted butter (allowing about 1 tablespoon for every 2 slices) until brown on both sides, but not mushy. Serve with pork dishes, or with ham and sausage for breakfast.

♦ GLAZED APPLE RINGS. Cook as above but sprinkle the rings as they cook with a little sugar and let it blend with the butter to glaze the apples slightly.

♦ SAUTEED PEARS. Peel, core, and quarter ripe but firm pears. Sauté them in hot butter (about 1 tablespoon per pear), sprinkling them with a little sugar as they cook so they glaze slightly. Cook only until lightly glazed, not until they get mushy or break up. Serve with a little pear brandy (*eau-de-vie de poire*) poured over them.

♦ SAUTEED PINEAPPLE. Sauté slices or fingers of fresh pineapple in hot butter (1 tablespoon per slice, or per two fingers). After turning the slices or fingers, sprinkle them with brown sugar so they glaze slightly. Serve plain or flavored with a little dark rum.

♦ BANANAS A L'ARCHESTRATE. Slice bananas very thin and sauté them in hot butter (1 tablespoon per banana) over a high flame, tossing them well and sprinkling them with 1 tablespoon sugar per banana, until they brown, caramelize, and get crispy. Flame with warmed cognac (1 tablespoon per banana) and serve spooned over vanilla ice cream—the hot bananas and the frigid ice cream make a sensational dessert.

# Frying

$F$rying is a very much misunderstood word. People tend to assume that any food cooked in a frying pan or skillet is fried. It isn't. It is sautéed, or pan-fried, which means that it is cooked in a minimum of fat.

To fry means to immerse completely in deep fat raised to a high temperature so that the entire surface of the food is quickly seared and becomes brown and crisp. Foods are fried in different ways, for different reasons. Some, like potatoes, are fried in their natural raw state, others are dipped in flour or batter, or first coated with flour, then dipped in egg, and finally in bread or cracker crumbs.

In these calorie-conscious days, deep-frying has gotten a bad name. People are prone to think of fried foods as being greasy and fattening, but if they are fried correctly, there will be minimum absorption of fat. The most important thing to remember is that the heat must be kept at the right frying temperature and allowed to reheat to that temperature between batches, so that the surface of the food is immediately sealed by the hot fat. Once fried, the food should be removed to paper towels to drain off any excess fat on the outside and then put in a low-temperature oven to keep warm until the rest of the food is fried and ready to serve. If you remember these simple rules, you'll have perfectly cooked food every time, not a soggy, grease-soaked disaster.

When we think of deep-frying, the first thing that comes to mind is the French fried potato, which you'll find (often abbreviated Fr. fr.) on the menus of luncheonettes, fast-food chains, and small restaurants all over the country. While good French fries can be very good indeed, unfortunately they have become so universal and universally bad that they are one of the curses of the American diet. Pity the poor potato, cut into thick chunks, soaked in cold water, dried, then rudely thrust into a cauldron of hot fat without any care as to the accuracy of temperature or timing, so it emerges limp and soggy on the outside and hard in the center. That needn't be so. If you follow my recipe for perfect French fries on page 205, you'll know how good this crisp little morsel can be.

While French fries have no coating of any kind, other vegetables, French fried zucchini, for example, may be lightly dusted with flour to give them a nice brown coating. Or, like French fried onion rings, they may be dipped in batter. Batter forms a light, crisp, puffy envelope for delicate things such as fruits, fish, vegetables, and tender little chunks of sweetbreads or brains and a protective insulation that prevents them from overcooking and becoming hard and inedible. Breading, where the food is first lightly coated with flour, then dipped in beaten egg and finally in crumbs, is another kind of insulation. As the coating meets the hot fat it creates a quick, crunchy, golden-brown crust, keeping the food inside tender or creamy.

*P*roperly fried food can be sublime. Just think of *beignets soufflés*, those little fritters of cream puff dough that puff up and expand in the hot fat to an ethereal lightness, delicate batter-coated tempura, the Japanese version of French-frying, and the very similar Italian *fritto misto* (or mixed fry) where pieces of fish or meat or vegetable are dipped into batter and deep-fried to a delicious crunchiness. I first encountered *fritto misto* at an Italian trattoria in London that I used to frequent when I lived there as a young man. The chef understood what frying should be. His *fritto misto* of early vegetables—tiny green beans, artichoke bottoms, small pieces of carrot, potato, and onion-dipped in batter and quickly and expertly cooked, was an inspiring example of this much maligned and misused technique.

Our forefathers, of course, were great exponents of cooking in deep fat. One of the staples of their diet was fried cakes of all kinds—crullers, doughnuts, and so on. Later, as they began to make bread from yeast, setting the dough to rise overnight in rooms that were much cooler than ours are today, chunks of the risen dough would be broken off in the morning, dropped into hot fat to puff and brown, then consumed for breakfast with maple syrup. There used to be a small inn on Nantucket that for many years kept this tradition going, serving "dough gobs," as they were called, two or three days a week. How homely, simple, and delectable they were! Then we all know cake doughnuts, doughnut holes, and those luscious jelly doughnuts made from bread dough that one bites into and encounters the hidden sweetness of jam or jelly—innocent, unpretentious food, but wonderfully exciting to the palate.

At a later period in our food history came croquettes, the elegant type of fried food considered proper for ladies' luncheons. These were made from ground poultry, meat, or fish bound together with a very heavy white sauce, seasoned, shaped into balls or ovals, coated with flour, egg, and crumbs, and cooked in hot fat until golden brown. Croquettes were usually served with a sauce, green peas, and sometimes (showing an unfortunate lack of judgment) another fried food—potato chips, or Saratoga chips as they were called because they were said to have originated in Saratoga, the unwitting invention of a chef who sliced his fried potatoes too thin and ended up with crispy chips.

All kinds of fats can be used for frying. In the early days of this country, many recipes called for lard, which, like rendered beef fat, gives very good flavor. Some people use solid vegetable shortening, which I don't happen to like. Nowadays oil, mainly peanut oil, corn oil, and cottonseed oil, is the preferred fat for frying because it is colorless, odorless, and can be heated to quite high temperatures without burning or darkening. Personally, my preference is for peanut oil, which I use almost exclusively because it satisfies my frying requirements better than any other.

Oil can be used over and over, provided you strain it after every use and now and then clarify and purify it by frying in it a few pieces of raw potato, which collect those little burned bits that get left behind. Discard it when it gets very dark or starts to smell rancid. Never be skimpy with the oil you use for frying and never overcrowd the pan. There should be enough oil comfortably to cover whatever is being fried and space for the food to move around.

The first requisite is a deep fryer. You can take your choice of an electric deep fryer with a thermostatic control; the traditional wide, deep pan designed for deep-frying that has a basket that fits into the pan and hooks on to the side handles to drain; any deep, heavy 4- or 5-quart pot, such as a Dutch oven; or an electric skillet. With a nonelectric pan you'll also need a deep-frying thermometer and, if you are using an electric skillet or a pan without a frying basket, something to fish the fried food out with, such as a slotted spoon, a wire skimmer, or one of the flat, mesh skimmer-lifters the Japanese use for tempura—anything, in fact, that will simultaneously lift and drain the food. For batter-fried foods, you'll also need tongs for dipping the foods in the batter and lowering them into the fat.

While there's no denying that deep-frying is a messy job that smells up the kitchen and one that needs care and attention if you are to get worthwhile results, it does have advantages. It is the fastest of all cooking techniques, and once you have acquired the skill and a sense of timing, you'll be able to turn out a meal in no time flat and serve the food immediately, crisp, hot, and deliciously tasty.

# ❧ Fried Zucchini

*This is one of the simplest and very best fried dishes I know—quick, easy, and delicious.*

*You need a good deep fryer (see introduction and illustrations, page 193). Be sure to check the oil temperature, remembering to let the fat heat between batches as the addition of cold food will cool it off. If you're using a frying basket, heat it in the fat first; otherwise it, too, will cool the fat. You should also keep at your side a baking sheet lined with paper towels on which the fried zucchini can drain and keep warm in the oven. Preheat the oven to 250° before you begin frying.*

**Makes 6 servings**

6 to 8 small, firm zucchini
Salt, freshly ground black
   pepper
Peanut oil for deep-frying
¼ cup flour

Wash and dry the zucchini and cut off the ends. Cut in half lengthwise and then into long strips of matchstick thickness. Place these sticks in a colander over a bowl, sprinkle with about 1 tablespoon salt, cover with a piece of waxed paper or foil, and allow to stand for 1 hour or more. This salting draws some of the liquid from the zucchini and results in quicker cooking and a better texture.

When you are ready to fry, put the oil in the deep fryer. Fill it no more than half full—fat foams up when food is added. If the fryer is electric, set the thermostat for 370°. If you are using a pot on a surface burner, have a deep-frying thermometer handy to test the temperature. Heat the frying basket in the oil. (If you don't have a frying basket, you can drop the zucchini pieces directly into the fat and remove them with a wire skimmer or slotted spoon, but with a basket you can remove all the fried zucchini at once and there is no risk of any getting overcooked.)

While the oil is heating, drain the zucchini sticks, first tasting one. If it is very salty, rinse the sticks briefly with cold water to remove the salt. Toss the zucchini, salted or rinsed, on paper or linen towels to dry them thoroughly.

Then remove to paper towels and dust with the flour, sifting it over them and shaking them around until lightly coated.

When the oil reaches 370° transfer a handful of the zucchini sticks to the frying basket and immerse in the hot fat. There will be a sizzling and the fat will bubble up, so stand back or you may get splashed with hot oil. The zucchini will cook very, very quickly. In about 2 to 3 minutes they will brown lightly and become crisp. Immediately remove to the baking sheet lined with paper towels and taste one to see if they are cooked through. Keep them hot on the baking sheet in the warm oven. Before adding more zucchini to the oil, let the temperature return to 370°. When all the zucchini are fried, serve immediately, fresh and hot—they will not hold or freeze. Salt and pepper them just as they are served. If they are salted ahead of time they can turn soggy.

# Batter-Dipped Foods

##  Fried Shrimp

*Deep-fried shrimp are one of the most popular dishes in this country. They can be sheer delight—crisp, tender, greaseless, and flavorful—or they can be a soggy mess. The secret of these fried shrimp is the lightness and crispness of the beer batter which encases them—the yeast in the beer has a leavening effect on the batter. Make the batter ahead of the time you plan to fry the shrimp and let it rest, anywhere from 1 to 2 hours to overnight. This allows the ingredients to expand and amalgamate after the vigorous beating and the batter will be crisper for it.*

**Makes 4 servings**

1½ pounds of raw shrimp in the shell (these should be fairly good-sized)

BEER BATTER
¾ cup flour
2 eggs, separated
1½ teaspoons salt
2 tablespoons salad oil
¾ cup beer, at room temperature
Freshly ground black pepper
Oil for deep-frying

Wash the shrimp very carefully and dry on paper towels. Take a pair of sharp kitchen scissors and cut along the curved back of the shell toward the tail, then break off the body shell with your finger, leaving the tail shell on. Cover the cleaned and shelled shrimp with plastic wrap until ready to fry.

To make the batter, put the flour in a bowl and add the 2 egg yolks (the whites will be used later), the salt, the oil, the beer, and a grind or two of pepper. Starting in the center, stir clockwise with a wire whisk until well mixed and free of lumps. Cover the bowl with plastic wrap and allow to rest for at least 1 to 2 hours or overnight. Then stir the batter. In a separate bowl beat the 2 egg whites with a wire whisk until stiff but not dry and very gently fold them into the batter.

Preheat the oven to 250°. Line a baking sheet with paper towels and put it near the stove. Half fill the deep fryer with oil and heat it to 375°.

Put the shrimp, one at a time, on a small ladle or large spoon and dip them into the batter so that they become completely coated, then lower them into the hot fat. Cook about 4 or 5, not more than 6, at a time—the batter expands in the fat and besides you don't want to lower the temperature too much. It will take about 3 to 4 minutes for the shrimp to brown and cook through.

As the shrimp are fried, lift them out in the basket or with a flat mesh skimmer (which can also be used to skim any stray pieces of batter from the fat) and let them drain and keep warm on the baking sheet in the oven.

Serve at once with either a tartare sauce (see page 283) or a Béarnaise sauce (see page 280), or merely with mayonnaise and wedges of lemon. These may be served as a first course, as a cocktail tidbit, or as a main course. For a main course, you could have coleslaw with them, which you will find on page 296.

# Fritto Misto

*Although it is not traditional for fritto misto, I like to use beer batter—and prepare it several hours ahead; it gives such a light, crisp finish to the food. The following version, made with tender meats, organ meats, and vegetables, is one I have used with great success.*

**Makes 6 to 8 servings**

*Double recipe beer batter*
*(see page 197)*
*1 pair sweetbreads*
*1 pair calf's brains*
*2 or 3 firm zucchini*
*1 teaspoon salt*
*1 tablespoon lemon juice*
*½ pound veal scaloppine*
*½ pound calf's liver*
*1 whole chicken breast,*
*skinned and boned*
*2 veal kidneys*
*1 cauliflower*
*Or 1 bunch broccoli*
*Oil for deep-frying*
*Flour*
*4 lemons, quartered in wedges*

Make the beer batter and leave it in the refrigerator for 3 to 4 hours. (Do not add beaten egg whites until just before using.) Meanwhile, prepare the sweetbreads, brains, and zucchini. First soak the sweetbreads and brains in ice water for 30 minutes. Peel off as much as possible of the covering membranes and dark thin veins from the brains.

Trim the zucchini, cut into ½-inch strips, and put in a colander. Sprinkle with salt, as for French fried zucchini, and set aside for about 1 hour to let the bitter juices drain out.

Put the sweetbreads and brains into a pan with 4 cups water, 1 teaspoon salt, and 1 tablespoon lemon juice. Bring to a boil; reduce the heat and simmer for 10 minutes. Drain and immediately plunge the sweetbreads and brains into cold water to stop them from cooking. When cool enough to handle, drain and dry, then remove any remaining membrane, connecting tubes, and fat on the sweetbreads. Cut sweetbreads, brains, veal, liver, and chicken breast into 1½-inch pieces. Skin the kidneys; make a slit in the top and remove the hard core of fat and tubes, then cut into 1½-inch pieces.

Wash the cauliflower or broccoli. Remove the flower heads, discarding the thick stalks of the cauliflower (the thick broccoli stems may be removed, reserved, then peeled, cut into julienne strips, and sautéed with other vegetables, as in the recipe on page 191). Break the heads of the cauliflower or broccoli into small flowerets; put in a pan; cover with lightly salted water; bring to a boil and boil for 3 minutes. Drain and plunge into cold water to stop them from cooking. Dry the parboiled flowerets well.

When ready to fry, remove the batter from the refrigerator; mix lightly with a wooden spatula, as some of the flour may have sunk to the bottom, then beat the egg whites until stiff but not dry with a wire whisk or an electric hand mixer and fold lightly into the batter. Preheat the oven to 250°.

Put enough oil in a deep fryer to half fill it. Heat to 375°. Have ready two baking sheets lined with paper towels.

Dust the pieces of meat and chicken lightly with flour to prevent moisture or juices from seeping out. Dip the meats into the batter and turn until well coated. Lift them out with tongs; hold over the bowl for a moment to let excess batter drip off, then drop them into the hot oil, no more than 6 pieces at a time. Fry, turning them once or twice with tongs, until golden brown, about 4 minutes, then remove to the paper-lined baking sheets to drain and keep warm in the oven. After frying the meats, dip the zucchini and flowerets into the batter and fry for 3 minutes.

Arrange the *fritto misto* on a platter lined with a plain white napkin and serve with wedges of lemon.

## French Fried Onion Rings

Makes 4 servings

3 *large yellow onions, peeled*
*Ice water*

BATTER
1 *egg, beaten*
1 *cup buttermilk*
1 *cup all-purpose flour*
½ *teaspoon salt*
½ *teaspoon baking powder*
*Oil for deep-frying*

Slice the onions about ¼ inch thick, separate them into rings, and soak in ice water for 2 hours. Drain and dry thoroughly on paper towels.

To make the batter, mix the egg and buttermilk and then whisk in the flour, which has been sifted with the salt and baking powder, until smooth.

Heat the fat to 375° in a deep fryer; dip the onion rings into the batter and fry in the hot fat, a few at a time, until brown and crisp, about 4 to 5 minutes. Drain well on paper towels.

# ❧ Fruit Fritters

*These are the dessert equivalent of the batter-dipped shrimp, meat, and vegetables, and they make a light delicious end to a meal. If you want a sauce for the fritters, serve them with crème anglaise (page 277) flavored with 2 tablespoons of the spirit you used to marinate the fruit.*

**Makes 6 to 8 servings**

BATTER
*2 cups flour*
*2 eggs, beaten*
*2 tablespoons melted butter*
*Pinch of salt*
*1 cup light beer, at room temperature*
*1 tablespoon kirsch or cognac*

*Oil for deep-frying*
*Flavored fruit (for choices, see below)*
*1½ to 2 cups stale macaroon crumbs or spongecake crumbs*
*Superfine or confectioners' sugar*

Sift the flour into a bowl and combine with the eggs, butter, salt, and beer, beating with a wire whisk until smooth. Or whirl until smooth in an electric blender. Mix in the kirsch or cognac. Let the batter stand 2 to 3 hours or longer before using.

When you are ready to fry, stir the batter with a spatula in case the flour has sunk to the bottom of the bowl. Heat the oil in a deep fryer to 375°. Roll fruit in crumbs, then dip into the batter and lower into the hot fat with tongs, a few pieces at a time. Fry until golden brown on all sides, about 4 to 5 minutes. Remove; drain on paper towels and serve hot, dusted with sugar.

## Variations

♦ APRICOT FRITTERS. Drain 12 whole canned apricots. Marinate them in ⅓ cup kirsch for 1 hour. Roll in macaroon crumbs; dip in batter and fry.

♦ PINEAPPLE FRITTERS. Marinate 12 slices of canned, drained pineapple or fresh pineapple in ⅓ cup kirsch for 1 hour. Coat with macaroon crumbs; dip in batter and fry.

♦ PEAR FRITTERS. Poach 6 small, peeled, cored, and halved pears in syrup (see directions for poached peaches, page 54) until just tender when pierced with a fork. Drain. Marinate for 30 minutes in kirsch or, preferably, *eau-de-vie de poire*. Coat with cake crumbs, pressing them in firmly; dip in batter and fry.

♦ APPLE FRITTERS. Peel, core, and quarter 4 apples and poach gently in syrup (see directions for poached peaches, page 54) until barely cooked through, not soft or mushy. Drain. Marinate for 30 minutes in applejack. Coat with cake crumbs; dip in batter and fry.

# Breaded Foods

## Shrimp and Dill Croquettes

Croquettes are mixtures of finely chopped or ground meat, poultry, fish, and vegetables, seasoned and bound together with a very thick white sauce, then shaped into balls, cylinders, or cones, rolled in fine bread crumbs and egg, and fried. The coating should cover the food completely, to protect it during the cooking and keep it soft and creamy and to prevent the fat from penetrating the interior and causing the croquette to burst open during the frying. Croquette mixtures are usually chilled, which makes them easier to shape and handle, and often chilled after coating, to help the coating adhere. Before frying, allow them to warm up at room temperature for an hour, or the inside may still be cold when the croquette is removed from the oil.

The trick in frying croquettes is to have the fat hot enough to form a quick, sealing crust immediately, keeping the inside moist.

While I seldom serve croquettes as a main dish, I find they do make very tasty little cocktail appetizers, or a simple first course.

**Makes 4 to 6 appetizer or first-course servings**

3 tablespoons olive oil
½ cup finely chopped onion
3 garlic cloves, finely chopped
3 tablespoons finely chopped green pepper
3 tablespoons finely chopped celery
½ cup peeled, seeded, and finely chopped tomato
3 tablespoons chopped almonds
⅓ cup finely chopped dill
¼ teaspoon dried oregano
Salt, freshly ground black pepper
3 slices white bread, crusts removed
½ cup light cream
2 tablespoons butter
¼ cup flour
¾ cup warm milk
2 cups coarsely ground cooked shrimp

Heat the olive oil in a skillet; add the onion and garlic and sauté over medium heat until limp and golden. Add the green pepper, celery, and tomato and sauté about 10 minutes, until softened. Stir in the almonds, dill, and oregano; taste, and add as much salt and pepper as the mixture needs. Remove from the heat.

Soak the bread in the cream until soft; then squeeze dry and add to the mixture in the skillet, mixing together well.

Melt the butter in a saucepan; add the flour and cook, stirring, over medium heat until smooth, golden, and bubbling. Slowly mix in the warm milk, stirring continuously so the sauce does not lump, then cook slowly, stirring, for 10 minutes or until the sauce is smooth and very thick. Remove from the heat and mix in the onion mixture, shrimp, and sherry. Taste again and add salt and pepper if needed.

Spread the croquette mixture evenly in a flat baking dish and chill for 45 minutes, until firm enough to handle. Take large spoonfuls of the mixture and roll between the palms of your

1 tablespoon dry sherry
2½ to 3 cups fine dry bread
    crumbs
2 eggs, beaten
Oil for deep-frying

hands into balls about 1½ inches in diameter. Have the bread crumbs and eggs in separate pie plates. Dip the balls first in the bread crumbs, completely covering the surface, then in the egg, and then again in the bread crumbs, making sure the surface is completely coated.

Chill for 30 minutes, then leave at room temperature for 1 hour before frying.

Preheat the oven to 250°. Heat the oil to 375°; drop in the croquettes, no more than 6 at a time, and fry until golden brown, about 3 minutes. You may use a frying basket or remove them with a skimmer. Remove and drain on paper towels and keep warm in a 250° oven until all are cooked, then serve immediately.

## ❧ Fried Fish

To deep-fry fish properly, without letting it get overly brown and overly cooked, is no mean task. It takes care and accurate timing. The fish should be no more than lightly browned. Overcooked fish may look beautifully brown and appetizing, but it will prove to be dry and dreary eating. Either fish fillets or cleaned small, whole fish, such as smelt, skinned small catfish, and small whiting (with the backbone removed), can be fried. They may be first dipped in flour, beaten egg and cream and rolled in crumbs, or fillets can be dipped in the beer batter, like shrimp. Measure the fish at the thickest point to determine the cooking time (10 minutes per measured inch).

First, see that the fish is thoroughly dry. Dredge it with flour, dip it into beaten egg and cream (in the ratio of 1 egg to 1 tablespoon cream), and then roll it in crumbs—bread crumbs, cereal or cracker crumbs, and cornmeal are all suitable. Completely cover the fish with the crumbs, pressing them in well. Heat the oil in the deep fryer to 370° or 375°.

Lower the fish, a few pieces at a time, into the hot fat, using a slotted spoon, and cook for 10 minutes per measured inch (see page 113). Immediately remove the fish to paper towels and drain. Season with salt and pepper. Let the fat return to the correct frying temperature between batches. Serve at once on a hot platter with a sprinkling of chopped parsley and wedges or slices of lemon or lime—the last gives a fine and rather different flavor. Accompanying the fish with boiled or straw potatoes (see page 206), fried parsley, and a tartar, rémoulade, or mustard sauce.

### FRIED PARSLEY
Wash and dry 1 bunch of parsley. Be sure it is thoroughly dry before frying or the fat will splatter. Remove the heavy stalks from the sprigs and drop them, a handful at a time, into 365° oil. Step back as you do so, as the oil will hiss and

sputter. When crisp, which happens almost immediately, in about 2 seconds, remove at once with a wire skimmer and drain on paper towels. The parsley should be crispy but not shriveled.

# Chicken Kiev

*The Russian specialty called chicken Kiev has become very popular in this country. The essence of the dish is that the boned chicken is rolled around a finger of butter so that when the chicken is cut into, the hot butter spurts out. The trick lies in having the butter frozen, so it doesn't ooze out during the frying, and the chicken very cold. Chicken Kiev is made with just the boned breast, as a general rule, but I like to leave the wing bone on, which forms a little handle. I also like to flavor the butter with chopped garlic and herbs, which make it much more flavorful, if not traditional.*

**Makes 6 servings**

6 tablespoons butter
2 garlic cloves, peeled and
   very finely chopped
1 tablespoon chopped parsley
1 tablespoon chopped fresh basil
   Or 1 teaspoon dried basil
3 whole chicken breasts, with
   the wings on
1 cup flour
2 eggs, beaten
1 to 1½ cups fine bread crumbs
Oil for deep-frying

Blend the butter with the garlic and herbs, either by beating them together with a wooden spatula or by putting everything in the food processor and processing until thoroughly mixed. Divide the seasoned butter into 6 equal pieces; shape them into long, tapered fingers and put in the freezer, covered with plastic wrap, until frozen hard.

Cut off the chicken wing tips, leaving the wing bone on. Skin and bone each breast (see page 167 for technique) and cut in half lengthwise, so you have 6 half breasts. Remove the meat about halfway up the wing bone, to make a little handle. Put the chicken breasts between sheets of waxed paper and flatten with a meat pounder (see page 137), pushing down and outward as you pound. Be careful not to hit the bone or sever it from the breast. The chicken must be very thin, almost transparent. Put a finger of frozen butter in the center of each pounded breast (on the inner, not the skin, surface) and roll the chicken around it, tucking in the ends, so the rolled-up breast makes a neat sausage-shaped package. The butter must be completely sealed in so that it cannot leak out during the cooking.

Dip the rolled breasts in flour, then in beaten egg, and finally roll in bread crumbs. Arrange on a cookie sheet covered with waxed paper; cover with plastic wrap and chill in the refrigerator for at least 4 hours. Or make them the day before you plan to serve them and chill until ready to fry.

Heat the oil in a deep fryer to 370°. Fry the chicken rolls, 2 or 3 at a time, until golden brown, about 4 minutes. Drain on paper towels; put a paper frill on each wing bone and serve immediately.

# Wiener Schnitzel (Deep-Fried Veal Scallops)

*The famous Viennese dish of Wiener schnitzel is one of the few examples of deep-fried veal scallops, tender morsels which are more often sautéed. There is another version, in which the veal is sautéed in butter, but this one is better known.*

**Makes 4 to 6 servings**

*1 cup flour seasoned with
    2 teaspoons salt and
    ½ teaspoon freshly ground
    black pepper
1½ to 2 cups fine, dry bread
    crumbs
2 eggs, lightly beaten
Oil for deep-frying
12 large veal scallops (about
    1½ pounds), pounded thin
Lemon slices, chopped parsley*

Put the seasoned flour on one sheet of waxed paper, the bread crumbs on another, and the beaten egg in a baking dish. Dip each scallop into the flour, then into the beaten egg, and finally into the bread crumbs. Arrange between sheets of waxed paper on a cookie sheet and refrigerate for 20 minutes.

Either heat oil to 370° in a deep fryer, or heat 2 inches of oil to 370° in a deep skillet or electric skillet. When hot, fry the scallops quickly, 2 at a time, until golden brown on both sides, about 2 to 3 minutes. Remove and drain on paper towels, then arrange on a hot platter. Serve garnished with lemon slices and chopped parsley.

## Variation

♦ Serve each person 1 large scallop topped with a fried egg, an anchovy fillet, and a slice of lemon.

# French Fried Eggplant

**Makes 4 servings**

*1½ pounds of eggplant
Oil for deep-frying
¾ cup flour
2 to 3 eggs, lightly beaten
2 cups fine bread crumbs
Salt, freshly ground black
    pepper*

Peel the eggplant. Cut into slices about ¾ inch thick, then cut each slice into strips ¾ inch wide.

Heat the oil in a deep fryer to 380°. Dip each eggplant strip first into flour, then into the beaten egg, and finally into the crumbs. Fry, a few strips at a time, in the hot fat until golden brown, about 4 minutes. Recheck the heat of the fat after frying each batch.

As the eggplant strips cook, remove to drain on a baking sheet lined with paper towels and keep warm in a 250° oven until all are fried. Then season to taste with salt and pepper.

# Uncoated Foods

## ❧ Perfect French Fries

*For making French fries, some like the mealy Idaho potato, others the waxier boiling potato. Either one will work, but you might, to amuse yourself, fry different types of potato, such as the long white California, the Idaho, and the Maine and decide which you like best.*

**Makes 4 servings**

4 medium-to-large Idaho, Maine, or California potatoes

Peanut oil or rendered beef fat for deep-frying

Potatoes are best if peeled and cut just before you fry them. If you can't do that, put the cut potatoes into a bowl of cold water, take them out just before frying, spread them out on a double layer of paper towels or a terry towel, and dry thoroughly.

Peel the potatoes and cut them into long strips from ¼ to ½ inch wide and thick. Have ready a baking sheet lined with paper towels. Heat the fat in a deep fryer to 325° and, if you are using a basket, heat the basket in the fat. See that the potatoes are completely dry; lift out the basket; toss a handful of the potatoes into it and lower them slowly into the hot fat. Cook for 5 to 6 minutes, or until they get rather flabby-looking. They should not brown. During the cooking, lift the basket and shake the potatoes around once or twice to prevent them from sticking together.

Remove the potatoes as they are cooked to a baking sheet lined with paper towels and leave at room temperature from 1 to 1½ hours, until you are ready to do your second frying. Then reheat the fat and basket to 375° or 380°; toss the prefried potatoes back into the hot fat, a handful at a time; and fry for 2 or 3 minutes, or until they are as brown as you prefer. Be sure to bring the fat back to the correct temperature after each batch. Keep warm in a 250° oven, on lined baking sheets.

Season your French fries with salt and freshly ground black pepper just before serving.

## Variations

♦ SHOESTRING POTATOES. Slice the potatoes thinner than for French fried potatoes and cut into long strips about as thick as a kitchen matchstick. Fry in deep fat heated to 375° for only 1 minute, until crisp and browned. Season and serve. (These are fried only once.)

♦ SLICED OR WAFFLE-CUT POTATOES. Slice the peeled potatoes about ⅛ inch thick, using a special vegetable slicer, such as a mandoline, which has plain and waffle-cut blades. Fry once only, in 375° fat, for 2 to 3 minutes.

♦ WEDGES. Cut the potatoes into wedges, either peeled or with the well-scrubbed skins left on. You should get about 8 wedges from an Idaho, 6 from a regular boiling potato, and 4 from a small potato. Fry once, in 375° fat, for 8 to 10 minutes.

♦ CUBES. Peel the potatoes and cut into ½-inch cubes. Fry once, in 375° fat, for 5 to 6 minutes.

# Straw Potatoes (Pommes Paille)

*These are tiny, julienne-cut potatoes, which come out crisp, golden, and very thin.*

**Makes 4 servings**

Peel and slice 4 or 5 large potatoes and cut the slices into very fine julienne strips, about ⅛ inch thick. If you can, use a food processor with a fine shredding attachment, or the fine shredding disk of the vegetable slicer called a Mouli-julienne.

Heat oil in deep fryer to 365° or 370°; plunge the potato strips, a handful or two at a time, into the oil; and fry very briefly, less than a minute, until just golden and crisp. Remove with a skimmer, drain on paper towels, sprinkle with salt, and serve very hot.

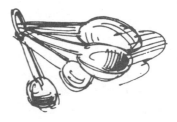

# Beignets Soufflés (Soufflé Fritters)

Beignets *are simply tablespoons of sweetened and flavored cream puff dough* (pâte à choux) *fried in deep hot fat until they rise into air-filled puffs—the eggs in the dough are the leavening agent. This most versatile dough can also be baked (for cream puffs).*

**Makes 6 servings**

8 tablespoons (1 stick) unsalted butter, cut into pieces
1 cup water
⅛ teaspoon salt
½ teaspoon sugar
1 cup all-purpose flour
4 eggs
2 tablespoons rum or brandy
Oil for deep-frying
Confectioners' sugar

Combine the butter, water, salt, and sugar in a heavy 2-quart saucepan and heat over medium heat until the butter is melted and the water boiling. Remove the pan from the heat; dump in the flour all at once and beat vigorously with a wooden spatula until well blended. Put the pan over medium heat and beat the mixture with the spatula for about 1 minute, or until the mixture forms a mass that clings to the spatula and comes away from the sides and bottom of the pan.

Remove the pan from the heat and leave for 5 to 6 minutes (or, if you have an electric mixer, transfer the dough to the bowl of the mixer and put on the paddle attachment). The dough should have time to settle before the eggs are added.

Make a well in the center of the dough with the spatula; drop in one egg and beat into the dough until thoroughly absorbed. Beat in the other eggs in the same way, one at a time, until the dough is smooth and glossy and the eggs completely absorbed. When adding the last egg, also beat in the rum or brandy. If you use an electric mixer, add the eggs one at a time, first at low speed, then, as the eggs become absorbed, at high speed. Beat only until dough is smooth and glossy—it should not be overbeaten.

Heat the oil in a deep fryer with a basket to 370°. Drop the dough into the hot oil by tablespoons, a few at a time, and fry for about 4 minutes or just until the *beignets* puff up and brown. When one side browns, the *beignets* will turn themselves over. Drain on paper towels and sprinkle lightly with confectioners' sugar, sifted over them through a fine sieve. Serve immediately with a sauce of raspberry purée (page 311) or crème anglaise (page 277).

*Note.* Cream puff dough is best used as soon as it is made. If you have to keep it, put it in a bowl and cover the bowl tightly with plastic wrap. If you store it in the refrigerator, remove and allow to come to room temperature 2 hours before using.

# Raised Doughnuts

*These are made with a yeast dough, which gives them a lovely lightness.*

2 tablespoons warm water
  (110° 115°)
½ package active dry yeast
½ cup granulated sugar
1 egg
1 cup warm milk
3 tablespoons melted butter
3¾ cups sifted all-purpose
  flour
Peanut oil, vegetable
  shortening, or lard for
  deep-frying
1 cup confectioners' sugar or
  superfine sugar for coating
  doughnuts

Warm water from the hot-water faucet can be used. Draw it off into a measuring cup and test the temperature with your meat thermometer; it should be between 110° and 115°. If the water is too hot it will kill the yeast, if too cool, the yeast will not proof properly.

Put the 2 tablespoons of warm water and the yeast into a large mixing bowl and stir. Add 2 teaspoons of the sugar and mix well. Leave for 10 to 15 minutes to give the yeast time to proof (become frothy and bubbly).

Using your hands or two wooden spoons, stir in the egg, milk, 2 tablespoons melted butter, the remaining sugar, and finally the flour. Continue to stir until the dough seems springy. Brush the top of the dough lightly with remaining melted butter and cover with waxed paper or foil. Place in a warm, draft-free spot (or in an oven heated only by the pilot light) to rise until doubled in bulk, about 1½ hours. Or you may put the dough in the refrigerator overnight, where it will rise very slowly.

When risen, punch the dough down by hitting it with your fist—this deflates it. Turn it out onto a floured board. Divide in half. Roll out half the dough at one time to a thickness of ½ inch. Cut into doughnut shapes with a floured doughnut cutter and place them on a board or cookie sheets covered with waxed paper to rise until doubled in bulk, about 45 minutes to an hour.

Heat 4 inches of oil, shortening, or lard in a deep fryer, or an electric skillet to 370°. Put in the doughnuts, a few at a time, top sides down. Fry about half a minute, until brown on one side, then turn them with a skimmer and brown on the other side for half a minute. When nicely browned, remove and drain on paper towels. Be sure that the fat returns to the correct frying temperature after each batch or the doughnuts will absorb too much fat and become soggy.

While still warm, put the doughnuts in a large paper or plastic bag with the sugar and shake gently until coated. Serve warm.

# Baking

One of the most vivid memories of my childhood is reading the story of King Alfred and how, during a lull in the battle, he sat by the fire in a peasant's hut watching the cakes that were being baked on hot stones. History tells us that he let the cakes burn, which proves he was no cook, but somehow this mental picture of that historic figure brooding over the cakes has always fascinated me. Who knows—it may well have influenced my choice of a career.

Nowadays baking is generally assumed to mean cooking in the oven, but that's only the half of it. We bake crêpes in a pan; we bake English muffins or scones on a griddle or, as the Scots like to call it, a girdle. Our many flat breads and pancakes are reminders that we baked over heat before ovens were ever thought of. Mexican tortillas, Indian poori, the Chinese pancakes one has with Peking duck are griddle foods with a long and honorable history. Much later, when ovens came into existence, they were very chancy affairs—great caverns of brick built into the side of the fireplace into which hot coals were put and raked out when the oven had reached the required heat. The only way of testing the temperature was to put your hand inside and count up to a given number—and then the heat was apt to drop in the middle of baking and ruin whatever you were cooking.

Baking is many-faceted. If you stop to think, you realize that you use the oven many times during the day for a widely varied range of foods. For breakfast, you may make muffins, heat coffeecake, bake shirred eggs. Later, you may bake bread or cakes, prepare a casserole or a stuffed fish for dinner, a pie, a soufflé, or a baked custard. It's all so easy with our modern temperature-regulated ovens equipped with timers and thermostats, well insulated, and even, glory be, self-cleaning. Of course, even with automatic controls, we still have to learn the right temperatures for various foods. We find out that puff pastry bakes best if started at rather high heat, then finished at a lower heat. We learn that some breads require high heat and that the majority of casseroles, vegetable dishes, and fruit dishes bake best at a moderate temperature of around 350°. Unlike surface cooking, you can't adjust quickly as you go along; you have to determine the degree of heat you will need beforehand.

What completely revolutionized baking as we know it was the discovery of leavening, in which heat combines with a rising agent, such as eggs, egg whites, yeast, baking powder, or baking soda, to make the food rise and expand. I wonder who first hit upon the miraculous leavening power of the egg? Long before baking powder was envisioned, the génoise and the other classic risen cakes depended for their lightness on eggs. Many of our cakes are entirely leavened by eggs. Some, like heavy, rich poundcake, are leavened with whole eggs, beaten in one by one. For the génoise, whole eggs are beaten over heat, so they partially cook as the sugar is beaten in, and this initial beating gives the cake its magical lightness and unmatched flavor and texture. Then there is the angel food cake, leavened with whites alone, and other cakes in which the yolks and whites are added separately, at different stages.

One of the most spectacular examples of the leavening power of the egg is the soufflé, where the yolks go into the basic sauce mixture and the whites, beaten until light and firm and folded in at the last minute, elevate the solid mass to a light puffy cloud with an almost ethereal texture.

Then there is that other kitchen miracle—yeast—which has played a vital part in baking since the time of the ancient Egyptians. Our ancestors made their own yeast, using formulas that were part of their heritage. Until standard commercial yeast was introduced at the end of the nineteenth century, yeast was made from many things, among them potatoes, corn, and hops. We still cleave to one of these—the sourdough of the pioneers, a yeast made from flour, water, sugar, salt, and sometimes milk, which, as it ferments, gathers wild yeast cells from the air.

Finally came the artificial leaveners like baking powder and baking soda. These gave rise to a whole new range of quick breads and baking-powder biscuits, which puffed and baked quickly at high temperatures and came out crisp on the outside, soft and rather crumbly inside. Quick breads, hot breads, muffins and biscuits and waffles, baked on a special iron, became the fashion all over the country and our roster of cakes was increased by light, fluffy baking-powder cakes that rose faster than, and had a texture completely different from, the poundcake or génoise.

Baking is one of the most versatile cooking techniques we have—almost unlimited in its uses. Consider for a minute some of the forms it can take. For a start, let's take that old New England dish, baked beans, one of the simplest of all baked dishes. The beans, prepared on Saturday night for Sunday dinner, were placed in a crock with salt pork, onion, maple syrup or brown sugar and baked in the oven at a low, steady temperature overnight, sometimes for as long as 12 hours, until all the flavors had melded together. There are many peasant dishes from Europe that are made this way. One is the incomparable *tripes à la mode de Caen*, in which tripe, onions, garlic, and white wine or cider are baked for 12 to 14 hours at a very low temperature in a pot sealed with a flour-and-water paste to lock in the steam and aromatic flavors. The longer it bakes, the more lip-smacking it becomes. Our modern crock-pot cookery is just a new-fangled version of this very old technique.

The casseroles that have become such a familiar part of the American way of cooking are another type of baked dish. Casseroles have been rather looked down on in the last few years, probably because at one point we suffered through a proliferation of all kinds of bastardized versions made with canned soups and other canned ingredients and revoltingly topped with crushed cornflakes or potato chips. Despite these lapses, casserole-cooking still remains one of the simplest and most satisfactory ways of turning out a good meal with a minimum of effort, or of using up leftovers that accumulate in the refrigerator. After all, when you come to think about it, all kinds of baked things, from stuffed vegetables to molded and scalloped foods and gratins, are really casseroles. The only difference is the container and the name.

Next we have a loaf of good, honest homemade bread, baked at a high temperature that makes the bread rise and expand, sometimes to one-third more than the size at which it went into the oven, and browns and crisps the outside to a delicious crust.

Then there is the custard, baked in a dish or pan of hot water with damp rather than dry heat. The warm water creates a buffer of moisture around the delicate custard, allowing it to bake slowly to a firm creaminess without curdling or breaking down. The quiche, custard baked in a pastry shell, needs no such protection. The insulation of the pastry, the shallowness of the mixture, and the speed of the cooking are sufficient.

So while baking is one of the oldest of all cooking processes, it is also one of the most complex and scientific. In baking, you have to learn the rules and go by them.

## ᴥ Baked Potatoes

The simplest of all baking recipes, and one that illustrates perfectly the importance of the correct oven heat, is the baked potato. The potato bakes best at a high temperature, from 400° to 450°, and it should be the mealy Idaho type. With this type of potato, which is different from the waxier potatoes used for boiling, the starch expands under the intense heat and the potato becomes fluffy on the inside, with a nice crisp skin.

Preheat the oven to 425°. Scrub the skin of the potato well and either make a very thin slit around the center of the skin with a sharp knife or prick it in two or three places with a fork. This gives the steam an escape route and prevents the skin from bursting during baking.

Put the potato on the oven rack in the center of the preheated oven. Bake for 1½ hours. Then cover your hand with a cloth or pot holder and gently squeeze the potato. If it feels soft and gives, it is baked. If not, give it a little while longer. Naturally, larger potatoes take longer to bake. When the potato feels soft, remove it from the oven and slit it open across the top at once to release the steam inside and keep the texture beautifully mealy and not soggy. Serve at once. Baked potatoes don't like to wait.

To savor a properly baked potato, don't gulp it up immediately with butter or sour cream. Just sprinkle it with salt and coarsely ground black pepper and the full taste and texture will come through. It should have a good potatoey flavor, a mealy texture, and a lovely earthy smell. If it is soggy and unpalatable, either it didn't bake long enough or you didn't let the steam escape properly.

### Variations

♦ Add butter to taste with the salt and pepper.

♦ Add sour cream and chopped chives or crisp, crumbled bacon to taste with the salt and pepper.

♦ STUFFED BAKED POTATO. Halve the baked potato lengthwise and scoop out the pulp into a hot bowl. For each baked potato, add 1 teaspoon salt,

1 teaspoon freshly ground black pepper, 1 tablespoon grated Cheddar or Gruyère cheese, and 1½ teaspoons light or heavy cream. Blend well, then heap back into the shells; dot each half with 1½ teaspoons butter cut into small pieces and sprinkle the tops with a little grated Parmesan cheese. Return to the oven to bake at 375° until the tops are nicely browned, about 15 minutes. These stuffed baked potatoes are excellent with roasted or broiled meats, but rather rich, so you need serve nothing more than a simple green salad.

## Potatoes Anna

*Potatoes Anna, a French dish that has become quite the vogue in this country, represents yet another way of baking potatoes. Sliced thin and well lubricated with butter, they form a kind of cake, crustily brown on the outside and meltingly tender inside.*

**Makes 6 servings**

6 medium Idaho potatoes
About ½ pound (2 sticks)
  butter, melted
Salt, freshly ground black
  pepper

Peel the potatoes and slice them into very thin, even rounds, ⅛ inch thick. You can do this more easily if you use a vegetable slicer with an adjustable blade. As the potatoes are sliced, drop them into a large bowl of salted ice water until ready to use.

When ready to cook, preheat the oven to 400°.

The best thing to use for baking is a heavy 8-inch cast-iron skillet, 2 inches deep. Lacking this, use a deep 8-inch round pie dish or baking dish of the same dimensions. Brush the bottom and sides of the skillet heavily with melted butter. Drain the potatoes and dry them thoroughly on clean cloth or paper towels. They must be completely dry, as excess moisture would ruin the dish. Arrange a layer of potatoes in the bottom of the skillet: put one slice in the center and arrange overlapping circles of potatoes around it, from center to sides. Sprinkle the potatoes very lightly with salt and pepper and spoon a tablespoon or two of melted butter over them.

Continue to make layers of potatoes, seasoning each layer and spooning butter over it, until the pan is filled. Spoon another tablespoon or two of butter over the top.

Put the skillet or dish on the center shelf of the oven and a baking sheet on the shelf below it to catch any butter that might bubble over. Bake for 30 to 45 minutes, until the potatoes are crisp and brown around the edges and tender when prodded with a fork or toothpick.

Remove the pan from the oven. Run a knife around the edge of the potatoes to loosen them. Put a large flat serving platter, big enough to hold the potato cake, on top of the pan and quickly invert it so the cake unmolds itself onto the platter. To serve, cut into wedges. Serve potatoes Anna with steak, roast meats, or chicken.


# ❧ Crêpes

In my classes, I always start the students off with crêpes, because it is one of the most basic of cooking processes and demonstrates very graphically the change that takes place when a mixture is baked. The element of participation also brings the students together and they gain confidence from their newly found ability to make the batter, handle the pan, and turn out a perfect crêpe.

Until a year or two ago I always used the traditional French iron crêpe pan. In many ways, this pan is unbeatable. If it is properly seasoned and cared for, it will maintain a nice patina. You must never sink an iron crêpe pan in a bath of detergent or put it into the dishwasher. Merely rub it out with a little coarse salt and a paper towel if it should chance to stick, and keep it for crêpes alone. It will do yeoman duty for many years.

However, other types of pan are equally good for crêpes. Teflon-lined frying pans, which have become a regular part of our cooking lives in the last decade or so, work beautifully. They cannot take as intense a heat as iron and so do not heat or cook as fast, but I think they produce a tenderer, more supple crêpe. I find my Teflon-lined aluminum omelet pan is ideal. It matters not one whit how often you wash it, or how many other things you cook in it, so it saves adding yet another specialized utensil to your kitchen. I am also prone to turn a crêpe over by flipping it, and it will slide with the greatest of ease in a Teflon-lined pan. Of course, with Teflon you can't use a metal spatula; it must be one of wood or plastic. You should have no trouble with crêpes provided you use the right kind of pan, make a smooth batter, and practice until you have mastered the baking technique.

You need a pan about 8 to 9 inches in diameter with sides sloping to a bottom 6 inches in diameter, such as the French iron crêpe pan, the Teflon-lined omelet pan, or a heavy frying pan of similar shape and material. Other necessities are a medium-sized mixing bowl, a wire whisk (or an electric hand mixer or blender), a 2-ounce ladle or a ¼-cup dry measure (the kind that looks like a little pan and has a handle), a pastry brush, a small pan to hold the melted butter, and either a thin-bladed, supple metal spatula with a blade about 1 inch wide and 8 inches long for turning the crêpes or, if you are using a Teflon-lined pan, a spatula of wood or plastic.

The first step is to make the crêpe batter. If you can, make it 2 or 3 hours ahead of time and let it rest, which enables the flour to expand and absorb the liquid. A batter that has rested will work better than one that is freshly made.

## BATTER FOR 16 TO 18 6-INCH CRÊPES

3 eggs
⅛ teaspoon salt
1 to 1¼ cups milk or beer (use beer only for nonsweet or savory crêpes)
⅞ cup (1 cup less 2 tablespoons) all-purpose flour
4 to 5 tablespoons melted butter

## FOR DESSERT CRÊPES, ADD

3 tablespoons sugar
2 tablespoons cognac
  Or 1 tablespoon vanilla extract

Break the eggs into the mixing bowl and beat until smooth with the wire whisk. Mix in the salt and 1 cup of the milk or beer. Beer gives a nice lightness to the crêpes and the taste goes well with savory fillings, but for dessert crêpes milk is preferable. Blend well. Stir in the flour with the whisk and, still stirring, add 2 tablespoons of the melted butter. Beat well until the batter is smooth, free of lumps, and has the consistency of heavy cream. Depending upon the dryness of the weather and, therefore, the flour, you may need to add the remaining ¼ cup liquid, but wait until the flour is thoroughly mixed in and then judge. It is better to underestimate the amount of liquid. You can always mix in more later if your batter seems too thick. Often you find that the batter thickens considerably after it has rested and needs to be thinned with a little more liquid.

If you are making dessert crêpes, add the sugar to the batter with the flour and stir in the cognac or vanilla when the batter is mixed.

A quicker and easier way of making the batter is to use an electric hand mixer instead of a whisk, or put all the ingredients in the blender or food processor at one time and blend until smooth and well mixed.

Cover the bowl of batter with plastic wrap and let it rest at room temperature for 2 to 3 hours, or up to 12 hours in the refrigerator if you wish to make the batter well ahead of time.

When you are ready to bake the crêpes, assemble your equipment: a small pan containing the remaining melted butter, the pastry brush for brushing the crêpe pan, the crêpe pan, the ladle and spatula, a plate to put the crêpes on, and some paper towels for wiping out the pan should it get too hot and the butter brown. Uncover the batter and beat with the whisk, as the flour will have settled. If the batter is thicker than heavy cream, add a little extra liquid.

Put a metal crêpe pan on medium-high heat, or a Teflon-lined pan on medium heat. Let the pan get good and hot, then brush it with melted butter. The butter should sizzle but not brown or burn. If it does, the pan is too hot. Wipe it out with paper towels and cool it off by putting it on a cold burner or waving it in the air a few times. Then start again, reheating the pan and brushing it with butter.

The secret of a perfectly thin and tender crêpe is to use just enough batter to cover the bottom of the pan in a thin layer. When the butter sizzles, dip your ladle or measure into the batter and scoop up about 3 tablespoons, or a little less than ¼ cup.

Pour the batter into the pan with your left hand and, holding the handle of the pan with your right hand, raise the pan from the heat and tilt it so the batter quickly swirls around and runs over the bottom of the pan. If there is too much batter, pour the excess back into the bowl. If there is too little, and it does not completely cover the bottom of the pan, add a touch more.

Replace the pan on the heat and bake the crêpe for about 1 to 1½ minutes, until the surface is set and the crêpe moves slightly when you shake the pan. If you poured off excess batter, there will be a little tongue of crêpe on the side of the pan, which you should lop off with your spatula. Now turn the crêpe. There are various ways to do this.

You can run the spatula around the edges of the crêpe to loosen it, then slide the spatula underneath, and with a quick movement flip it over, using your hand if needed. Or, if you are a hardy soul, you can tip and shake the pan until

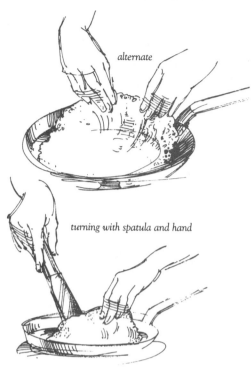

*alternate*

*turning with spatula and hand*

the crêpe hangs over the front edge a bit, then pick it up with your fingers and turn it over (if you do this quickly, you won't burn your fingers) or use a spatula and one hand. Or, if you can flip a pancake, shake the pan once or twice to loosen the crêpe and then give the pan a quick jerk so the crêpe flips over of its own accord. If the crêpe does not lie completely flat in the pan, pat it down with your fingers. I find the flipping or hand-turning methods are safer and more professional. With a spatula there is always the chance that you will break or cut the crêpe.

Return the pan to the heat to bake the second side, which will take only about half a minute, then turn the crêpe out by quickly inverting the pan over the plate. The second side will be less brown than the first side but that doesn't matter. This is the side on which you put the filling.

Continue to heat the pan, brush it with butter, and make crêpes until all the batter is gone. If you are using the crêpes right away, simply stack them on the plate. Should you wish to make them ahead of time, put waxed paper between the crêpes as you stack them and, when they are cool, cover the stack and the plate with plastic wrap and leave at room temperature or in the refrigerator until you are ready to use them. To store crêpes, put waxed paper between them, remove them from the plate when cool, wrap them in aluminum foil, and freeze them. If you have made batches of both sweet and savory crêpes, identify them by writing "sweet" or "savory" on the outside of the package so you don't get them mixed up.

It's a lot of fun to make crêpes. If you have never done it before, take some time to practice until you become deft at pouring in just the right amount of batter and turning the crêpes. Don't overbake crêpes or they will be crisp and difficult to roll. A crêpe should be rather pale and supple. If you are going to fill, roll, and sauce the crêpes, don't worry if every one is not impeccable, for they are still perfectly usable.

For a main course, allow 2 to 3 filled crêpes per serving. For a dessert or first course, allow 2 crêpes per serving.

# Chicken Crêpes

**Makes 4 to 6 servings**

2 cups white and dark meat
  from poached chicken, cut
  into ½-inch cubes
2 cups sauce suprême (page
  274), made with chicken
  broth
12 savory crêpes
¼ cup heavy cream
3 tablespoons grated
  Parmesan cheese

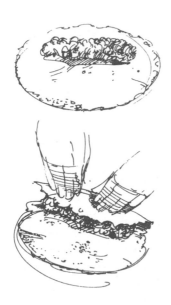

Mix the chicken cubes into the sauce and heat in a pan over very low heat until thoroughly warmed through. Do not overheat or the sauce will curdle. Rub an 8 x 11-inch baking dish with softened butter. Spread the crêpes flat on a board or the countertop, paler side up. Place about 2 tablespoons of the filling on each crêpe, fairly near the edge closest to you; roll the crêpe up carefully and place it in the buttered dish, seam side down. Continue until you have used up all the crêpes and most of the chicken mixture, pushing the crêpes close together so they don't unroll. Put the remaining chicken and sauce back on the heat, stir in the heavy cream, and let it warm through. Pour this over the rolled crêpes and sprinkle with the Parmesan cheese.

Just before you are ready to serve, preheat the oven to 375°. Put the dish on the center shelf of the oven and bake until the crêpes are heated through and the cheese melted, about 15 minutes. Serve the crêpes on hot plates, 2 or 3 per serving. As a main course, serve with a vegetable, such as broccoli, or a green salad and crisp French bread.

## Variations

♦ You can vary the fillings for the savory crêpes, using different combinations of poultry, meat, or fish and sauces. Some fillings you might use are cooked shrimp or crabmeat with the sauce suprême (made with milk or fish stock) or curry sauce; diced ham with the sauce suprême and a touch of sherry; sliced sautéed mushrooms and cubed cooked turkey with mornay sauce.

♦ QUICK CANNELLONI. Spread the crêpes with a thin layer of ricotta cheese; top with a tablespoon of poached, skinned, and shredded Italian sweet or hot sausages, a sprinkling of grated Parmesan cheese, and a little freshly ground black pepper. Roll up, and put into a baking dish. Cover the rolled crêpes with 1 cup tomato sauce, sprinkle with grated Parmesan cheese, and heat as above.

# Crêpes Directoire

*There are many different types of dessert crêpes, ranging from the simplest of all—crêpes spread with fruit preserves, rolled, placed in a buttered skillet, sprinkled lightly with sugar, and flamed with ½ cup warmed cognac or bourbon—to the ever-popular crêpes Suzette and crêpes soufflées, crêpes filled with a soufflé mixture and baked in the oven until the soufflé puffs up inside the crêpes. The following recipe is very easy and very good.*

**Makes 6 servings**

6 firm ripe bananas
12 dessert crêpes
2 tablespoons grated lemon zest (the yellow part of the rind)
½ cup kirsch
4 tablespoons sugar
4 tablespoons butter
Juice of 1 orange
Grated zest of 1 orange

Bake the bananas in their skins in a 350° oven for 20 to 25 minutes, until the skins are black. Split the skins, remove the bananas, and cut in half crosswise. Spread out the crêpes, pale side up, and arrange a half banana on each crêpe. Sprinkle each one with lemon zest and 1 teaspoon kirsch and roll up.

Melt 3 tablespoons of the sugar in a metal skillet over medium heat until it becomes caramelized, or brown and bubbly. Stir in 2 tablespoons of the kirsch and then the butter, stirring rapidly so the batter and kirsch blend with the caramelized sugar, then add the orange juice and zest and stir to make a smooth sauce. Arrange the banana-filled crêpes in the pan, seam side down, and spoon the sauce over them. Turn off the heat. Heat the remaining kirsch in a small pan. Sprinkle the crêpes with the remaining tablespoon of sugar, light the kirsch with a match, and pour it flaming over the crêpes. Shake the skillet until the flames die. Serve immediately.

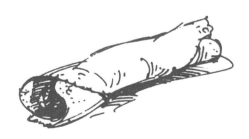

# Soufflés and Rolls

I have always said that the one thing that makes a soufflé fall is letting it know you are afraid of it. A soufflé is not the difficult, temperamental dish it is made out to be. I have let a completely mixed soufflé stand in the refrigerator for half an hour before putting it into the oven and I have even opened the oven door while it was baking without mishaps.

The secret of making a good soufflé lies in the egg whites. Provided they are beaten until they are full of little air bubbles and firm enough to stand in upright peaks, then folded into the soufflé base gently so that they do not lose that aeration, the soufflé will rise perfectly.

You may have been told that the only way to beat egg whites properly is in a large, unlined copper bowl with a big balloon whip. I don't agree. In my classes students beat the egg whites by hand in the copper bowl and by machine in the heavy-duty electric mixer and though there may be more initial expansion with the bowl and whip, it doesn't seem to make any noticeable difference in the volume of the finished soufflé. However, if you do beat egg whites in the mixer, or in any other noncopper bowl, you should add a pinch of cream of tartar to the egg whites when they have been beaten to the first, foamy stage. Cream of tartar supplies the acidity that unlined copper provides naturally, and it is this acidity that helps the whites to rise and to keep their stability after they have been beaten.

There are two other things to bear in mind if your beaten egg whites are to rise as they should. First, the whites should be at room temperature before beating. Second, there must not be so much as a speck of egg yolk in them, or any trace of grease on the bowl or beater.

To bake a soufflé, you don't have to invest in the classic, straight-sided porcelain soufflé dish, the kind that comes in sizes from 1 pint to 3 quarts. There are other types of dish or mold that will do just as well. In one class we made soufflés in twelve different containers and they all worked. Metal charlotte molds make superb soufflé dishes, and they have one very valuable attribute the classic type lacks—handles on the sides. You can lift them out of the oven easily by the handles, whereas a soufflé dish must be grasped awkwardly around the belly. Then there are the ovenproof glass soufflé dishes now on the market. To me, these are the ultimate in elegant containers, so beautiful to the eye. The thin glass conducts heat more rapidly than thicker porcelain, so if you use this kind of soufflé dish you should lower the oven temperature by 25 degrees. The straight-sided, square Corning Ware cooking pots are also excellent for soufflés.

It is my contention that tying a collar of waxed paper or aluminum foil around a soufflé dish is unnecessary, unless you have added so many extra egg whites that there is a danger the soufflé might rise to spectacular heights and topple over. The standard soufflé contains only one additional white and can be counted on to support itself without assistance.

If you have a suitable, straight-sided 1½-quart dish to bake a soufflé in, plus a 2-quart size for larger soufflés or those with more egg whites, you really don't need any other special equipment. For making the sauce you will use a 2- to 2½-quart saucepan, a wooden spatula, and a wire whisk. For separating the eggs, you will need a couple of small bowls. For beating the egg whites, you can use a copper bowl and balloon whip or an electric mixer, or a large bowl, about 10 inches in diameter, of stainless steel, plastic, or Pyrex plus a big whisk or an electric hand beater. For folding in the egg whites, you will need a broad rubber or plastic spatula.

The most basic of all soufflés is the one with a béchamel sauce base, into which the yolks, seasonings, and flavoring ingredients are mixed and the beaten egg whites folded. This is the type used for almost all savory soufflés and many dessert soufflés. I have chosen for our example a cheese soufflé, for others are merely variations, with different ingredients and flavorings.

## ❧ Cheese Soufflé
Makes 4 servings

FOR A 1½-QUART
(6-CUP) SOUFFLÉ DISH
OR MOLD
1 teaspoon butter
4 eggs
1 extra egg white
3 tablespoons butter
3 tablespoons flour
1 cup hot milk
1 teaspoon salt
¼ teaspoon freshly ground
   black pepper
Pinch of grated nutmeg
½ cup grated sharp Cheddar
   cheese
   Or 1 cup grated Parmesan
   cheese
   Or ¾ cup grated Emmenthaler
   or Gruyère cheese
   Or ¾ cup crumbled
   Roquefort cheese
⅛ teaspoon cream of tartar
   (optional)

With your fingers, grease the bottom and sides of a 1½-quart soufflé dish or mold with 1 teaspoon butter. This will help the soufflé to rise and give it a nice shiny crust.

There are four steps in making a soufflé: separating the eggs, making the béchamel sauce base and adding the yolks and flavorings, beating the egg whites, and folding the egg whites into the soufflé base.

Start by separating the eggs, which should be at room temperature. Have beside you two small bowls and the large bowl in which you will beat the egg whites. Crack the center of the egg on the rim of one small bowl so the shell divides neatly into halves. Hold the egg over the bowl and tip it back and forth between the halves of the shell so the white slips into the bowl, leaving the yolk in the shell. When all the white is in the bowl, tip the egg yolk into the second small bowl and transfer the white to the bowl in which you will beat the whites. This is a precautionary measure. If by mischance a yolk should break and part of it mingle with the white, you only have to discard one egg white, not a whole batch. Continue this process until all the egg yolks are in one small bowl and all the egg whites have been transferred to the large beating bowl.

There is a safer way to separate eggs, and you should at least try it once to get the feel of the separating. Break the eggshell and tip the whole egg into the palm of your hand. Let the egg white run between your slightly parted fingers into the small bowl. Your hand is softer than an eggshell and there is less chance of the yolk breaking.

You'll have one extra yolk in this recipe—don't throw it away after it has been separated from the extra egg white. Store it in the refrigerator in a small screw-topped jar and use it for mayonnaise or hollandaise.

With the eggs separated, turn your attention to the sauce. Make a thick béchamel sauce as directed on page 272. Melt the butter in the saucepan over medium-low heat; stir in the flour; cook the roux until frothy and then mix in the hot milk. Stir and cook until it comes to the boiling point and thickens to a rather stiff sauce consistency. Season with the salt, pepper, and nutmeg and remove from the heat. Stir the egg yolks into the sauce with a whisk or spatula until thoroughly mixed, and then mix in the cheese with the spatula.

Preheat the oven to 375°. Remove the two top racks. The soufflé will be baked in the center of the oven and needs room to rise.

If you are beating the egg whites by hand, use the large balloon whip. Beat with a vertical circular motion, at first fairly slowly and then, as the whites become foamy, more rapidly, so as to incorporate as much air as possible into the whites. If you are not using a copper bowl, add the cream of tartar when the whites are foamy. Continue to beat rapidly until the whites are thick and stiff enough to hold their shape when the beater is lifted—they should just droop over in soft peaks. Do not overbeat until they are dry and stand stiffly upright, as for a meringue. When a recipe directs you to beat egg whites until "stiff but not dry" or to the "soft-peak stage," this is what is meant. If you are using an electric mixer or electric hand beater, watch the whites carefully as it is very easy to overbeat them.

The beaten egg whites must be folded into the soufflé mixture immediately, before they have a chance to subside. With the rubber spatula take up about one-quarter of the whites and mix into the cheese-sauce mixture in the pan, which lightens the rather heavy soufflé base.

Then tip the lightened cheese mixture into the bowl of egg whites and, with your rubber spatula, fold the egg whites lightly into it. Cut down through the center of the mixture with the edge of the spatula, then draw it toward the side of the bowl; pull it up and over and then cut down again. Continue to fold very rapidly and lightly for about a minute, turning the bowl as you do so, just until the cheese sauce has mixed with the egg whites. Don't overfold, or the egg

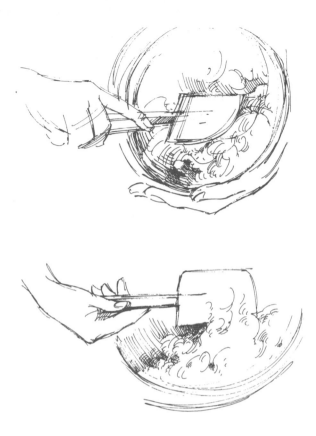

whites will deflate. There should still be little bits of unincorporated egg white visible. Immediately pour into the prepared soufflé dish and smooth the top with the rubber spatula. Put the dish in the center of the preheated oven and bake for 30 to 35 minutes, until the soufflé has risen about 2 inches above the rim of the dish and is browned on top. After 30 minutes the soufflé will be firm on the sides and still slightly creamy in the center. If you like a firmer center, bake the extra 5 minutes.

Serve the soufflé the minute you take it from the oven—soufflés can't wait. To serve, puncture the top of the soufflé with a serving spoon and fork, pull it gently apart, and spoon onto hot plates, giving each person some of the center and some of the crusty brown exterior. All you need with this is a green salad.

For a larger soufflé, to serve 6, use a 2-quart (8-cup) dish or mold. Increase the quantities to 4 tablespoons each of butter and flour, 1½ cups of milk, 6 egg yolks, 7 or 8 egg whites, and 1¼ cups of cheese or other ingredients. Also increase seasoning to taste, and increase cooking time to 35 to 45 minutes.

## Variations

♦ For a spicier cheese soufflé, add to the seasonings a dash or two of Tabasco and 1 tablespoon Dijon mustard or 1 teaspoon dry mustard (don't add mustard and Tabasco if using Roquefort, which has a very strong flavor).

♦ Instead of cheese, use ¾ cup of any of the following: finely ground chicken; finely ground ham plus 1 teaspoon dry mustard; well-drained puréed, cooked spinach plus 2 teaspoons grated onion; puréed, cooked broccoli; canned tuna, drained and flaked, plus 1 teaspoon lemon juice; poached, flaked finnan haddie; well-drained canned minced clams.

# Spinach Roll

*A roll is really a fallen soufflé baked flat in a jelly-roll pan, and, according to the mixture involved, may be either savory or sweet. The beaten egg whites cause the mixture to rise slightly during the baking, but after it is taken from the oven and turned out it quickly deflates. Rolls are delicate things and care must be taken not to break them when they are being rolled up. Spinach roll, filled with either creamed ham or scrambled eggs, makes an excellent brunch or luncheon dish.*

**Makes 8 servings**

## FOR PREPARING THE JELLY-ROLL PAN

1½ tablespoons butter
½ cup freshly made white bread crumbs

## FOR THE ROLL

3 pounds fresh spinach
  Or 3 packages frozen spinach
1 teaspoon salt
½ teaspoon freshly ground black pepper
¼ teaspoon grated nutmeg
6 tablespoons melted butter
4 eggs, separated
⅛ teaspoon cream of tartar (optional)
5 tablespoons grated Parmesan cheese

## FOR THE FILLING

1 teaspoon Dijon mustard
2 tablespoons Madeira
1 cup béchamel sauce (page 272) made with ham or chicken broth
½ cup heavy cream
2 cups diced boiled or baked ham

Butter a 15 x 11-inch jelly-roll pan, then line the pan with waxed paper, leaving an overhang of about 2 inches at each end. Butter the waxed paper heavily and sprinkle the surface with the bread crumbs. Preheat the oven to 350°.

If you are using fresh spinach, wash it well and remove the heavy stems. Put into a large pot with only the water clinging to the leaves; cover and cook over high heat until the leaves have wilted down, turning the top leaves to the bottom with tongs or a wooden spoon. When wilted, drain very well, pressing out as much water as possible, then chop very fine. If you use frozen spinach, thaw it in a pan over low heat, drain well, and chop fine.

Put the spinach in a bowl and mix in the salt, pepper, nutmeg, and melted butter. Beat in the 4 egg yolks, one by one, blending well. Beat the egg whites as for a soufflé, adding ⅛ teaspoon cream of tartar when they are at the foamy stage if you are not using a copper bowl.

Fold the stiffly beaten egg whites into the spinach mixture with a rubber spatula. It is not necessary to do this in two stages, and they should be more thoroughly incorporated than for a soufflé, with no bits of egg white showing. Do not overfold, however, or you will break down the air bubbles in the egg whites.

Spread the spinach mixture evenly in the prepared pan with a rubber spatula and sprinkle the top with 4 tablespoons of the grated cheese. Bake in the center of the oven for 15 to 16 minutes, or until the top feels just firm when touched, but not dry or hard. The roll will have come away from the sides of the pan. Remove from the oven.

Butter a large sheet of waxed paper or aluminum foil. Very quickly invert the pan onto the paper or foil so the roll falls onto it, top side down. Carefully peel off the waxed paper adhering to the roll, loosening it, if necessary, with a small, sharp knife. If some of the surface sticks to the paper it is not too important, as the filling will go on this side.

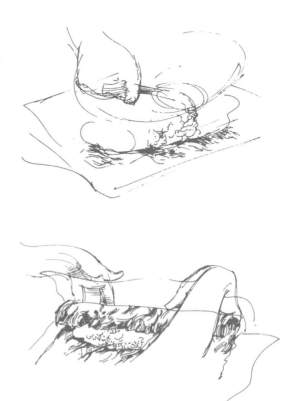

Mix the Dijon mustard and Madeira into the béchamel sauce, then add the cream and stir over medium heat until heated through. Mix in the ham. Spread some of this fill-ing over the spinach roll, leaving about a 1-inch margin around the edge.

Lift up the edge of the waxed paper or foil and gently roll up the roll. With the aid of the waxed paper, roll it onto a serving platter. Sprinkle the top with the remaining cheese and serve at once, slicing it ¾ to 1 inch thick. Leftover filling may be served on the side.

# Grand Marnier Soufflé

*This type of dessert soufflé is made without a béchamel base and with a great many eggs, to produce a very light, delicate, and high-rising result. In this case, it is advisable to use a paper collar.*

**Makes 8 servings**

FOR PREPARING A
2-QUART SOUFFLÉ
DISH
*1 tablespoon butter*
*1 tablespoon sugar*

Take a piece of waxed paper or aluminum foil long enough to fit around the soufflé dish with a little overlap, fold it in half, and butter one side heavily. Tie the waxed paper or foil around the soufflé dish, buttered side inward,

## FOR THE SOUFFLÉ

8 eggs
1 extra egg white
1¼ cups sugar
Grated zest (orange part of
    the rind) of 1 orange
⅓ cup Grand Marnier
Pinch of salt
¼ teaspoon cream of tartar
    (optional)

so it rises about 3 to 4 inches above the rim. Butter the inside of the soufflé dish, sprinkle it with the sugar, and tilt the dish so the sugar rolls around and coats the bottom and sides completely. Tip out any excess sugar. This helps the soufflé to rise and gives it a crusty, sugary exterior. The butter and sugar coating is standard for dessert soufflés.

Preheat the oven to 375° and remove the two top oven racks.

Separate the eggs, putting the whites in the bowl in which they will be beaten and the yolks in a large mixing bowl or the bowl of the electric mixer. Beat the yolks with a whisk, rotary or electric hand beater, or the whip attachment of the mixer, until the yolks are light and lemon-colored. Gradually beat in 1 cup of sugar and continue beating until the mixture is very thick, pale, and ribbony, which means that when the beater is lifted the mixture falls from it in a thick, broad ribbon. Add the orange zest and Grand Marnier to the egg-and-sugar mixture and beat in.

Beat the egg whites, adding the salt (and cream of tartar if you are not using a copper bowl) when they are foamy. Beat until they reach the soft-peak stage, then gradually beat in the remaining ¼ cup sugar and continue to beat until the egg whites form stiff, glossy peaks. Fold one-quarter of the egg whites into the egg-and-sugar mixture to lighten it, then lightly fold in the rest of the whites, as for any soufflé (see page 222).

Pour the mixture into the prepared soufflé dish, smoothing the top with a rubber spatula, and bake in the center of the preheated oven for 25 to 30 minutes, according to how cooked you like your soufflé. This type of soufflé is best if baked 25 minutes—the center will still be slightly liquid and creamy and will form a little sauce for the crustier, firmer part of the soufflé.

Remove from the oven and untie the paper collar. Very gently peel it away from the risen soufflé, being careful not to puncture the crust or the soufflé will collapse. Serve immediately.

# Chocolate Soufflé

*Like the Grand Marnier soufflé, this is made without flour. It is much lighter and more delicate than a chocolate soufflé made with a béchamel base. The basic mixture may also be baked as a chocolate roll or "fallen soufflé."*

**Makes 6 servings**

## FOR PREPARING A 1-QUART SOUFFLÉ DISH
*1 teaspoon butter*
*2 teaspoons sugar*

## FOR THE SOUFFLÉ
*6 eggs*
*½ cup sugar*
*¼ teaspoon salt*
*6 ounces semisweet chocolate*
*1 teaspoon vanilla extract*
*¼ teaspoon cream of tartar*
  *(optional)*

## FOR THE WHIPPED CREAM
*1 cup chilled heavy cream*
*2 tablespoons sifted*
  *confectioners' sugar*
*1 tablespoon cognac, Grand*
  *Marnier, or dark rum*
  *Or 2 tablespoons kirsch*

Butter the soufflé dish and sprinkle with sugar, as for previous soufflé. Chill the bowl in which the cream will be whipped. Separate the eggs, putting the yolks in a mixing bowl and the whites in the bowl in which they will be beaten. Beat the yolks until light and lemon-colored, then gradually beat in the sugar and salt until the mixture is very thick, pale yellow, and ribbony.

Meanwhile, melt the chocolate in the top of a double boiler over hot water or in a small pan in a 300° oven.

Stir the chocolate and vanilla into the egg-and-sugar mixture and beat until well mixed. Preheat the oven to 375°.

Beat the egg whites until foamy; add the cream of tartar (unless you are using a copper bowl) and continue to beat until they hold soft, unwavering peaks. Fold into the chocolate mixture as for other soufflés, first folding in one-quarter of the egg whites to lighten the mixture and then lightly folding in the rest. Pour into the prepared soufflé dish and bake in the preheated oven for 45 minutes—this soufflé needs a longer baking time because of the density of the chocolate.

Just before the soufflé is ready to come out of the oven, put the chilled cream in a chilled bowl and beat with a rotary or electric beater until it has doubled in volume and holds its shape when the beater is lifted. Gently fold in the sugar and cognac, or other flavoring. Put in a serving bowl and serve with the soufflé, as a sauce.

# Chocolate Roll

For this, use the chocolate-soufflé mixture for the roll and the sweetened whipped cream as the filling.

Butter a 15 x 11-inch jelly-roll pan, then line the pan with waxed paper, leaving an overhang of about 2 inches at each end. Butter the waxed paper, to prevent the cake from sticking. Or, if you have kitchen parchment, line the pan with parchment, which does not need to be buttered. Preheat the oven to 350°.

Make the soufflé mixture as before, but fold in the egg whites rather more completely—it is not essential to have bits of unincorporated egg white, as this version of the soufflé is meant to fall. Spread the mixture evenly in the prepared pan, smoothing it with a rubber spatula so it is the same overall thickness. Bake on the center shelf of the preheated oven for 15 minutes, or until the top feels firm and springy when touched.

Have ready a large sheet of waxed paper or aluminum foil sprinkled with cocoa or sifted confectioners' sugar. Remove the jelly-roll pan from the oven and, holding it carefully with pot holders, very quickly invert the pan onto the paper or foil so the cake falls onto it, top side down. Carefully peel the paper or parchment from the cake, loosening it, if necessary, with a small, sharp knife. If some of the surface sticks, this is not too important as the filling will go on this side.

Let the cake cool, and then spread it with the whipped cream, not quite to the edges. Lift one long edge of the waxed paper or foil and raise it so the cake rolls inward. Then, with the aid of the waxed paper, roll the cake onto a long narrow chocolate-roll board, or a flat serving tray. To serve, cut in diagonal slices.

## Variation

♦ NUT ROLL. Substitute 1 cup finely ground nuts (pecans, walnuts, filberts) for the chocolate, folding them into the egg-and-sugar mixture before folding in the egg whites.

# Prune Soufflé

*Another type of dessert soufflé is made with a fruit purée and nothing more except egg whites and sugar, beaten to stiff, glossy peaks, or the meringue stage.*

**Makes 6 servings**

FOR PREPARING A
1½-QUART SOUFFLÉ
DISH
*1 teaspoon butter*
*2 teaspoons sugar*

Prepare the soufflé dish as for other dessert soufflés (see page 225). Preheat the oven to 400°.

Drain the prunes and purée them by putting them through a food mill, rubbing them

## FOR THE SOUFFLÉ

1 pound pitted prunes, soaked
   for 1 to 2 weeks in Port or
   Madeira to cover
6 egg whites
Pinch of salt
¼ teaspoon cream of tartar
   (optional)
⅓ cup sugar

through a fine sieve, or puréeing in a blender or food processor.

Beat the egg whites until they are foamy; add the salt and cream of tartar (unless you are using a copper bowl) and continue beating until they hold soft peaks. Gradually beat in the sugar and continue to beat until the whites stand in stiff, glossy, upright peaks. Fold in the prune purée, incorporating it lightly but completely. Do not overfold. Turn into the prepared soufflé dish; smooth the top with a spatula and bake in the preheated oven for 25 to 30 minutes.

## Variations

♦ APRICOT SOUFFLÉ. Soak 1 pound dried apricots in water or white wine to cover for 3 hours, then simmer in the water or wine with ⅓ cup sugar for 5 minutes. Cool. Purée the apricots, and use in place of the prunes.

♦ ORANGE SOUFFLÉ. Substitute a 1-pound jar of orange marmalade for the prunes.

♦ OTHER FRUIT SOUFFLÉS. Substitute 2 cups puréed fruit, such as raspberries, strawberries, or peaches.

# Pastry

There are many types of pastry, starting with the simple American pie crust, which is merely flour sifted with salt into which butter or shortening is cut (with a pastry blender or two knives) or rubbed with the fingers and just enough water added to make a firm ball of dough. However, the pastry I teach in my classes is the French *pâte brisée*, or rich tart pastry, which is shorter—meaning that it will have a more brittle crumb—richer, and more versatile. It may be used unsweetened for pies and savory quiches (the open-faced custard tart that originated with the classic quiche Lorraine and now has almost unlimited variations) and sweetened for dessert tarts.

For a flakier crust, suitable for meat pies or for cocktail or dessert turnovers, I find a simple, quick version of puff pastry works very well.

A third type of pastry is *pâte à choux*, or cream puff pastry which, as you have seen in a previous chapter, can not only be baked but also deep-fried. These three pastries will give you a good working knowledge of the pastry-making processes and a repertoire that should cover most of the pastry dishes you might want to begin with.

# ❧ Rich Tart Pastry (Pâte Brisée)

*This pastry can be prepared well in advance and refrigerated or frozen. The dough, formed into a ball, is wrapped airtight in waxed paper, plastic wrap, or aluminum foil, or it may be rolled out, fitted into a pie pan, covered, and stored either unbaked or partially or fully baked, according to your needs.*

*Two methods for making this pastry follow. One calls for mixing by hand or in an electric mixer with a paddle (not a beater) attachment, the other for almost-instant mixing in a food processor.*

## HAND OR MIXER METHOD FOR PÂTE BRISÉE

**Makes enough pastry for a 9-inch pie or
tart shell or about 8 2-inch tartlets**

1¾ cups sifted flour
8 tablespoons (1 stick)
  unsalted butter, firmly
  chilled, cut into small pieces
1 egg yolk, slightly beaten with
  2 tablespoons ice water
1 tablespoon lemon juice
¼ teaspoon salt
2 tablespoons sugar (optional,
  for dessert pastry only)

Put the flour in a mixing bowl; make a well in the center and put the butter in the well. Work the butter and flour together quickly with the fingertips (do not let the warm palms of your hands come near pastry—they cause the butter to soften, melt, and become very difficult to work with) until the mixture forms small, flaky granules, like oatmeal. Blend in the egg-yolk mixture, lemon juice, salt, and sugar, if needed.

If you are using a mixer with a paddle attachment, the method is the same: first combine flour and butter and beat until mixture forms small, flaky granules, then add egg-yolk mixture, lemon juice, salt, and sugar, if desired, and beat until pastry forms a ball on the paddle.

Cupping your hands tightly, gather the dough into a rough ball, pulling in any crumbs from the sides and bottom of the bowl. The dough should feel moist but not sticky. If it seems too sticky, sprinkle with 2 to 3 teaspoons flour and blend in; if it feels dry, sprinkle with a few drops of water and knead in. Break off small pieces, about 2 to 3 tablespoons each, and smear them across the board by pushing hard with the heel of your hand. This process, called the *fraisage*, ensures the complete blending of the butter and flour. When all the dough has been worked this way, gather it together with a pastry scraper or spatula; form it into a ball; wrap in waxed paper, plastic wrap, or foil and chill for 30 minutes or until the dough is firm, but not so firm that it cracks at the edges when rolled out.

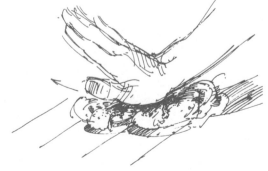

# FOOD PROCESSOR METHOD FOR PÂTE BRISÉE

*2 cups flour*
*8 tablespoons (1 stick) butter,*
    *frozen, cut into small pieces*
*¼ teaspoon salt*
*1 tablespoon lemon juice*
*2 eggs*
*2 tablespoons sugar (optional,*
    *for dessert pastry only)*

Put the metal chopping blade in place in the food processor beaker. Add the flour, frozen butter, and salt to the beaker. Process for 8 to 10 seconds, turning on and off, until the butter is cut into the flour and the mixture forms very small, flaky granules. Add the lemon juice, eggs, and sugar to the beaker and process until a ball of dough forms on top of the blades, about 15 seconds. The dough should be damp but not sticky. If it seems too soft, sprinkle with 1 to 2 tablespoons flour and process for an additional 5 to 6 seconds, until well combined. If it feels too dry, sprinkle with a few drops of water and process to blend well.

Pastry made in the food processor needs no *fraisage*. Wrap the ball of dough in waxed paper, plastic wrap, or foil and chill until firm but still malleable.

## ROLLING OUT THE PASTRY

When the pastry is chilled and firm but still malleable, it is ready to be rolled out. (For frozen dough, defrost in the refrigerator until it is the correct firmness, or defrost at room temperature and then refrigerate to firm if necessary. Do not keep in the freezer for longer than 3 to 4 weeks.) Roll out on as cool a surface as possible: a marble slab is ideal, but a countertop or one of the new heat-and-cold-proof "counter-savers" works almost as well, as long as it is in a cool part of the kitchen. If the dough gets too warm, the butter melts and the pastry becomes extremely difficult to work with. To prevent this, work as quickly as possible on a cool surface.

A good way to roll out a rich pastry such as this is between sheets of waxed paper: roll smoothly and evenly, and turn dough over often. With every turn, loosen the top paper to prevent it from sticking to the dough and wrinkling.

Or roll the pastry out on a lightly floured marble slab or other smooth surface. Rub the rolling pin lightly with flour and begin by flattening the ball of dough. Roll in one direction, not back and forth, smoothly, evenly, and

quickly, rotating the pastry a quarter turn each time and stopping just short of the edge so that you get a fairly even circle. While rolling, lift the pastry occasionally to see if it is sticking to the board; if it is, sprinkle the board lightly with flour. Also flour the rolling pin if the pastry is sticking to it. Roll the pastry out about ¼ inch thick, until you have a circle 11 to 12 inches in diameter, or large enough to fit into a 9-inch pie or tart pan or a 9-inch flan ring without skimping. There should be a little overlap. To check, hold the pan or ring over the rolled-out pastry and gauge with your eye. Use this method of gauging the size of your pastry whatever type of pan or flan form you are using—for a rectangular flan form, roll the pastry into a rectangle rather than a circle.

## TO LINE A FLAN MOLD, PIE PAN, OR TART PAN

A flan mold (or form) is a bottomless piece of metal which may be round, square, or rectangular and it is ideal for baking open-faced tarts because after baking, the tart, mold and all, may be slipped onto a serving dish and the mold lifted off, leaving a perfectly shaped tart, a much more attractive form of presentation than if it were served from a pie plate. There are also heavy tinned tart pans with a fluted edge and removable bottom that serve much the same purpose. Again, the outer ring may be easily removed after baking. Flan molds or forms come in tin, stainless steel, or other metals, in various sizes and shapes. The standard flan mold is 1 inch deep, but you can sometimes find deeper ones, which are better for baking tarts or quiches with a liquid, custard filling. Flan molds will last a long time and are well worth buying. If you have never tried one, look at our illustration and see how it works. As the flan mold has no bottom, it must be put on a baking sheet of heavy aluminum, or the heavier cast iron, open on at least one side so the baked pastry case may be easily slid from the sheet onto the serving dish.

The method for lining a flan mold, removable-bottom tart pan, or standard pie pan is much the same. If the dough has been rolled on a board, roll it loosely but carefully over the rolling pin, lift, then unroll carefully over the flan mold. Lift the edges of the dough and let it fall gently into place, patting it lightly into the bottom, without forcing or stretching it. If the pastry is stretched, it will shrink during baking. Press it snugly into the sides and trim edges with a sharp knife or scissors, allowing an overlap of about ¼ to ½ inch —you need the excess because the pastry will shrink. Crimp the edges of the pastry by pinching it between two fingers, making a firm edge.

If the dough has been rolled between sheets of waxed paper, remove the top sheet, slip one hand under the bottom sheet, and lift up the rolled dough, inverting it over the flan mold or tart pan. Lift the edges of the dough and let it fall gently into place in the mold or pan without forcing or stretching it. Peel off the waxed paper and let the dough sink into place in the mold, then pat it snugly into place.

Trim the edges by rolling your pin over the top or use scissors. Then with the flat of a paring knife, press the dough gently against the sides in an even pattern so it adheres.

When using a tart pan with a removable bottom, be sure the pastry is pushed well (without being stretched) into the fluted sides of the pan. Also be certain it is completely sealed and free of cracks or the filling will run out the bottom. If a traditional American pie plate is used, let the dough flop over the rim, trim it, and crimp the top by pressing together thumb and finger, thus pinching the dough in the middle, at even intervals to give a scalloped pattern on the rim. Or flute the edges by pressing the back of the tines of a fork lightly into the dough.

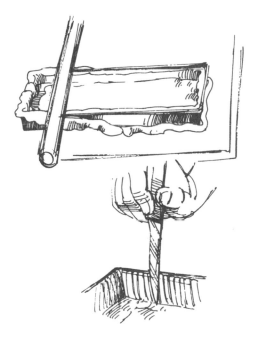

Should the pastry break while you are lining the mold or pan (this can happen, as this short pastry is very fragile), don't worry. Just patch it by pressing the broken edges together with your fingertips. Patch any holes in the pastry with some of the trimmings.

If the pastry shell is to be baked and has become quite soft after rolling and fitting into the mold or pan, refrigerate or freeze it for 10 to 15 minutes, until firm.

## TO BAKE A TART SHELL

Baking an unfilled tart shell is called "baking blind." There are various ways to do this: one method is to prick the dough well with a fork and bake the shell in a 425° oven for 14 to 16 minutes, until the bottom is set and the edges slightly browned. Or prick the dough lightly, line the shell with foil, shiny side down, pressing it well into the pastry, then bake the shell in a 425° oven for

14 to 16 minutes. The third method, which gives a better-looking, better-textured shell, is to line the shell with foil or waxed paper, weigh it down with raw rice or beans (they may be kept in a jar and used repeatedly), and bake it in a 425° oven for 14 to 16 minutes, until the bottom is set and the edges lightly browned.

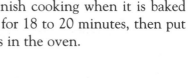

After the initial baking, remove the shell from the oven, remove the lining if you have used one, brush the bottom with beaten egg yolk (or Dijon mustard for a savory tart), and return to the oven for 2 minutes. This seals the bottom and prevents a soggy crust.

The timing of 14 to 16 minutes and the 2-minute period with the yolk glaze is for a partially baked shell; the pastry will finish cooking when it is baked with its filling. For a fully baked shell, bake it for 18 to 20 minutes, then put on the egg-yolk glaze and dry out for 2 minutes in the oven.

# Dessert Tarts

## Swiss Apple Tart

**Makes 6 to 8 servings**

4 tablespoons (½ stick) unsalted butter

5 to 6 cooking apples (see page 340), peeled, cored, and thickly sliced

1 teaspoon vanilla extract

⅛ teaspoon mace

9-inch pastry shell, partially baked in a 425° oven for 10 minutes (see recipe and directions, page 233)

2 eggs

½ cup sugar

1 cup heavy cream

½ cup heavy cream, whipped just until stiff, and lightly flavored with ⅛ teaspoon mace

Melt the butter in a heavy skillet and cook the apples very gently in the butter until just tender, but not falling apart. Add the vanilla and mace. Carefully transfer the apples to the partially baked pastry shell, arranging the slices in an even layer. Beat the eggs and sugar together until light, creamy, and lemon-colored, then stir in the cream. Pour over the apples and bake in a 350° oven until the custard has set and the crust is golden, about 30 minutes. Serve warm with mace-flavored whipped cream.

# Simple Strawberry Tart

**Makes 6 to 8 servings**

1 recipe for pâte brisée
  (see page 230)
1 egg yolk, beaten
1-pound jar currant jelly
1 tablespoon kirsch
1½ to 2 pints perfect ripe
  strawberries, of more or
  less even size, washed and
  hulled
½ cup heavy cream whipped
  just until stiff and favored
  with 1 tablespoon kirsch

Roll out the pastry and fit it into a rectangular flan mold or a 9-inch ring set on a cookie sheet (or use one with a removable bottom). Bake blind until it is browned and crisp, about 18 to 20 minutes. Brush with egg yolk and return to oven for 2 minutes to set the glaze. Cool.

Heat the currant jelly in a heavy saucepan over moderate heat until it comes to the boiling point; add the kirsch and let it cool slightly. Brush the bottom of the cooled flan shell with 1 or 2 tablespoons of this glaze.

Arrange the strawberries in the pastry shell, building from the sides toward the center. You may make a double layer in the center to give a feeling of elevation. Spoon the currant glaze over the berries. Serve the tart with kirsch-flavored whipped cream.

# Quiches

The French quiche is one of the most popular of American culinary adoptions—and small wonder. While essentially a simple dish, it is infinitely accommodating, for the basis is nothing more than a custard tart to which different ingredients are added. A quiche can be served as a cocktail appetizer, a first course, a luncheon dish, or with an entrée as a substitute for both the starch and the vegetable: a pea quiche with chicken; onion quiche with steak, roast beef, or pork; spinach quiche with roast lamb.

For most quiches, a 9-inch aluminum or Pyrex pie plate or a flan ring about 1½ inches deep set on a cookie sheet is recommended for baking the shell. (Rings 1½ inches deep can be found in shops specializing in cookery equipment. I don't find rings shallower than that are satisfactory.) To make small squares of quiche to serve as a cocktail appetizer, use an 11 x 14-inch jelly-roll pan, or a large, shallow, square pan. You can also make cocktail quiches in small tart pans, although this takes more time and work.

After years of sampling quiches, I have learned that the most common failing is a soggy crust. The secret of a crisp one is simple: the pastry shell is partially baked and then brushed with egg yolk and returned to the oven to dry. Some chefs use egg yolk, others prefer egg white or whole egg, and a new trick which lends excellent flavor is to use Dijon mustard, but the results are the same—a perfect, crisp, nonsoggy crust.

To prevent any trouble in preparing quiches, follow these rules:

1. Partially bake the pastry shell in a 425° oven for 14 to 16 minutes, until the bottom is set and the edges slightly brown. Remove from oven; remove the lining if one was used, brush with lightly beaten egg yolk, white, whole egg, or Dijon mustard, and return it to the oven for 2 minutes. This seals the crust and prevents it from soaking up the custard mixture and becoming soggy.

2. Do not pour the filling into the pastry shell until just before baking; this also prevents a soggy crust.

3. When baking in a Pyrex pie plate, reduce heat by 25 degrees as glass conducts the heat more quickly than aluminum.

4. To test a quiche for doneness, shake the pan gently to see whether or not the custard is set (it should be just firm), or slide a knife tip into the custard at the center—if it comes out clean (or almost clean), the quiche is cooked. Remember that the custard will continue to cook by internal heat after it is removed from the oven, so the very center of the quiche should be slightly underdone.

5. Do not overcook or the custard will curdle and become watery. It is better to risk a quiche that is slightly underdone.

6. Allow the quiche to cool for a few minutes before serving (unless prepared in individual tart pans). This will give the custard time to settle and it will slice better.

# ❧ Classic Quiche Lorraine

**Makes 4 to 6 servings**

6 to 8 thick slices streaky (lean) bacon
Partially baked 9-inch pastry shell (see page 233)
4 eggs
1½ cups light cream
Or 1 cup milk and ½ cup heavy cream
Salt, freshly ground black pepper, freshly grated nutmeg

Cook the bacon in a skillet until it is cooked through but not crisp. Drain on paper towels. Cut the slices into small pieces and spread evenly in the partially baked pastry shell. Beat the eggs lightly and combine with the cream or milk and cream. Season to taste with salt, pepper, and nutmeg. Pour the custard over the bacon. Bake in a 350° oven for about 30 minutes or until the custard is set, puffed, and lightly browned. Serve hot, cut into wedges.

*Note.* Buy bacon that is not flavored with artificial smoke and oversugared, as most brands are today. Genuine bacon can still be found in many farmers' markets and good pork stores.

## Variations

♦ Substitute 1 cup cream cheese or 1 cup cottage cheese for 1 cup milk. Beat the eggs with the remaining cream, combine with the cheese, and rub through a sieve or strainer before adding to the pastry shell. Bake as directed.

♦ Instead of bacon, use about 1½ cups Virginia or country ham of good flavor, cut into small strips and distributed in the shell. Add the custard and bake as directed.

# Chicken Quiche

**Makes 4 to 6 servings**

2 whole eggs
2 egg yolks
¾ cup milk
¾ cup heavy cream
1 tablespoon chopped fresh tarragon
Or ½ teaspoon dried tarragon
Salt, freshly ground pepper
2 cups diced cooked chicken or turkey
Partially baked 9-inch pastry shell (see page 233)

Beat the eggs and yolks lightly; blend with the milk and cream, season with tarragon, and salt and pepper to taste. Spread the chicken or turkey evenly in the pastry shell. Pour the custard over it. Bake in a 350° oven about 30 minutes, until the custard is barely set and still a little creamy.

# Clam Quiche

4 thick slices good-quality
   bacon
2 tablespoons minced onion
8-ounce can minced clams,
   drained (reserve juice)
Partially baked 9-inch pastry
   shell (see page 233)
4 eggs
½ cup clam juice (drained
   from clams)
1 cup heavy cream
Salt, freshly ground black
   pepper
Freshly grated nutmeg
Several drops of Tabasco

Cook the bacon in a skillet until crisp; drain on paper towels, then crumble. Pour out all but 1 tablespoon of the fat from the skillet and sauté the onion in the fat until soft but not browned. Spread the bacon, clams, and onion evenly in the pastry shell. Beat the eggs lightly and combine with the clam juice and cream. Season to taste with salt, pepper, nutmeg, and a few drops of Tabasco. Pour the custard mixture over the clams and bake in a 350° oven about 30 minutes, until custard is just set.

# Spinach Quiche

1½ pounds fresh spinach,
   cooked and drained
   Or 1 package frozen
   spinach, thawed and
   drained
⅛ teaspoon freshly grated
   nutmeg
1 tablespoon chopped fresh
   tarragon
   Or 1 teaspoon dried,
   crushed tarragon
1 tablespoon lemon juice
Salt, freshly ground black
   pepper
2 tablespoons chopped parsley
Partially baked 9-inch pastry
   shell (see page 233)
½ cup crumbled feta cheese
4 eggs
¾ cup heavy cream
½ cup plain yogurt

Cook the spinach as for spinach roll (page 224) and thoroughly drain off all liquid by squeezing small handfuls between the palms of your hands. Chop very fine.

Combine the spinach with the nutmeg, tarragon, lemon juice, salt and pepper to taste, and parsley and spread it in the bottom of the pastry shell. Sprinkle the cheese on top. Beat the eggs lightly; add the cream and yogurt and blend well. Pour over the spinach mixture. Bake in a 350° oven for about 30 minutes, until the custard is just set. This is excellent as an accompaniment to roast lamb or chicken.

# Swiss Onion Quiche

4 tablespoons (½ stick)
  unsalted butter
4 to 6 onions, peeled and
  thinly sliced
Salt, freshly ground black
  pepper
Partially baked 9-inch pastry
  shell (see page 233)
1 cup shredded Gruyère
  cheese
2 whole eggs
2 egg yolks
1½ cups heavy cream
  Or 1 cup milk and ½ cup
  heavy cream
⅛ teaspoon freshly grated
  nutmeg

Melt the butter in a very heavy pan; add the onions; cover tightly and steam over medium-low heat until the onions are soft but not browned, shaking the pan occasionally. Season with salt and pepper to taste. Drain the onions; arrange in the pastry shell and sprinkle with the cheese. Beat the eggs, yolks, cream, and nutmeg together and pour into the shell. Bake in a 350° oven for about 30 minutes, until the custard is just set and puffed. This is an excellent accompaniment for steak, roast beef, or roast pork.

# Puff Pastry

## ✒ Simple Puff Pastry

*This type of pastry is made by rolling butter between layers of dough. When baked, it puffs up into a many-layered, light, flaky, and richly buttery pastry that is excellent for the top crust on meat or game pies, for tartlets, for meat baked en croûte, such as beef Wellington, or for cocktail appetizers. Any leftover scraps of dough can be rolled out and used for little turnovers of Roquefort cheese or other savory fillings.*

*To give puff pastry the desirable light and tender texture, you need a soft flour, either a combination of cake flour and all-purpose flour, or a very fine granular flour such as Wondra. Puff pastry freezes beautifully and will keep for six months to a year, if securely wrapped and airtight.*

**Makes about 2 pounds pastry, or 2 9-inch crusts**

DOUGH MIXTURE
2¾ cups all-purpose flour and
⅓ cup cake flour
Or 3 cups Wondra flour
¼ cup vegetable oil
½ teaspoon salt, mixed with
¾ cup ice water

If using the mixture of all-purpose and cake flour, blend well with a rubber spatula in a bowl. Remove and reserve ½ cup of the flour mixture or the Wondra flour. Stir the oil into the flour with a rubber spatula and mix thoroughly. Stir in the salt and water. Cut and press mixture firmly with a spatula and then the cupped fingers of one hand until it forms a mass. Lift the mixture from the bowl; sprinkle any remaining bits of flour with a few drops of ice water and gather them up and lightly press into the rest of the dough. The dough should be pliable but not damp or sticky. Sprinkle very lightly with flour. Wrap dough in waxed paper, then put in a plastic bag and refrigerate for 1 hour.

BUTTER MIXTURE
¾ pound (3 sticks) unsalted
butter, chilled
Reserved ½ cup flour

If working by hand, pound the butter with a rolling pin to make it softer and more pliable, then gather into a mass. Break off bits of about 2 to 3 tablespoons and smear across the work surface with the heel (not palm) of the hand, a process just like the *fraisage* described on page 230. Sprinkle the butter with flour, then gather the butter into a mass and knead it until it is smooth and completely mixed with the flour. Work quickly so that the mixture remains chilled but supple; if it melts because of the warmth of your hands, it becomes very difficult to work with and will have to be refrigerated until firmer. Gather into a mass.

If using an electric mixer, break each stick of butter in half, sprinkle with the flour, and work with the paddle at slow speed until it is thoroughly mixed, smooth, and supple, but still chilled. Gather into a mass.

Refrigerate uncovered for not more than 20 minutes.

## MAKING THE PUFF PASTRY

Flour the work surface very lightly (again, as with all pastry, marble is best, but any cool surface will do). Lightly flour the dough, both top and bottom (whisk off any excess flour with a soft pastry brush), and your hands. Push and pat the dough with the heels of your hands into a 16 x 8-inch rectangle (to measure quickly, use a piece of paper cut to these dimensions). Lay the dough out lengthwise away from you. Cut small pieces of the chilled butter and arrange them evenly spaced over two-thirds of the dough farthest from you, leaving a ½-inch margin around the edge. Fold the unbuttered third of the dough over half the buttered dough, then fold the remaining buttered third over, just like folding a letter. Pinch the edges together to prevent possible leakage of butter. Rotate the dough a quarter turn clockwise, so the dough is once more lengthwise away from you. With a rolling pin, gently but firmly roll out to a 16 x 8-inch rectangle. As you roll, try to keep the dough in as even a rectangle as possible: if the edges become ragged, even the sides with the side of the rolling pin. Roll across the width once or twice if necessary to widen it. Check to make sure the dough is not sticking to the work surface. If

it is, either dust the work surface lightly with flour or brush the dough lightly with flour. Should the dough split and butter start to ooze out, dust the split area lightly with flour.

Now fold the top and bottom ends of the rectangle to meet in the center, then fold these two halves together, as if you were closing the pages of a book. Wrap the dough in waxed paper, put into a plastic bag, and refrigerate for 1 hour.

You have now completed the first "turn": rolling out the dough to a 16 x 8-inch rectangle, bringing the ends to the center, and folding them together. Do two more turns in the same way; chill for 1 hour after each turn. After each, mark the number of turns you have made by making depressions on the dough with your fingers. Each time start with the dough lengthwise on the work surface so the open ends of the "book" are at top and bottom; roll into a 16 x 8-inch rectangle; fold opposite ends to meet in the center and then fold these two halves together. Should the dough be too cold and hard to roll easily after chilling, beat it firmly and evenly lengthwise and crosswise with the rolling pin to soften it a little. When the three turns have been completed, wrap the pastry well and refrigerate for 2 hours or until ready to use. It is now ready to be rolled out and used.

## ❧ Beefsteak and Kidney Pie

*For this famous old English dish, the beef is first braised and then cooked in a pie dish or baking dish under a puff-pastry crust.*

**Makes 6 servings**

2 pounds round or rump
  steak, cut into 1½-inch
  cubes
½ cup flour
1 teaspoon salt
½ teaspoon freshly ground
  black pepper
¾ teaspoon thyme
4 tablespoons chopped
  beef suet
2 medium onions, peeled and
  chopped
1 onion, stuck with 2 cloves
2 to 3 cups beef broth

Put the beef, flour, salt, pepper, and ½ teaspoon thyme into a plastic bag and shake until the beef is well covered with flour. Remove and shake off the excess. Render the beef suet over medium heat in a large, heavy skillet with a cover and when the suet is melted and hot, add the meat cubes, a few at a time, and brown on all sides over high heat. Remove the cubes, reduce the heat, add the chopped onions, and sauté over medium heat until just limp. Replace the meat in the skillet with the clove-stuck onion, the remaining thyme, and just enough beef broth to cover the meat. Cover and simmer for 1½ hours, or

*3 veal kidneys*
*12 firm white mushroom caps*
*    of the quick puff pastry*
*    (see previous recipe)*
*2 egg yolks, beaten*

until the beef is tender when tested with a fork or knife point. Discard the clove-stuck onion and let the beef cool for 1 hour.

Clean the kidneys. Peel off the covering membrane and remove the white core in the center with a small, sharp knife, making a slit in the top and then working around it. Slice the kidneys thin. Wipe the mushrooms with a damp cloth and slice them thin. Arrange layers of the cooled beef and onions, kidneys, and mushrooms in a baking dish or pie dish about 9 x 12 x 3 inches. Put in the center of the dish an inverted ovenproof custard cup or egg cup that comes as high as the rim of the dish (this is to hold up the crust). Pour the juices from the braised beef into the dish and add just enough extra beef broth barely to cover the contents of the dish.

Roll out the puff pastry about ⅜ inch thick and 1½ inches larger than the dish. From this, cut off a strip 1 inch wide and long enough to fit the circumference of the dish. Arrange this around the rim of the dish, dampen the top of the strip lightly with cold water (this makes it adhere to the top crust), and drape the remaining pastry over it to form the top crust. Press to seal the two edges together and trim off any pastry that overhangs the dish. Crimp the edge of the pastry by pressing it between thumb and forefinger. Cut a V-shaped slit in the center of the top crust and place a small cone of waxed paper in it, to form a vent for the steam to escape. Roll out leftover pastry and cut into simple flowers and leaves with pastry cutters. Moisten the underside of the dough with cold water and lay on the crust as decoration. Brush top crust and decorations with beaten egg yolks, which give it a brown glaze when baked. Preheat the oven to 450°. Bake the pie at 450° for 10 minutes, then reduce the heat to 375° and bake 25 to 30 minutes longer.

# Choux Pastry

## ❧ Cream Puffs with Chocolate Sauce

*The name* choux, *or cabbage, for this pastry probably originated because when the little puffs rise, they resemble tiny cabbages.* Choux *pastry can be used for beignets soufflés (page 207) or, without the rum or brandy flavoring, it can be baked as little cream puffs, then filled with ice cream or whipped cream and served with a chocolate sauce. If the sugar is omitted from the following recipe, the puffs can be filled with a savory mixture, such as creamed fish or mushrooms, and served as a hot first course or a cocktail appetizer. For cocktail appetizers, make bite-size puffs, using 1 teaspoon of the* choux *pastry instead of 1 tablespoon.*

**Makes 24 puffs, or enough for 8**

CHOUX PASTRY
8 *tablespoons (1 stick) butter, cut into pieces*
1 *cup water*
⅛ *teaspoon salt (for savory puffs, use 1 teaspoon)*
½ *teaspoon sugar (omit for savory puffs)*
1 *cup all-purpose flour*
4 *eggs*

GLAZE
1 *egg beaten with 1 teaspoon water*

CHOCOLATE SAUCE
12 *ounces semisweet chocolate*
2 *ounces unsweetened chocolate*
1 *cup heavy cream*
1 *tablespoon cognac or Madeira or dark rum*

FILLING
1 *pint ice cream*

Combine the butter, water, salt, and sugar in a heavy 2-quart saucepan over medium heat and heat until the butter is melted and the water boiling. Remove the pan from the heat; dump in the flour and beat vigorously with a wooden spatula or spoon until well blended. Put pan over medium heat and beat the mixture with the spatula for about a minute or until it forms a thick mass that clings to the spatula and comes away from the sides of the pan. Remove the pan from the heat and leave for 5 to 6 minutes. Preheat the oven to 425° and butter two baking sheets.

Make a well in the center of the dough and beat in the eggs, one at a time, beating thoroughly after each addition. When the eggs are absorbed and the pastry is smooth and glossy, drop small mounds of the *choux* pastry onto the buttered baking sheets using either a tablespoon or a pastry bag fitted with a ¾-inch plain tube, spacing the puffs 2 inches apart to allow room for expansion.

If you use the pastry bag, turn the top back about 3 inches to form a cuff, then fill the bag with the *choux* pastry, using a rubber spatula. Fold the top back again, then twist the bag tightly, forcing the pastry to the bottom.

Squeeze it onto the sheet, making a circular mound about 2 inches in diameter at the base, tapering to about 1 inch at the top.

If you use a table-spoon, push the pastry from the tablespoon onto the sheet with another spoon.

Brush the tops of the puffs with the egg glaze, using a pastry brush, but don't allow any of the egg to drip onto the sheet as it would set and prevent the puffs from rising. Put one baking sheet on the upper shelf of the preheated oven and one on the lower, spacing them so one is not directly above the other, to allow for heat circulation. Bake for 10 to 15 minutes, or until the puffs are golden brown, puffed to twice their original size, and firm to the touch. To make sure they are baked, remove one puff and cut it open. If the inside is doughy, bake the puffs a minute or two longer. When puffs are baked, turn off the oven; remove the baking sheets and pierce the side of each puff with a sharp knife to allow the steam to escape. Replace the sheets in the oven for 10 minutes to allow the puffs to dry out, leaving the door ajar, then transfer the puffs to wire cake racks to cool.

Meanwhile, make the chocolate sauce. Either melt the chocolate in the top of a double boiler over hot water or put it in a small, heavy pan in a 300° oven until it melts. Stir the cream into the melted chocolate and flavor with the cognac, Madeira, or rum. Keep warm over hot water until ready to use.

When the puffs are cool, split them in half horizontally with a knife. Scrape out any moist paste inside with a small spoon, then put a scoop of the ice cream on the bottom of each puff and cover with the top. Serve immediately, with a bowl of the hot chocolate sauce to spoon over the puffs at the table.

# Bread

In these days when commercially made bread often has the quality of a plastic sponge, many people have fortunately discovered the enjoyment of making their own, both for the comforting and rewarding experience breadmaking is, and even more for the pleasure of producing and eating a well-flavored, beautifully textured loaf.

Before you start to make bread, there are a few things you should know. The first is that flours differ a great deal, not only in various locales, but also from one batch to another. Thus the balance of liquid to flour can be so changeable that an absolutely accurate measure cannot be given. You will have to learn to know your dough by the feel. Good dough should be firm, elastic, and smooth and should blister easily on the surface when it has been well kneaded. Sticky, lumpy dough is not good and will never make a well-textured loaf.

Proofing yeast is a very important step in breadmaking. To proof means to test to see if the yeast is still active. This is done by dissolving the yeast in warm water, about 110° to 115° (take the temperature the first time to get the feel of how hot this is—water from the hot tap is usually perfect), to start the fermentation. You can test the temperature with your sensitive meat thermometer. The bubbling of the mixture is proof that the yeast is active.

Risings are equally important. The double-in-bulk rule given in many recipes means that after the kneaded dough has been placed in a buttered bowl and set in a warm, draft-free place, the bulk should increase until it is double in volume. An oven is an excellent place for the rising—either a gas oven with the faint warmth given off by the pilot light or an electric oven that has been heated very slightly and then turned off. The place should be draft-free because the yeast must be pampered with constant warmth to keep it active. The rising time will differ for various types of breads. Some will rise in less than 1 hour, whereas others will take as long as 2½ to 3 hours to double in bulk. Some recipes call for two risings, meaning that when the dough has risen once it is punched down and left to rise again before being shaped into loaves and given a third and final rising in the pan. Others need to rise only once before being shaped into loaves and put into the pan to rise again before baking. Rising bread should be covered with a towel or a sheet of plastic wrap, unless otherwise noted, to prevent the surface from drying and cracking.

# ❧ Basic White Bread

*This is my idea of a good, simple loaf of bread—firm, honest in flavor, tender to the bite yet with a slight chewiness in the crust. It is also excellent for toast. Once you have mastered the procedures given here, you can go on to more complex recipes without difficulty.*

*As I have said, there are many variables in breadmaking. As far as flours are concerned, for example, hard-wheat flour produces the best results in wheat breads but it is not always easy to find, so we'll use a common, unbleached (or bleached) all-purpose flour. Compressed or cake yeast is also difficult to find and the active dry variety is everywhere, so we'll use that. Water may be used for the liquid; the milk used in this recipe makes a richer bread. The amount of salt may be varied according to taste: my rule of thumb is 1 tablespoon for each pound (3¾ cups) of flour. Even the weather has an effect on breadmaking. The degree of humidity and warmth will govern the absorption quality of the flour and the action of the yeast.*

**Makes 1 large or 2 smaller loaves**

1 package active dry yeast
¼ cup warm (110° to 115°) water
2 teaspoons sugar
1 cup milk
1 tablespoon salt
3 tablespoons butter
About 3¾ cups all-purpose flour
Egg wash: 1 egg white beaten slightly with 1 tablespoon water

In a small bowl mix the yeast and ¼ cup warm water; add the sugar, stir well, and set aside until proofed. It is proofed when fermentation is apparent: the mixture will swell and small bubbles appear on the surface. (If it doesn't proof at all, it means the yeast is not fresh.)

Heat the milk with the salt in a small saucepan and stir in the butter until it melts. Set aside to cool until it is no warmer than the yeast mixture. Put 2 cups of the flour in a large mixing bowl and stir in the milk mixture. Beat well with a wooden spatula, add the yeast mixture, and continue beating the dough until it is smooth, adding an additional cup of flour to make a firm dough. Turn the dough out onto a floured work surface and begin the kneading process, which evenly distributes the fermenting yeast cells through the dough.

Knead for about 10 minutes, kneading in additional flour as necessary, until the dough is smooth and no longer sticky, and blisters form on the surface. There are several kneading methods, but the basic one is to flour the dough and your hand lightly, then push the heel of your hand down into the dough and away from you. Fold the dough over, give it a quarter turn, and push down again. Repeat pushing, folding, and turning until the motion becomes rhythmic. If you have a heavy-duty electric mixer with a dough-hook attachment, knead the dough with the hook and finish it off on the board. To test whether the dough has been kneaded enough, make an indentation in it with your fin-

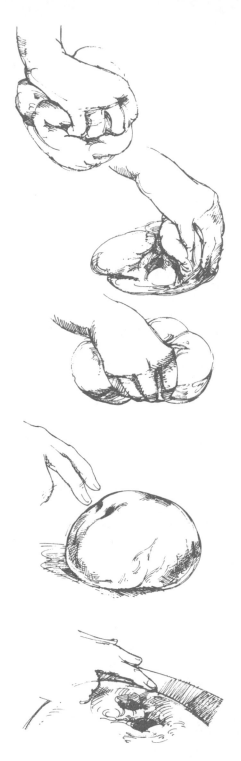

gers; it should spring back. If blisters form on the surface of the dough and break, this is another sign that the kneading is sufficient.

Butter a large bowl, transfer the dough to it, and turn the dough in the bowl until the dough is well coated with butter on all sides. Cover the dough with a dish towel and let it rise in a warm, draft-free place for 1 to 1½ hours, until it is double in bulk.

To test further if the dough has risen properly, make an indentation in it with two fingers: if the dough does not spring back, then it is ready.

Butter a 9 x 5 x 3-inch loaf pan, or two pans that are about 8 x 4 x 2 inches. Punch the dough down with your fist to deflate it; transfer it to a floured board and knead well for about 3 minutes. Pat it into a smooth round or oval shape and let it rest for 4 to 5 minutes. Then form into 1 large or 2 small loaves, by shaping the dough into an oval the length of your bread pan, then gently stretching, rounding, and plumping it in the palms of your hands, tucking the edges underneath and pinching them together. Lift carefully; drop the dough into the pan or pans and smooth out. Cover the dough with a towel and let it rise again in a warm, draft-free place for about 45 minutes to 1 hour, until it is double in bulk.

Preheat the oven to 400°. Brush the egg wash over the top of the dough. Bake in the center of the oven for 20 minutes; reduce the heat to 350° and bake for 20 to 25 minutes longer, until the crust is well browned and the bread sounds hollow when removed

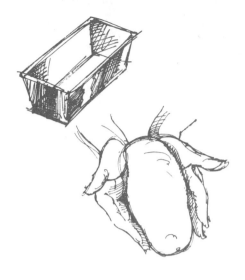

from the pan and tapped on the bottom with the knuckles. If you like a crusty loaf, remove it from the pan about 5 to 10 minutes before the end of the baking time and let it finish baking on the oven rack. It will get brown and crusty all over. Remove the bread from the oven and let it cool on a rack before slicing. The bread may be stored in a plastic bag in the refrigerator after it has cooled (if you seal it in a bag before it is completely cooled, the crust will become soft); it will keep about a week. It also freezes well if wrapped tightly in plastic wrap and sealed in a plastic bag and can be kept for up to 3 months.

## Batter Bread

*Batter breads are extremely popular with people who feel that kneading is too much work. There's nothing complicated or arduous about making a real loaf, but if you want to start modestly, begin with batter breads and work up to the others.*

**Makes 1 large round loaf**

2 packages active dry yeast
2 cups warm (110° to 115°) water
⅓ cup nonfat dry milk
2 tablespoons sugar
2 tablespoons butter
2 teaspoons salt
2 garlic cloves, finely chopped (optional)
4 cups all-purpose flour
Egg wash: 1 egg white lightly beaten with 1 tablespoon water
3 to 4 tablespoons sesame seeds

Proof the yeast in the water in a large mixing bowl or the bowl of an electric mixer. Add the dry milk, sugar, butter, salt, optional garlic, and 2 cups flour. Beat the batter by hand or with an electric mixer at medium speed for 2 minutes. Stir in the remaining flour by hand and stir the mixture well to make a soft dough. Cover it with a damp towel and let it rise in a warm, draft-free place for about 40 minutes or until it is double in bulk.

Preheat the oven to 375°. Uncover the risen dough and stir it vigorously for 1 minute. Butter a 1½-quart straight-sided casserole or soufflé dish and put in the batter. Brush the top with the egg wash and sprinkle with sesame seeds. Bake the bread in the center of the oven for about 1 hour, or until it is delicately browned and sounds hollow when rapped with the knuckles. Remove from the casserole or dish and serve warm, cut into wedges.

# ❧ Corn Bread

*There are innumerable recipes for corn bread, which is leavened by baking powder. This one, which is very moist and rich, happens to be my favorite.*

**Makes 6 servings**

½ cup flour
1½ cups yellow cornmeal
1 teaspoon salt
1 teaspoon sugar
3 teaspoons baking powder
3 eggs, well beaten
1 cup milk
¼ cup cream
⅓ cup melted butter

Preheat the oven to 400°. Butter an 8½ x 11-inch baking pan. Sift the flour, cornmeal, salt, sugar, and baking powder into a large bowl, to mix the ingredients thoroughly and distribute the baking powder evenly. Beat in the eggs and milk with a wooden spoon until well mixed. Beat in the cream and, lastly, the melted butter. Pour into the buttered pan and bake for 18 to 20 minutes. While still hot, cut into squares and serve wrapped in a napkin.

# Cakes

In cake baking, it is very important to use the size of pan specified in the recipe. Most recipes call for a round or square 8-inch or 9-inch pan, 1½ or 2 inches deep. There are, of course, other sizes and types, such as the flat 15 x 11-inch jelly-roll pan, the deep rectangular loaf pan, the deep, round tube pan, and the ring mold in which a savarin is baked, but the 8- or 9-inch pans are those you will find you need most often. Keep pans of different sizes separate and check them before you bake. If you use a pan that is too small for the recipe the batter is likely to overflow during baking, while with a too-large pan the cake may bake too rapidly.

Whatever you bake in or on, whether it is a cake pan, a jelly-roll pan, a pie pan, or a baking sheet, it should be made of heavy-duty aluminum, not a flimsy material that would warp or buckle with the heat. Keep your pans clean. Burned pans or those darkened with grease may make a batter scorch or over-bake, as dark surfaces conduct more heat than light ones. Some aluminum cake pans and cookie sheets have a Teflon coating, which works extremely well and enables you to remove the baked cake or cookies from the nonstick coating with a minimum of effort. Otherwise, you should prepare your pan according to the type of cake you are baking. For certain cakes, such as angel food, the pan needs no preparation but for the majority of cakes the inside of the pan should be buttered, or buttered and floured, or buttered and lined with buttered waxed paper cut to fit the pan. To do this, place the pan bottom side down on the paper, trace around it with a pencil, and then cut out the shape.

If you are using more than one layer-cake pan, fold the waxed paper in layers and trace and cut out all the liners at one time. An extremely valuable baking accessory that not too many people seem to know about is cooking parchment or kitchen parchment, which is sold in sheets and rolls. Cooking parchment is far more useful than waxed paper because it doesn't need greasing, won't discolor or scorch, and is easy to cut and fit into the pan. Using a pastry bag with one of its various-shaped tubes, you can pipe sticky things like meringues onto a parchment-lined cookie sheet and be confident that you'll be able to get them off without any problem.

If you are baking more than one cake, or cake layer, in the oven, don't put the pans directly above each other. Stagger them on the oven racks so that the hot air can circulate around them, and keep the pans about 2 inches away from the back and sides of the oven where the heat tends to be more intense or your cake may bake more on one side than the other. If you are baking only one cake, put it in the center of the oven. Unless the heat is right, the cake won't bake properly. It is heat that makes the leavening expand and "sets" the cake when it has expanded. A cake with a gummy texture or a soggy bottom is an indication that the heat was too low.

Be sure to have both dry and liquid measuring cups in your kitchen. Accurate measurements are essential in baking and you can't be accurate if you pour liquid into a dry measure, where it will spill over the top, or put flour and sugar, which need to be leveled off, into a liquid measuring cup. You can pick up sets of liquid and dry measures for next to nothing in any dime or hardware store. The most accurate system of all is to weigh, rather than measure, dry ingredients, but unlike the British and French we are not given to using scales in our kitchens, though we may well have to once the metric system is adopted here. So watch your measuring habits, and don't ruin your cake by using too much or too little flour or liquid.

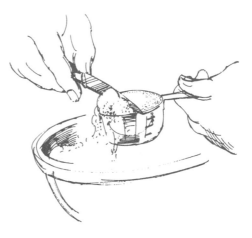

Another inexpensive essential is a flour sifter, the kind you operate by squeezing the handle. For cakes, flour is practically always sifted—to aerate it and make it lighter—and measured after sifting. In the first cake recipe, I'll explain the best way to sift flour into your dry measuring cup. All-purpose flour, made from a mixture of hard and soft wheat, is used for most cakes, except those in which cake flour, made from all soft wheat, is called for.

Apart from your basic cake pans and cookie or baking sheets, measures, and sifter, the only equipment you will need in addition to the normal kitchen complement of mixing bowls, beaters, whisks, spatulas, and rolling pin and board are a couple of wire cake racks, for cooling the cakes, and a set of cookie cutters.

A final tip. Your cake will be easier to mix, lighter, and better-textured if you have all your ingredients at room temperature. This is particularly important when you are using eggs, for both yolks and whites will have greater volume if they are allowed to warm up before being beaten.

# ⮞ 1-2-3-4 Cake

*This layer cake was a standard in our house. The recipe is a very old one that people could keep in their heads because of the utter simplicity of the formula that gave the cake its name—1 cup of butter, 2 cups of sugar, 3 cups of flour, and 4 eggs. Here baking powder is the leavening agent, so this is a very easy cake to make. You might like to try mixing it the first time with your hands, which will give you a good idea of the basic techniques of beating and folding. If you don't want to use your hands to mix the cake, use a whisk, a rotary hand beater, or an electric beater or mixer to cream the butter and sugar and to beat in the egg yolks, milk, flour, and vanilla. Fold in the egg whites by hand.*

**Makes 1 3-layer cake**

FOR PREPARING 3
9-INCH LAYER-CAKE
PANS, 1½ INCHES DEEP
*1 tablespoon softened butter*
*2 tablespoons flour*

FOR THE CAKE
*3 cups sifted cake flour (if you*
*can't find cake flour, the*
*same amount of all-purpose*
*flour can be substituted)*
*4 teaspoons double-acting*
*baking powder*
*½ teaspoon salt*

Preheat the oven to 350°. Butter the bottom and sides of each layer-cake pan with the softened butter, using your hands, then sprinkle the flour inside and shake this around so you get a thin coating on the butter. *Tip out any excess.*

8 ounces (2 sticks) unsalted
   butter, at room temperature
2 cups granulated sugar
4 eggs, at room temperature
1 cup milk, at room
   temperature
1 to 1½ teaspoons vanilla
   extract

## FOR THE FILLING
## AND TOPPING

¾ cup strained orange juice
2 tablespoons lemon juice
¾ cup granulated sugar
1 tablespoon finely grated
   orange rind

Now to sift your flour. Lay a large piece of waxed paper on a board, put a dry measuring cup in the center, hold a sifter directly over it, scoop cake flour from the package into the sifter, and sift the flour directly into the cup. When the cup is full, draw the back of a knife blade lightly across the top of the cup (don't shake the flour down, or it will become dense) and then tip the measured flour into a mixing bowl. Repeat with the other 2 cups of flour (you can put any flour that spilled onto the waxed paper back in the sifter). When you have 3 cups of sifted flour in the bowl, put the baking powder and salt in the sifter, holding it over the mixing bowl, and sift it over the flour. Then mix the baking powder and salt lightly with the flour, using your hands.

Next, put the butter into a second, large mixing bowl. If it is very firm (it shouldn't be, if you have left it out of the refrigerator), squeeze it through your fingers until it softens up. When it is soft enough to work, form your right hand into a big fork, as it were, and cream the butter—which means that you beat it firmly and quickly with your hand, beating and aerating it, until it becomes light, creamy, and fluffy. Then whirl your fingers around like a whisk so the butter forms a circle in the bowl. Gradually cream the 2 cups of sugar into the butter with the same fork-like motion, beating until the mixture is very light and fluffy. As the sugar blends in it will change the color of the butter to a much lighter color, almost white.

Now wash and dry your hands thoroughly and separate the eggs, as you would for a soufflé, letting the whites slip through your slightly parted fingers

into a small bowl and dropping the yolks into a second, larger bowl. Beat the yolks for a few minutes with a whisk until they are well blended. Then, again with your hand, beat them very thoroughly into the butter-sugar mixture. Now beat in the milk alternately with the sifted flour—first one, then

the other—this time keeping your fingers close together as if your hand were a wooden spatula. Beat, beat, beat until the batter is well mixed, then add the vanilla and beat that in for a minute or two.

Put the egg whites in your beating bowl and beat them with a large whisk or an electric hand beater until they mount first to soft, drooping peaks and then to firm, glossy peaks. Do not overbeat until they are stiff and dry.

Tip the beaten whites onto the cake batter and fold them in with your hand. Slightly cup your hand and use the side like a spatula to cut down through the whites and batter to the bottom of the bowl and then flop them over with your cupped hand, rotating the bowl with your other hand as you do so— exactly the technique you use when folding egg whites into a soufflé mixture with a rubber spatula. Repeat this very lightly and quickly until the whites and batter are thoroughly folded and blended. Once you have mastered this hand technique you can use it for a soufflé, too.

Again using your hand like a spatula, pour and scrape the batter into the three prepared pans, dividing it equally between them. Give the filled pans a little knock on the countertop to level the batter. Put the three pans in the center of the oven, or, if you have to use more than one rack, stagger them on the two middle racks of the oven so they do not overlap. Bake for 25 minutes, then touch the center of each cake lightly with your fingertip. If it springs back, it is done. Remove the pans from the oven and put them on wire cake racks to cool for a few minutes, then loosen the layers by running the flat of a knife

blade around the sides of the pans, put a rack on top of each pan, and invert so the cake comes out onto the rack, top side down. Then reverse the layers so they are top side up.

Mix the orange juice, lemon juice, sugar, and orange rind together and drizzle the mixture over the still-warm cake layers, being careful not to let it all soak into one spot; then pile the layers on top of each other. The juice mixture will give the cake a lovely, fresh, fruity flavor and it is not rich like an icing. Leave the cake to cool.

# ✆ Savarin with Apricot Glaze

*A savarin is a rich spongy cake leavened by yeast and baked in a ring mold. The technique is different from that of other cakes and the soft, sticky dough requires quite a lot of beating by hand. The cake is not sweet and is usually saturated with a rum syrup or, in this case, coated with an apricot glaze.*

TO PREPARE THE
8-CUP RING MOLD
*2 teaspoons soft butter*

FOR THE SAVARIN
*½ cup lukewarm milk
(110° to 115°)
1 package active dry yeast*

Butter the inside of the ring mold well and set aside.

Pour the milk into a cup measure and test the temperature with a meat thermometer. Sprinkle the yeast into the milk, add a pinch of sugar, and stir. Leave it until it proofs (becomes frothy), which shows that the yeast is working.

1 tablespoon sugar
2 cups all-purpose flour
4 eggs
½ teaspoon salt
⅔ cup (about 11 tablespoons)
   softened butter, cut into
   small pieces

FOR THE GLAZE
AND FILLING

1-pound jar pure apricot
   preserves (without added
   pectin)
1 pint strawberries, washed,
   hulled, and lightly sugared
1 cup sweetened whipped
   cream

Sift the flour (using the technique described for the previous cake) into a large mixing bowl or the bowl of an electric mixer. Beat the eggs slightly with a fork or whisk and add to the flour with the salt, the rest of the sugar, and the yeast mixture. Beat with a wooden spoon or spatula, or the dough-hook attachment of the electric mixer, until it forms a soft, sticky dough. You may have to add a little more milk to get the right consistency.

When thoroughly mixed, beat for 2 minutes with your hands, pulling the dough up and letting it drop back into the bowl, until it becomes elastic, smooth, and no longer sticky. Cover the bowl with a towel and let the dough stand in a warm place (on top of the stove, or in the oven, heated by the pilot light) for 45 minutes, or until doubled in bulk.

Deflate the risen dough by gathering it from the sides of the bowl toward the center. Then beat the pieces of softened butter into the dough with your hands or a wooden spatula, beating for about 4 minutes. Use the same beating technique you used when making the 1-2-3-4 cake.

Turn the dough into the buttered ring mold and let it stand in a warm place, uncovered, until the dough has risen to the top of the mold, about 1 hour or more. Meanwhile, preheat the oven to 450°.

Put the mold in the center of the oven and bake the cake for 10 minutes, then reduce the heat to 350° and continue baking until nicely browned, about 20 minutes longer. Test by inserting a cake tester or skewer into the cake; if it comes out clean, the cake is baked.

Take the mold from the oven and put a wire rack on top of it. Invert so the savarin comes out onto the rack. Let it cool slightly while making the glaze.

Put the apricot preserves (be sure to use pure preserves, without added pectin, or the jam won't melt properly) into a small, heavy saucepan and stir over medium heat until the preserves come to a boil. Reduce the heat and cook for 2 minutes, stirring, until liquid. Rub through a fine sieve with a wooden spatula, then put the savarin on a plate and pour the apricot glaze over it. Allow the savarin to cool. Just before serving, fill the center with sugared strawberries and top with whipped cream.

# ❧ Génoise

*This light cake, leavened entirely by eggs, is of Italian origin but French by adoption. Mostly it is used as a layer cake, with a butter-cream filling and frosting, but it can also be baked flat in a jelly-roll pan, filled with a fruit-flavored Bavarian cream and rolled, or used as a base for trifle (see page 323).*

## FOR PREPARING 2 9-INCH ROUND LAYER-CAKE PANS, 1½ INCHES DEEP

1 tablespoon soft butter
2 tablespoons flour

## FOR THE GENOISE

8 tablespoons (1 stick)
    unsalted butter
6 eggs (standard large size)
1 cup superfine sugar
1 cup cake flour
½ teaspoon salt
1 teaspoon vanilla extract

## FOR THE BUTTER CREAM

Makes 2 cups
2 egg yolks
¼ cup sugar
⅛ teaspoon salt
½ cup light cream
½ teaspoon vanilla extract
½ pound (2 sticks) unsalted
    butter

First, prepare the pans. Put one pan on a double sheet of waxed paper or kitchen parchment and trace the diameter of the bottom with a pencil. Cut out the circles, which will be used to line the pans. Grease the bottom and sides of each pan with butter, then put a waxed-paper circle in the bottom of each pan and butter the paper. Put a tablespoon of flour in each pan. Toss it around until the greased pans are lightly coated with flour, then shake out the excess. Set the pans aside. If you use parchment, there is no need to butter and flour the paper.

For this cake, the butter must be melted and clarified and only the clear yellow part of the melted butter used. Melt the butter in a small saucepan over low heat until the clear yellow fat and the whey (the whitish, curdlike substance that sinks to the bottom) separate. Put the pan of melted butter in the refrigerator to chill until the fat solidifies on top, then remove it from the moist whey underneath. Reheat the solidified fat until it melts and leave to cool until just tepid. You should have ½ cup clarified butter. Preheat the oven to 350°.

Combine the eggs and sugar in the top of a double boiler over hot (not boiling) water, which should not touch the bottom of the upper pan. Set the double boiler over low heat (the water must not even simmer) and beat the eggs and sugar for about 15 minutes with a whisk or an electric hand beater until the mixture is very thick, pale in color, and falls in a thick ribbon when the beater is lifted. Remove the top of the double boiler from the water and put the contents into a mixing bowl.

Sift the flour through a sifter, letting it fall lightly into a 1-cup dry measure set on a sheet of waxed paper (pour spilled flour back into box). When you have 1 cup flour, put it back in the sifter with the salt and sift twice again, letting the flour fall on a large piece of waxed paper.

Sprinkle one-quarter of the sifted flour over the egg-sugar mixture and quickly fold in with a rubber spatula, rotating the bowl as you do so, using the same folding technique as for a soufflé or the 1-2-3-4 cake. Add the rest of the flour and the ½ cup melted butter and vanilla in the same way, a third at a time, rotating the bowl as you fold. (If you have an electric mixer, put the egg-sugar mixture into the bowl and beat in the flour, butter, and vanilla at low speed, using the beater attachment. Add all the flour, butter, and vanilla at one time and beat just until mixed. Do not overbeat.)

Immediately turn the batter into the prepared pans, smoothing the tops lightly with a rubber spatula. Tap the pans lightly on the countertop to settle the batter. Bake in the center of the preheated oven for 25 to 35 minutes, or until the top of the cake springs back lightly when touched with a fingertip. Remove the pans from the oven and cool on wire racks for 15 minutes, then hold the racks over the pans and quickly reverse them, turning the cakes out onto the racks. If the waxed paper sticks to the cake, remove it. Again reverse the cakes so the top side is uppermost. Cool for 1½ to 2 hours on the racks, meanwhile preparing the butter cream.

To make the butter cream, first make a crème anglaise or custard with the egg yolks, sugar, salt, light cream, and vanilla, as directed on page 277. Cool the custard. Put the butter into a bowl and beat with a whisk, rotary beater, or electric hand beater until very thick, light, and creamy. Beat this vigorously, a little at a time, into the cooled custard. Chill slightly before using. If the mixture separates, heat it gently in the top of a double boiler over hot water, beating until re-emulsified.

Sandwich the génoise layers with the chilled butter cream and spread a layer of butter cream on the top, if you wish. Or sift confectioners' sugar over the top. If you don't fill and ice the cake, cool it and wrap in plastic wrap and foil to keep it from drying out. It will keep under refrigeration for several days, or it may be frozen and kept in the freezer for several months.

# Cookies

There are all types and shapes of cookies. Easiest to make are the bar type, for which ingredients are simply mixed, spread on a pan, and baked. Rolled cookies are made from a stiff, chilled dough, rolled until thin between sheets of waxed paper or on a lightly floured board, and cut out with cookie cutters. Dropped cookies are pushed from a spoon onto the cookie sheet with the aid of another spoon. These cookies are usually thick and round, with a soft center, and as they spread more than the other types it is important to leave plenty of space—about 2 inches—between them. Pressed cookies are pushed through a cookie press with a shaping tip. Molded or shaped cookies are made with chilled dough and are either shaped into balls and flattened or molded into all kinds of different shapes, such as crescents and rings. Refrigerator cookies are made from dough shaped into a roll, chilled thoroughly, and then sliced thin with a sharp knife. The following cookies belong to the bar, rolled, and dropped types.

For baking cookies, you need large flat pans without sides or with very shallow sides, known as cookie sheets or baking sheets, from which the cookies can be removed easily after baking. Jelly-roll pans can also be used. Large pans are better than small ones, but the pan shouldn't be so large that it impedes the circulation of the hot air in the oven—there should be at least 2 or 3 inches between the pan and the oven sides.

As you usually bake more than one sheet of cookies and cookies bake fast, you can set up an assembly-line system. Put the first sheet of cookies on the lower rack of the oven and when they are almost baked move this pan to the top rack to finish baking and slide another sheet onto the lower rack. In this way the cookies bake evenly. However, if you are baking meringue-type cookies, bake only one pan at a time as the cookies might fall if the oven door is opened and they are exposed to the cold air.

## Scotch Shortbread

*This is a very rich, short, buttery type of bar cookie. The dough can either be pressed into 8-inch pie plates and marked in wedges with a knife so it can be broken into pieces after baking, or patted out on cookie sheets and cut into fingers.*

**Makes about 5 dozen cookies**

¾ pound (3 sticks) unsalted
   butter
1 cup granulated sugar
4 cups sifted all-purpose flour

Preheat the oven to 300°.

Beat the butter in a bowl with a wooden spatula or an electric hand beater until creamy and fluffy, then gradually beat in the sugar and continue beating until very light and thick. Mix in the flour until thoroughly incorporated, then turn the dough out onto a lightly floured board and knead the dough, as you would knead bread, until it is very smooth and forms a ball that breaks slightly when the thumb is run from the center to the edge. Divide the dough in half. Put each half on an ungreased cookie sheet, flatten it with your palms, and then pat the dough out about ½ inch thick. Trim the edges of the dough with a knife and cut it into fingers about ½ inch wide and 3½ inches long. Prick the surface well to prevent it from blistering during baking.

Bake the shortbread until it turns a very pale brown around the edges, about 30 minutes. Remove from the oven and cool slightly, then remove the shortbread with a metal spatula to a rack to cool completely. Store in an airtight tin, or place in freezer bags and seal. Shortbread may be eaten fresh, but is best if allowed to age for a week in a cool place.

# ❧ Sand Tarts

*One of the most popular kinds of rolled cookie is sand tarts. Make sure the dough is thoroughly chilled before rolling.*

**Makes about 2½ dozen cookies**

FOR THE COOKIES
8 *tablespoons (1 stick)*
    *unsalted butter*
1 *cup sugar*
¼ *teaspoon salt*
1 *egg*
2 *cups sifted cake flour*
½ *teaspoon vanilla extract*

FOR THE TOPPING
2 *egg whites*
2 *tablespoons sugar*
½ *teaspoon ground cinnamon*

Beat the butter in a bowl until creamy and fluffy, then beat in the sugar, salt, and egg and continue to beat until very light, fluffy, and pale. Beat in the sifted flour and the vanilla until thoroughly combined. When the dough is well blended, form it into a ball, wrap in waxed paper, and chill in the refrigerator for at least 3 hours.

Roll out the dough between sheets of waxed paper until very thin, less than ¼ inch, and cut into 3- or 3½-inch rounds with a plain or fluted cookie cutter. Preheat the oven to 375°.

Butter 3 cookie sheets. Arrange the cookies on the sheets, lifting them from the paper with a flexible, thin-bladed metal spatula.

Beat the egg whites lightly with a fork and, using a pastry brush, brush the tops of the cookies with the beaten egg white. Sprinkle the tops with the sugar and cinnamon, to taste. Do not overdo either sugar or cinnamon.

Bake the cookies until they turn a deep yellow around the edges, 10 to 12 minutes. Remove from the oven and cool slightly, then remove from the pans with a metal spatula and put on wire racks to cool. These cookies are better used within a week, but they will stay crisp 3 or 4 weeks if stored in an airtight tin in a cool place.

# ❧ Meringue Kisses

*These are dropped cookies made with a meringue mixture and are therefore very sticky. Preferably they should be baked on a cookie sheet lined with cooking parchment. If you don't have parchment, the cookie sheets should be both buttered and floured.*

**Makes 5 dozen cookies**

3 egg whites
½ teaspoon cream of tartar
1 cup superfine sugar
1 teaspoon vanilla

These meringues are most easily made in an electric mixer or with an electric hand beater. If you don't have either one, beat in a large bowl with a wire whisk. Prepare 3 cookie sheets, either by lining them with parchment or by buttering them well, then dusting them lightly with flour.

Beat the egg whites in a bowl until foamy, add the cream of tartar, and beat until white, fluffy, and just beginning to hold their shape when the beater is lifted. Gradually beat in the sugar, 3 or 4 tablespoons at a time, adding the vanilla when half the sugar has been added. Beat until the sugar is dissolved and the whites are smooth, glossy, and stand in stiff, upright peaks—the meringue stage. Preheat the oven to 275°.

Take up a teaspoon of the meringue mixture and push from the tip of the teaspoon with the back of another teaspoon onto the prepared cookie sheet. Space the meringues at least 1 inch apart to allow for expansion. Bake one sheet at a time on the center shelf of the oven for about 20 minutes, or until the meringues are set and very lightly colored. Remove from the oven and cool slightly, then remove them from the sheets to a wire rack to cool, sliding a flexible metal spatula under them. Cool completely. Store in an airtight container between sheets of waxed paper or aluminum foil.

# Casseroles and Other Baked Dishes

## Gratin of Greens

Makes 6 to 8 servings

2 pounds fresh spinach
¾ cup olive oil
2 pounds Swiss chard
2 pounds zucchini
Salt
1 cup cooked rice
3 garlic cloves, finely chopped
6 eggs
½ cup fine bread crumbs

Wash the spinach well. Remove the coarse stalks; dry the leaves thoroughly and chop rather fine. Cook in 2 tablespoons oil in a heavy skillet over medium heat until just wilted. Drain and put into a large bowl. Wash, dry, and chop the chard and cook in 2 tablespoons oil in the same skillet until wilted. Drain and add to the spinach. Wash, dry, trim, and dice the unpeeled zucchini; add about 4 more tablespoons oil to the skillet, and sauté the zucchini, tossing well until just tender. Add to the spinach and chard, season with salt to taste, and mix in the rice and garlic. Combine well and transfer to a well-oiled, heavy 2-quart baking dish. Spoon 3 to 4 tablespoons oil over the top and bake in a 300° oven for 20 minutes. Beat the eggs well; pour them over the vegetable mixture; sprinkle the top with crumbs; return to the oven and bake until the eggs are just set, about 10 to 15 minutes. Eat warm or cold. This makes an excellent luncheon or supper dish.

## Scalloped Oysters

*One of the most popular of all baked oyster dishes, this is a traditional feature of the Thanksgiving or Christmas dinner menu. It can also be served as the hot dish for a supper of cold turkey or ham, or as a luncheon entrée.*

Makes 4 to 6 servings

8 tablespoons (1 stick) butter
1 to 1½ cups freshly rolled
   soda-cracker crumbs
1½ pints oysters
Salt, freshly ground black
   pepper, Tabasco
½ cup liquid from oysters
½ cup heavy cream
½ cup fine bread crumbs

Melt half the butter in a pan and brush a little of it on the bottom and sides of a 1½-quart baking dish. Reserve the rest of this melted butter for sautéing the bread crumbs. Cut the other 4 tablespoons into small pieces.

Cover the bottom of the dish with a layer of cracker crumbs (to make the crumbs, put crackers in a plastic bag and crush coarsely with a rolling pin). Arrange on them a layer of half the oysters, then another layer of cracker crumbs. Dot with half the pieces of butter and sprinkle lightly with salt and pepper and a dash or two of Tabasco. Make another layer of oysters and another layer of crumbs; dot again with butter and sprinkle with salt, pepper, and Tabasco. Pour the liquid from the oysters and the heavy cream over the top. Lightly sauté the bread crumbs in the remaining melted butter until golden, tossing and turning them well. Sprinkle over the top of the oyster mixture. Bake in a 400° oven for 25 minutes. Serve hot.

# Stuffed Eggplant

*Hollowed out, stuffed, and baked vegetables represent one of the best ways to use up leftovers—cold meat, cooked rice or other grains, a few mushrooms, some bread crumbs, whatever you have around. Half the fun is making up your own combinations. Good candidates for stuffing are eggplants, zucchini, green peppers, onions, and tomatoes. When baking eggplant or zucchini, there should always be some water in the dish to create steam and keep the shell soft.*

**Makes 4 to 8 servings**

4 medium eggplants
3 tablespoons butter
4 tablespoons oil
1 large onion, finely chopped
2 garlic cloves, finely chopped
1 cup cooked rice or cooked
    cracked wheat
1½ to 2 cups finely ground
    cold lamb
4 tablespoons chopped parsley
½ cup chopped walnuts or
    whole pine nuts
2 tablespoons tomato paste or
    catsup
Salt, freshly ground black
    pepper
2 eggs, well beaten
½ cup fine bread crumbs

Trim off the stem end and the brown part of the rounded end of the eggplants and wash and dry them. Halve the eggplants lengthwise and cut around the inside with a sharp knife or grapefruit knife, about ⅜ inch from the skin, then scoop out the pulp with a spoon, leaving a ⅜-inch layer around the sides and bottom of the shell. Chop the pulp and set aside. Preheat the oven to 350°.

Heat the butter and 2 tablespoons oil in a skillet and sauté the onion and garlic over medium heat until limp and golden. Add the eggplant pulp and sauté for 5 minutes, until it has cooked down and some of the liquid has evaporated. Stir in the rice or cracked wheat, lamb, parsley, nuts, tomato paste or catsup and season with salt and pepper to taste. Blend well, stir in the beaten eggs, and cook over low heat for 2 minutes. Fill the eggplant shells with this mixture; spoon a little of the remaining oil over the filling and sprinkle the tops with the bread crumbs. Arrange the stuffed shells in a large baking dish or pan and add about ½ inch hot water.

Bake for 40 minutes. If the stuffing seems to be getting too dry on top (it should be brown but not too crisp), baste it with a little oil or with melted butter. Serve one-half eggplant as a first course or a main course at luncheon or two halves as a dinner main course.

# Celery and Pecan Ring

*You can serve this ring hot, filling the center with creamed mushrooms, chicken, shrimp, crabmeat, lobster, or sweetbreads; or cold with seafood or chicken salad.*

**Makes 6 to 8 servings**

½ cup very finely chopped or
  ground celery
2 tablespoons finely chopped
  parsley
¾ cup finely chopped or
  ground pecans
⅓ cup very finely chopped or
  ground onion
⅓ cup very finely chopped or
  ground green pepper
1 cup fine bread crumbs
3 large eggs, slightly beaten
3 tablespoons melted butter
1½ teaspoons salt
¾ teaspoon freshly ground
  black pepper
1½ cups milk

Either chop the vegetables and nuts by hand or, if you have a blender or food processor, process them until you have a more finely ground texture. Combine the celery, parsley, pecans, onion, green pepper, crumbs, eggs, butter, salt, pepper, and milk and mix together thoroughly. Heavily butter a 6-cup ring mold and pour the mixture into it.

Preheat the oven to 350°.

Put the ring mold into a large pan, such as a roasting pan, and place on the center shelf of the oven. Pour into the pan enough hot water to come about halfway up the mold (this prevents the ring from drying out as it bakes) and bake for 1 hour.

Remove from the oven and let the ring mold stand in the hot water for 10 minutes before unmolding. To unmold, loosen the baked mixture from the edges of the mold by running a thin-bladed knife or metal spatula around it; put a round serving platter on top of the mold and invert. Fill the center with desired creamed filling and serve at once. Or cool, cover with plastic wrap, and chill in the refrigerator. When ready to serve, unmold in the same way.

# Lentil Casserole with Sausage

*Lentils are nutritious, delicious, and too often ignored. They combine extremely well with any kind of pork product. You can vary this casserole by substituting for the sausages such meats as well-browned pork chops; braised pork tenderloin, cut into thick slices; quartered roast duck; braised lamb shanks.*

**Makes 6 servings**

2 cups quick-cooking lentils
1 onion, stuck with
  2 cloves
1 bay leaf
1 tablespoon salt

Cover the lentils with water, add the clove-stuck onion and bay leaf, and simmer until just tender, about 25 to 30 minutes, adding the salt after the lentils have cooked for 15 minutes. Drain. Preheat the oven to 350°.

12 Italian sausages, either
    sweet or hot
4 tablespoons (½ stick) butter
½ cup finely chopped onion
Salt, freshly ground black
    pepper
1 cup dry red wine

While the lentils are cooking, prick the skins of the sausages well and poach in water to cover for 5 minutes (see page 29). Drain. Melt the butter in a skillet and sauté the onion until just limp and golden. Butter a 2½-quart baking dish or casserole. Arrange half the sausages in the bottom, cover with half the lentils and half the sautéed onion, and sprinkle lightly with salt and pepper. Make another layer of lentils, then top with sausages and the rest of the onion. Pour in the wine and bake for 25 to 35 minutes or until the top sausages are nicely browned.

## Variation

♦ If you prefer, you can use 6 knockwurst in place of the Italian sausages. Before adding to the casserole, split them in half lengthwise and sauté in butter or bacon fat until browned on both sides.

# Corned Beef Hash Ring

*This is a rather more elegant way of serving corned beef hash, good for a luncheon party. You can use the leftover corned beef and potatoes from the recipe on page 16.*

**Makes 4 servings**

1 large onion, finely chopped
2 tablespoons butter
1½ cups finely chopped cold
    corned beef
3 cups finely chopped boiled
    potatoes
Salt, freshly ground black
    pepper
¼ to ½ cup heavy cream

### TO FILL THE RING
2 cups sliced or quartered
    hard-boiled eggs (about 4
    to 5 eggs) mixed with 1 cup
    béchamel sauce, or 2 cups
    succotash mixed with 1 cup
    béchamel sauce (canned or
    frozen succotash may be
    used)

Sauté the onion in the butter until just golden and limp. Mix with the chopped meat and potatoes and season to taste with salt and pepper. Add enough cream barely to moisten the mixture.

Preheat the oven to 350°. Butter a 6-cup ring mold and pack the corned beef hash into it. Bake for about 45 minutes. Allow to stand for a few minutes after removing from the oven, then loosen around the edges with a knife or spatula, put a serving platter on top of the mold, and invert the mold. Fill the center with the creamed eggs or succotash.

# Casserole of Turkey with Rice

*A good finale for the leftover Christmas turkey, stuffing, and ham.*

**Makes 4 to 6 servings**

5 tablespoons unsalted butter

2 medium onions, peeled and chopped

½ pound firm white mushrooms, sliced

2 cups diced cold turkey

½ cup diced baked ham

1 cup crumbled leftover bread stuffing

2 tablespoons chopped parsley

¼ teaspoon dried thyme

Salt, freshly ground black pepper

1 tablespoon curry powder

1 cup uncooked rice

2 cups hot chicken or turkey broth

Melt 4 tablespoons of the butter in a skillet, add the onions, and sauté over medium heat until limp and golden. Add the mushrooms and sauté for 2 or 3 minutes, until just cooked through. Combine the vegetables in a casserole with the turkey, ham, stuffing, parsley, and thyme. Mix well, taste, then add salt and pepper—the amount will depend on the seasoning in the stuffing. Preheat the oven to 375°.

Melt the remaining tablespoon of butter in the skillet, add the curry powder and the rice, and sauté lightly over medium heat until the rice is just translucent (curry powder should always be cooked in fat to take away the raw taste before being added to a dish). Add to the casserole; pour in the hot broth; cover the casserole and bake until the rice is tender and the liquid absorbed, about 25 to 30 minutes. If the rice does not seem quite tender, add a little more heated broth and continue cooking.

# Baked Fish

Baking is an excellent way to cook a whole fish, and if you stuff it the fish will go even farther. Have the fish gutted and the scales and fins removed, but the head and tail left on—the fish will look better and stay moister and juicier. If the fish is to be stuffed, also have the backbone removed. Good choices for baking among the less expensive fish are cod and haddock. Sea bass, red snapper, striped bass, and whitefish are more costly, but the flesh has a delicacy and flavor that is worth the extra money. A whole fish weighing from 4 to 6 pounds will easily serve 4.

For stuffings, you can choose one with a bread-crumb base, a vegetable stuffing, or one containing seafood such as minced clams, oysters, or crabmeat. To my taste, a simple vegetable stuffing is best.

The baking temperature, time, and method are the same whether the fish is baked stuffed or unstuffed.

# ⤖ Stuffed, Baked Striped Bass

**Makes 4 servings**

1 striped bass or other fish
weighing about 5 pounds,
backbone removed

2 medium onions, thinly sliced

4 or 5 ripe tomatoes, thinly
sliced

2 to 3 tablespoons butter, cut
into small pieces

½ cup chopped parsley

1½ teaspoons salt

½ teaspoon freshly ground
black pepper

Preheat the oven to 450°. Line a baking dish large enough to hold the fish with a double layer of heavy-duty aluminum foil (this makes it easy to lift the fish out and transfer it to a platter after baking). Butter the foil well.

Wash the fish well, dry it, and stuff with alternating layers of the sliced vegetables, dotting each layer with pieces of butter and sprinkling with chopped parsley. Salt and pepper the filling well. Close the opening with small skewers or toothpicks. Measure the fish at its thickest point, from back to belly. Rub the skin of the fish with butter, salt and pepper it, and place in the foil-lined baking pan. Bake for 10 minutes per measured inch—it should take about 30 to 35 minutes. Test with a fork or toothpick; the fish is done when the flesh flakes easily.

Transfer to a hot platter and remove the skewers. Decorate with lemon wedges and watercress and serve with small boiled potatoes.

## Variation

♦ BAKED, STUFFED FISH STEAKS. Substitute 2 large fish steaks for the whole fish; sandwich the stuffing between them and bake as before, allowing 10 minutes per measured inch of thickness of the combined steaks.

## Baked Fish Fillets or Fish Steaks

Arrange fish fillets or steaks in a foil-lined baking dish or a foil-lined broiler pan. Brush with the basting mixture given for broiled fish fillets (page 113) and bake for 10 minutes per measured inch of thickness in a preheated 450° oven, basting once or twice during cooking.

# Thickeners and Liaisons

"*L*iaison" is a very useful word that explains a lot—in the language of cooking, the language of love, and the language of diplomacy. In each case it means very much the same thing: a bond or relationship that in cooking binds the solids and liquids in a sauce, in love binds two people together, and in diplomacy binds countries.

In cooking, the most basic and most valuable of liaisons is the roux, the mixture of fat and flour that thickens a sauce. In a great many of our southern recipes (and, of course, French recipes), you find the instruction "first make a roux." You may not have realized it, but when as a child you watched gravy being made in the pan in which chicken had been fried or meat roasted, this was exactly what was happening. First some of the fat was poured off, then flour was added and cooked over low heat in the remaining fat to make a roux, with all those little bits of browned goodness scraped up in the process. Finally, hot milk or cream or stock was mixed in to make a cream or a brown gravy. The flour was what brought and held everything together, forming a liaison between the fat and the liquid.

This, in a rather more refined and classic form, is what happens when you make one of the great French mother sauces (so called because so many other sauces spring from them) such as a béchamel sauce or white sauce, or a sauce Espagnole or brown sauce. In each case, butter and flour are cooked together until completely amalgamated and frothy. However, the roux for a béchamel is cooked only until it is a light golden color, while for a brown sauce it is cooked until it turns a rich nut-brown, which colors the sauce and gives a more pronounced flavor.

The trouble with the sauces many people make is that the flour in the roux is not cooked long enough, which gives the sauce an unpleasant raw-flour taste. The flour must be stirred and cooked in the fat until it is smooth, golden, and lightly frothing in little bubbles before the liquid is added. Three tablespoons each of butter and flour will make a thick roux that will take about 1 cup of liquid and give you a heavy, stiff sauce of the type used as a base for a soufflé. Two tablespoons of each to about 1 cup of liquid will make a medium roux and a medium sauce, the kind we call a cream sauce or a white sauce. When you make a sauce, it is better to make it too thick than too thin. It's an easy matter to thin it down by adding more liquid, but if you have to thicken it, you'll need to add another type of liaison called *beurre manié*, which I'll tell you about in a minute.

To make a good béchamel sauce takes time and care. I remember visiting a cooking class in London, given by one of my colleagues, where nine girls were being taught béchamel. This was a repeat performance, as the one they had made the previous week had been very poor. Their teacher, a Frenchwoman, showed them how, after the liaison had taken place and the sauce had thickened, the sauce should be simmered very gently while occasionally a pat of butter was stirred in—not enough to cause the sauce to separate or become very fatty, just enough to enrich it and give it a beautiful glossy finish. This gives you a much richer white sauce, and while you don't have to do it, especially if you are going to add other enrichments or flavorings to your basic sauce, you might try it sometime and discover the difference it makes. You'll also find that some of the older French cookbooks will tell you to simmer a béchamel as much as 45 or 50 minutes, which might seem a hell of a long stretch, but again it does make a difference to the texture and flavor.

Once you know how to make a béchamel and a brown sauce, recipes for which I will give you later, you'll have a whole repertoire of other sauces at your fingertips. The addition of cream makes a béchamel a velouté sauce; with cream and egg yolks it becomes a sauce suprême; with cheese it is a mornay; with white wine and fish stock as the liquid you have a white wine sauce for fish. From the basic brown sauce springs a sauce Bordelaise, a sauce diable, a sauce piquante, a Madeira sauce, and many other brown sauces for meat, poultry, game, fish, or vegetables.

The other type of butter and flour liaison evolved by the French, *beurre manié*, is made quite differently. Instead of being cooked together at the beginning, the equal quantities of butter and flour are worked together with a fork or your fingers until they form a thick paste, with the flour completely absorbed by the butter. The paste is rolled into tiny balls, or patted out and cut into squares, and these little pieces are used to thicken a liquid at the end of the cooking time. The mixture, called *beurre manié* because the butter is manipulated or kneaded with the flour, is something you can make up ahead of time and store in the refrigerator for 2 or 3 weeks and bring out whenever you find your sauce is too thin or your soup or stew needs thickening.

Say you have made a stew and it seems a little too thin. You remove the meat and vegetables, bring the liquid to a boil, and then drop in your little balls of *beurre manié*, one or two at a time, cooking and stirring constantly until the liquid is thickened to your liking. The *beurre manié* has to break up, allowing the flour to cook and expand in the liquid, so it takes a little while before you can judge how much you will need to get the right thickness. It's better to underestimate at the beginning, as you can always add more. Once the liquid has thickened, taste it. If there is a floury taste, let it simmer gently for a few more minutes. Then return your meat and vegetables to the pan and let them reheat. *Beurre manié* is also an easy way to thicken a soup to just the consistency you want, or you may use it to thicken a sauce that is too thin.

While butter and flour is the classic, and to my mind the best, liaison, occasionally you'll find a recipe where flour alone is used. The flour is mixed to a heavy paste with water or milk, stirred into simmering liquid, and cooked until thickened. Should this lump, as it is inclined to do, it must be beaten vigorously with a wooden spoon or wire whisk until the lumps disappear or, if that doesn't work, the sauce must be rubbed through a fine strainer.

The Chinese thicken their fast-cooking sauces with cornstarch, adding it in the same way as the flour, after mixing it to a paste with water. Cornstarch does not require long cooking and it makes a sauce very smooth. While it is a serviceable liaison, it has, to my mind, one great drawback. As it thickens, it gives the dish a translucent glaze that I find aesthetically displeasing. My great bone of contention with many Chinese chefs is that they overdo the cornstarch and their dishes have a sticky, glazed look instead of being smooth, velvety, and glossy. Nor do I like pies or fruit desserts in which cornstarch has been used to thicken the juices. They look like cheap bakery products to me.

There are other starches that are mixed with water and used for thickening, usually at the last minute because, like cornstarch, they don't need the long cooking that flour does. Arrowroot, potato starch, and rice flour serve this purpose, but as their thickening power is greater than that of flour, you use proportionately less. One teaspoon of potato starch or arrowroot, or 2 teaspoons of cornstarch or rice flour, have the thickening power of 1 tablespoon of flour.

Arrowroot, more delicate in texture than cornstarch, is often used to thicken desserts as well as sauces. Potato starch is frequently resorted to by chefs and cooks to thicken a sauce that has thinned out or shows signs of separating after cooking. It cooks clear quickly, has no raw taste, and gives a rather glossy finish. Rice flour, which also cooks clear and is almost tasteless, is often used to thicken vegetable soups. Yet another starch used for thickening soups and the juices for fruit pies is quick-cooking tapioca (not the pearl tapioca used for puddings), for which I can find no good words. It has an unpleasant, glutinous quality, and becomes stringy if allowed to boil. While these starches are easy to use and have their place in cooking, I do not care for the rather shiny, artificial-looking finish they give a dish. I prefer to stick with the roux and *beurre manié*.

There are, of course, other thickeners, like ground nuts, grated potato or mashed potato, bread or cake crumbs, that you find indicated in various recipes. These, naturally, give a very different texture and result. The famous English sauce for poultry and game, as common there as cranberry sauce for turkey is here, is bread sauce. This isn't a smooth, velvety kind of sauce; it has a thick, almost porridgelike consistency, but it is nevertheless delicious and unusual. A traditional thickener for certain brown sauces is the blood of an animal or bird. In old recipes for *coq au vin*, beef *bourguignon*, *civet* of hare, and other French dishes, blood was added at the last minute and brought to a boil to both thicken and give great color to the sauce. *Boudin noir*, which we call "blood pudding," is made from pigs' blood. Certain butchers in my neighborhood sell pig and beef blood, but it isn't something you are likely to encounter at your local supermarket.

Finally, there is that masterpiece of nature, the egg. In the preceding chapter on baking we discussed the miraculous leavening power of eggs. They have an equally miraculous thickening power as a liaison. Egg yolks are the liaison with milk or cream that thickens a custard; stirred into chicken broth they produce the velvety *avgolemono*, or Greek egg-lemon soup, and in combination with heavy cream they turn pan juices into an exquisitely, delicately thickened sauce. Probably the most common use of the egg yolk in the kitchen is in the making of the two other mother sauces, hollandaise and mayonnaise. These are known as emulsified sauces because the butter or oil is beaten into the egg yolks in such a way that the egg absorbs and holds the fat in a thick emulsion.

Making mayonnaise and hollandaise is not complicated, but it must be done slowly and with great care and patience and the ingredients must be at the right temperature, otherwise the yolks will curdle and the sauce will break or separate, at which point you must start over with a fresh egg yolk.

In the old days (and even now) people made mayonnaise with a fork or a whisk, beating the egg yolks by hand and then beating in the oil, drop by drop. There is no doubt that to make mayonnaise by hand is a praiseworthy accomplishment, but now that we have perfected electric appliances that do the same job in a great deal less time, I think that anyone who spurns the modern methods is either a fanatic or a masochist. I have come to adopt the food processor or blender method of making mayonnaise. It is unbelievably speedy and enables one to use the whole egg, not just the yolk. The terrific centrifugal power that emulsifies mayonnaise in a matter of seconds produces a stabler and firmer sauce than the old hand method and I, for one, am all for this type of operation. I have yet to tell the difference between a mayonnaise made by hand and one made in the food processor. I'll bet that the great chefs, like Escoffier and Carême, would have used one had it been around in their day.

# Roux-Thickened Sauces

## ❧ Basic White Sauce (Béchamel Sauce)

*This is the most valuable and versatile of all the sauces. It can be used, in its many variations, for seafood, poultry, meat, vegetables, crêpes, pasta, eggs, and for dishes that are to be gratinéed, or browned under the broiler. A thin white sauce (1 tablespoon butter and 1 tablespoon flour to 1 cup liquid) is the base for certain cream soups. A thick white sauce (3 tablespoons butter and 3 tablespoons flour to 1 cup liquid) is the base for soufflés. Very thick white sauces act as the binding agent for croquettes and mousses. In each case, the method is the same, only the proportions of butter and flour to liquid differ.*

*According to the recipe you are following, or the food for which the sauce is to be used, the liquid may be any of the following, or a combination of two (usually broth and milk or cream): milk; cream; chicken or turkey broth; veal, beef, lamb, pork, or ham broth; game broth; clam, fish, or shellfish broth; mushroom or other vegetable broth; dry white wine or dry vermouth combined with broth.*

**Makes 1 cup medium white sauce (béchamel)**

| | |
|---|---|
| *2 tablespoons unsalted butter*<br>*2 tablespoons all-purpose flour* | Melt the butter over low heat in a heavy-bottomed 1½-quart saucepan. This can be of |

1 cup heated milk or broth, or
  other specified liquid
Salt, freshly ground black
  pepper, nutmeg

any suitable material such as stainless steel with an aluminum core, enameled cast iron, lined copper, heatproof porcelain, or Corning Ware. Uncoated iron and aluminum are not recommended as they may discolor a white sauce that contains wine or egg yolks.

Mix the flour into the melted butter with a wooden spatula or spoon and cook slowly, stirring all the time, for 2 or 3 minutes, or until the roux of butter and flour is well blended and frothy. This initial cooking removes the starchy taste of the flour. Gradually stir in the hot liquid—when the liquid is hot there is less likelihood of the sauce lumping, but you should also stir vigorously while adding it to thoroughly mix the liquid and the roux. Or you may, if you prefer, remove the pan from the heat while adding the liquid, which makes it easier to control the thickening of the sauce as the flour absorbs the liquid. Return to the heat as soon as the liquid is mixed in.

Increase the heat to medium and cook, stirring all the time with a wooden spatula or a wire whisk, until the sauce is smooth, thick, and at the boiling point. Let the sauce simmer, stirring, for 3 or 4 minutes, then season to taste with salt, pepper, and nutmeg. Many people tell you to use white pepper in a white sauce, but I am against this. The flavor of black pepper is so much better. If you do see a fleck or two of black in the sauce, so what? I also think a little touch of freshly grated (not ready-ground) nutmeg improves the flavor of a white sauce, but this is for you to decide.

The sauce is now ready to be used, or ready for the enrichments and flavorings that turn it into a sauce of another name. If you are not using it right away, butter a piece of waxed paper large enough to fit inside the pan and lay it on the surface of the sauce, buttered side down, to prevent a skin from forming.

## HOW TO COPE WITH MISHAPS

If your sauce should lump, don't despair. Force it through a fine sieve to remove lumps, return to the pan, and reheat.

If your sauce is too thin (which may happen if you have to remove lumps), make *beurre manié* by working together equal quantities of butter and flour—2 teaspoons of each. Roll into tiny balls, bring the sauce to a boil, drop one or two of the balls into the sauce, and beat them in with a wire whisk, stirring until the sauce thickens. Do not add them all at once, wait and see how thick the sauce becomes before adding more—the amount of thickening depends on how thin your sauce was.

If your sauce is too thick (a medium white sauce should be of a good, thick coating consistency, not stiff and pasty, but not so thin that it slides off the spatula), add a little extra liquid, a tablespoon at a time, until thinned to the right consistency.

## Variations

♦ SAUCE VELOUTE. Enrich the finished sauce by adding ½ cup heavy cream. Simmer a few minutes to blend. Just before using the sauce, beat in a further enrichment of 3 tablespoons butter, 1 tablespoon at a time.

♦ SAUCE SUPREME. Use chicken or veal stock as the liquid. Enrich the finished sauce with cream and egg yolks. Lightly beat 3 egg yolks and mix with 1 cup heavy cream. Stir a little of the hot béchamel sauce into the mixture, to warm and temper the yolks (prepare them for the shock of heat), then stir the yolk mixture into the sauce. Reheat, but do not let the sauce get too hot or boil or the yolks will curdle.

♦ WHITE WINE SAUCE FOR FISH. Use ¾ cup fish stock and ¼ cup dry white wine for the liquid. Beat 2 egg yolks lightly and mix in ½ cup heavy cream. Blend into the finished sauce, as for sauce suprême.

♦ SAUCE MORNAY. Stir ¼ to ½ cup grated Parmesan cheese into the finished sauce and 1 or 2 tablespoons butter, 1 tablespoon at a time. Simmer 3 or 4 minutes. This is a favorite sauce for vegetables, pasta, fish and shellfish dishes, and for dishes that are gratinéed under the broiler. If the sauce is for a gratinéed dish, use the smaller quantity of cheese and omit the final butter enrichment. Then sprinkle the sauced dish with grated Parmesan cheese before putting it under the broiler.

♦ CHEESE SAUCE. This is a sharper and spicier American version of sauce mornay, and a favorite sauce for vegetables. Stir ½ cup grated sharp Cheddar cheese (or, if you prefer, grated Swiss Gruyère or Emmenthaler cheese) and a dash of Tabasco or dry mustard into the finished sauce. Heat only until the cheese melts into the sauce, or it may become stringy from overheating.

♦ TARRAGON SAUCE. Use chicken broth for the liquid. Add 2 tablespoons chopped fresh tarragon or 2 teaspoons dried tarragon and an enrichment of 2 eggs and ½ cup heavy cream, as for white wine sauce. Serve with poached or roast chicken.

♦ FRENCH CURRY SAUCE. This is not a true curry sauce, but a mildly curry-flavored white sauce. Cook 2 teaspoons good-quality curry powder in the butter for 2 minutes before adding the flour (this precooking in butter takes away the acrid rawness of the curry powder), then make the sauce in the usual way. Use for chicken, turkey, veal, and egg dishes and for savory crêpes.

♦ MUSTARD SAUCE. Stir 2 tablespoons Dijon mustard into the finished sauce. Simmer for 2 to 3 minutes. This makes a fairly hot sauce, excellent with broiled fish and strong-flavored oily fish such as herring and mackerel. For a milder sauce, add less mustard.

♦ HORSERADISH SAUCE. Stir 1 to 2 tablespoons drained bottled horseradish, or to taste, into the finished sauce. Or use fresh-grated horseradish to taste and 1 tablespoon lemon juice. Serve with boiled beef.

◆ CAPER SAUCE. Add 3 tablespoons bottled capers and 1 tablespoon liquid from the bottle to the finished sauce. Caper sauce is traditional with boiled leg of mutton or lamb and poached fish.

◆ EGG SAUCE. Peel and slice 2 hard-boiled eggs and add to the finished sauce. This is another traditional sauce for poached fish, especially salmon.

◆ PARSLEY OR DILL SAUCE. Stir ¼ cup finely chopped parsley or 1 tablespoon finely chopped fresh dill and a few drops of lemon juice into the finished sauce. Serve with fish, chicken, or veal.


# ꙮ Basic Brown Sauce

*There are various ways of making the classic French brown sauce, most of them quite time-consuming and requiring many different ingredients and long simmering. One method is first to make a brown roux by cooking the butter and flour very slowly over low heat in a heavy skillet until the roux turns a delicate nut-brown, then mixing this roux into brown stock or beef broth. This would appear to be simplicity itself, but I have found that once a roux has been browned, the parched starch granules in the flour no longer expand as they do in a white roux and a lot more of the roux is needed to thicken the liquid.*

*After working out various methods over the years, I have settled on two brown sauces that work well for me. One is made with a white roux and beef broth, to which I add a drop or two of homemade caramel coloring (similar to the commercial gravy browner) or, if I have any on hand, some glace de viande, to color the sauce a rich, deep brown. Or, if I am in a rush and don't have homemade beef broth on hand, I make a quick brown sauce by simmering canned beef bouillon with red wine and seasonings, to give it a good flavor, and then thickening it with beurre manié.*

**Makes 1 cup basic brown sauce**

2 tablespoons unsalted butter
2 tablespoons all-purpose flour
1 cup brown stock or beef broth
Salt, freshly ground black pepper
1 or 2 drops of caramel coloring (*see below*)
Or ½ teaspoon glace de viande (*see page 24*)

Make a roux of the butter and flour, cook until frothy, and then stir in the liquid and simmer as for basic white sauce. Season the sauce to taste with salt and pepper. Stir in just enough caramel coloring to turn the sauce a rich brown or stir in *glace de viande* and simmer for 2 or 3 minutes. If you are not using the sauce right away or are adding other flavorings, lay a piece of buttered waxed paper on the surface to prevent a skin from forming.

CARAMEL COLORING
Heat 2 cups granulated sugar over low heat in a heavy metal skillet until the sugar melts and begins to bubble and turn a very dark brown. Stirring

constantly with a long-handled wooden spoon, add 1 cup water. Stand back as you pour in the water; the liquid sugar will hiss, bubble up, and may splash on you. Cook the mixture over low heat until it begins to smoke and turn very black and gives off a strong, caramelized smell. What you are really doing is burning it. Add 2 cups water and simmer until blended, about 2 to 3 minutes, then strain and bottle the liquid, which will be thick and syrupy. Store in the refrigerator; it will keep indefinitely.

*Note.* Never use tin-lined copper when making caramel, as the great heat of the caramelized sugar will melt the tin lining.

# Quick Brown Sauce

Makes 1½ cups brown sauce

3 tablespoons unsalted butter
3 shallots or green onions,
    finely chopped
1 cup dry red wine
10½-ounce can beef bouillon
    (not consommé)
Pinch of dried thyme
3 tablespoons soft butter
3 tablespoons flour
Salt, freshly ground black
    pepper

Melt the butter in a heavy-bottomed 1½-quart saucepan; add the shallots or green onions and sauté over medium heat until limp and golden. Stir in the wine and bouillon and bring to a boil. Season with the thyme and cook over high heat until the liquid is reduced almost by half. While the liquid is reducing, work the butter and flour together to a paste with your fingers and then roll it into tiny balls. Drop the *beurre manié* balls, one or two at a time, into the boiling liquid, and cook, stirring constantly with a wooden spatula or a whisk, until the sauce is thickened to your liking. Don't add all the *beurre manié* at once as it will take a little time to break up and thicken the liquid. Three tablespoons butter and 3 of flour will thicken 1½ cups liquid, the same proportions as a roux. Season to taste with salt and pepper, then put the sauce through a strainer to eliminate the bits of cooked shallot or scallion.

## Variations

♦ SAUCE BORDELAISE. Put 6 chopped shallots or green onions, 1 teaspoon dried thyme, and 1 cup dry red wine into a pan; bring to a boil and cook down over high heat until reduced to ⅓ cup. Strain this into 1 cup of brown sauce; add 1 tablespoon cognac and simmer for 3 minutes. Stir in 1 tablespoon chopped parsley. Serve with steaks, roast beef, or roast lamb. Makes 1½ cups.

♦ MADEIRA SAUCE. Combine 1 cup brown sauce and ⅓ cup Madeira; bring to a boil, then reduce the heat and simmer until reduced to 1 cup. For sauce Périgueux, add 2 tablespoons finely chopped black truffle to the sauce. Serve either sauce with roast fillet of beef, or the Madeira sauce with ham or chicken livers. Makes 1⅓ cups.

♦ SAUCE DIABLE. Boil ½ cup tarragon vinegar, ¾ cup dry white wine, 1 finely chopped shallot, and 1 teaspoon dried tarragon until reduced by half. Combine with 1½ cups brown sauce, a dash of Tabasco, and 2 teaspoons dry mustard. Simmer for 3 minutes. Add several grinds of black pepper (the sauce should be very spicy) and strain. Serve with broiled flank steak, broiled chicken, or deviled beef bones. For sauce piquante, add 1 tablespoon chopped capers and 1 tablespoon finely chopped sour pickle to the sauce diable. Serve with roast pork, pork chops, or boiled beef. Makes 1¾ cups.

♦ ORANGE SAUCE FOR ROAST DUCK. Combine 1½ cups brown sauce with ⅓ cup undiluted frozen orange juice, 2 tablespoons orange rind (the orange part only, no white pith) cut into very fine julienne strips, and 1 tablespoon lemon juice. Simmer 5 minutes, then add 1 tablespoon Grand Marnier, Cointreau, or cognac. Just before serving, add ½ cup orange sections and heat through. Makes 2½ cups.

# Egg-Yolk-Thickened Sauces

## ❧ Custard Sauce (Crème Anglaise)

*The French may call it crème anglaise, but this egg-yolk-thickened dessert sauce was known as "boiled custard" to early American cooks, although boiled it is certainly not and never should be. A custard is a delicate thing that should always be approached with respect. It is absolutely essential to have the right implements. Choose a heavy-bottomed saucepan of enameled cast iron, stainless steel with an aluminum core, or lined copper. Or use a double boiler. The glass type is the best, although those with earthenware tops and metal bottoms are also good (the drawback being that you can't see if the water starts to boil in the bottom). You will also need a wire whisk or electric hand mixer and a wooden spatula.*

*This simple, basic custard may be used as a sauce for fruit, fritters, or soufflés and as a base for desserts such as Bavarian cream and ice cream.*

**Makes 2½ cups custard sauce (crème anglaise)**

4 egg yolks (preferably from extra-large or jumbo eggs)
¼ cup granulated sugar
Pinch of salt
1 cup milk
1 cup heavy cream
2 teaspoons vanilla extract
Or a 1½-inch piece vanilla bean

Combine the egg yolks, sugar, and salt in a 1½-quart or 2-quart saucepan or the top of a double boiler. Beat with a wire whisk or electric hand mixer until well mixed, pale, and creamy.

Put the milk and cream in another heavy-bottomed saucepan and heat them just to the boiling point—until tiny bubbles appear around the edge—stirring occasionally to make sure the liquid does not scorch on the bottom

of the pan. (If you are using a vanilla bean, heat it in the liquid and remove before adding the liquid to the egg mixture.)

Slowly pour the hot liquid into the egg mixture in a thin stream, stirring constantly. Put the saucepan over medium-low heat, or put the top of the double boiler over simmering, not boiling, water. The water should not touch the pan but be about ½ inch below it. Cook, stirring constantly with an electric beater turned to low or with a wooden spatula all over the bottom and sides of the pan, until the custard thickens to a light, creamy consistency that just coats the spatula. The custard must not overheat or approach the simmering point, or it will curdle and there is no way to save a curdled custard. Timing cannot be estimated; it may take 20 to 25 minutes, depending on the thickening power of the egg yolks, and whether you use a saucepan or the double boiler, which takes longer but is safer.

Remove the custard from the heat. Stir in the vanilla extract and any desired liqueur flavoring, such as those given below. If you are serving the custard hot, let stand over warm water, covered, until ready to use. To serve cold, pour into a cold bowl and cool. When cool, cover the bowl with plastic wrap and refrigerate.

## Variations

♦ COFFEE FLAVOR. Dissolve 1 tablespoon instant coffee in the hot liquid before adding to the egg mixture.

♦ CHOCOLATE FLAVOR. Dissolve 1 or 2 ounces of semisweet chocolate in the hot liquid before adding to the egg mixture, and reduce the vanilla extract to 1 teaspoon.

♦ LIQUEUR FLAVOR. Add 1 tablespoon rum, cognac, or flavored liqueur to the finished custard with the vanilla extract.

*Note.* Some cookbooks recommend that you mix 1 teaspoon arrowroot or cornstarch with the egg yolks and sugar to stabilize the yolks and help the custard to thicken. While I don't think this is necessary, if you haven't had good luck with your first custard, by all means try it.

# Emulsified Sauces

## ~ Hollandaise Sauce

This rich, suave butter and egg sauce which tastes so elegant with freshly cooked asparagus, artichokes, poached fish, or eggs Benedict takes care and patience unless you make it in a blender or food processor, in which case it is practically foolproof. When you make hollandaise by hand, over direct heat or hot water, you have to be very careful that the sauce doesn't overheat or you'll end up with scrambled eggs.

### HAND METHOD

Makes 1 cup hollandaise sauce

3 egg yolks
½ teaspoon salt
Pinch of cayenne pepper
  Or dash of Tabasco
1 tablespoon lemon juice
8 tablespoons (1 stick) butter,
  cut into small pieces

To make your sauce, use a small, heavy saucepan (enameled cast iron is ideal) or the top of a double boiler over but not touching hot (not boiling) water. If you use the saucepan, make the sauce over low heat.

Put the egg yolks, salt, pepper or Tabasco, and lemon juice in the pan over low heat. Beat with a wire whisk or electric hand mixer until the eggs and seasonings are well blended and the egg yolks have thickened to the consistency of heavy cream. You should be able to see the bottom of the pan between strokes. The egg yolks must be beaten until thick or they will not absorb and hold the butter properly and the sauce will not thicken as it should.

Have the pieces of butter at your elbow, on a warm plate. The minute the yolks are thick, drop one piece of butter into them and stir rapidly with a wire whisk in a circular motion until it has been absorbed by the eggs. Then stir in another piece. Continue to add the butter, one piece at a time, each time stirring until absorbed, until you have a sauce of a consistency that coats the whisk heavily.

If by any chance the sauce seems to be thickening too fast, add a tablespoon of cold water to slow the process. If it is too thin, you are adding the butter too quickly.

As soon as the sauce is made, remove it from the heat and serve. If you have to keep it for a short time, cover the pan with plastic wrap and let it stand over warm water, then reheat slowly over the water until the sauce is just warm. Hollandaise should not be served hot. However, it is my contention that hollandaise should be served freshly made and not reheated, because there is always the chance that the warm sauce will develop bacteria.

### COPING WITH MISHAPS

Should your sauce break and curdle because you have let it get too hot, try stirring a tablespoon of hot water or an ice cube into it, which often works. If it doesn't, start over again with a clean pan and 1 egg yolk. Beat the yolk until thick and then gradually beat in the curdled sauce until it smooths out (this is the same technique you use for saving a curdled mayonnaise).

## BLENDER METHOD

**Makes ¾ cup hollandaise sauce**

*4 egg yolks*
*½ teaspoon salt*
*Dash of Tabasco*
*1 tablespoon lemon juice*
*8 tablespoons (1 stick) butter*

Combine the egg yolks, seasonings, and lemon juice in the container of a blender and turn the blender on and off, at high or "blend" setting, to just blend the mixture. Heat the butter until it is bubbling and very hot, but not browned. Remove the insert from the lid of the blender, turn the blender to high or "blend," and pour in the hot butter in a thin, continuous stream—do not pour too fast or the eggs will not absorb the butter properly. When the butter is absorbed and the sauce thick, turn off the machine. If the sauce should start curdling while you are adding the butter, pour 1 tablespoon hot water into the sauce while the blender is running.

## FOOD PROCESSOR METHOD

**Makes ¾ cup hollandaise sauce**

*4 egg yolks*
*2 tablespoons lemon juice*
*½ teaspoon salt*
*Dash of Tabasco*
*8 tablespoons (1 stick) unsalted*
  *butter, melted and hot*

With the metal blade in place, add egg yolks, lemon juice, salt, and Tabasco to the beaker. Process for 3 seconds and, still processing, pour in bubbling melted butter. It is essential that the butter be bubbling hot or the sauce will not thicken.

## Variations

♦ BEARNAISE SAUCE. Put 1 tablespoon finely chopped shallots or scallions, 1 tablespoon chopped fresh tarragon or 1 teaspoon dried tarragon, 1 teaspoon chopped parsley, ¼ cup white wine, and ¼ cup white wine vinegar into a small pan; bring to a boil and boil until it is reduced practically to a glaze—about 2 tablespoons. Cool. Press this through a strainer into the beaten egg yolks before starting to add the butter. Serve with steak, broiled liver, chicken, or fish.

♦ TOMATO HOLLANDAISE (*Sauce Choron*). Add 1 or 2 tablespoons tomato paste to Béarnaise sauce. Serve with steaks, fish, or chicken.

♦ MUSTARD HOLLANDAISE. Add 1 or 2 teaspoons Dijon mustard or 1 teaspoon hot dry English mustard to the seasonings for the hollandaise. Serve with steak or fish.

♦ SAUCE MOUSSELINE. Fold 1 cup whipped cream into the finished sauce. Serve with fish, asparagus, or soufflés.

♦ ANCHOVY HOLLANDAISE. Add 4 very finely chopped anchovy fillets, 1 finely chopped or crushed garlic clove, and 1 teaspoon capers to the finished sauce. Serve with steak.

# ~ Mayonnaise

*I learned to make mayonnaise when I was just about tall enough to reach the work table. I would stir the mixture constantly with a fork in a deep plate to the slow drip, drip, drip from the oil cruet. Later, I made the sauce with a Dover beater (now called a rotary beater), which was to me a much trickier process than the slow, sure, productive technique of the fork. Nowadays I prefer to make mayonnaise in a food processor or blender. Or, if a large quantity is needed, I use an electric mixer with a whisk attachment. I start the mixer on a rather slow speed and increase it as the mixture becomes a true emulsion.*

*I have always, since childhood, preferred mayonnaise made with a good, fruity olive oil. However, I'm aware that many people do not like the definite flavor of olive oil and would rather have a bland and tasteless oil, in which case I consider peanut oil as good as anything else.*

*In making mayonnaise, it is imperative that both the eggs and the oil be at room temperature. Often mayonnaise made with refrigerated eggs and warm oil will curdle. Here, then, is the traditional way of making mayonnaise by hand.*

## HAND METHOD

Makes 1¾ cups mayonnaise

2 egg yolks (from large or
  extra-large eggs)
1 teaspoon salt
½ teaspoon dry or Dijon
  mustard
1½ cups good, fruity olive oil
  Or half olive oil and half
  peanut oil
1 tablespoon lemon juice
  Or white wine vinegar

Put the egg yolks, salt, and mustard into a mixing bowl and beat with a wire whisk or electric hand mixer until the yolks become thick and sticky. Begin adding the oil, drop by drop, beating it in thoroughly after each addition.

As the mayonnaise begins to thicken, stiffen, and become light in color, which means it has emulsified, you can beat in the remaining oil more rapidly, but be sure it is all incorporated before adding the next batch. When thick and stiff, beat in the lemon juice or vinegar, which gives a nice tartness and thins it out slightly.

Transfer the mayonnaise to a bowl or jar, cover, and refrigerate. You can safely keep it for a week under refrigeration.

## COPING WITH MISHAPS

Should the mayonnaise start to curdle, this indicates you have added the oil too fast. Start over again in a clean bowl. Beat 1 egg yolk until thick, then beat in a few drops of oil. Gradually beat in the curdled mixture until it becomes thick and smooth. This method also works if the mayonnaise does not thicken properly but remains liquid.

## BLENDER METHOD

*The main difference between the hand and the blender method is that with the blender you use whole eggs and add the lemon juice to them. Because of the great speed of the machine, the mayonnaise will begin to stiffen almost immediately and you can add the oil more quickly.*

**Makes 1¾ cups mayonnaise**

2 whole eggs
1 teaspoon salt
½ teaspoon dry or Dijon
   mustard
Dash of Tabasco (optional)
1 tablespoon lemon juice
   Or white wine vinegar
1½ cups olive oil
   Or half olive oil and
   half peanut oil

Put the eggs, salt, mustard, Tabasco (if used), and lemon juice or vinegar in the container of the blender or processor. Blend at "blend" or high-speed setting for no more than 5 seconds, remove the cover insert, and, with the machine running, dribble in the oil in a slow, thin, steady stream, adding it more quickly as the sauce emulsifies. Blend only until smooth and thick; do not overblend.

## FOOD PROCESSOR METHOD

**Makes 1¾ cups mayonnaise**

1 whole egg
1 tablespoon vinegar or lemon
   juice
1 teaspoon salt
¼ teaspoon freshly ground
   pepper
1½ cups oil

With the metal blade in place, add the egg, vinegar, salt, and pepper to the beaker. Process until blended, about 2 to 3 seconds. Continue processing and gradually pour oil through feed tube, slowly at first. As mayonnaise thickens, the sound of the machine will become deeper. Taste for additional vinegar or lemon juice, salt, and pepper. Transfer to a covered container and refrigerate until needed. This mayonnaise will hold for a week to 10 days in the refrigerator.

If mayonnaise should separate, pour the separated mixture into a liquid measuring cup. Using the metal blade and a clean beaker, add 2 egg yolks, and process, pouring the separated mixture through the feed tube very slowly. The mayonnaise will rebind.

## Variations

♦ SAUCE VERTE. Chop ½ cup very dry raw spinach until it is practically a purée (or purée in a blender or food processor). 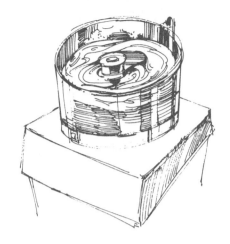 Add to 1½ cups mayonnaise with 1 tablespoon finely chopped fresh tarragon, 2 tablespoons finely chopped parsley, 1 tablespoon finely chopped capers, and, if you can get it, 1 table- spoon finely chopped fresh chervil. You can substitute finely chopped fresh dill for the tarragon and capers, if you serve the sauce with fish. Or you can use finely chopped watercress leaves in the mixture. This sauce is especially good with cold seafood, such as poached salmon, trout in aspic, or cold shrimp. Sauce verte does not keep very well.

♦ MUSTARD MAYONNAISE. Add 1 tablespoon Dijon mustard or 1 tea- spoon dry mustard to each cup of mayonnaise. This is an excellent sauce for shrimp, for celery root salad, or for cold meats such as roast pork.

♦ SOUR CREAM MAYONNAISE. Combine equal quantities of mayon- naise and sour cream. Use for seafood or poultry salads or for coleslaw.

♦ TARTAR SAUCE. Mix 1½ tablespoons finely chopped onion, 2 tea- spoons chopped parsley, 1 teaspoon lemon juice, and 1 tablespoon finely chopped dill pickle into 1 cup mayonnaise. This is just about the most popu- lar sauce for fried fish and shellfish. It is also good with baked fish.

♦ REMOULADE SAUCE. Mix 1 finely chopped hard-boiled egg, 2 table- spoons finely chopped capers, 1 tablespoon finely chopped parsley, a squeeze of lemon juice, and salt and pepper to taste into 1½ cups mayonnaise. You may also add ½ teaspoon anchovy paste and omit the salt. This is perfection with crabmeat, raw scallops, lobster, or shrimp, as a first course, and also with cold chicken or on hard-boiled eggs.

♦ THOUSAND ISLAND DRESSING. Mix 1 tablespoon finely chopped onion, 3 tablespoons chili sauce, 1 finely chopped hard-boiled egg, and salt and pepper to taste into 1½ cups mayonnaise. Allow to stand 1 hour. Serve with salads of crabmeat, avocado, hearts of palm.

♦ RUSSIAN DRESSING. Mix 1 teaspoon dry mustard, 2 tablespoons finely chopped onions, 2 teaspoons Worcestershire sauce, and 2 tablespoons red or black caviar (*not* the best quality) into 1½ cups mayonnaise. If you don't want to use caviar, add 1 tablespoon chili sauce, but caviar makes it an authentic Russian dressing. Great with cold meats and for cold meat sandwiches.

♦ TOMATO MAYONNAISE. Peel, seed (see page 396), and finely chop 2 ripe tomatoes and mix into 1½ cups mayonnaise with 1½ tablespoons chopped fresh basil or 1 teaspoon dried basil. If you can't get really ripe tomatoes, substitute 2 tablespoons tomato paste or strained chili sauce, but the tomatoes give the best flavor. Serve with crabmeat or lobster salad, or on sliced tomatoes.

♦ TUNA MAYONNAISE FOR COLD ROAST VEAL. Combine 1 cup drained and flaked French or Italian white-meat tuna (packed in olive oil) with 6 to 8 finely chopped anchovy fillets, ¼ cup drained and rinsed capers, ¼ to ½ teaspoon finely chopped garlic (to taste), and 1½ cups mayonnaise. Add salt and freshly ground black pepper to taste. Let the sauce mellow for 3 to 4 hours before serving. Thinly slice cold roast leg or shoulder of veal and cover each slice with a thin layer of the tuna mayonnaise, which gives you a short-cut version of the classic Italian *vitello tonnato*.

♦ SMOKED SALMON MAYONNAISE FOR COLD ROAST VEAL. Combine 1 cup finely slivered smoked salmon, preferably Scotch or Nova Scotia, with ¼ cup drained and rinsed capers, ¼ cup finely chopped onion, ¼ cup finely cut fresh dill, ¼ cup finely chopped parsley, and 1½ cups mayonnaise. Season to taste with salt and freshly ground black pepper. Mellow the sauce for 2 to 3 hours before serving. Serve with thinly sliced cold roast leg or shoulder of veal.

# Greek Garlic Sauce (Skordalia)

*Skordalia is basically a mayonnaise with a great deal of garlic, further thickened by finely ground almonds (you can make these by chopping blanched almonds in a blender or food processor until they are pulverized to the consistency of very fine bread crumbs). Traditionally, the sauce is made with a mortar and pestle. First the whole garlic cloves are ground to a paste with the pestle, then raw egg yolks are pounded, into the garlic with the pestle until thick and sticky, then the olive oil is pounded in drop by drop until it forms a mayonnaise. (This is also the way aïoli, the garlic mayonnaise of Provence, is made and it is a long and arduous business.) The other ingredients are then mixed into the mayonnaise.*

*I find it much easier to be less traditional and make the sauce in a blender or food processor. It is delicious with hot or cold poached fish, with fried fish, as a dip for shrimp, raw vegetables, or artichokes, and as a sauce for rather bland vegetables such as cauliflower and boiled potatoes.*

**Makes about 1¾ cups sauce**

4 to 6 garlic cloves, very finely chopped

2 whole eggs

3 or 4 tablespoons lemon juice

1 teaspoon salt

Put the chopped garlic (the amount depends on your taste), the eggs, 2 tablespoons lemon juice, and the salt into the blender or processor, blend or process until just mixed, and then add the oil in a thin, steady stream,

1 cup olive oil
  Or half olive oil and
  half peanut oil
½ cup finely ground blanched
  almonds
1 tablespoon finely chopped
  parsley

according to the directions for blender or food-processor mayonnaise (page 282). Remove to a bowl and stir in the ground almonds and remaining lemon juice, to taste. Mix in the parsley and chill before serving.

## Variations

♦ For a thicker sauce, stir in 1 cup fresh white bread crumbs with ground almonds.

♦ Instead of ground almonds, mix 1 cup plain mashed potatoes (with no butter or milk added) into the sauce. After the mayonnaise is made, put the potatoes into the blender or processor and blend with the mayonnaise until just combined.

# Bread-Thickened Sauce

## Bread Sauce

*This is the traditional British sauce for roast turkey and game birds, such as pheasants. Bread crumbs, the thickening agent, give the sauce its almost porridgelike consistency.*

**Makes about 2½ cups sauce**

1 onion, peeled and stuck with
  2 cloves
2½ cups milk
1 bay leaf
2 cups fresh white bread
  crumbs, made from
  unsweetened, day-old bread
2 tablespoons unsalted butter
Salt, freshly ground black
  pepper

Put the onion, milk, and bay leaf into a 2-quart saucepan and bring slowly to a boil, being careful not to let the milk stick to the bottom and scorch. Remove the pan from the heat, cover with the lid, and leave to steep for 15 minutes, until the onion and bay leaf flavor the milk. Stir in the bread crumbs and the butter and cook the sauce over very low heat, stirring occasionally, for 15 minutes or until the bread crumbs have expanded to make a very thick sauce. Season to taste with salt and pepper. Remove the onion and bay leaf before serving.

# Soups

Like sauces, soups may be thickened by a roux or *beurre manié*, by egg yolks, or by various other starches. You'll also find soups, especially those of Spain and Mexico, in which ground almonds or filberts are the thickening agents. Then, of course, many vegetable and dried legume soups are thickened by the natural starchiness of potatoes, split peas, or dried beans. Another natural thickener is puréed avocado, much used for cold blender soups.

## Cream of Mushroom Soup
Makes 6 servings

1 pound mushrooms
4 cups chicken broth
2 tablespoons butter
3 tablespoons flour
2 cups heavy cream
2 tablespoons sherry or cognac
  (optional)
1½ teaspoons salt, or to taste
¼ teaspoon Tabasco

Wipe the mushrooms with a damp cloth and break off the stems. Simmer the stems in the chicken broth for 35 to 40 minutes, or until the mushroom flavor has thoroughly permeated the broth. Strain the broth through a sieve and return to the pan. Discard the stems. Mix the butter and flour to a paste and roll into tiny balls. Bring the broth to a boil; drop in the balls of *beurre manié* and beat in with a whisk until the *beurre manié* is absorbed and the broth slightly thickened. Slice the mushroom caps thin and add them to the thickened broth. Simmer for 8 to 10 minutes. Meanwhile, heat the cream in another pan, stirring, until just at the simmering point. Add the sherry or cognac to the mushroom broth and then stir in the cream. Add salt to taste and the Tabasco. Reheat the soup until hot, but not boiling, and serve in heated soup plates or cups.

## Egg-Lemon Soup (Soupa Avgolemono)

*This famous Greek egg-lemon soup is kin to the equally well-known, basic egg-lemon sauce for vegetables, meat, and fish.*

Makes 6 servings

8 cups double chicken broth
  (see page 20)
½ cup long-grain rice
Salt to taste
2 whole eggs
2 egg yolks
½ cup lemon juice

Bring the broth to a boil in a pan and add the rice. Simmer until the rice is tender, about 15 to 20 minutes. Taste, and add salt if needed (this depends on how seasoned the broth is).

Beat the eggs and egg yolks together in a bowl with a whisk or rotary beater until light and frothy. Slowly beat in the lemon juice.

Add a cup of the hot broth to the mixture, little by little, beating it in until well blended, then slowly add the mixture to the pan, stirring constantly. Heat through, stirring, but do not allow to overheat or come to a simmer or the eggs will curdle. The soup should be lightly and delicately thickened, of a thin custardlike consistency.

# Cold Spinach and Seafood Soup

*An unusual combination with a lovely, fresh taste, this refreshing soup is excellent for a summer luncheon or dinner party. The thickening is supplied by instant mashed potatoes.*

**Makes 8 to 10 servings**

3 pounds fresh spinach
2 quarts strong chicken stock
　(see page 20)
Juice of 1 lemon
1 tablespoon chopped fresh
　tarragon
　Or 1 teaspoon dried
　tarragon
1 garlic clove, peeled and
　finely chopped
Salt, freshly ground black
　pepper
¾ cup mashed potatoes (made
　with instant mashed
　potatoes, according to
　package directions)
1½ cups finely chopped
　cooked shrimp, crabmeat,
　or lobster
8 to 10 tablespoons sour
　cream or crème fraîche
　(see below)
2 to 3 tablespoons chopped
　parsley

Wash the spinach well in cold water to get rid of all the sand. Break off the heavy stems and put the spinach in a large pot with only the water clinging to the leaves. Cover the pot and cook over high heat until the spinach has just wilted down, turning it with tongs so the top leaves fall to the bottom. Remove, drain well, and press to remove excess liquid. Chop as fine as possible. Combine in a large bowl with the stock, lemon juice, tarragon, garlic, and salt and pepper to taste. Beat in just enough mashed potato to give a smooth but light consistency. Chill well, taste, and correct the seasoning, if necessary. Serve in chilled bowls and sprinkle the top of each serving with chopped seafood, a tablespoon of sour cream or *crème fraîche*, and a teaspoon of parsley.

## CREME FRAICHE

Buttermilk, like yogurt, has been thickened by warmth and a bacterial culture. It can also be used, in turn, to thicken heavy cream, producing a reasonable approximation of the French *crème fraîche*, a matured cream thickened by lactic acids and natural fermentation. Combine 2 cups heavy cream and 5 tablespoons buttermilk in a jar. Cover and shake the jar, as if you were shaking a cocktail, for 2 minutes. Let the jar stand at room temperature for at least 8 hours, or overnight, until the cream has thickened. This will keep under refrigeration for a week.

# Noncooking

Several years ago a young man I know came out with a book for children called *The No-Cook Cookbook*, and if you think that is a contradiction in terms, just stop for a minute and consider how many of the dishes we eat are actually uncooked. It's amazing how much can be done without resorting to the range or oven. Given all our vegetables, fruits, salad greens, cheeses, and breads, the range of dishes that may be eaten *au naturel* is impressive.

*F*or a beginning, let's take that old favorite, steak tartare. All right, so it does require a little muscle, a little effort, to do the chopping and blending, but it is a no-cook process. If you have that latest kitchen miracle worker, the food processor, it's no trouble to chop the beef with onion, maybe a little garlic, capers, anchovies (if you like them), season it, form it into little mounds, top them with an egg yolk, and garnish with chopped onion or chopped parsley. Again, let me repeat that modern equipment can produce just as perfect food as the old, time-consuming hand methods. I've tried just about everything both ways and I can assure you that there is no difference.

Then there's the delicious Middle Eastern raw lamb dish, *kibbeh nayé*, which again can be done completely in the food processor, and the Italian *carpaccio*, slices of raw beef pounded paper-thin and served with a mustard mayonnaise.

One of the more interesting of the world's fish dishes is seviche, from Latin America. Tender raw fillets of fish, little bay scallops, or raw crabmeat are covered with lime juice which "cooks" them by the action of the acid in the citrus, turning the translucent flesh opaque. Now that can't really be called cooking. Scandinavia has *gravlax*, raw salmon cured with salt, sugar, and dill until the flesh becomes beautifully, fragrantly edible. The Japanese, of course, eat a lot of raw fish in the form of *sushi* and *sashimi*, which takes a deft hand, a sharp knife, and the very freshest of firm-fleshed fish. The French latched on to this idea and came up with salmon tartare, raw salmon chopped, seasoned, and served in the same manner as steak tartare.

If you look through cookbooks, you'll find many soups that involve absolutely no cooking, from the Spanish gazpacho and the Turkish soup of cucumber and yogurt to blender soups made with raw or canned vegetables and buttermilk or yogurt. Canned goods are very handy for no-cook dishes. One of my favorite quick soups is made with condensed tomato soup, sour cream, onion, and basil, shaken up like a cocktail.

Raw fruits are among the best and easiest of all desserts. All you have to do is flavor them with a little liqueur or serve them with whipped cream, sour cream, or the American version of *crème fraîche* given on page 287.

Turning to the vegetable world, we have a vast assortment of things that are eaten raw, either freshly tossed in salads or after they have marinated in a vinaigrette sauce—among them mushrooms, tomatoes, cucumbers, avocados, zucchini, celery, onions, radishes, snow peas, carrots, fennel, and green peppers.

First, let's consider the basic dressing for any salad, a sauce vinaigrette, the universal mixture of oil, vinegar, and seasonings that is widely (and incorrectly) known as French dressing.

# Green Salad

## ❧ Basic Vinaigrette Sauce

You can't make a good salad without a good vinaigrette sauce. A true vinaigrette is as simple as one, two, three—oil, vinegar, salt and pepper—and the success depends on the quality of the ingredients.

First, a good oil, preferably a rich, fruity, and flavorful olive oil. Other oils don't have enough flavor to make a good vinaigrette.

Second, a vinegar that is not sharp or acid, either red or white wine vinegar (white tends to be milder). There are some fine imported French wine vinegars available and a few excellent ones from California. If you can't find a good wine vinegar, use cider vinegar or lemon juice. I don't recommend that you buy an herb-flavored vinegar—if you want an herb flavor in your salad it's better to use real herbs, fresh or dried.

Third, salt and pepper. I like to use coarse (kosher) salt for salads, as for other cooking, because it has more flavor and guts than iodized table salt, and a better texture. Freshly ground black peppercorns have more spiciness and taste than ready-ground pepper which, as far as I'm concerned, is worse than useless.

As to proportions, after years of experimenting I find that I prefer to use 3 or 4 parts of oil to 1 of vinegar, depending on the heaviness of the oil and the sharpness of the vinegar. This is something you must learn to adjust so there is a perfect balance. Start with less vinegar than you think you will need, then taste and see if you need more. You can always add, but you can't subtract.

**For a green salad for 4
(about 8 cups loosely packed greens)**

1 teaspoon coarse (kosher) salt
½ teaspoon freshly ground black pepper
1½ to 2 tablespoons wine vinegar
6 tablespoons fruity olive oil

Blend the ingredients together with a wooden spatula or a fork, using 1½ tablespoons vinegar. Then taste, and add more if you feel the dressing needs it. This makes about ½ cup.

Never add sugar to a vinaigrette. If the vinegar is mild, as it should be, no sweetening is necessary. Always mix your vinaigrette just before you intend to use it. The fresher it is, the better. Don't follow that reprehensible practice of making the vinaigrette days ahead and keeping it in a jar in the refrigerator. For that matter, don't store oil in the refrigerator. It gets cloudy, thick, and sluggish. If you are afraid of opened oil going rancid in hot weather, buy a small quantity at a time and use it up quickly.

# Variations

♦ GARLIC. If you like garlic flavor in a salad, either crush a clove of garlic and rub it into the salt you are using for your dressing or impale the crushed clove on a toothpick, put it in the vinaigrette, and remove it just before tossing the salad. Or adopt the French way of giving salad a garlic flavor. Rub the crushed clove on a small cube of dry bread (called a *chapon*), toss the bread with the salad, and let some garlic-lover eat it. Never, ever, use garlic salt or garlic powder; the flavor is ersatz and disagreeable and will ruin your salad.

♦ MUSTARD. There are times when mustard is needed in a vinaigrette—for instance, when you are dressing a vegetable that needs some extra punchiness, such as the coarse, bitter greens like chicory, or green beans. Use either the French-style Dijon mustard or dry, hot mustard and adjust the amount to the salad. First blend the mustard (about ½ teaspoon) with the salt, pepper, and vinegar, then mix in the oil.

♦ HERBS. The outstanding salad herbs are tarragon, chervil, parsley, chives, and, if you are using tomatoes, basil. Dill goes well with cucumber salads or tomato salads, but is rather limited as a regular salad herb. Use either 1 tablespoon chopped fresh herbs or 1 teaspoon dried herbs, crushed in the palm of your hand with your thumb, to ½ to ¾ cup of vinaigrette. Don't throw a bouquet of herbs into your dressing—they will just cancel each other out. One herb, possibly with parsley as a companion, is ample.

## CHOOSING AND PREPARING GREENS FOR SALAD

Too many simple green salads suffer from a lack of imagination. I've known people to use nothing but iceberg lettuce, although this is just one of the salad greens available, and by no means the best. (You'll find a detailed list of salad greens on page 356.) Select from such leafy types as Boston, Bibb, romaine, escarole, chicory, watercress, leaf lettuce, field or corn salad, dandelion greens, arugula, endive, and tender young leaves of spinach and sorrel. Finely shredded cabbage and Chinese cabbage can also be used in salad. Pick one type of green or a combination—but consider their texture and nature. Delicate Boston lettuce or field salad would be overpowered by coarse, tough greens such as escarole and chicory.

Wash the greens ahead of time. The reason salads are limp, soggy, and insipid is because the greens are not thoroughly dried and crisped before being tossed. Separate the leaves and wash the greens carefully, removing all sand and dirt (certain types of lettuce, notably Bibb, are great harborers of dirt). Discard wilted or discolored leaves. Shake off excess water, or spin dry in a salad dryer, if you have one. Then roll the washed greens loosely in several thicknesses of paper towels or in a clean dish towel; put them in plastic bags and store in the vegetable crisper section or on the bottom shelf of the refrigerator for 12 to 24 hours. Don't put them in a part of the refrigerator that gets too

cold, or they may freeze and become unusable.

How much salad should you calculate per serving? That's hard to say, but it is my feeling that you should allow about 2 cups of loosely packed greens per person, or slightly less if you are putting other ingredients in your salad.

Prepare the salad at the last minute so it will stay fresh and crisp. Break or tear (do not cut) large leaves into bite-size pieces with your hands, leaving smaller ones whole. Put the greens in the salad bowl, pour some of the vinaigrette sauce over them, and toss gently, with salad tossers or your hands. Add more vinaigrette as needed, until each leaf is lightly coated. I like to use my hands to toss. It's a good practice for a beginner because your hands will tell you when the greens are coated with just enough dressing. Don't drown your salads. Serve at once. You can vary your plain tossed green salad by adding other vegetables.

Here are some suggestions:
♦ Sliced raw mushrooms
♦ Slices or cubes of avocado and chopped chives
♦ Finely cut celery and thin strips of green pepper, topped with onion rings
♦ Sliced radishes, sliced cucumber, and chopped green onions
♦ Onion rings or finely chopped raw onions or green onions
♦ Thin shreds of cooked or canned beets in a salad of bitter or peppery greens, such as endive, chicory, arugala, or watercress.

I'm not an advocate of adding tomatoes to a green salad, except for whole cherry tomatoes. The flavors are complementary, but the addition of slices or wedges of tomato tends to make the salad watery. If you like tomatoes as a salad, have a platter of sliced tomatoes vinaigrette.

# Vegetables Vinaigrette

Salads of vegetables, cooked, canned, or raw, served with a vinaigrette sauce, are more commonly known as vegetables vinaigrette. They can be served alone as a salad or first course, or as part of an hors d'oeuvre selection, along with other vegetables vinaigrette, canned, fresh, and cured fish and shellfish, pâtés, ham, and sliced sausages such as salami and mortadella. Some vegetables benefit from being marinated first for an hour or two.

## Fresh Mushroom Salad

**Makes 6 to 8 servings**

2 pounds very firm
  mushrooms
½ cup vinaigrette sauce
  (see page 290)
1½ tablespoons chopped fresh
  tarragon
  Or 1½ teaspoons dried
  tarragon
2 tablespoons finely chopped
  parsley

Contrary to what you are often told, white, cultivated mushrooms don't need washing. Just wipe them with a damp cloth or dampened paper towels.

Wipe the mushrooms, break off the stems and reserve them for some other use (they can be chopped and cooked down in butter until all the liquid evaporates, then used for an omelet filling or swirled into scrambled eggs). Slice large mushroom caps lengthwise about ¼ inch thick. Small mushrooms may be left whole, or halved. Put the mushrooms into a mixing bowl, add the vinaigrette sauce and tarragon, and toss well. Let the salad stand for 1 or 2 hours. To serve, put into a serving bowl or dish, add additional oil and vinegar, if needed, and sprinkle with the parsley.

### Variation

♦ Use chopped fresh dill instead of tarragon. This gives the salad another dimension that is extraordinarily agreeable.

## Cucumber Salad

**Makes 4 servings**

2 large or 3 medium cucumbers
2 teaspoons salt
½ cup vinaigrette sauce (see
  page 290)
2 tablespoons chopped fresh
  dill or parsley

Peel the cucumbers with a paring knife or vegetable peeler, cut them in half lengthwise, and remove the seeds with a spoon. Slice the cucumbers thin, put them in a colander or sieve and sprinkle them with the salt Let them drain in the sink or over a bowl for 1 to

2 hours or until the bitter juices have been drawn out by the salt and the slices are limp. Rinse them quickly with cold water, pat dry on paper towels, and toss them with the vinaigrette sauce. Add the dill or parsley and toss again, lightly. Serve on lettuce leaves as a salad or first course.

## Variation

◆ Instead of vinaigrette sauce, dress the wilted cucumber with ½ to 1 cup sour cream or yogurt mixed with 1 tablespoon lemon juice, and toss with the dill or parsley.

# Tomato Salad

*Really ripe tomatoes usually need no peeling, but if the skin is thick and coarse, they are better peeled. To peel, drop the tomatoes into a bowl; pour boiling water over them to cover; leave for 30 seconds, then remove by piercing the core of the tomato with a fork or knife point and lifting it out of the bowl. Cut out the core and remove the skin, which will slip off easily. No salt, vinegar, or oil should touch the sliced tomatoes until they are ready to be eaten. Tomatoes that are left to stand in a vinaigrette sauce become slimy and gooey. I also feel that tomatoes should not be chilled before serving; they taste better at room temperature.*

**Makes 6 to 8 servings**

6 firm ripe tomatoes, cored
   and peeled (if necessary)
½ cup vinaigrette sauce (see
   page 290)
1 tablespoon chopped parsley,
   preferably Italian
1 tablespoon chopped fresh
   basil or dill

Slice the tomatoes thin and arrange them on a serving platter or in a glass or earthenware salad bowl. Just before serving, pour the vinaigrette sauce over them and sprinkle with the chopped herbs.

## Variations

◆ Add 2 tablespoons finely chopped green onions.
◆ Use chopped chives instead of basil or dill.
◆ Add 1 small garlic clove, peeled and very finely chopped.

## Other Vegetables

Other raw or canned vegetables that may be dressed with a well-seasoned or an herbed vinaigrette sauce, in the proportions of ½ cup vinaigrette to 4 cups vegetable, are:

### FRESH VEGETABLES

- ♦ FAVA BEANS. Use a basil-flavored vinaigrette.
- ♦ CABBAGE, GREEN OR RED, SHREDDED. Use a mustard-flavored vinaigrette and 1 teaspoon celery seed.
- ♦ CARROTS, GRATED. Use a basic vinaigrette.
- ♦ CAULIFLOWER, THINLY SLICED. Use a basic vinaigrette.
- ♦ CELERY, THINLY SLICED. Use a mustard-flavored vinaigrette.
- ♦ ONIONS, THINLY SLICED. Crisp in ice water for several hours. Drain, dry, and dress with a basic vinaigrette flavored with 1 small garlic clove, peeled and very finely chopped.
- ♦ SWEET GREEN OR RED PEPPERS, PEELED AND THINLY SHREDDED. Use a basic vinaigrette. (For directions for removing skins, see page 119.)

### CANNED VEGETABLES

Drain the canned vegetables, rinsing them if they are in a thick fluid, like kidney beans and cannellini (white beans), and arrange on a platter or in a bowl.

- ♦ ARTICHOKE BOTTOMS OR HEARTS. Use a basic vinaigrette.
- ♦ ASPARAGUS TIPS OR SPEARS. Use a tarragon-flavored vinaigrette.
- ♦ WHOLE GREEN BEANS. Use a basic vinaigrette. They may also be combined with thin rings of white onion and chopped parsley.
- ♦ KIDNEY BEANS. Use a basic vinaigrette and thinly sliced white onion.
- ♦ CANNELLINI BEANS. Use a basic vinaigrette.
- ♦ BEETS, WHOLE OR SLICED. Use a basic vinaigrette.
- ♦ WHOLE-KERNEL CORN. Use a basil-flavored vinaigrette.
- ♦ CELERY ROOT, SLICED. Use a basic vinaigrette.
- ♦ CELERY HEARTS. Use a basic vinaigrette and drape with anchovy fillets.
- ♦ HEARTS OF PALM. Use a basic vinaigrette. They may also be combined with anchovy fillets and sliced boiled potato.

# Mayonnaise-Dressed Vegetables

## Celery Root Rémoulade

*Celery root is a knobby root vegetable that is most generally used for a purée (see page 52), or sliced in fine julienne and combined with a spicy mayonnaise. There are two schools of thought about the preparation of celery root. Some blanch the celery root for a minute or two in boiling water before slicing it. Personally, I prefer to peel it and slice it raw, using a mandoline slicer, a Mouli-julienne, or the coarse shredding attachment of a food processor. If you have none of these aids, slice thin and then cut into fine julienne with a sharp knife. Celery root rémoulade is usually served as a first course, either alone or as part of the hors d'oeuvre selection.*

**Makes 4 servings**

1 pound celery root, peeled
    and cut into fine julienne
    strips
1 cup mayonnaise (see
    page 281)
1 tablespoon Dijon mustard
1 tablespoon Dusseldorf
    mustard
    Or 1½ teaspoons English
    mustard
Salt

Put the celery root strips in a mixing bowl. Blend the mayonnaise and mustards (for a spicier sauce, use English mustard), mix with the celery root, and let it mellow for 1 hour. Taste for seasoning and add salt if necessary. Serve as a first course, on lettuce leaves. It also makes a good accompaniment to thinly sliced, dry (ready-to-eat) sausages like salami and cervelat.

## My Favorite Coleslaw

*Coleslaw must be one of the oldest and certainly one of the most popular American dishes. There are innumerable ways of making it, some with a boiled dressing, others with a very spicy vinaigrette, but to my mind it is best when simply tossed with homemade mayonnaise and sour cream.*

**Makes 6 to 8 servings**

1 firm white cabbage,
    weighing 2 to 3 pounds
1 cup homemade mayonnaise
    (see page 281)
1 cup sour cream
1 teaspoon salt
½ teaspoon freshly ground
    black pepper

Wash and dry the cabbage, then trim it, cutting off the stalk end and removing discolored or limp outer leaves. Cut into quarters, lengthwise; cut out the hard core at the bottom with a small sharp knife; then put the cabbage on a board and cut the quarters into thin shreds with a large sharp knife, cutting down through the rounded side. Put the shreds into cold water and leave for 1 hour to crisp. Drain well and combine with the mayonnaise, sour cream, salt, and pepper. Toss well and let stand for 30 minutes, or longer if you like a wilted slaw.

## Variations

♦ For a sweet-and-sour slaw, mix together 2 tablespoons sugar, ¼ cup cider vinegar, 1 teaspoon dry mustard (or to taste), and ¼ teaspoon Tabasco. Mix into the mayonnaise, sour cream, and seasonings before combining with the cabbage.

♦ For a spicy slaw, add 1 tablespoon freshly grated horseradish or drained bottled horseradish to the mayonnaise mixture.

# Composed Salads

These salads are composed in two senses of the word: composed of a variety of ingredients and allowed to compose or rest themselves, rather than being agitated like a tossed salad. Composed salads can encompass anything from a modest mixture of different vegetables to an elaborate combination of greens, vegetables, seafood, meat, poultry, and fruit that is a main dish in itself—and almost a work of art. Arrangement is one of the secrets of a perfect composed salad. There should be a blend of colors, tastes, and textures. The ingredients should be attractively cut and the salad beautifully arranged on a large platter or in a bowl so that it becomes almost a centerpiece for the table.

While a very simple composed salad, such as one of Bibb lettuce and raw mushrooms, may be served with meat or poultry, the majority are eaten alone, either as a first course, or as a main course with French bread or rolls. More substantial composed salads of cold cooked meats and fish, such as beef salad or lobster salad, are generally served as a main course. The following composed salads are made chiefly with raw or canned ingredients.

# Salade Niçoise

*This Provençal salad is one of the best of all luncheon dishes. You can vary it to taste, adding other vegetables of your choice. The only constants are the tuna, anchovies, hard-boiled eggs, tomatoes, and tiny black olives. You can also serve small helpings of this salad as a first course, as they do in Provence.*

**Makes 4 to 6 main-course servings**

1 head Boston or romaine
   lettuce, washed, dried,
   and crisped
2 7-ounce cans white-meat
   tuna, drained
20 to 30 anchovy fillets,
   drained on paper towels
4 to 6 ripe tomatoes, cored
   and quartered
   Or 12 to 18 cherry
   tomatoes
4 to 6 hard-boiled eggs,
   quartered
½ cup small black olives,
   preferably Niçoise olives
1 tablespoon chopped fresh
   basil
   Or 1 teaspoon dried basil
1 cup vinaigrette sauce (see
   page 290)

OPTIONAL
INGREDIENTS
½ cup finely chopped yellow
   onion
   Or 1 red Italian onion,
   sliced into thin rings
¼ cup pimiento strips
1 green pepper, sliced into
   thin rings
½ cup canned, drained
   artichoke hearts

Cover a large platter or line a large salad bowl with the lettuce leaves. Place the tuna in the center and surround it with the anchovy fillets. Arrange the tomatoes and eggs around the edge of the platter or bowl and sprinkle the olives on top. Add any of the optional ingredients—onion is good in a salade Niçoise, and so are green pepper rings. Sprinkle the salad with the basil. When you are ready to serve, pour the vinaigrette sauce over the salad at the table and toss lightly. Serve with French bread.

## Variations

♦ Certain cooked vegetables may also be added to the salad, such as tiny, boiled new potatoes or sliced boiled potatoes, green beans cooked until just bitey-crisp, or cooked artichoke hearts rather than canned. Little croutons of bread, sautéed until golden brown in oil with a garlic clove, are another good addition.

# Tomato, Onion, and Avocado Salad

*Basically a variation on the simple tomato salad, this combines three ingredients with complementary flavors and textures, and so becomes a composed salad.*

**Makes 6 servings**

6 firm ripe tomatoes
1 large red Italian onion
1 ripe avocado
1 to 2 tablespoons chopped parsley
1 tablespoon chopped fresh basil, if available
½ cup vinaigrette sauce (see page 290)

If the tomatoes have coarse, thick skins, peel them (see page 294). Otherwise, remove the core with a small, sharp knife and slice them thin. Peel and thinly slice the onion. Halve the avocado lengthwise; remove the pit; peel and slice into ½-inch-wide strips. Do not peel and slice until just before serving, as avocado darkens quickly when exposed to the air. (If the avocado is fully ripe and easily separated from the skin, you may find it easier to first slice the avocado with the skin on and then peel it off with your fingers.) Arrange alternating slices of tomato, onion, and avocado on a platter and sprinkle with the chopped herbs. Pour the vinaigrette sauce over them and serve.

# Health Salad

*This delicious and attractive salad of raw vegetables is often served in health-food restaurants, hence the name. To shred the vegetables, use a food processor or Mouli-julienne with a coarse shredding attachment, the coarse side of a grater, or cut into fine shreds by hand.*

**Makes 6 servings**

1 head lettuce of your choice, washed, drained, and crisped

1 cup freshly shredded raw carrots

1 cup freshly shredded raw young beets

½ cup freshly shredded Japanese radish (daikon) or icicle radish

¾ cup freshly shredded raw, young, white turnips

1 small cucumber (peeled if waxed), seeded and shredded

12 cherry tomatoes

6 ribs celery, cut into julienne strips

½ to ¾ cup vinaigrette sauce (see page 290)

OPTIONAL
INGREDIENTS

1 cup of any of the following: raw young green peas, thinly sliced snow peas, sliced raw mushrooms

Arrange the lettuce leaves on a platter or in a shallow bowl. Heap shredded and julienne vegetables in individual mounds to make an appealing color pattern and arrange the cherry tomatoes around the edges. Serve the vinaigrette sauce in a separate bowl, so the guests can help themselves to their choice of vegetables and add vinaigrette to taste.

# Avocado, Onion, and Grapefruit Salad   Makes 4 servings

1 large avocado
1 large grapefruit
1 red Italian onion
1 head lettuce, washed dried,
    and crisped
½ cup vinaigrette sauce (see
    page 290)

Halve the avocado lengthwise; remove the pit; peel and cut into crescent-shaped strips, about ½ inch wide. Remove the peel and pith from the grapefruit by cutting it off in a long spiral, around the fruit, with a sharp knife (hold the grapefruit over a bowl to catch the juice). Then remove whole sections, one by one, by cutting downward on either side of the membrane surrounding them. Peel the onion and slice thin. Arrange the lettuce leaves on a platter or in a bowl, then put alternating slices of avocado, onion, and grapefruit on top of them. Dress with the vinaigrette sauce.

*Note.* Oranges can be peeled, sectioned, and used in the same way.

# Gruyère Cheese Salad

*An excellent salad to take on a picnic, as it improves with age.*

Makes 6 servings

2 pounds Swiss Gruyère
    cheese (imported, not
    domestic), finely shredded
2 cups finely sliced green
    onions
1 cup sliced stuffed green
    olives
1 cup vinaigrette sauce (see
    page 290) flavored with
    1 tablespoon Dijon mustard
Salad greens

Combine the cheese, onions, and olives; add the vinaigrette sauce and toss until well combined. Let the salad stand at least 30 minutes to mellow the flavors, then arrange it in a bowl lined with salad greens. If you wish, garnish the top with a few more sliced onions and olives—about 2 tablespoons of each. Serve with French bread or rolls.

# White Bean and Tuna Salad

A delicious summer salad for a buffet or a luncheon main dish that may be made either with cooked white beans or canned Italian cannellini beans, which can be found in any supermarket.

**Makes 6 servings**

6 cups cooked white beans (see page 49)
Or 3 20-ounce cans cannellini beans
1 cup vinaigrette sauce (see page 290) flavored with 1 tablespoon chopped fresh or 1 teaspoon dried basil
1 cup finely chopped onion
2 7-ounce cans white-meat tuna, drained and flaked
1 tablespoon chopped fresh basil
¼ cup chopped parsley
Additional oil and vinegar if necessary

If you use the canned beans, after draining them, rinse them well under cold running water in a colander to get rid of the thick, gummy liquid that clings to them. Shake well to free of excess water, then put the canned or the freshly cooked beans into a serving bowl or dish. Pour the vinaigrette sauce over the beans, letting it run through to coat them, then toss very lightly to distribute the vinaigrette—don't toss too much or the beans will break up. Put the onion and tuna on top of the beans. Sprinkle with the basil and parsley. Just before serving, add a little more oil and vinegar, if the salad seems to need it, and toss lightly to combine ingredients.

## Variations

♦ Add ½ cup small black olives and 6 chopped anchovy fillets with the onion and tuna.

♦ Use canned salmon, or boneless, skinless canned sardines instead of tuna.

♦ Omit the tuna. Serve bean salad in tomato shells, as a first course. To prepare the shells, slice off about ½ inch of the top, scoop out all the seeds and pulp, and turn the hollow shells upside down to drain.

# Tabbouleh

This Middle Eastern salad is immensely refreshing on a hot day and especially good with broiled chicken or kebabs. Be sure to use the fine grade of bulghur (cracked wheat); the others are too coarse for this salad. You can buy it in Middle Eastern groceries or health-food stores.

**Makes 4 to 5 servings**

½ cup fine bulghur (cracked wheat)
3 medium-sized ripe tomatoes, peeled, seeded, and finely chopped

Soak the bulghur in cold water to cover for 30 minutes. Drain in a sieve, lined with cheesecloth to prevent the fine grains from falling through, then twist the cheesecloth into a bag and wring out the remaining moisture from

1 cup finely chopped parsley
1 cup finely chopped green
    onions
⅓ cup lemon juice
Salt
⅓ cup olive oil
¼ cup finely chopped fresh
    mint leaves
    Or 2½ tablespoons dried
    mint, crushed with your
    fingers
Boston or romaine lettuce
    leaves

the bulghur. Put the bulghur on a clean dry dish towel, pat out flat, and leave until fairly dry. Then place the bulghur in a large bowl; add the tomatoes, parsley, onions, lemon juice, and salt to taste. Mix gently but thoroughly, using your hands or wooden spoons. Just before serving, mix in the oil and fresh or dried mint. Taste, and correct seasoning if necessary. Serve on lettuce leaves.

# Guacamole

*There are innumerable versions of this Mexican sauce-cum-salad, which seems to have become American by adoption, and I'm going to give you my favorite, with variations.*

*Buy avocados that are ripe and soft enough to be easily mashable, but not so ripe that they have turned dark. Avocados discolor very quickly when cut and exposed to air. Use a stainless-steel knife, make the guacamole a short time before you plan to serve it, and keep it tightly covered with plastic wrap. Putting the avocado pit in the center of the guacamole helps to prevent darkening and so does the acidity of lime juice.*

**Makes about 4 cups**

1 to 2 canned, peeled green
    chilies
    Or 1 canned jalapeño or
    serrano chili
2 large, fully ripe avocados
2 tablespoons lime juice
Salt

Split the canned chilies, scrape out and discard the tiny seeds, which are very hot, then chop the flesh very fine. Jalapeño and serrano chilies are hotter than those sold as "peeled green chilies," so use less. Never touch your fingers to your eyes when working with chilies, as the juice is highly irritating, and wash your hands well with soap and water afterward.

Halve the avocados, remove the pits, and scoop the pulp into a bowl with a spoon. Mash until smooth with a fork. Mix in the chopped chili, lime juice, and salt to taste. The mixture should be spicy, not bland. Put the avocado pit in the center; if you are not serving it right away cover the bowl tightly with plastic wrap until ready to use. Serve as a dip with tortilla chips, as a salad on lettuce leaves, or as a sauce for Mexican foods, such as tacos. It is also delicious on top of hamburgers or charcoal-broiled steaks or as a sauce for fried chicken which has had a little chili powder added to the flour coating.

## Variations

♦ For a more traditional guacamole, add 1 peeled, seeded, and finely chopped tomato, ½ cup finely chopped white onion, and 1 tablespoon finely chopped cilantro, or fresh coriander (sold as Chinese parsley in Asian markets).

♦ Add ½ cup of any of the following: crisply cooked, crumbled bacon; chopped roasted peanuts or chopped salted almonds; thin strips of Smithfield or country ham.

# Soups

## California Gazpacho

*The Spanish gazpacho has become one of the most universally popular uncooked, cold soups and, as was to be expected, variations have proliferated. Traditionally, the soup is a combination of puréed raw vegetables, garlic, bread crumbs, oil, vinegar, water, and seasonings—served well chilled with an ice cube in the plate and a garnish, passed in separate bowls, of the same vegetables, finely chopped, and sometimes small croutons. This version has more texture and needs no vegetable garnish.*

**Makes 6 servings**

3 pounds ripe tomatoes
2 cucumbers
½ cup finely chopped green
    pepper
½ cup finely chopped onion
2 garlic cloves, very finely
    chopped
2 cups chilled tomato juice
⅓ cup olive oil
3 tablespoons wine vinegar
¼ teaspoon Tabasco
Salt, freshly ground black pepper
6 cubes tomato juice, frozen
    in ice cube trays

CROUTONS
1 cup ¼-inch cubes of white
    bread
2 to 3 tablespoons olive oil
1 garlic clove, finely chopped

Peel and seed the tomatoes and chop fine, saving as much of the juice as possible. Peel cucumbers, split lengthwise, scoop out seeds with a teaspoon, and chop fine. Combine tomatoes and their juice, cucumbers, green pepper, onion, garlic, tomato juice, oil, vinegar, Tabasco, and salt and pepper to taste in a large mixing bowl. Stir well, cover with plastic wrap, and chill until very cold, 3 or 4 hours.

Sauté the bread cubes in the olive oil with the garlic over medium-high heat until lightly browned on all sides, tossing them well. Do not let the bread or garlic burn. Remove to paper towels to drain and cool.

Taste the gazpacho for seasoning and add more salt, pepper, Tabasco, and garlic, if needed. Serve in chilled bowls or soup plates with a tomato-juice cube in each and pass the croutons in a bowl.

# Turkish Cucumber and Yogurt Soup   Makes 4 to 6 servings

1 large or 2 small cucumbers
Salt, freshly ground black
  pepper
2 to 3 garlic cloves, peeled
3 cups yogurt
3 tablespoons finely chopped
  fresh mint
  Or 1 tablespoon dried mint,
  crushed

Peel the cucumber and either shred or dice fine. If diced, sprinkle lightly with salt and put in a colander over a bowl to drain for 30 minutes (shredding will remove most of the water from the cucumber), then taste. If salty, rinse with cold water, then drain.

Crush the garlic cloves to a paste with ¼ teaspoon salt with a mortar and pestle, mix in 3 tablespoons of the yogurt, then mix the garlic paste into the rest of the yogurt. Beat the yogurt with an electric hand mixer or rotary beater, which will liquidize it slightly (or whirl it briefly in the blender). Mix in the cucumber and mint. Taste and add more salt, if needed, and 1 teaspoon pepper. If the soup seems rather thick, thin with a little cold water to the desired consistency, but do not make it too liquid. Serve in chilled soup cups.

## Variation

♦ For the Iranian version of this soup, omit the mint and add ½ cup seedless raisins, 1 tablespoon finely chopped fresh dill, and, just before serving, 2 chopped hard-boiled eggs.

# Quick Iced Tomato Soup

*This very easy tomato soup can be made as quickly, and in the same fashion, as a cocktail.*

**Makes 4 servings**

10½-ounce can condensed
  tomato soup
1½ cups sour cream or yogurt
1 tablespoon chopped fresh
  basil
  Or 1 teaspoon dried basil
1 tablespoon grated onion
½ teaspoon salt
½ teaspoon freshly ground
  black pepper
6 or 7 ice cubes
1 tablespoon chopped parsley
  or hard-boiled egg

Just before you are ready to serve, combine all the ingredients, including the ice cubes, in a large cocktail shaker, a screw-top jar, or a plastic container with a tight-fitting lid and shake vigorously until well blended and chilled. Pour into chilled cups and garnish with chopped parsley or chopped hard-boiled egg. The soup can also be mixed in a blender.

# Cold Avocado and Buttermilk Soup

**Makes 4 servings**

1 large ripe avocado
2 tablespoons grated onion
1 tablespoon fresh chopped
    tarragon
    Or 1 teaspoon dried
    tarragon
1 teaspoon salt
½ teaspoon freshly ground
    black pepper
3 cups buttermilk

Split the avocado lengthwise; remove the pit and scoop out the pulp. Put the avocado pulp in a blender with the other ingredients and whirl until smooth. If you don't have a blender, put the avocado pulp through a stainless-steel sieve or food mill and combine with the remaining ingredients.

# Meat

## Kibbeh Nayé

*This delicious Middle Eastern dish of ground raw lamb, cracked wheat, and onions is even easier to make if you have a food processor. It does everything from chopping the onions to grinding the lamb and mixing all together in a matter of minutes.*

**Makes 6 servings**

1½ pounds leg or shoulder of
    lamb
1½ cups fine bulghur (cracked
    wheat)
3 medium-sized onions, peeled
    and grated or finely
    chopped
1 or 2 ice cubes
1½ to 2 teaspoons salt
1 teaspoon freshly ground
    black pepper
½ teaspoon allspice
Shredded green onions,
    radishes, cherry tomatoes

If you are using a food processor, trim the lamb of all fat and tendons; cut it into cubes; put into the processor and mince until fairly fine. Otherwise, have the butcher trim the lamb and put it through the meat grinder twice. The lamb must be used while very fresh.

Soak the bulghur in cold water to cover for 1 hour, then drain it through a cheesecloth-lined sieve and squeeze the cheesecloth well with your hands to remove all excess water. Spread the soaked bulghur on a clean dish towel and pat dry. Put the bulghur, lamb, grated or chopped onion, ice cubes, salt, pepper, and allspice into a bowl and blend the

mixture well with your hands. The ice cubes keep the mixture cold and fresh and add moisture. When well blended, taste and add any necessary seasoning. Remove and discard any fragments of ice. If you use a food processor, add the soaked bulghur, onion, and seasonings to the ground lamb and process until well mixed. Omit ice cubes.

Spread the *kibbeh* flat on a chilled serving platter and decorate with shredded green onions and radishes, putting a few cherry tomatoes around the edge for more color. Serve immediately as a cocktail spread with thinly sliced French bread or the flat, round Arab bread called pita.

# ❧ Steak Tartare

*Probably the most famous of all raw meat dishes, steak tartare requires beef that is very tender and absolutely fresh.*

**Makes 6 servings**

2 pounds beef fillet, sirloin, or
   top round, with no fat
2 medium onions, peeled and
   finely chopped
½ cup capers
2 teaspoons Dijon mustard
2 egg yolks
⅓ cup cognac
¼ cup chopped parsley
2 teaspoons salt
1 teaspoon freshly ground
   black pepper
Tabasco
6 anchovy fillets (optional)

GARNISH
1 tablespoon chopped parsley
6 egg yolks (optional)

The best steak tartare is made of chopped (not ground) fillet. Cut the meat into finger strips and then chop it very fine, using a heavy chef's knife. If this seems too arduous, buy sirloin or top round and have it ground twice.

If you have a food processor, cut the meat into cubes and put into the processor with the onions, roughly cut up, capers, mustard, cognac, parsley, salt, pepper, Tabasco, and anchovy fillets. Do not add egg yolks.

Process until the meat is finely ground and well mixed with the other ingredients.

If you do not have a food processor, combine the chopped or ground meat with the onions, capers, mustard, egg yolks, cognac, parsley, salt, pepper, and Tabasco to taste. You may, if you wish, add finely chopped anchovy fillets (in which case, reduce the salt, as anchovies are very salty), or serve the whole anchovy fillets on the side. Mix everything together very well and taste for seasoning.

Steak tartare can be served in a bowl, sprinkled with the parsley, or formed into 6 mounds and placed on serving plates with a hollow made in the top of each mound. Drop a raw egg yolk into every mound (to be mixed into the beef by each person) and garnish with chopped parsley. Serve as a light main course for luncheon with toast fingers on the side, or as a snack.

For cocktail food, form the mixture into balls about ¾ inch in diameter, roll them in chopped parsley or chopped hazelnuts, and pile them in a mound, to be speared with toothpicks.

Editor's note: *Because of the risk of foodborne illness associated with raw and undercooked meat, the USDA recommends cooking ground beef to an internal temperature of 160°F.*

# Marinated Raw Beef

*While almost everyone knows the delights of steak tartare, few know the pleasures of sliced raw beef as an hors d'oeuvre. Ask the butcher to slice the beef with his meat slicer.*

**Makes 6 servings**

1 ½ pounds fat-free fillet of beef, sliced paper-thin

MARINADE
½ cup olive oil
¼ cup wine vinegar
¼ cup soy sauce (preferably Chinese or Japanese)
¼ cup cognac
1 ½ teaspoons salt
1 teaspoon freshly ground black pepper
1 teaspoon dried thyme
1 large onion, peeled and very finely chopped
2 garlic cloves, peeled and very finely chopped

GARNISH
6 thin slices of lemon
2 tablespoons chopped parsley

Arrange the beef in a serving dish. Combine the marinade ingredients and pour them over the beef. Marinate for 4 to 6 hours, turning the beef several times. Serve garnished with lemon slices and chopped parsley.

## Variation

♦ For the Italian raw beef dish, *carpaccio*, put the beef slices between sheets of waxed paper and pound until practically transparent with a meat pounder. Serve 2 or 3 slices of the raw beef to each person as a first course, with mustard mayonnaise (see page 283), flavored with 1 very finely chopped garlic clove and 1 tablespoon chopped parsley, crusty French or Italian bread, and red wine.

# Fish

## Seviche

*This spicy Latin-American dish of pickled fish "cooked" in lime juice is delicious served with cocktails or as a first course.*

**Makes 4 to 6 servings**

1 ½ pounds firm sole fillets, cut into thin strips about ½ inch wide
1 cup fresh lime juice
½ cup olive oil

Arrange the fish strips in a baking dish and pour the lime juice over them. Refrigerate for 4 hours, by which time the citrus juice will have turned the fish opaque and made it firm. Drain off the lime juice; combine the

¼ cup finely chopped green
  onion
¼ cup finely chopped parsley
2 tablespoons finely chopped,
  canned, peeled green chilies
1 garlic clove, finely chopped
1½ teaspoons salt
1 teaspoon freshly ground
  black pepper
Dash of Tabasco
1 tablespoon chopped fresh
  coriander
  Or cilantro or Chinese
  parsley

remaining ingredients (except the fresh coriander) and pour over the fish, tossing the
pieces lightly in the mixture. Chill for ½
hour, then sprinkle with the chopped coriander and serve.

## Variations

♦ Substitute tiny raw bay scallops, raw crabmeat, or raw red snapper fillets for the sole.

♦ Add slices of avocado and whole-kernel
corn (either canned or sliced from freshly
cooked ears) to the sauce.

# Gravlax

*For this dish, native to Scandinavia, the raw salmon is cured with salt and sugar, a
process that, like the action of lime or lemon juice on fish, "cooks" the flesh and gives
it a most exciting and interesting flavor.*

**Makes 6 to 8 servings**

3 to 3½ pounds center cut of
  fresh salmon
⅔ to ¾ cup coarse (kosher)
  salt
¼ cup sugar
1 to 2 tablespoons coarsely
  ground peppercorns
Large bunch of fresh dill

SWEET MUSTARD
SAUCE
4 tablespoons seasoned
  German mustard (not hot,
  but very spicy)
1 teaspoon dry mustard
3 tablespoons sugar
2 tablespoons wine vinegar
⅓ cup vegetable oil
3 tablespoons finely chopped
  dill

When you buy the salmon, tell the fish market to leave the skin on but to split the
salmon lengthwise and remove the backbone
and the little bones surrounding it. This will
give you two pieces of boneless salmon.

Place one half, skin side down, in a large
dish or casserole in which it can lie flat. Combine the salt, sugar, and peppercorns and rub
the flesh of the salmon very well with this
mixture. Place the dill on top. Rub the rest of
the salt-sugar-peppercorn mixture into the
flesh of the second piece of salmon and place
over the dill, skin side up, re-forming the
salmon shape. Cover salmon with foil, then
put a board or large plate on top and weigh
this down with canned goods. Refrigerate for
36 to 48 hours, turning the salmon over each
day so that it cures evenly, and basting with
the liquid that accumulates from the curing
process. Each time, weigh it down again.

About 4 hours before the fish is done, make the sweet mustard sauce. To make the sauce, put the mustards, sugar, vinegar, and oil in a small bowl and beat well with a whisk until it has the consistency of a thin mayonnaise (the mustard thickens the liquid). Mix in the dill and refrigerate for 3 or 4 hours before serving to let the flavors mellow.

At the end of the curing time, remove the fish from the liquid, scrape away the dill and seasonings, and dry it well on paper towels. To serve, place on a carving board (I like to put a bouquet of dill at one end, parsley at the other, as a garnish) and slice thick on the diagonal, detaching the flesh from the skin as you do so. Serve with the sweet mustard sauce and buttered rye bread as an appetizer or a main course for luncheon or supper, or with other fish dishes on a cold buffet.

# Fruit

Of all the desserts in the spectrum of cuisines, I find those made with fruit the most rewarding. If you are serving fresh fruit at the end of a meal, only the freshest and ripest are worthy of your attention. Give them a sprinkling of sugar if they are not sweet enough in themselves, but keep the preparation simple. A little macerating, or steeping, in fruit juice or a liqueur of a complementary flavor, a spoonful or two of raspberry purée, a touch of whipped cream or *crème fraîche* (see page 287) are all that good fruit needs.

## Strawberries Romanov

*If there is one satisfactory version of strawberries Romanov, there are twenty-five. The classic is probably that of the great Escoffier. As served at the Carlton in his day, it was a simple but extraordinarily good dish notable for the interesting contrast of flavors.*

**Makes 4 servings**

Wash and hull 1 quart large, ripe strawberries. Put them into a bowl and sprinkle them with sugar, if necessary. Add 1 cup freshly squeezed orange juice and ⅓ cup orange-flavored liqueur and let the strawberries macerate for 1 hour. Transfer the berries to a chilled serving dish, draining off some of the liquid. Whip 1½ cups heavy cream and sweeten it with 2 tablespoons sugar. Spread the cream over the berries and decorate the dish with candied violets.

# Strawberries with Raspberry Purée

**Makes 4 servings**

Thaw 2 packages frozen raspberries and pour off three-fourths of the syrup. Using a wooden spatula or spoon, force the raspberries and the remaining syrup through a fine sieve. Discard the seeds.

Wash and hull 1 quart large, ripe strawberries and pile them pyramid fashion in a serving dish. Sprinkle them very lightly with sugar and spoon over them some of the syrup from the frozen raspberries. Spoon raspberry purée over the strawberries and top with macaroon crumbs or finely chopped pistachio nuts. Serve the dessert with a bowl of sweetened whipped cream flavored with Madeira or *eau-de-vie de framboise*.

# Sugared Peaches

Few things in the food world equal the flavor of a ripe peach.

The earliest ones in season are usually the white variety, which are among the more luscious fruits. To ripen them, keep them out of the refrigerator in a plastic bag in a dark place for a day or two; or put them in a paper bag with a ripe apple, make a hole in the bag, and store it in a dark place. When peaches are really ripe you can peel them the way Spanish and Portuguese waiters do: rub each peach with the dull side of a table knife without breaking the skin. This loosens the skin so that, with practice, it can be removed in one piece with a squeeze of the hand, a spectacular trick.

The same problem of ripeness applies to the peaches having yellow and orange pulp, which are available later in the season. I have bought hard yellow peaches in New York markets and tried in vain to coax them into a fully ripe, juicy state. If nothing works, including storage in darkness, it is better to do without fresh peaches.

Depending on size, allow 1 to 3 peaches for each serving. Slice the peaches at the last possible moment to prevent them from discoloring. Add sugar to taste; the amount will vary greatly with the acidity of the peach. Some peaches require a mere sprinkling; others require no sugar at all. Several sugars can be used—confectioners' sugar, granulated sugar, brown sugar, Demerara sugar, or maple sugar. Maple syrup is also good. Light cream, sour cream, and *crème fraîche* are natural companions to peaches. We lack true *crème fraîche* in this country, but a fairly good substitute can be made with heavy cream and buttermilk (see recipe on page 287).

# Peaches with Raspberry Purée

Makes 8 servings

Peel and halve 8 peaches and arrange them in a serving dish. Sprinkle them with 2 tablespoons sugar and 1 tablespoon lemon juice, or more to taste. Spoon raspberry purée (page 311) over the peaches and serve them with light cream or kirsch-flavored whipped cream.

Raspberry purée may also be spooned over peeled and sliced peaches. Serve with heavy cream or *crème fraîche* (see page 287).

# Sugared Raspberries

Ripe raspberries have an exquisite bouquet, a subtle flavor, and a silky texture that make them ambrosial whether served with just a dusting of sugar, with sugar and heavy cream, or with a touch of crème de cassis, the liqueur made from black currants. I also like them with sugar and crisp, toasted, sliced almonds, which provide a bold contrast of textures and flavors. Madeira enhances raspberries too, as does *eau-de-vie de framboise* if it is incorporated in whipped cream or crème anglaise. Straight kirsch or *framboise*, on the other hand, is perhaps too harsh for raspberries and overshadows their delicacy. If you use these fruit brandies, first heat them to evaporate the alcohol.

# Raspberry Fool

Makes 4 servings

Purée 1 quart raspberries by forcing them through a fine sieve or the fine disk of a food mill. Sweeten the purée to taste. (Two packages of frozen raspberries, with some of the syrup poured off, flavored with several drops of lemon juice, may be substituted.) Combine the purée with 1 cup heavy cream, whipped not too stiff (see page 319), or with 1½ cups sour cream. The purée may also be combined with yogurt, which might require additional sugaring of the berries. Serve the dessert very cold in small glasses with thin butter cookies or fingers of shortbread.

# Pineapple with Raspberries

*Raspberries and pineapple have a great affinity for each other, and they are combined to wonderful effect in this recipe.*

**Makes 4 to 6 servings**

Cut about 1 inch from the top of a large, ripe pineapple and reserve it. Remove the pulp from the shell by cutting around the inside edge with a long-bladed, sharp knife and then slicing downward toward the center. Scoop out loosened pulp with a spoon. Discard the less tender pulp and the core. Sprinkle the pulp with 3 tablespoons sugar and, if desired, ¼ cup *eau-de-vie de framboise* and chill it for 2 hours. Make alternating layers of the pineapple and fresh raspberries, sugared, in the pineapple shell and replace the top. Stand the pineapple on a serving platter and surround it with fresh raspberries sprinkled with confectioners' sugar and garnish with a few pistachio nuts, finely chopped. Serve the fruit directly from the shell.

# Sugared Oranges

Sometimes people forget how satisfying good oranges can be when served as a dessert.

For each serving peel 1 or 1½ oranges very carefully with a sharp knife, removing all the white pith, and cut them into ⅜-inch slices. Sugar them lightly, sprinkle them with orange-flavored liqueur, and chill them.

In Spain and Mexico the oranges are peeled and sliced as above and arranged in layers in a serving dish. Each layer is sprinkled with confectioners' sugar and cinnamon. Extra orange juice is sometimes added.

# Melon with Port

Cantaloupe, honeydew, or Cranshaw melons are all perfect for this dish. Be sure the melons are fully ripe and sweet. Cut them into halves or slices, depending on type and size, and make 2 or 3 gashes in the flesh of each piece with a spoon. Add 2 ounces of Port to each piece and let it stand half an hour to mellow. Serve a half cantaloupe or a slice of larger melon per person.

# Drunken Watermelon

Cut a deep plug about 2 inches square out of the top of a ripe watermelon. Remove the plug and slowly pour in as much light rum, brandy, or champagne as the melon will absorb. Replace the plug and seal with masking tape. Refrigerate the melon for 24 hours, turning it 4 or 5 times to allow the liquor or wine to seep through the pulp. Serve in slices, like ordinary watermelon.

# Coeur à la Crème

*Cream cheese and fresh fruit are good companions. This is the classic French dessert, for which fresh cream cheese is drained in little heart-shaped molds or baskets.*

**Makes 6 servings**

2 8-ounce packages cream
    cheese
1 cup sour cream
1 quart fresh strawberries,
    washed and hulled

Blend the cream cheese and sour cream together with a fork to a smooth paste. If the mixture seems too firm, add a little heavy cream. It should be soft, but not sloppy.

Line one large or two small, heart-shaped porcelain molds or straw or reed baskets (the type sold in kitchen shops for this dessert) with cheesecloth. Press the cheese mixture into the mold or molds and place them on a rack over a bowl in the refrigerator. Let them stand for several hours, until the liquid part has drained off and dripped through and the cheese mixture is firm. If you don't have any suitable molds, the cheese can be drained through a cheesecloth-lined sieve.

When ready to serve, unmold the dessert by inverting it into a flat serving dish. Remove the cheesecloth and surround with fresh strawberries. Or tip the cheese out of the cheesecloth-lined sieve and form into a mound on the plate. Serve with more strawberries (or homemade strawberry preserves) and slices of French bread or brioche bread.

# Chilling and Freezing

A very different, but extremely useful and necessary aspect of cooking is chilling and freezing, the action of extreme cold on such foods as aspics, jellies, and creams in order to shape and solidify them.

I have always been struck by the expression "congealed salad," which is much used in certain parts of the South to refer to gelatin salads. This rather unappetizing phrase defines exactly what the application of cold does—causes the contents to congeal and become firm yet delicate, fragile yet shapely. The process applies to many dishes that contain gelatin, such as mousses, Bavarian creams, charlotte russes, soufflés glacés, and to certain desserts thickened with eggs and cream or cornstarch—custards and blancmanges, for example; all these dishes depend on chilling for their final texture and edibility.

In its simplest form, chilling plays a great part in retaining texture and flavor. We chill lettuce to keep it crisp and refreshing; we chill cold soups to give them a velvety smoothness; we chill pâtés to make them firm and easy to slice, or marinated seafood and vegetables to let them absorb and blend with the spicy flavors. While we are on the subject of chilling, I'd like to stress that there are times when chilling can damage flavor. If roast meats and poultry have been cooked to eat cold, they will taste far more delicious, juicy, and flavorful if they are cooled at room temperature and eaten just tepid (slightly above room temperature) instead of being chilled in the refrigerator. A roast chicken with crisp, buttery skin and moist flesh, a squab, a roast of beef or pork will have a better taste and texture if cooled this way.

Another interesting aspect of cooling or chilling food is cooling with pressure, which you do when making a pâté or terrine, or cold boiled beef or tongue. When cooling a pâté, you take a board or plate that fits inside the mold or dish and press it down with weights from a scale or canned goods so that as the meat mixture cools and settles, the excess fat is forced out and it becomes firmer. For cold beef or tongue, or jellied chicken, the hot meat is put into a bowl or mold and weighted down in the same way until it congeals and sets. This makes it more solid and easier to slice and the slight jelly that forms around the edge looks very attractive when the food is unmolded onto a platter.

An extension of these "set" dishes are aspics, one of the glories of *haute cuisine*. Aspics date back to those prerefrigeration days when a means had to be found of keeping cold, cooked foods succulent and unspoiled. Even today, aspic is used to protect the tender, moist flesh of a dish like poached salmon that may have to stand on a buffet table for hours. Sealed in its aspic coat, it won't dry out, but stays fresh and flavorful.

I once knew someone in New York who taught nothing but aspics. She did a certain amount of catering in that field as well, for she was a specialist in clarifying, molding, decorating, and chilling the most exquisite dishes ever put on a table. That's an art in itself and one that few people can master. Anyone can whip up a wine jelly, or a "perfection" salad, or a fruit gelatin, but to produce a perfect, firm, and shimmering aspic is a feat.

The most extreme application of cold is freezing, on which we depend for the success of frozen mousse, sherbet, ice cream, or any one of a number of frozen desserts. Whereas in the old days one had to make ice cream in a hand-cranked freezer or embed molded mixtures in salt and ice and freeze them for hours, today, with freezers that go as low as 20° below zero, electric ice cream makers and *sorbétières*, it is a very easy process indeed.

Frozen dishes, by the way, taste better if the mousse or ice cream or sherbet is removed from the freezer to the refrigerator and allowed to soften a little before you serve it. It improves both the texture and the flavor and is certainly pleasanter for the palate than the assault of something icy and hard as a rock.

# Mousses

A cold mousse is one of the best examples of "cooking" through the action of chilling temperatures. The most basic type of mousse is a combination of ground or puréed food mixed with gelatin for firmness and whipped cream for an airy, velvety smoothness, put into a mold, and chilled until firm and set. There are, of course, variations on this formula. Some savory mousses, like the ham mousse on page 320, have as a base a thick egg-and-cream-enriched béchamel sauce and do not include whipped cream. Or sour cream, cream cheese, or mayonnaise may replace all or part of the whipped cream. However, it is the mousses made with whipped cream, which doubles in volume when beaten, that have the lightest, softest, and creamiest texture.

Cold mousses, sweet or savory, are usually molded, chilled, and then turned out onto a chilled platter for serving. Metal molds, which chill fast and well, are the easiest to use. Before adding the mousse mixture you should brush the inside of the mold with vegetable oil, which will prevent the mousse from sticking to the mold when it is turned out.

## ❧ Roquefort Mousse with Seafood Salad

*This delicious mousse, which I have often used in my classes, was the inspiration of Helen Corbitt, Director of Restaurants for Neiman-Marcus in Dallas.*

**Makes 6 to 8 servings**

¼ cup strained lemon juice

1 envelope unflavored gelatin

1 cup boiling water

¼ pound Roquefort cheese, left at room temperature for 1 hour

1 cup peeled and grated cucumber

4 tablespoons finely chopped parsley

2 tablespoons finely chopped canned pimiento

1 tablespoon finely chopped capers

1 teaspoon grated onion

1 teaspoon salt

½ teaspoon or more freshly ground black pepper

Before you start the recipe, put the bowl in which you will whip the cream into the refrigerator or freezer—beating the chilled cream in a chilled bowl prevents it from breaking down. Brush the inside of a 6-cup ring mold with 1 tablespoon vegetable oil, using a pastry brush. Coat the bottom and sides thoroughly, then turn the mold upside down on paper towels to drain off the excess oil.

Put the lemon juice into a bowl and sprinkle the gelatin on top. When softened, add the boiling water and stir until the gelatin is completely dissolved.

Put the cheese into a mixing bowl and mash with a wooden spoon or a fork until smooth. After grating the cucumber, wrap it in a dish towel and squeeze out all the water, then spread it out on a clean dish towel or

1 cup chilled heavy cream
3 to 4 cups seafood salad

GARNISH
Chopped parsley or parsley
  sprigs

paper towels and pat dry—excess water in the mousse might prevent it from setting properly.

Combine the cheese, cucumber, 4 tablespoons parsley, pimiento, capers, onion, salt, and pepper; mix well and taste for seasoning. Adjust the pepper to taste—you probably will not need any more salt because of the sharpness of the Roquefort cheese. If you have a food processor, you can mash the cheese and combine with the other ingredients in the processor, using the steel blades.

Combine the cheese-and-gelatin mixture and mix until smooth (this can also be done in the processor). Put into the refrigerator for 20 minutes, or until the mixture is slightly thickened—the whipped cream should be folded in when the gelatin has thickened to the point where it will support the air bubbles in the cream.

Take the cream and bowl from the refrigerator; pour the cream into the bowl and beat, using a whisk, a rotary beater, an electric hand beater, or, if you have an electric mixer, the whip attachment. Whip the cream until it has doubled in volume and is just firm enough to hold soft peaks when the beater is lifted from the bowl. Remove the cheese-and-gelatin mixture from the refrigerator and lightly but thoroughly fold the whipped cream into it with a rubber spatula, using the technique with which you fold egg whites into a soufflé (see page 222). Pour the mousse mixture into the prepared ring mold, cover the top with plastic wrap, and chill in the refrigerator for 4 hours, or until the surface is firm when pressed with a finger. Also chill a round serving platter large enough to hold the mousse.

To unmold, remove platter and mold from the refrigerator. Run a thin-bladed knife or metal spatula blade around the edges of the mousse to loosen it from the sides of the mold. Tilt the mold to one side and rap sharply with your hand to shake the mousse free; then tip the rounded part of the mold quickly in and out of hot water to free the top of the mousse. Place the platter on the bottom of the mold, next to the mousse and, holding platter and mold firmly, invert them, giving a sharp shake downward as you do so to release the mousse. Lift off the mold. If the mousse does not come out of the mold, either dip again briefly in hot water, or rub the top with a dish towel wrung out in very hot water. Return the unmolded mousse to the refrigerator for another 10 minutes to firm up, then fill the center with 2 to 2½ cups of the seafood salad. Sprinkle the salad with a little chopped parsley. You can also put sprigs of parsley or a ring of chopped parsley around the base of the mousse, if you wish.

## SEAFOOD SALAD

Combine 3 to 4 cups cooked lobster chunks, or whole shrimp, or crabmeat (or a combination of the three) with ½ cup tarragon-flavored vinaigrette dressing (see page 324). Heap in the center of the mousse (serve excess salad separately, in a bowl) and sprinkle with 1 tablespoon chopped parsley.

# Frozen Lemon Mousse

*This very simple form of frozen dessert mousse is made with a thick, cooked lemon mixture which the English call "lemon curd," lightened by whipped cream, that can also be used, unfrozen, as a filling for a jelly roll. As this mixture is not quite as firm as one containing gelatin, it is advisable not to unmold it.*

**Makes 6 servings**

8 tablespoons (1 stick) butter
Grated rind of 1 large lemon
   (the yellow part only)
Juice of 3 large lemons
¼ teaspoon salt
1½ cups sugar
3 egg yolks
3 whole eggs
1 cup chilled heavy cream

Chill the bowl in which you will whip the cream in the refrigerator or freezer. Chill a 6-cup metal charlotte mold.

Melt the butter in the top of a double boiler over hot water (the water should not touch the upper pan but come about ½ inch below it). Mix in the lemon rind and juice, salt, and sugar. Beat the egg yolks and eggs together with a whisk and add to the ingredients in the pan. Cook over hot water (which should not be allowed to boil), beating constantly with a whisk, until the mixture is smooth, glossy, and very thick. Remove from the heat and cool.

When the lemon curd is cold, whip the cream in the chilled bowl with a whisk, rotary beater, or electric hand beater, or in an electric mixer with a whip attachment, until doubled in volume and firm enough to hold soft peaks when the beater is lifted. Fold the whipped cream into the lemon curd with a rubber spatula until thoroughly combined. Pour into the metal mold, cover the top with plastic wrap, and freeze until firm and set, about 6 hours. Serve from the mold.

# Cold Ham Mousse

*Another variation on the mousse theme, with a béchamel sauce base, this is an easy and good way to use up leftover cooked ham. You might serve it for a summer luncheon party or as part of a cold buffet.*

**Makes 6 servings**

4 tablespoons (½ stick)
    unsalted butter
4 tablespoons flour
1 cup milk
Salt
⅛ teaspoon cayenne pepper
½ teaspoon grated nutmeg
¼ cup cognac
2 egg yolks
½ cup heavy cream
1 envelope unflavored gelatin
½ cup cold water
½ cup hot chicken broth or
    ham broth
2 cups very finely ground
    cooked ham

## CUCUMBER GARNISH

2 medium cucumbers, peeled,
    seeded, and very thinly
    sliced
3 tablespoons white wine
    vinegar
2 tablespoons sugar
3 tablespoons chopped parsley
2 teaspoons chopped fresh dill

Prepare a 3½-cup ring mold by brushing it with 1 tablespoon vegetable oil, then turning it upside down on paper towels to drain off the excess oil.

Melt the butter in a saucepan, blend in the flour, and cook over medium heat, stirring, until golden and bubbling. Slowly mix the milk into this roux, and continue to stir, over low heat, until very thick and smooth. Season to taste with salt (be sparing if the ham is salty), the pepper, and the nutmeg. Stir in the cognac. Mix the egg yolks and cream in a small bowl with a fork, then stir a little of the hot sauce into them to warm up the yolks. Stir into the sauce in the pan and cook over low heat, stirring, until blended. Do not let the sauce get too hot or boil, or the eggs will curdle. Remove pan from the heat.

Sprinkle the gelatin on the cold water. When softened, stir into the hot broth until thoroughly dissolved. Blend this into the sauce, then thoroughly mix in the ground ham. Fill the prepared mold with the ham mousse, smoothing it evenly with a rubber spatula. Cover the mold with plastic wrap and chill in the refrigerator until firm and set, about 2 to 3 hours.

Meanwhile, put the cucumbers into a bowl. Stir the vinegar and sugar until the sugar dissolves; mix with the parsley and dill; pour over the cucumbers and mix. Leave to marinate until the mousse is set.

When ready to serve, remove the plastic wrap from the mold; loosen the edges with a knife or spatula, dip the top of the mold in hot water for a second or two to release it, then invert onto a serving platter, as for Roquefort mousse (see page 317). Drain the marinated cucumbers. Put them in the center of the molded ring.

# Soufflé Glacé Benedictine

*A soufflé glacé, which can be either chilled or frozen (when frozen, it does not contain gelatin), has very little in common with an oven-baked soufflé, apart from name and appearance. In fact, if you analyze it, a soufflé glacé is merely another, fancier form of mousse. The illusion that the soufflé has, by some magic, risen in the refrigerator, is produced by containing the mousse within a paper collar that comes some 3 or 4 inches above the rim of the dish and is removed before serving.*

**Makes 8 servings**

10 eggs, separated
1⅓ cups sugar
3 envelopes unflavored gelatin
½ cup cold water
2 cups chilled heavy cream
⅔ cup Benedictine or other
  liqueur
¼ teaspoon cream of tartar
½ cup finely crushed
  macaroons

First, prepare a 1½-quart soufflé dish. Take a piece of waxed paper or aluminum foil long enough to fit around the soufflé dish with about 1 inch of overlap and fold it in half. Brush one side of the paper or foil with vegetable oil (this prevents the soufflé mixture from sticking when the collar is removed). Wrap the collar around the soufflé dish so that it extends 3 or 4 inches above the rim, oiled side inward, and tie securely around the dish with string (see illustration, page 226).

Combine the egg yolks and sugar in the top of a double boiler and beat over hot water (which should not boil or touch the bottom of the pan) until the mixture is warmed and thick. Meanwhile, sprinkle the gelatin on the cold water to soften. When softened, stir into the hot egg-sugar mixture until completely dissolved.

Whip the cream in a chilled bowl until it has doubled in volume and holds soft peaks when the beater is removed. Put into the refrigerator until ready to use.

Put the top of the double boiler containing the egg-sugar mixture over a bowl of ice cubes and beat it over the ice until the mixture is cold. Then beat in the Benedictine. Fold the whipped cream into the mixture, before it starts to set.

Put 10 egg whites in a bowl with the cream of tartar, or in the bowl of the electric mixer, and beat with a whisk or the mixer until stiff but not dry, as for a soufflé. The cream of tartar helps the egg whites to mount, but if you are beating them in an unlined copper bowl, cream of tartar is not necessary. Lightly but thoroughly fold the beaten egg whites into the mousse mixture and then carefully pour into the prepared soufflé dish, so that it mounts inside the collar. Smooth the top with a rubber spatula.

Chill in the refrigerator until set and firm, about 4 to 6 hours. To serve, untie the string and very carefully peel off the collar without disturbing the molded mousse. Sprinkle the top with the crushed macaroons.

If you are not serving the dessert right away, replace in the refrigerator to keep firm until ready to use, which should be within an hour or two.

## Variation

♦ Instead of Benedictine, use a coffee-flavored liqueur, such as Tia Maria, and decorate the top with macaroon crumbs and the little candies that look like coffee beans.

# Chilled Custards

## ❧ Orange Bavarian Cream

*The Bavarian cream or* bavarois *is a rich but delicate mousselike dessert usually made by combining crème anglaise with gelatin, whipped cream, and any desired flavorings—one of the pleasantest is orange.*

**Makes 8 servings**

CREME ANGLAISE
*8 egg yolks*
*¾ cup sugar*
*⅛ teaspoon salt*
*1 cup milk*
*1 cup heavy cream*
*1 teaspoon vanilla extract*

FLAVORING
*1 envelope unflavored gelatin*
*¼ cup strained orange juice*
*2 tablespoons finely grated orange zest (the orange part of the rind)*
*2 tablespoons Grand Marnier*
*1 cup chilled heavy cream*

The Bavarian cream may be chilled in a mold, in the same way as a mousse, or spooned into individual glass serving dishes or one large glass serving bowl, which is easier and equally attractive.

Put the bowl in which you will whip the cream into the refrigerator or freezer to chill.

Prepare the crème anglaise according to the directions on page 277, using the proportions given above. Sprinkle the gelatin on the orange juice to soften it.

Immediately after the crème anglaise is made, pour it into a bowl and blend in the softened gelatin. The gelatin must be thoroughly dissolved in and distributed through the hot custard, otherwise you will get hard little lumps of gelatin in your Bavarian cream.

Add the orange zest and Grand Marnier and stir until well mixed. Cool the custard, then lay a piece of plastic wrap on the surface to prevent a skin from forming, and chill in the refrigerator until it is thick and just at the point of setting.

Whip the cream in the chilled bowl until it holds soft peaks when the beater is lifted—do not let it get too stiff. Fold lightly but thoroughly into the chilled custard mixture with a rubber spatula.

Spoon into 8 individual glass serving dishes or 1 large glass serving bowl and chill until set and firm, about 6 to 8 hours for the large bowl, about 1 to 2 hours for individual dishes. You may, if you wish, decorate the top with peeled orange segments (see page 301) and rosettes of whipped cream piped through a pastry bag with a rosette tube.

# Trifle

*This most delectable of English desserts is very easy to make and quite spectacular on a buffet table or for a summer dinner party. As it is very rich, it will serve a lot of people.*

**Makes 8 to 10 servings**

9-inch génoise (see page 257)
  or spongecake layer
  Or 10 to 12 ladyfingers
½ cup or less cream (sweet)
  sherry
½ cup raspberry preserves
  Or ¾ cup raspberry purée
  (see page 311)
2½ cups chilled crème anglaise
  (see page 277)
1 cup chilled heavy cream
2 tablespoons superfine sugar
1 tablespoon cognac

GARNISH
¼ cup chopped pistachio nuts
¼ cup candied cherries
4 to 6 pieces of angelica

You will need a crystal serving bowl or soufflé dish, 9 inches in diameter —the crystal dish is more effective, as you can see the different layers. Put the cake layer or the ladyfingers on the bottom and sprinkle liberally with the sherry. Use just enough to dampen and flavor the cake, but not enough to make it soggy. Let the cake stand 15 minutes.

Spread the cake or ladyfingers with a ⅜-inch-thick layer of raspberry preserves, or with the raspberry purée. (The purée is not as concentrated as the preserves and also has a more delicious flavor and texture.) Cover with the crème anglaise and chill for 3 or 4 hours.

Just before serving, whip the cream in a chilled bowl until it stands in soft peaks, then beat in the sugar and cognac. Cover the surface of the custard with the cream, smoothing it evenly with a rubber spatula. Sprinkle chopped pistachio nuts over the top and decorate with candied cherries and angelica or other decoration of your choice. Serve chilled, but do not let it stand in the refrigerator for more than 30 minutes or it will become soggy.

# Chilled Soups

## Chilled Minted Pea Soup

*This soup is made with dried split peas, which may or may not need soaking, according to the type you buy. Some dried peas are the quick-cooking, processed variety. Check the package directions as to the length of cooking time required.*

**Makes 8 servings**

1½ cups dried, green split peas
8 to 12 cups chicken broth
2 garlic cloves, crushed
Salt, freshly ground black pepper
6 tablespoons sour cream
2 tablespoons chopped fresh mint

Soak or preboil the peas according to package directions. Drain and put in a deep pot with 8 cups chicken broth and the garlic. Bring to a boil; reduce the heat and simmer, covered, until the peas are completely cooked. Strain the peas, reserving the broth. Purée the peas by putting them through a food mill, whirling them in a blender, or processing them in a food processor, then measure the purée and combine it with an equal amount of chicken broth. Taste, correct the seasoning, adding salt and freshly ground black pepper as needed, and chill.

When you are ready to serve, stir in the sour cream and serve in chilled soup cups; sprinkle with the chopped fresh mint.

## Cold Clam Bisque

*If you can get fresh clams on the half shell, use them for this recipe and substitute the liquor from the clams for part of the clam broth. If not, use canned clams.*

**Makes 6 to 8 servings**

½ cup rice
4 cups clam broth or bottled clam juice
2 cups cherrystone or razor clams, or canned minced clams
3 tablespoons butter
Salt, freshly ground black pepper
1½ cups heavy cream
2 to 3 tablespoons finely chopped parsley and chives

Simmer the rice in the clam broth for 45 to 50 minutes, or until it is very soft. Purée it in a blender or food processor or rub through a very fine sieve. If you are using fresh raw clams, either purée them in the blender or food processor or chop them very fine. Combine the rice-broth mixture, the clams, and the butter. Bring to a boil, then reduce the heat and simmer for 5 minutes. Season to taste with salt and pepper. Cool. Combine with the heavy cream and chill thoroughly. Serve in soup cups set in bowls of crushed ice. Sprinkle each serving with chopped parsley and chives.

# Chilled Avocado Soup

1 large ripe avocado
1½ cups hot chicken broth
1 tablespoon chopped fresh
    tarragon
    Or 1 teaspoon dried
    tarragon
¼ teaspoon Tabasco
1 tablespoon lemon juice
½ cup heavy cream
½ cup sour cream

GARNISH
1 tablespoon chopped fresh
    tarragon or chives

Cut the avocado in half lengthwise; remove the pit and either peel off the skin (if the avocado is really ripe, it should come off easily), or scoop the avocado pulp out with a spoon. Put the avocado into a blender with the chicken broth and seasonings and whirl until smooth. Chill well in a covered bowl. Just before serving, mix with the heavy cream and sour cream and chill again, briefly. Serve in chilled soup cups, topped with a sprinkling of chopped tarragon or chives.

# Gelatin Molds and Aspics

## ❧ Cucumber and Carrot Ring with Crabmeat

*This is a very simple jellied salad, the kind popular for buffets and luncheons. You can fill the center with crabmeat or with shrimp or lobster meat.*

½ cup cold water
2 envelopes unflavored gelatin
1½ cups boiling water
2 tablespoons lemon juice
1 cup white wine
1 teaspoon salt
¼ teaspoon Tabasco
1½ cups peeled, seeded, and
    grated cucumber
½ cup grated carrot
2 tablespoons chopped parsley
2 to 3 cups crabmeat
1 head of Boston lettuce or
    other salad greens, washed
    and chilled

Put the cold water into a bowl. Sprinkle the gelatin on top of the water.

When the gelatin has softened, pour in the boiling water and stir until thoroughly dissolved. Add the lemon juice, wine, salt, and Tabasco and cool in the refrigerator until the gelatin is thick and syrupy, but not set.

Squeeze the grated cucumber in a dish towel to get rid of the excess water. Rinse a 6-cup ring mold with cold water and shake out the excess (for gelatin molds, the ring should be rinsed with water rather than brushed with oil, which would cloud the surface of the clear gelatin).

Mix the cucumber, carrot, and parsley into the syrupy gelatin mixture and spoon into the

*3 hard-boiled eggs, peeled and sliced*
*1 cup mayonnaise (see page 281)*

prepared ring mold. Cover the top with plastic wrap and chill until set and firm, about 3 hours. Also chill a round platter large enough to hold the unmolded ring.

To unmold, run a thin knife blade or metal spatula around the edge of the mold, put a plate over the bottom of the mold, and invert quickly. If the mold does not release, rub the top with a cloth wrung out in very hot water, then, holding mold and plate, give it a sharp shake. Return to the refrigerator until ready to serve, or to set, if the top of the mold has been softened by the heat of the towel.

To serve, pile crabmeat in the center of the ring, passing any excess in a separate bowl, and garnish the edges of the platter with lettuce leaves and slices of hard-boiled egg. Pass mayonnaise separately to dress the crabmeat.


# Jellied Veal

*This recipe for a jellied veal that can double as a mock headcheese is one I have used most of my life for picnics, on the hors d'oeuvre table, and for supper. It originated with a most remarkable cook who worked for a family I knew years ago. This is my adaptation of one of her specialties.*

**Makes 8 to 10 servings**

*3 pounds veal shanks*
*2 pounds veal neck*
*1 tablespoon salt*
*3 peeled garlic cloves*
*1 onion, stuck with 2 cloves*
*3 or 4 sprigs of parsley*
*1 bay leaf*
*1 teaspoon dried basil*
    *Or several leaves fresh basil*
*2 tablespoons Worcestershire sauce*
*½ teaspoon Tabasco*
*6 to 8 hard-boiled eggs*

Put the veal shanks and neck in a deep kettle with the salt, garlic, onion, parsley, bay leaf, basil, and water barely to cover. Bring to a boil and boil rapidly for 5 minutes, skimming off the scum that rises to the surface. Reduce the heat; cover the pot and simmer the veal for 2 hours, or until the meat is very tender but not overcooked. Remove the veal from the pot and take all the meat from the bones. Return the bones to the pot with the Worcestershire sauce and Tabasco and simmer the broth briskly for 15 minutes. Strain the broth through a double thickness of cheesecloth or a linen towel into a clean pot. Cut the meat into small pieces and add them to the strained broth. Bring to a boil, then taste and season with salt and pepper, if needed. Remove from the heat.

Peel and slice the eggs. Rinse a 2-quart metal melon mold or an 8-cup ring mold with cold water. Put in a layer of the veal and broth, then a layer of sliced egg, and continue making layers until all the veal and eggs have been used, finishing with a layer of veal and enough broth to cover. Cover the mold with foil and chill for at least 8 hours. Unmold the jellied veal according to the directions for the previous recipe. Cut into fairly thick slices and serve with a vinaigrette sauce (see page 290).

# Cold Poached Salmon in Red Wine Aspic

*A whole poached salmon in aspic is a glorious sight on a buffet table. You should get fish bones and heads to provide a strong, concentrated, flavorful stock with natural gelatin, and clarify it for your aspic. This recipe is rather unusual in that red wine is used in the poaching court bouillon, rather than the usual white.*

**Makes 12 servings**

## COURT BOUILLON

*2 to 3 pounds fish bones and heads*
*2 quarts water*
*4 to 5 cups red wine*
*1 onion, peeled and stuck with 2 cloves*
*1½ tablespoons salt*
*1 tablespoon thyme*
*2 bay leaves*
*1 carrot, scraped*
*1 lemon, sliced*
*½ cup red wine vinegar*

*6- to 7-pound salmon*
*2 egg whites, lightly beaten*
*3 envelopes unflavored gelatin*
*¼ cup cold water*

## DECORATION

*Thin slices of lemon, tarragon leaves, cucumber slices, sprigs of dill*

Cook the fish bones and heads in the water until they practically fall apart, 1 hour or more. Strain this fish stock and transfer it to a fish poacher with a rack, or a pan large enough to hold the salmon. Add the remaining court bouillon ingredients, bring to a boil, reduce the heat, and simmer for 10 minutes.

Measure the salmon at its thickest point, from belly to backbone, to determine the cooking time (10 minutes per measured inch). Put it on the rack of the fish poacher or on a large piece of heavy-duty foil; lower it into the simmering liquid and poach at a simmer for the necessary time. Test for doneness with a fork or toothpick. If the flesh flakes easily, it is done. Transfer to a platter and cool completely. When cool, carefully peel off and discard all the skin; put the fish on a board or serving platter, cover with plastic wrap, and chill while making the aspic.

Boil the poaching liquid rapidly until reduced to about 7 cups, then strain it through several thicknesses of cheesecloth into a deep pan and clarify with the beaten egg whites (see description of technique on page 21). Strain the clarified stock through a sieve lined with a linen towel or several thicknesses of cheesecloth into a pan. Reheat the liquid.

Sprinkle the gelatin on the ¼ cup cold water to soften, then stir it into the hot, clarified liquid until dissolved. Let the aspic mixture cool, then stir over a bowl of ice cubes until it starts to get syrupy. Remove the salmon from the refrigerator, take off the wrap, and coat the flesh on the best-looking side of the salmon with a thin coat of the syrupy aspic, pouring it over with a large spoon. Chill the fish until the aspic sets, then give it another coat and again chill until set. You may find when working with aspic that it gets too cold and sets. In this case, you have to melt it over low heat and chill again until it starts to get syrupy. Decorate the fish with thin slices of lemon or cucumber arranged in overlapping rows to look like fish scales and with sprays of tarragon leaves or sprigs of dill. Dip the decorations in aspic first so they will adhere to the coating. Then, very carefully, apply a final coat of aspic over the decorations and chill until set. Remove any aspic that ran onto the board or platter.

To serve, garnish the board or platter with tomato shells (see page 302) filled with Russian salad (cold, diced cooked vegetables bound with mayonnaise) and tuck sprigs of parsley or watercress in between. Leftover aspic can be chopped fine on a sheet of waxed paper and scattered around the fish. You might also serve a cucumber salad if you didn't use cucumbers for decoration.

# Sherry and Grapefruit Jelly

*This is a very easy and pleasant dessert to serve after a rich main course.*

**Makes 8 servings**

2 envelopes plain gelatin
¾ cup sugar
1½ cups water
2 tablespoons lime juice
½ cup medium sherry
1 tablespoon angostura bitters
2 cups grapefruit juice
¾ cup grapefruit sections (for technique, see page 301)
4 teaspoons grated orange zest (the orange part of the rind)
1 cup chilled heavy cream
2 tablespoons sweet sherry

Mix the gelatin and sugar in a small, heavy saucepan; add the water and stir over low heat until the gelatin and sugar are completely dissolved. Remove from the heat and stir in the lime juice, sherry, bitters, and grapefruit juice. Pour into 8 individual molds or 1 large 6-cup mold. Chill until firm. Unmold onto chilled plates or a platter, as for other gelatin molds (see page 326); garnish with the grapefruit sections and sprinkle with the orange zest. Whip the cream in a chilled bowl until it just holds its shape, then add the sweet sherry and whip until doubled in volume. Serve the sherry-flavored cream with the jelly.

# Pâté

## Veal and Ham Pâté

*This is a rather different pâté because it is made with whole pieces of meat, rather than the usual ground-meat mixture, or forcemeat. A pâté is baked in an oval or a long, deep, rectangular dish (known as a terrine), which is lined with very thin strips of salt pork or bacon to lubricate the meat and prevent it from drying out during cooking. The classic terrine, which may be made of glazed earthenware, ovenproof porcelain, or enameled cast iron, has a cover and comes in a range of sizes. If you don't own a terrine, you can make this recipe in a 9-inch loaf pan of glass or metal, the kind you would use for meat loaf, and cover it with heavy-duty aluminum foil.*

**Makes 10 to 12 servings**

1 pound bacon or very thinly
    sliced salt pork
2 pounds veal scaloppine,
    pounded until very thin
1¾ pounds thinly sliced ham
    or Canadian bacon
About 1 tablespoon salt
1 teaspoon freshly ground
    black pepper
10 shallots, peeled and finely
    chopped
½ cup finely chopped parsley
1 teaspoon dried thyme
1 bay leaf
½ cup dry white wine

Line a 9-inch oval or rectangular terrine or loaf pan with the bacon or salt pork, draping the strips across the bottom and up the sides, first crosswise and then lengthwise. Leave overhangs at the top to cover the pâté.

Before putting in the meat, check to see how salty the ham or Canadian bacon is. Sauté a small piece in a tablespoon of butter in a skillet and taste. The amount of salt used for seasoning depends on the saltiness of the meat.

Preheat the oven to 325°.

Beginning and ending with veal, alternate layers of scaloppine and layers of ham or Canadian bacon in the lined pan, sprinkling each layer with salt, pepper, shallots, parsley, and thyme. Drape the ends of the bacon or salt pork slices over the mixture. If they don't cover completely, add a few more strips, placing them down the length of the meat, and fold the ends over these strips. Arrange the bay leaf on top of the slices and pour the white wine over all.

Put the cover on the terrine or cover the top of the loaf pan with a double layer of heavy-duty foil, tucking it around the sides of the pan. Put the terrine or pan on a baking sheet (to catch any overflow of juices that might bubble out during the baking) and bake in the center of the oven for 2 to 2½ hours, or until the fat and juices bubbling up around the sides of the pan are clear. Remove cover or foil and check after 2 hours. If the juices are cloudy, more cooking is needed.

When the pâté is cooked, remove it from the oven, uncover, and cool for about 20 minutes. It should then be weighted down, which firms the texture and forces out excess juices from the meat, and refrigerated until cold. For this you will need something flat and heavy that will fit inside the pan, such as a piece of board or plywood, cut to size and weighted down with canned goods, or a foil-covered brick. Pâté should be weighted for 12 hours before unmolding.

When the pâté is cold and firm, remove the board and weights and refrigerate, covered with the lid or with foil, until ready to serve. Do not store a pâté for more than 3 or 4 days in the refrigerator, as the juices are apt to sour. If you wish to store it for longer, remove excess liquid or jelly and cover the top of the pâté with a layer of melted pork fat to seal it. Most pâtés do not freeze well; they lose texture and flavor.

To serve, unmold by inverting the pâté onto a serving dish and cut into slices about ⅜ inch thick. The fat should be left on and removed at the table.

# Ice Cream

I well remember the simple homemade ice creams of my childhood. They were turned by hand in a freezer packed with cracked ice and rock salt—a strenuous task, particularly toward the end when the cream froze solid and turning the handle required a fair amount of brute force. Nowadays electric ice-cream freezers have made the whole business effortless, and if you are a lover of ice cream, it's well worth buying one. Some people make ice cream in refrigerator ice trays, but it is my feeling that the finished product seldom equals that made in an ice-cream freezer, which churns the mixture to a perfect, smooth creaminess.

There are different kinds of ice creams. Those with a base of custard, often called French ice cream, have a distinctly different taste and texture from the ice creams made of light or heavy cream.

## ◆ Basic Vanilla Ice Cream

*This is the simplest of all ice creams to make. For a rich ice cream, use heavy cream instead of light.*

**Makes about 1½ quarts**

4 cups light or heavy cream
¾ cup granulated sugar
1½ teaspoons pure vanilla
   extract
   Or a 2-inch piece of vanilla
   bean
Cracked ice and rock salt
   Or coarse (kosher) salt for
   freezing

Stir the cream and sugar together for 5 or 6 minutes to dissolve the sugar. Add the vanilla extract or slit the vanilla bean lengthwise with a sharp paring knife and scrape the tiny black seeds inside into the cream.

Pour the mixture into the can of an electric or hand-operated ice cream freezer (the can should be about three-quarters full, to allow for expansion), put in the dasher, and cover the can tightly with the lid. Lower it into the freezer and pack the freezer with alternating layers of cracked ice and rock salt or coarse salt in the proportions of about 1 cup salt to 6 cups ice, or whatever proportions are recommended by the freezer manufacturer. Connect the dasher to the crank or shaft mechanism, according to manufacturer's directions, and turn the mixture by hand or electrically, again following operating directions, until the ice cream is frozen. With a hand-operated freezer this will be at the point when the crank can barely be moved. With a machine, the motor will slow down or stop. When operating by hand, do not stop turning until the mixture is frozen, or the ice cream may be lumpy.

When the ice cream is frozen, disconnect the mechanism, remove the can, and wipe it carefully to remove any salt. Remove the lid and dasher, press the ice cream down firmly with a spoon, and cover the can again, plugging the hole in the top of the can where the dasher was with a piece of aluminum foil (this prevents salt from seeping through). Drain the water from the freezer, replace the can, and repack with more ice and salt until ready to serve, which will keep it firm. The ice cream may be kept this way for up to 4 hours. If you are going to serve it right away, it need not be repacked.

## Variations

♦ BANANA ICE CREAM. Peel and remove strings from 5 or 6 very ripe bananas. Crush them well with a fork and combine them with 1 cup sugar, 1 tablespoon vanilla extract, 1½ tablespoons lime or lemon juice, and ⅛ teaspoon salt. Stir this mixture into 4 cups heavy cream and freeze as for basic vanilla ice cream.

♦ GINGER ICE CREAM. Follow the recipe for basic vanilla ice cream, but use half the amount of vanilla and add ⅔ cup finely cut preserved ginger and ⅓ cup of the syrup in which the ginger is packed. Combine well and freeze.

♦ CASSIS ICE CREAM. Follow the recipe for basic vanilla ice cream but use only ¾ teaspoon vanilla extract. Add ¾ cup cassis syrup or crème de cassis liqueur (made from black currants) and 1 cup sieved black currant preserves (rubbed through a strainer with a wooden spoon). Mix well and freeze. Serve this with additional cassis syrup or crème de cassis blended with raspberry purée (see page 311), if you wish. In peach season, this ice cream can be served with halved or sliced, sugared peaches in addition to the raspberry and cassis purée.

# French Vanilla Ice Cream
Makes about 2 quarts

6 egg yolks
1 cup sugar
⅛ teaspoon salt
2 cups milk
4 cups (1 quart) heavy cream
1½ to 2 tablespoons pure
    vanilla extract
    Or 2½ inches of vanilla
    bean

The first step is to make a crème anglaise or custard. Combine the egg yolks, sugar, and salt in a heavy, 3-quart, enameled cast-iron saucepan or the top of a double boiler and beat together with a wire whisk, rotary or electric beater, or wooden spatula until well mixed, pale, and creamy. Meanwhile, in another pan, heat the milk until little bubbles appear around the edges of the pan. Gradually pour the hot milk into the egg mixture, stirring constantly. Cook over medium heat or hot water (if using the double boiler), stirring constantly, until the custard thickens sufficiently to coat lightly a wooden spatula or spoon. Remove from the heat and cool. Stir in the heavy cream and the vanilla extract or seeds scraped from the vanilla bean. Freeze as for basic vanilla ice cream (see previous recipe).

## Variations

♦ LEMON ICE CREAM. Before freezing, add ½ cup lemon juice and 3 tablespoons grated lemon zest (the yellow part of the lemon rind) to the ice cream. Serve topped with chopped pistachio nuts.

♦ STRAWBERRY ICE CREAM. When the ice cream is half frozen (after about 15 minutes in a hand-cranked freezer, or 10 minutes in an electric freezer), add 2 cups fresh, crushed strawberries and 1 tablespoon lemon juice. Stir well and continue freezing.

♦ PEACH ICE CREAM. When half frozen, add 3 cups sliced, sugared peaches and 1 tablespoon lemon juice. Stir well and continue freezing.

*Note.* When you remove the lid and add any of the above ingredients, be very careful not to let any of the salt mixture drip into the ice cream.


# Ice-Tray Apricot Ice Cream

*If you are making ice cream in an ice tray, I find it advisable to use a slightly different mixture and to whip the cream, the result of which is nearer a frozen cream or a very rich, creamy version of sherbet. As it is very difficult to get luscious, ripe apricots these days, I make this ice cream with apricot preserves, which work beautifully.*

**Makes 6 servings**

1-pound jar pure apricot
  preserves
1 cup water
⅓ cup sugar
1½ cups heavy cream

Rub the preserves through a strainer with a wooden spoon or put through a food mill.

Boil the water and sugar together for 5 minutes to make a simple syrup, then cool until cold. Combine the apricot purée and the syrup, mixing well.

Whip the heavy cream in a chilled bowl with a rotary beater or electric hand mixer (or in the bowl of an electric mixer) until it has doubled in volume and holds its shape when the beater is lifted. Fold the cream thoroughly into the apricot mixture with a rubber spatula, then pour the mixture into refrigerator ice trays and put in the coldest part of the freezing compartment or freezer until frozen around the edges and mushy in the center. Remove, turn into a bowl, and beat with a wooden spatula until smooth. Return the trays to the freezer. Repeat this beating process 1 or 2 times, then return to the freezer and freeze until hard. The beating process keeps the ice cream from forming crystals and makes it smooth.

# Sherbet

Sherbets, or *sorbets*, as the French call them, and *granités* are water ices made with a simple syrup, or sugar, and flavorings—fruit juice, coffee, champagne, and puréed fruit are the most usual. The main difference seems to be that while the sherbet may contain other ingredients such as beaten egg whites or milk (for a milk sherbet), the *granité* is simply frozen liquid and has a more crystalline, grainy texture. Ice-tray freezing works well for sherbets and *granités*, provided they are taken out of the freezer and beaten smooth 2 or 3 times while still mushy. Sherbet may also be turned in an ice cream freezer until it is just softly frozen, not hard like ice cream. Before serving a sherbet, remove it from the freezing compartment to the refrigerator to soften a little.

The freezing time for sherbet or *granité* depends on how often you beat it and how cold your freezer or freezing compartment is—to speed the process, set it at the lowest possible temperature.

## ❧ Strawberry Sorbet

Makes 8 servings

3 pints fresh strawberries
  Or 3 packages frozen
  strawberries
2 cups sugar
  Or 1 cup sugar if using
  frozen strawberries
1½ cups orange juice
¾ cup lemon juice
⅓ cup Grand Marnier

Wash and hull the fresh strawberries or slightly thaw the frozen strawberries. Combine the strawberries, sugar, and fruit juices in a bowl and let stand 2 to 3 hours for the strawberries to absorb the flavors. Put the mixture through a food mill, rub through a sieve, or purée in a blender or food processor. Stir the Grand Marnier into the purée and pour it into refrigerator ice trays. Freeze until about 1 inch of the mixture has frozen around the sides of the trays, then remove; turn the mixture into a bowl and beat until smooth. Return to the trays and freeze until firm. For a more delicate *sorbet*, beat the mixture twice, freezing between beatings until just solid around the edges.

# Lemon Granité

½ cup sugar
1 cup water
⅓ to ½ cup lemon juice

Boil the sugar and water together for 5 minutes to make a simple syrup. Cool completely, then mix in the lemon juice—the amount depends on how tart you like your *granité*. Pour into ice trays and freeze as for strawberry *sorbet* (see previous recipe), removing and beating once or twice. Serve in sherbet glasses.

## Variation

♦ COFFEE GRANITE. Combine 8 tablespoons Italian-roast coffee, ground for espresso (or instant espresso), 2 to 4 teaspoons sugar to taste (according to how sweet you like your *granité*), and 4 cups boiling water in a glass or pottery coffee maker. Leave to steep for 30 to 40 minutes. Cool completely, then pour into ice trays (if you use coffee ground for drip pots, strain it through a paper filter cone to remove the grounds). Freeze, beating twice. Serve in sherbet glasses topped, if you wish, with a spoonful of whipped cream.

# Cooking Terms and Methods

# The Concordance

# Carving

# Cooking Terms and Methods

I have never thought that the glossary of terms given in most cookbooks was particularly helpful. Processes such as clarifying or folding are defined in the abstract, without relating them to the recipes. To me, you learn a technique by doing it, not by reading a definition. Therefore, in the list that follows you'll find, instead of a definition, a page reference to the place in the text where that particular term or technique is first described and fully demonstrated, so you can turn there, immediately get your hands in, and learn all about it as you cook.

# The Concordance

APPLES. For cooking, one needs tart apples. On the East Coast I shop for Greenings or Granny Smiths, which are firm, well-textured, and highly satis-factory. In other parts of the country I buy Pippins in the spring, Gravensteins in the early fall. Both are flavorful, with a good bouquet and excellent texture. Many authorities recommend Golden Delicious and Rome Beauties, but I find they don't cook as well. Apples are good stewed for applesauce (see page 55), baked, sautéed (see page 158), as fritters (see page 200), and, of course, there's nothing like them for tarts (see page 234), pies, certain cakes and cookies, fruit stuffings for poultry (see page 82), and with certain game birds (see page 149). For eating apples, McIntosh and Delicious are the most generally available year round, but look for other firm, juicy varieties, particularly in farm markets in the fall.

APRICOTS. One of our finest fruits when fully ripe. They should be tender to the touch, sweet to the tongue, and full of flavor, but are seldom found that way in the markets today because they are picked too green. You may be better off using dried apricots and reconstituting them by bringing them to a boil in water and letting them stand. They have a fine flavor. A good brand of canned apricots can be substituted in some dishes, such as fritters (see page 200).

ARTICHOKES. For most purposes, the large green globe artichokes are best. Choose big ones with firm heads and tight leaves. Tinges of brown on the leaves are frost marks. These do not affect the flavor, only the appearance. To cook, break or cut off the stalk and pull off the small hard leaves around the base. Slice off ¼ inch of the prickly top with a sharp knife, then snip off the prickly tips of the remaining leaves with sharp scissors. Boil uncovered in plenty of salted water with a slice of lemon and 2 garlic cloves. Allow 40 min-utes for large artichokes, less for the small ones. They are done when a leaf pulls out easily. Drain upside down, on paper towels. Serve hot with melted butter or hollandaise sauce, or cold with vinaigrette sauce. Artichokes can also be steamed, braised, or stuffed and baked. To remove the unpalatable choke (the fuzzy core), spread the leaves, pull out the tight center cone of pale leaves, and scrape the choke from the artichoke bottom with a teaspoon. Very tiny, immature artichokes in which the choke has not developed, sometimes found in Italian markets, may be eaten raw or sautéed whole.

ASPARAGUS. In most parts of the country, asparagus is in the markets from 10 to 12 months a year—at a price. It is most plentiful and inexpensive in the spring Most fresh asparagus needs no peeling, unless the stalks are very thick and woody. Merely break off the tough lower part of the stalk where the tender spear begins. There are many ways of cooking asparagus. My favorite is to lay it flat in a skillet and boil very rapidly in salted water (see page 53). Serve hot with melted butter or hollandaise or cold with vinaigrette sauce or mustard mayonnaise. Young asparagus may be eaten raw. Frozen asparagus is limp, tasteless, and not worth buying. Canned asparagus tastes like an entirely different vegetable—either you enjoy it as a salad or you hate it.

AVOCADOS. One of the pleasantest fruits we have, in season most of the year. There are many varieties, of which the russety-green-skinned California, or Calavo, is probably the best. A ripe avocado will be yielding to the touch, soft but not mushy, with buttery-tender green flesh. If the flesh is dark or brown, the avocado is overripe. If firm when bought, avocados will ripen if left in a dark place for a day or two. Avocados are usually served in their natural state, peeled and cut up in salads (see page 292), split and stuffed with seafood or other salads, mashed with a fork or in a blender to a soft purée (see guacamole, page 303), or blended in cold soups (see page 306). They may also be stuffed and baked. In Central and South America they are blended with sugar and lime juice for a dessert. When cut and exposed to air, avocados discolor quickly so serve as soon as possible after cutting. To keep a leftover piece, rub cut surfaces with lemon juice and cover tightly with plastic wrap. Some say that leaving the pit in puréed avocado prevents discoloration.

BAKING POWDER. In the markets today you are likely to find only baking powder marked "double-acting." This means that the baking powder acts twice—when it is first mixed into the batter and again after the cake goes into the warm oven. Some home bakers were distressed recently to learn that the famous old-fashioned Royal baking powder is no longer being manufactured, owing to the rising cost of cream of tartar. They claim that the chemical double-acting powders leave a slightly bitter aftertaste. If you want to pay the price, you can make your own natural mixture by combining 2 parts cream of tartar to 1 part baking soda (bicarbonate of soda); don't try to store it, though, because it won't keep well.

In a recent test we found that 1 teaspoon of double-acting baking powder worked as the equal of 2 teaspoons of the Royal baking powder. Directions on a tin of double-acting baking powder recommend 1 teaspoon for each cup of flour (for Royal, or for your own homemade equivalent, simply double the amount—2 teaspoons to 1 cup of flour). Exceptions to the double-acting formula: mixtures containing fruits such as raisins or made with heavy flours like whole wheat, cornmeal, or bran, require 1½ teaspoons per cup of flour; in recipes calling for more than 3 eggs, use ½ teaspoon less for each extra egg.

BAKING SODA. Baking soda or bicarbonate of soda is another leavening agent, mostly used for doughs mixed with sour milk, buttermilk, orange juice, and molasses, which have a rather high acid content. It is a valuable leavener, but take care not to use too much or it will adversely affect the taste and color of the finished product.

BANANAS. Considered a great source of potassium, if that means anything to you and your diet. Never refrigerate bananas. If you buy them yellow and firm, they will ripen quite quickly at room temperature. The riper they become, the more brown-speckled the skin and the more intense the flavor. For desserts, bananas are used whole, sliced, or puréed. Good broiled (see page 121); baked (see crêpes directoire, page 219); sautéed (see page 192); in pies; puréed for breakfast breads, soufflés, ice cream (see page 332); and, of course, sliced raw and eaten with cream. In season all year, widely available.

### BEANS

One of America's great gifts to the world. Always plentiful, both fresh and dried.

*Green beans.* Look for those that are firm, crisp, and small. They should snap when you break them—and don't be afraid to test one in the market. Green beans no longer need stringing. Just trim off the ends and cook whole in rapidly boiling salted water to cover until crisply tender—there should always be some bite left in them. Very young tender beans can be simply sautéed in a little butter. It's smart to cook more beans than you need and save some to have cold in vinaigrette (coated with the sauce, they last several days). Frozen green beans are acceptable, and canned ones, rinsed off, are possible in a pinch.

*Wax beans.* Pale-yellow version of the green bean. Cook in the same way.

*Lima beans.* Shell and cook in boiling salted water to cover until tender, from 10 to 20 minutes, according to size. Drain and dress with butter, or serve in a béchamel sauce.

*Fava beans or broad beans.* Rather like a lima bean, but with a thicker, fleshier pod, varying in size from half an inch to an inch in diameter. Often found in Italian markets, occasionally in supermarkets. Shell and cook in boiling salted water to cover until just tender, about 10 to 20 minutes, according to size. Cool slightly, slip off the heavy skin, and serve with butter, or with oil, garlic, and a touch of lemon juice.

*Cranberry beans.* During the summer, when mature, they have a pink-flecked, dry pod and a pink-speckled bean inside. Shell and boil in plenty of salted water until tender, which depends on how old and hard the beans are—it can take 30 minutes or more. Dress with butter, with crisp, crumbled bacon, bacon fat, and a tiny bit of vinegar, or with olive oil and garlic. A deliciously starchy accompaniment to meats.

These three kinds of shell beans may be combined with fresh, frozen, or canned corn kernels and butter to make different versions of succotash. Use equal amounts of each vegetable and enough butter to coat them well.

*Dried beans.* All dried beans require either overnight soaking or the following quick treatment: Cover the beans with enough water to come 1 inch above the top, bring to a boil, and boil 2 minutes. Turn off the heat and let stand in the water for 1 hour—no longer. Add salt, seasonings, extra water, if needed, bring to a boil again, and simmer until just tender, but not mushy. Drain and use for various recipes, such as baked beans, bean casseroles, bean salad (see page 49), and white bean and tuna salad (see page 302).

BEETS. One of the few vegetables that is equally good canned or fresh. Fresh beets bought in the market should be small and firm (larger ones tend to be woody and tasteless), with the tops still on. (For cooking beet tops, see "Greens Primarily for Cooking.") Never peel fresh beets before cooking, or they'll bleed to death. Cut off the stem an inch above the bulb and leave the roots on. Boil in salted water to cover until tender. Small beets will take 25 to 30 minutes, larger ones 35 to 40 minutes. Drain and cool a little until you can peel them by slipping off the skins. Leave whole if small, or slice or cut into thin julienne strips. Serve hot with butter or cold in salads, especially salads of slightly bitter greens such as endive or chicory that welcome the sweetness of the beet. Tiny baby beets take less cooking time and are usually served whole. Beets may also be wrapped in foil and baked in a 325° oven for about the same length of time as for boiling. Test with a fork.

BLACKBERRIES. The little wild blackberries that trail through the woods are full of flavor, though hard to pick, and make delicious pies, jams, and jellies. Large cultivated blackberries are somewhat seedy but heavenly with sugar and cream, baked in pies, or puréed for sauce.

BLUEBERRIES. It is hard to differentiate between wild huckleberries and wild blueberries. I think the wild huckleberries gathered in hilly or mountainous regions have greater flavor and bouquet. Wonderful for pies, preserves, and syrups. Wild blueberries can often be found in country markets in the summer. Cultivated blueberries, the kind sold in supermarkets, are much larger and should be relished with sugar and heavy cream, sour cream, or yogurt; stewed; or baked in pies, muffins, and pancakes. Buy only firm berries. Look below the top level of the basket. Both blueberries and huckleberries freeze successfully. Do not wash. Freeze in the basket, just as they are, wrapped in foil or plastic wrap. That way they hold their color and shape.

BROCCOLI. In season most of the year. Don't be deceived just because it looks green. If the stems are thick and woody and the buds beginning to open, it is old. Look for tender young buds, tiny and tightly packed. I like to cook the buds, or flowerets, separately from the stems, cutting or breaking them off and cooking them in boiling salted water to cover until crisply tender, about 10 to 12 minutes, or steaming them. Serve dressed with butter, with hollandaise, or with olive oil and garlic, or chill and use in salads. For another meal, save the stems, peel, cut into fine julienne strips, blanch for 2 minutes in boiling water, drain, and sauté in butter for 2 to 3 minutes, until crisply tender. Also good combined with rutabaga and turnip (see three-vegetable sauté, page 191). Broccoli also makes a lovely purée. Frozen broccoli, if not overcooked, merely blanched briefly in boiling water, is quite acceptable.

BROCCOLI RABE. A more vigorously flavored member of the broccoli family, with longer, thinner stems, small leaves, and tiny, open yellow buds, all of which can be eaten. The flavor is strong, slightly bitter, and the vegetable, boiled and puréed in a food mill or a food processor, is an interesting departure from the usual purée. Cook in plenty of boiling salted water for 10 to 12 minutes, or until crisply tender, drain, and serve whole or finely chopped with garlic and olive oil, or cold with vinaigrette sauce. Or chop coarsely, put into a skillet with hot oil and a few garlic cloves, and steam until tender, covered, over low heat in just the water clinging to the leaves.

BRUSSELS SPROUTS. A much maligned member of the cabbage family, probably because they are invariably served overcooked, soggy, and not fit for human consumption. Look for small, compact heads, not the large, loose ones. As with most vegetables, the smallest are the best. Trim off the stems and any discolored leaves, and wash. May be served raw if tiny, tender, and crisp, or sautéed (see page 185). Small frozen Brussels sprouts are good if blanched briefly in boiling salted water. They need minimum cooking. Canned ones are to be avoided at all costs.

BUTTER

*Salt butter.* Comes in ¼-pound sticks, 1- and 2-pound blocks, and sometimes in tubs, to be sold by the pound. Even though the salt does help to preserve the flavor and quality, it is highly possible and fairly common to find strong-tasting, even rancid salt butter in stores. Buy in small quantities and, if the butter doesn't taste right, switch to another brand. If you buy in quantity, freeze the butter you are not using immediately.

*Unsalted butter.* Commonly referred to as sweet butter, it is more perishable than salt butter, but more delicate in flavor and by far the more desirable for cooking, especially for baking. Keep butter you are using in a covered container in the refrigerator away from strong-flavored foods, or it will absorb the flavors very quickly. Freeze what you aren't using. One uses sweet butter for flavor, so keep it pure.

*Clarified butter.* Something you make, rather than buy. Melt sweet butter in a heavy pan over low heat, to prevent it from browning. The white froth that rises to the top should be skimmed off with a spoon, and the clear yellow "clarified" liquid butter carefully poured off into a container, leaving the white curdlike dregs in the pan. Clarified butter will remain fresh for 2 or 3 weeks, so you may make it in quantity and use as needed. Use it for sautéing when you need high heat, and for delicate cakes such as génoise (see page 257).

CABBAGES. You'll often find in the markets not only the familiar green-to-white cabbages, but also red cabbages and the curly leafed savoy cabbages, which have a looser head. Both the green and red cabbages should have firm heads and fresh, unwilted leaves. The leaves of savoy cabbages should be crisp and dark green. Heads vary from 1 to 5 pounds. If you use only part, cover the rest tightly with plastic wrap and refrigerate. Trim off the stalk and any discolored or limp outer leaves. Cut into wedges, remove the hard core with a large sharp knife, and shred. Soak the shreds well in cold water for an hour to crisp. Drain well for coleslaw. To cook, shred or cut into wedges and either boil in plenty of salted water until crisply tender (about 5 to 8 minutes for shredded cabbage, 10 to 12 minutes for wedges) or braise. Blanched individual cabbage leaves may be stuffed and rolled (see *poule au pot*, page 25). For stuffing and cooking whole, savoy cabbage is best, as the leaves are easy to separate for stuffing (blanch the head first to soften them). Cabbage is a great friend of boiled dinners (see boiled corned beef and cabbage, page 16) and a classic combination with pork, ham, sausages, and sautéed game birds, such as pheasant (see page 171). Braise red cabbage with apples, or with chestnuts (see page 152). Raw cabbage is used for coleslaw and other salads, with red and green sometimes combined for color.

CARROTS. For best flavor, look for small young carrots, either those sold in bunches with the feathery tops on, or the packaged small California carrots. Old carrots have a woody core. Large carrots, which are what you find most of the time, should be soaked in water before preparing, to crisp them. To cook, trim the ends, scrape the carrots, then boil in salted water to cover, anywhere from 7 or 8 to about 20 minutes, depending on the size and the way you have cut them. Small carrots may be left whole; large ones can be sliced or cut into fine julienne strips. Don't overcook. Carrots may be roasted (see page 92), sautéed (see page 186), or poached à la Grecque (see page 53), and are excellent puréed, especially in combination with puréed potatoes (see page 51). They, of course, are delicious eaten raw, crisp, and chilled. Canned carrots are not very good—and why use them when carrots come fresh in the market all year?

CAULIFLOWER. Look for heads with firm, tightly packed buds that are snowy white, not yellow or discolored. Wash well, cut off the heavy stem end and green leaves. Cook whole, stem down, or broken into flowerets, in lots of boiling salted water: 12 to 20 minutes for a whole head, depending on size, 5 or 6 minutes for flowerets. Do not overcook until dark and mushy. Serve dressed with butter, or cover with béchamel sauce, grated cheese, browned bread crumbs and bake until the cheese melts and the top browns. Cauliflower may be puréed after boiling, or sautéed after being parboiled, then sliced or chopped (see page 186). Flowerets may be cooked à la Grecque (see page 53) or used raw as a vegetable hors d'oeuvre, with a dip. Frozen cauliflower is acceptable, but I don't really recommend it.

CELERIAC. Also called celery root or knob celery. A large, knobby, brownish root vegetable. Cook in boiling salted water until tender, peel, and purée (see page 51). Also good braised. Celeriac may be peeled raw (rub with lemon to prevent discoloring), cut into very fine julienne, and mixed with mustard mayonnaise for celery root rémoulade (see page 296), a fine hors d'oeuvre. Difficult to find in some markets, but may be ordered ahead.

CELERY. Buy the green or Pascal celery; it is tastier and crisper. Wash well to get rid of dirt at the base of the ribs and trim off the bottom and leafy tops (save tops for flavoring soups or stocks, or use in salads). Remove the coarse outer ribs; use for stock or mirepoix for braised meat (see page 132). Celery, to my mind, is better sautéed (see page 187) than boiled. The inner ribs, known as the heart, are delicious split and braised (see page 151). The tiny leafy ribs in the center are good as a raw vegetable hors d'oeuvre or in salads. Canned celery hearts are quite acceptable for braising and need only to be heated through.

## CHEESE

Among the enormous and constantly growing range of cheeses in the market today are some old faithfuls we cannot cook without. Cheese, whether for cooking, eating, or both, should be kept in the refrigerator (the warmer, not the colder part) tightly covered in plastic wrap or foil, or in plastic bags. If a cheese is to be eaten, remove and bring to room temperature an hour before serving.

*Cheddar*. This firm cheese can be white or orange, sharp, medium sharp, or bland. Sharp is best for cooking. A good Canadian, English, or American Cheddar from the Northeast or Northwest is fine, but be sure it is natural Cheddar, please, not processed. Buy aged Cheddar—it has the most flavor. Cheddar keeps well, and if you buy a whole wheel, it will last you several months. Grate or shred for soufflés (see page 221), cheese sauce (see page 274), or omelets (see page 184), or as a topping for baked dishes, or use for toasted cheese sandwiches and Welsh rabbit. And, of course, eat with salad or fruit, especially apples.

*Cottage cheese*. In its many variations, the fresh soft cheese favored by dieters. Try to find a natural cottage cheese, without preservatives (healthfood stores have them). *Ricotta*, a very soft, light, and creamy fresh cheese, is mostly used for Italian dishes such as lasagne and cannelloni, for cheesecake or cheese pie and other desserts.

*Cream cheese*. Soft fresh cheese mixed with cream to a smooth consistency, for cheesecakes, cheese pie, *coeur à la crème* (see page 314), salad dressings. It is bland and very receptive to strong flavorings such as chives, onions, and anchovies. Eat it with lox and bagels, fruit, or with preserves for breakfast or tea. May be bought by the package or the pound—if you use a great deal, there are 3-pound blocks. The packaged cream cheese sold in supermarkets contains vegetable gum, and the texture leaves much to be desired. Whipping it with a little heavy or sour cream improves both texture and flavor.

*Gruyère.* A cooking and table cheese with a fine-grained, rather firm texture and a few holes or eyes. Nutty aroma and flavor. Not to be confused with *Emmenthaler*, a similar Swiss cheese that has much larger eyes. The best comes from Switzerland, other versions from France, Austria, and Finland. Sold by the piece. Never buy the processed Gruyère in small, foil-wrapped triangles— it will not do the job at all. Used extensively in cooking because of its superb melting qualities. The only suitable cheese for fondue, and perfect for topping casseroles and gratinéed dishes, such as onion soup (see page 34), for soufflés (see page 221), quiches (see page 239), and other custardy dishes. A salad of Gruyère and olives (see page 301) makes a lovely summer lunch. Also to be eaten with salad and fruit, especially pears. Keeps well, wrapped in foil or plastic. Should a slight mold form, cut it off; it will not affect the cheese.

*Monterey Jack.* A California-born cheese, smooth, semisoft, creamy, and excellent for melting. Much used on the West Coast for Mexican-style dishes, such as chiles rellenos. Most Monterey Jack has an extremely bland taste, which has made it popular for sandwiches, cheeseburgers, and some baked dishes. Sometimes used for pizza, like *mozzarella*, although I feel it does not have the quality of the Italian mozzarella, a super melting cheese which in its best version comes in bell-shaped pieces. Absolute hell to slice but essential for pizza, lasagne, eggplant Parmigiana, and veal Parmigiana.

*Parmesan or Parmigiana.* A rock-hard, very pungent, sharp, and slightly salty grating cheese, the very essence of Italian cooking. The ground domestic version of Parmesan sold in jars is third rate and should be shunned save for emergencies. Imported Italian Parmesan, sold by the piece and, in some cheese stores, grated, is very expensive. Don't buy more than you need. Keeps well wrapped in foil or plastic, and may be grated in the food processor or blender or on the finest side of a hand grater. Used more extensively than almost any other cheese, as a topping for pasta and gratinéed dishes, for soufflés (see page 221), quiches, and other egg and cheese dishes, for Mornay sauce (see page 274), risotto (see page 42), and gnocchi (see page 46). A less costly substitute for Parmesan is *asiago*, a hard Italian skim-milk cheese with a sharp, piquant flavor. Some good asiago is made here.

CHERRIES. For cooking, buy the tart Kentish or pie cherries, or the Montmorency. They are best for poaching, pies, or as a garnish for meats and poultry. The large, lusciously sweet Bings and Lamberts are used for open-face tarts and other desserts and, of course, eaten raw.

## CHICKEN

Fresh chickens are infinitely preferable to frozen. Some are of higher quality than others. In the San Francisco area, look for the fresh-killed Petaluma chickens. On the East Coast the Perdue chickens from the Delmarva Peninsula have a considerable reputation. If chicken is wrapped in polyethylene, remove it. Wrap loosely in waxed paper and refrigerate. Use fresh chicken within 3 days. Estimate about ¾ pound of chicken per serving, to allow for the bone.

*Broiling chickens.* Small birds, weighing 1½ to 2½ pounds, should be split in two lengthwise by you or your butcher. Be sure to cut out the backbone (see illustration, page 164) and the part that goes over the fence last so the broiler will lie flat in the pan. Marinate before broiling, if you wish, in red wine, oil, and garlic, or teriyaki marinade (see page 103). Or push flavored butter under the skin (see page 104).

*Frying chickens.* Weighing 3 to 3½ pounds, these fowl represent by far the largest part of all chicken production. Though plentiful, the way they are raised and fed affects the flavor and texture, so shop around until you find those most satisfactory to your palate. Use for fried chicken, for sautés (see pages 164 and 166), fricassees, or for braised dishes such as *coq au vin* (see page 147). Whole fryers may be roasted (see page 72) or poached (see page 25). If, like me, you are a lover of dark meat, you'll buy your frying or sautéing chicken in parts and get only legs and thighs. The chicken-in-parts business has done us all a great service. The breasts may be boned and sautéed (see page 164), deep-fried (see page 203), or poached, chilled, and glazed with aspic, and the less-expensive wings and thighs used for sautés, fricassees, and casseroles.

*Poaching chickens.* The mature, fairly good-sized hens or stewing fowls that once gave rich flavor to our chicken stock are now very hard to find. If you do run across them in the market, remember they have worked hard for a living producing eggs and need long, slow cooking to achieve tenderness. The poached flesh is excellent for chicken hash, creamed chicken, and chicken à la king. Usually an economical buy. Nowadays we are more often forced to buy expensive roasting chicken for stock and poached chicken dishes such as *poule au pot* (see page 25).

*Roasting chickens.* Usually run 4 to 5 pounds. They should be plump and tender with a good amount, but not an overabundance, of fat. It is difficult in most parts of the country to find roasters larger than 5 pounds, but occasionally you can find them in the frozen-poultry section, or frozen 8- to 9-pound capons (the desexed male birds), which are expensive but beautifully meaty and tender. Chickens may be roasted stuffed (see page 76) or unstuffed (see page 73).

*Squab chickens.* Tiny birds weighing about 1 pound. Once quite common but now hard to find outside specialty markets. Serve 1 to a person. Best split and broiled (see page 103) or stuffed and roasted (see page 77).

CHOCOLATE. There's a good deal of artificial chocolate in the markets today, so be careful to read the label. Most recipes call for unsweetened or semisweet chocolate, and occasionally for sweet. Shop around for uncommon brands (some kitchenware shops carry good imported cooking chocolate) and make a taste comparison with the supermarket variety—there is often a vast difference. To melt chocolate, put it in the top of a double boiler over hot water, or in a pan set in a second pan of hot water, or in a dish in a 300° oven. If it seems to tighten up when melted, stir in a small amount (1 to 2 table-spoons) of vegetable shortening to reliquefy. Chocolate keeps well, if tightly covered with plastic wrap. If it "blooms" (gets dusty-looking on the outside), that is because of exposure to air; it doesn't mean the chocolate is stale.

CORN. Naturally, the shorter the time from field to pot, the better the eating. Whenever possible, buy corn freshly picked from the farm and cook as soon as you can. However, the corn on the cob sold in markets nowadays has been specially chilled after picking to keep the kernels moist and juicy and prevent starch from forming. It is also much easier to find the desirable white ears than before. Never buy corn with coarse, dry kernels. To check, peel down the husk and silk at the top (you can also spot any worm damage). To my way of thinking, corn on the cob should be put into cold water, just brought to a boil, without cooking further, and served at once with lots of butter, salt, and pepper. Corn is often cut from the cob and sautéed, sometimes combined with other vegetables, such as chopped sautéed onion, green pepper, or cooked lima beans. Both frozen and canned whole-kernel corn are most acceptable and can be used in many dishes.

CORNMEAL. There are two grades of cornmeal, one quite coarse, the other rather fine. The coarse is best for polenta and cornmeal mush (see page 44) and the fine for muffins and corn bread (see page 250). Also excellent used like bread crumbs for breading sautéed fish, or for thickening casseroles.

CRACKED WHEAT. A coarsely ground wheat, sold in health-food stores and in Middle Eastern stores, usually under the names bulghur or burghul. A nutritious alternate to rice, with a nutty texture and flavor. Fine-grade cracked wheat is best for uncooked dishes where the grain is merely soaked, such as *tabbouleh* (see page 302) and *kibbeh* (see page 306), medium and coarse grades for pilaf (see page 44) and cooked dishes. Also used in porridge, and, in small amounts, in some breads, as a substitute for other ingredients.

CREAM
Rich natural cream is almost impossible to find. Dairies in various parts of the country differ greatly in what they have to offer. The most commonly found forms of cream are:
*Half and Half.* Supposedly half cream and half milk, but more like very rich

milk. Can be used in coffee, for hot chocolate, some soups and sauces, and with some fruits.

*Light cream or coffee cream.* Called one or the other, depending on which part of the country you are in. A very light cream with a lower butterfat content than heavy cream, which means it will not whip. Works well in sauces and soups and with fruits.

*Heavy cream or whipping cream.* Although the butterfat content varies somewhat from one area to another, this is the heaviest cream available, and may be whipped and used as a topping for desserts, or in mousses and other chilled or frozen desserts, such as orange Bavarian cream (see page 322). Unwhipped, it is often added to soups and sauces as an enrichment.

*Sour cream.* A cultivated product, rather thick in texture and slightly acid in flavor. Excellent on fruits and baked potatoes and in some soups, and good mixed half and half with mayonnaise for salads or coleslaw (see page 296). Traditional in Central European and Russian cooking, including such recipes as beef Stroganoff. If used in sauces, it should be stirred in slowly and with great care, and never allowed to come to the boiling point, or it will break and curdle.

*Sterilized cream.* A specially treated heavy cream found in some communities. Sterilization is supposed to give it a longer shelf life and stability. I have found that if sterilized cream is bought in quart containers and kept for several days before using, it whips quite well, almost as well as heavy cream, but others have reported that they find it totally unsatisfactory as a substitute. Best try it out for yourself.

*Crème fraîche.* Another cultivated cream only recently produced in this country and close to the famous French cream of the same name. It can be purchased at relatively few specialty shops throughout the United States and is undeniably expensive. High in butterfat, it makes a beautiful topping for fruits and desserts, and adds new quality to many sauces. It may be stirred into sauces such as béchamel, suprême, and sauces for braised veal or fish, as an additional thickener. For a homemade approximation of *crème fraîche*, see page 287.

CUCUMBERS. Cucumbers range in size from the minute gherkins of late fall, used for pickling, to the supermarket standards—absolute whoppers, coated with wax, which are full of seeds, watery, and not at all reminiscent of the delicious cucumbers grown in the garden. These giants must be carefully peeled, split down the center, and the seeds removed with a spoon. Slice, or cut into thin julienne shreds. To remove excess water, put in a colander, sprinkle with salt, and leave for an hour. Rinse, drain, and dry. A better buy, if you can find them, are the small, old-fashioned, unwaxed cucumbers, or a variety known as the Chinese or English cucumber now to be found in our markets. This is long, thin, bright green, and needs no peeling or seeding. Just slice paper-thin and eat in sandwiches or salads or marinate in vinaigrette sauce.

The pale-yellow lemon cucumber, found in parts of the West, is small, round, crunchy, never bitter, and delicious in salads. To cook cucumbers, peel, seed, cut into strips or oval lozenges, and poach briefly in salted water to cover, just until translucent. Serve with butter. Or blanch for 1 minute in plenty of boiling salted water, drain, and sauté quickly in butter, adding seasonings and perhaps a little cream. Cucumbers also make a delicious soup (see page 305).

DUCKS. Except for cities such as New York, San Francisco, and Los Angeles, where there are Chinese neighborhoods and markets, ducks are, alas, available only in the frozen state. In Chinese markets you can always buy fresh-killed ducks, often with the feet and heads on, and in certain country areas you may find a farmer who raises ducks and will sell them to you live, or freshly killed. Otherwise, you'll just have to make do with frozen duck, which should be thawed before use (see page 84). Thawed ducks are pretty wet. Dry them well inside and out by rolling them in and stuffing them with paper towels. If you have an electric fan, blow it on the duck for a little while to help dry it out. Ducks vary in weight from 5 to 8 pounds. Long Island ducks, the ones most widely available, have a thick layer of fat under the skin and not very much meat, so a 5-pound duck will serve 4 only scantily. It is not too extravagant to gauge half a duck per person, whether you roast it (see page 84), broil it (see page 105), or braise it (see page 149). This is not true of ducks raised for Chinese markets which have a different structure, less fat, and more breast and leg meat. Be sure to prick the skin of Long Island ducks well during roasting or broiling to let the fat drain out, and don't, whatever you do, overcook the meat or it will be dry and tasteless. Don't discard the duck liver, either. This is a great delicacy. If you don't cook it with the duck, accumulate livers in the freezer until you have enough for a pâté or terrine, or some other duck liver dish.

Wild duck is a very different bird, with no thick layer of fat. While the breast is usually well-meated, the legs and thighs are less tender. Roast (see page 87) to taste, but don't overcook. Wild ducks are really hell to pluck. Try to find an accommodating butcher or, if you live in a community where duck hunting is common, someone who makes a business of plucking ducks during the season. Wild ducks weigh only from 1 to 2 pounds. A small duck, such as teal, will serve 1; a larger duck, 2.

EGGPLANTS. Versatile vegetables, by themselves and in combination with others, and in the markets most of the year. Eggplants vary in size and color, from the large bell-shaped purple eggplants and white eggplants (the latter more or less curiosities) to small, thin, elongated purple ones about 4 to 6 inches long. Buy eggplants that are firm to the touch, with smooth, unblemished skins. If eggplant is to be cooked for a short time, it is best to peel, salt, and drain it, to draw out the water and bitter juices. If it is to be cooked for a long time, peeling is not necessary and salting is a matter of taste, as the liquid will evaporate in cooking. Eggplant may be sliced with the skin on and broiled (see page 118); or sautéed, cut into strips, and French fried (see page 204); combined with other vegetables in a melange such as ratatouille (see page 145); stuffed and baked (see page 263); or used in various casseroles and dishes, especially Middle Eastern, Oriental, French, and Italian.

EGGS. For the most part, the eggs we buy are produced in vast quantities on poultry ranches, graded, packed, and shipped to market. In country districts, or in some markets and health-food stores, you will be able to buy eggs from free-range (as opposed to battery-fed) hens. These tend to be richer in flavor and darker in yolk—and more expensive. Egg sizes range from the very small pullet eggs, not widely available, to small, medium, large, extra-large, and jumbo, based on minimum weight per dozen according to U.S. Department of Agriculture standards, and grades AA and A to B and C (B and C are seldom seen in markets; the usual grade is A). Despite what some people may tell you, there is absolutely no difference, in flavor or nutrition, between white eggs and brown eggs. Pick the color that appeals to you. Unless a recipe specifies a certain size of egg, you can take it for granted that it should be the large size. Naturally, the fresher the egg when you use it, the better. It has been my experience that most supermarkets have a quick turnover of eggs, more so than the neighborhood grocery store where they may be left on the shelf for a longer time. Store eggs in the refrigerator, but don't let them hang around for months, getting stale and absorbing food odors and flavors. Buy them by the half dozen and use them up, unless you are a great egg eater.

For most recipes, it is better to remove the eggs from the refrigerator 30 minutes to an hour before using, to come to room temperature. Room-temperature eggs beat better and have greater volume. For mayonnaise, there's the likelihood that the sauce will curdle unless the egg yolks and oil are the same temperature. When separating eggs, be careful not to get whites in the yolks or vice versa, especially important for soufflés, where the oiliness of the yolks can prevent the whites' beating to their greatest volume (see page 221 for separating technique). If you need only whites for a recipe, store the yolks in a tightly covered jar in the refrigerator, or freeze them, first labeling the jar so you know how many are in the container. Egg whites freeze well. Put them in 1-cup or ½-cup containers (8 to 11 egg whites, or 12 to 14 egg yolks, according to size, equal 1 cup). Use the egg whites for meringues (see page 261), certain cakes such as angel food, or for clarifying stock (see page 24); the egg yolks for emulsified sauces such as mayonnaise (see page 281), hollandaise, and Béarnaise (see pages 279–281), to enrich sauces (see page 274), and in rich custards such as crème brûlée (see page 123). For scrambling and omelets, beat eggs with a little water to lighten them.

FENNEL. There are two kinds of fennel. One, correctly called Florence fennel, is cultivated and sold commercially. The other, less well known, is wild fennel, which grows in profusion in California, Oregon, and throughout the Middle West. Florence fennel, a bulbous plant of broad, fleshy ribs with a strong anise flavor, is a cousin of celery. The rather feathery, dill-like leaves are sometimes used as a seasoning. The bulb may be halved or quartered and braised (see page 150); sliced or quartered and included in vegetable mixtures, such as ratatouille; poached à la Grecque (see page 53); or sliced and used raw, like celery, in salads and as a vegetable hors d'oeuvre. Wild fennel grows quite tall and the long stalks are dried and used as a flavoring. A dried fennel stalk may be thrust through a loin of pork before roasting, or a whole broiled fish may be placed over a bed of fennel stalks and flambéed with cognac-it takes on the taste of the burning fennel. If you live near a patch of fennel, gather and dry it. Or buy packaged stalks imported from France.

FISH

We are blessed in this country in having many varieties of fish that are caught along our shores and in our waters. Although it is harder to get a good selection of fish in the interior sections of the country than along the coastal regions, you should always be able to find some of the more popular prolific types, either fresh or frozen, and, of course, the ubiquitous fish fillets. Whole fish should look and smell fresh and have bright eyes, shiny scales, and flesh that springs back when pressed with a finger. After buying, wrap fish in waxed paper or place in a covered dish and refrigerate. Cook as soon as possible. Estimate ⅓ to ½ pound boneless fish per serving or 1 pound of whole fish, to allow for head, tail, and bone.

Cod. A fish with rather coarse white flesh, less expensive than many others and a familiar sight in our markets, especially on the East Coast. Fresh cod can be bought whole, in steaks, and in fillets. Whole cod run from 5 or 6 pounds to large specimens of 30 or 40 pounds. Cod may be poached, broiled, baked, and sautéed, and is excellent cold. Salt cod is much used all over the world, especially by the Italians and Portuguese. The hard, dried, salted fillets must be soaked overnight in cold water to soften them and remove the salt, then drained, covered with fresh water, and simmered until tender, about 15 minutes. Serve with melted butter or béchamel sauce; or use in codfish cakes, soufflés, in a salad with potatoes, onions, and vinaigrette sauce, or in other codfish dishes.

Haddock. Another coarsely textured fish, similar to cod, with excellent flavor. At its best poached or baked whole. Fillets must be handled carefully as they tend to break easily. Poach, broil, sauté, or bake them in aluminum-foil packages. Haddock takes kindly to strong flavors, such as onion, garlic, and tomato mixtures. Smoked haddock, commonly known as finnan haddie, is a great breakfast favorite. Poach in milk and serve with parsley butter or béchamel sauce, or broil. Also good flaked and used for fish cakes and soufflés, like salt cod.

*Halibut.* A white-fleshed fish with a rather coarse texture and a pleasant but slightly bland flavor, which, to my mind, needs dressing up. It is very friendly to strong seasonings such as garlic, onion, capers, to herbs like rosemary and thyme, to olive oil and tomato sauce, and is excellent prepared in the Italian manner. Halibut comes in sizes from 6 to 8 pounds (known as chicken halibut), up to 100 pounds or more. Usually cut into steaks. Steaks from halibut, cut 1 to 2 inches thick, may be poached (see page 31), sautéed (see page 178), baked, or broiled (see page 114). Leftover halibut is delicious cold with vinaigrette sauce or mustard mayonnaise.

*Salmon.* A splendid though expensive fish caught on the Pacific and Atlantic coasts. In fairly good supply throughout the country, either fresh or frozen. Fresh salmon in season is extraordinarily good, with rich but delicate flesh. When it is not available, frozen is quite acceptable. Whole salmon or large cuts of salmon may be poached (see page 31) and served hot with hollandaise, cold with mayonnaise, or glazed with aspic (see page 327). They can also be stuffed and baked, like other large fish. Salmon steaks are good almost any way—poached, broiled (see page 114), sautéed (see page 178), or baked. One of the more unusual ways to prepare salmon is to pickle it with salt and sugar for the Scandinavian *gravlax* (see page 309). Salmon smokes and cans extremely well. The best and most expensive smoked salmon comes from Scotland and Nova Scotia. The less expensive lox is much saltier, and though it can be used like better-grade smoked salmon, it is more at home with bagels and cream cheese, scrambled eggs, or steamed over potatoes. Smoked salmon is a very elegant first course, sliced paper-thin and dressed with oil, lemon juice, capers, and freshly ground pepper, but try it sometime slivered in a risotto (see page 42) or a quiche. Both choice and inferior cuts of salmon are canned, so shop carefully. Only the best grades are worth the money canned salmon costs these days.

*Striped bass.* One of the greatest eating fish we have. Commercially fished in the East and a sports fish on the West Coast, striped bass weigh from 3½ to 12 or 15 pounds. Most often cooked whole, either poached (see page 30) or stuffed and baked (see page 267). The boned fillets may be poached in a court bouillon or in water and white wine (see page 31). Serve in the bouillon, or with a sauce made from the reduced poaching stock, or chill and glaze with aspic.

*Trout.* An adaptable fish with delicate flesh. Large trout may be prepared like salmon. The small trout, usually served whole, with head and tail on, are handy little fish, for one is usually just enough for a serving. Brook trout, speckled (mountain) trout, and the frozen rainbow trout widely available throughout the country can be cooked in all manner of ways—poached, sautéed (see page 177), French fried, stuffed and baked, broiled in the oven or over charcoal, or poached, chilled, and glazed with aspic. Live trout, fresh from the stream or the tank, may be tossed straight into the pot and cooked *au bleu* (the skin turns blue and the fish curls up).

*Fish fillets*. Fillets comprise the major part of the fish bought in this country, no doubt because they are easy to prepare and satisfy those who shun fish with bones. Fillets come both fresh and frozen, varying from ⅓ to 1½ or 2 inches in thickness, depending on the type and size of fish they are taken from. A tremendous amount of fish is filleted—cod, haddock, flounder, sole, snapper, ocean perch, and many others. More often than not, the fish from which the fillets come is not identified, but try to find out, for some have a poorer taste and texture than others. The finest fillets are from members of the flounder family of flat fish found on both coasts. This includes grey sole, lemon sole, rex sole, and petrale sole, for there is no true sole in this country. Most "fillets of sole" are really flounder, for at this point the words have become interchangeable in our shopping language. The most expensive, delicate, and fragile fillets are lemon sole. They break easily and are best poached (see page 32) or marinated for seviche (see page 308). Don't attempt to fry them. Fillets of petrale sole and flounder can be stuffed and rolled for paupiettes; flounder or haddock fillets can be deep-fried (see page 202). Flounder can be baked, broiled, sautéed, or fried. Haddock, cod, and ocean perch, coarser in texture, lend themselves to any style of cooking. Ocean perch are the cheapest and most widely available of all the frozen fillets. Bland in flavor, they cry out for sauces, stuffings, and strong seasonings.

## FLOUR

There are many different types of flour on the market today, some generally available, others mainly sold by mail order or in health-food stores. Always use the flour specified in a recipe, if it is a type other than all-purpose. Substitutions can ruin a recipe.

*All-purpose flour*. The most commonly used flour for cooking, for everything from sauces to cakes and cookies. It is a mixture of hard-wheat (high-gluten) and soft-wheat (low-gluten) flours and now comes both bleached and unbleached. I much prefer the unbleached, which retains more of the natural qualities and nutrition of the wheat, for breadmaking.

*Cake flour*. Cake flour, made from soft wheat, is fine and soft and may contain cornstarch. At one time much used for the kind of cakes popular in the earlier part of the century, such as 1-2-3-4 cake (see page 252), but now less frequently called for.

*Hard-wheat flour*. A high-gluten flour used for certain breads. It makes a loaf with a firmer, tougher texture, similar to French and Italian breads. Sold in many health-food stores and by mail from mills. Use only if specified in a recipe.

*Instant flour.* Very fine, powdery, presifted all-purpose flour sold under various brand names. Good for thickening sauces and gravies, as it does not lump. Preferred by some people for making puff pastry.

*Self-rising flour.* Flour to which baking powder and salt have been added. Much used in the South. Use only in recipes calling for this type of flour, such as certain cakes and quick breads. Because it contains baking powder, which with age loses its leavening power, self-rising flour does not have a long shelf life.

*Stone-ground flours.* Flours from mills that grind the old-fashioned way, with millstones, rather than with modern steel rollers. They do not keep as well as commercial all-purpose flour and should be stored in a cool place, or the refrigerator.

*Whole-wheat or graham flour.* Not two different flours, but the same thing. Whole-wheat flour comes in a number of different grinds, some coarser than others. There is also a finely ground whole-wheat pastry flour, made from soft wheat, sold in health-food stores. Whole-wheat flour is a whole-kernel flour that still retains the wheat germ, which white flour does not.

GEESE. Geese, for the most part, come to the market frozen. At holiday time you may find fresh-killed ones. Geese weigh from 5 to 20 pounds and are the bearers of a good deal of fat. The packaged, frozen geese are usually smaller, more compact birds. A 6-pound goose will serve 4. An 8-pound goose will serve 6 to 8. Geese are best stuffed with a fruit, crumb, and chestnut stuffing (see page 82). Goose fat is useful in many types of cooking, particularly for sautéing potatoes.

GINGER. In its various forms, a spicy, sometimes fiery, accent for dishes—a major spice. Ground ginger, the least pungent, goes into spice cakes and gingerbread, and a touch adds an interesting fillip to codfish cakes. Fresh ginger root, subtler in flavor, enhances many marinades, such as teriyaki (see page 103) and most Asian dishes. Look for young, plump, juicy ginger root. As it ages, it dries out and becomes woody, stringy, and much hotter. Ginger root can be kept for quite a long time in the refrigerator if peeled and put into a small jar of vodka. The vodka, tasteless itself, takes on a spicy ginger flavor and can be used for seasoning. If you cut a piece of ginger root, wrap it tightly in plastic wrap and refrigerate. Candied ginger can often be substituted for ginger root if the sugar is washed off. Finely chopped, it is good for such things as teriyaki marinade, fruit compotes, and syrups. Preserved ginger, in syrup, can also be used for fruit compotes and for ginger-flavored ice cream (see page 332). Avoid dried ginger root, sometimes found in jars on the spice shelves of supermarkets—it is virtually useless.

GREENS FOR SALADS
Wash and dry thoroughly before using (see page 291), wrap loosely in paper

towels, put into a plastic bag, and refrigerate. Before washing head lettuce, such as Boston, cut out core. Hold head, core side up, under running water; leaves will then separate easily. Salad dryers with a centrifugal action are good for all but very delicate Bibb lettuce, which bruises easily. Use faded outer leaves of lettuce in stuffings for turkey, chicken, and meat to add moisture and texture.

*Bibb lettuce.* Small tender head lettuce with very crisp leaves. Soak and rinse well to get rid of sand and dirt that cling to the leaves. The small leaves should be left whole.

*Boston or butter lettuce.* Pale-green, deliciously tender head lettuce. Use in salads or as a garnish. Small leaves may be left whole, the larger ones broken with the fingers. Add coarse outer leaves, not good for salads, to soup stocks. Whole heads may be braised (see page 151).

*Chicory.* Sometimes called curly endive. A robust, crisp salad green with a slightly bitter tang. Best combined with other greens. Use the feathery leaves for garnishing. May be braised.

*Dandelion greens.* Commercially grown or wild dandelion leaves are excellent in salads, with a refreshingly bitter taste. Use alone or with other greens. Pick wild dandelions before the flowers form, dig up the root, and use the tender inner leaves.

*Endive, also called Belgian or French endive* (true name, witloof chicory). A small elongated lettuce with a tight head, blanched for marketing and carefully packed, so it requires little cleaning. Usually it is sufficient to wipe it off with a damp cloth and remove any discolored outer leaves. Crisp in texture with a delicately bitter flavor. One of the choicest and most expensive salad greens. However, the heads have no waste and go a long way. Use leaves whole, shred, or cut into julienne strips or rings. The sweetness of chopped beets is almost a must with endive salads. Separated leaves may be stuffed with various hors d'oeuvre mixtures. Braises or sautés beautifully.

*Escarole.* Rather coarse-leafed, slightly bitter green. Preferably, use only the tender greeny-yellow inner leaves for salads. Outer leaves may be added to soup. May be braised.

*Field salad, corn salad, lamb's lettuce.* A less common type of green with small tongue-shaped leaves, usually sold with roots attached. Flavor is tangy and "wild." Best combined with blander greens. Difficult to find, except in eastern markets in fall and winter.

*Iceberg lettuce.* Many people damn it, but when broken up (not cut) it adds good flavor and a wonderfully crisp texture to a salad, with other greens. Keeps longer than other lettuce.

*Leaf lettuce.* Lettuce with loose leaves that do not form a head but branch from the stalk. Comes in various colors—green, red, and coppery brown—and is sold under such names as salad bowl, oak leaf, ruby. The curly, fringed leaves are very decorative and add great color to mixed salads. Wash, dry, and use immediately, as leaves wilt quickly.

*Romaine or cos lettuce.* Head lettuce with long, crisp leaves shading from bright green to yellow. Excellent texture and flavor. Recommended for salads that need a lot of tossing, such as Caesar salad, as it does not wilt. Break large leaves into pieces, leave small ones whole. Coarse outer leaves may be added to soups or shredded, blanched, drained, and added to a cheese soufflé mixture, to give a crunchy texture.

*Rugola or arugola.* Small, flat-leafed greens with a bitter, slightly peppery flavor and rather coarse texture. Extremely popular for salads. Usually sold with the roots on. Wash thoroughly. Known in English as rocket, it is easy to grow from seed.

*Watercress.* Sold in bunches. Look for those with crisp, bright green leaves, not limp or yellowed. The small leaves have a refreshing bite and are usually mixed with other greens in salads. Watercress wilts quickly when dressed. A big bowl of plain watercress is good to munch on with steaks or chops. Or roll sprigs in soft white, buttered homemade bread for a lovely sandwich.

### GREENS PRIMARILY FOR COOKING

The leafy green tops of beets and turnips, mustard greens, collards, kale, spinach, Swiss and rhubarb chard, and dandelion greens are all good cooked. Remove damaged or discolored leaves and heavy stems and wash thoroughly. Boil, steam, or sauté. Cooking time depends on the age and coarseness of the different greens. Heavy, coarse greens like kale and collards take longest to cook. A pound of greens will serve 2.

*Beet greens.* Wash, put into a heavy pan with just the water clinging to the leaves. Sprinkle lightly with salt. Cover and cook over medium heat about 5 minutes or until just wilted—the leaves will lose most of their water, reduce in bulk, and become limp. Turn once or twice with a wooden spoon or spatula so top leaves fall to the bottom during cooking. If water evaporates too fast and leaves show signs of sticking, add a very little boiling water. Drain, leave whole or chop, dress with butter, and serve with lemon wedges.

*Chard.* Swiss chard has green leaves and long white ribs. The less common rhubarb chard, more often found on the West Coast than the East, has red ribs and reddish-green leaves. Cook the leaves like beet greens, about 10 minutes. Or sauté in oil, like mustard greens. Cook the white or red ribs as a separate vegetable, like asparagus, in boiling salted water to cover until just tender. Serve hot with melted butter or hollandaise, or cold with a vinaigrette sauce.

*Collards.* Unlike most other greens, collards are best cooked in the southern way, for 2 hours in water to cover with a piece of ham or bacon. Drain and serve.

*Dandelion greens.* Delicious sautéed with bacon. Fry squares of bacon in a heavy skillet until the fat has been drawn out, add the washed and dried dandelion greens, and toss in the fat with the bacon, a little chopped garlic, finely chopped fresh mint, and a touch of wine vinegar until wilted, about 5 minutes.

*Kale*. A heavy, coarse green with curly leaves. Best cooked like collards, for 1 hour. Drain and serve.

*Mustard greens*. Pungent, flavorful greens beloved of the Chinese, the French, and Southerners. I like to chop them coarsely and sauté in olive oil (about 4 tablespoons or just enough to cover the bottom of a heavy skillet) with a clove of garlic in the Italian manner. Cover the pan and cook for 10 minutes, or until wilted, shaking the pan occasionally to keep the greens from sticking.

*Spinach*. A very versatile vegetable, with many uses in cooking. Prewashed spinach packaged in bags is not a good buy; it is damp, has many small broken leaves and a lot of waste. Whenever possible, buy fresh, loose spinach with crisp, undamaged leaves. Wash well in several changes of water to remove all the sand, and pull off the heavy stems. May be cooked in just the water that clings to the leaves, like beet greens, for about 5 minutes until wilted, or sautéed in oil (see page 188). Plainly cooked spinach may be puréed (try combining it with a purée of cooked watercress), or drained very well and chopped fine to use in spinach roll (see page 224), soufflés, crêpes, stuffings, quiche, or omelet fillings. Frozen spinach is an acceptable substitute, but it holds a great deal of water and yields less than fresh.

*Turnip greens*. Cook like mustard greens, for 10 minutes.

## HERBS

With the vastly increased use of fresh herbs in cooking, herb-growing has become more popular in this country and it is easier than ever before to find herbs, both cut and potted, in vegetable stores and supermarkets. There is no doubt that the herbs you grow and dry yourself are vastly superior to the packaged ones. If you do buy dried herbs, shop around for a good brand. Some companies powder their herbs too much. Look for large leaves with a strong perfume, such as the dried herbs from Provence, sold in many specialty shops. Dried herbs lose their potency very fast. Always keep them in a dark place, away from heat, and replace them frequently. Most dried herbs are improved by crushing, either in a mortar and pestle or in the palm of your hand with your thumb, before being added to a dish. Soaking them in a little wine also helps to release the flavor. When substituting dried herbs for fresh, the standard ratio is 1 teaspoon dried herb for 1 tablespoon chopped fresh herb. Some of the more essential kitchen herbs are:

*Basil*. The sweet basil used for cooking (there are also ornamental basils) is an annual that grows abundantly, with a deliciously pungent leaf. There are two types: the large-leafed basil and the tiny-leafed bush basil. Basil is the definitive herb for tomatoes, whether they are sliced as a salad (see pages 294 and 299), turned into tomato sauce (see page 39), or used in a sautéed zucchini (see page 190) or salade Niçoise (see page 298). Ground with oil, garlic, and pine nuts, it makes that most glorious of pasta sauces—the Italian pesto. Chopped fresh basil leaves or the whole tiny leaves give lovely flavor to a green salad. Basil is easy to grow on your windowsill.

*Bay leaf.* The dried leaf of the bay tree is essential in a bouquet garni and for flavoring stocks, court bouillon, marinades for game and meat, stews, and many meat dishes. It can also impart an unusual and interesting flavor to custard and some sauces. The imported Mediterranean bay leaf has a better and more lasting flavor than the California floral bay.

*Bouquet garni.* Not a single herb, but a little bundle of herbs that flavor stocks and stews. Bay leaf, thyme, and parsley are the usual assortment, tied with string to a rib of celery or a leek which holds them firmly together so the bouquet can be easily removed after cooking. Or the flavorings, perhaps with the addition of an onion and a clove or two, may be tied in a cheesecloth bag. Sometimes a sprig of rosemary is included.

*Chives.* This slender green member of the onion family (see page 379) is one of the favorite herbs for salads, sauces, or garnishes for soups and vegetable dishes and is part of the classic fines herbes trio for an omelet (see page 184). Often mixed into cream cheese or cottage cheese, or the horseradish cream that goes with roast beef. Chives should be finely cut, not chopped, as their moist tubular stalks bruise easily. A hardy perennial for garden or flowerpot.

*Coriander.* Also known as Chinese parsley and, in Spanish, cilantro. Fresh coriander has pale-green leaves, rather like those of Italian parsley. Much used in Chinese, Indian, and Latin-American cooking, coriander has had quite a vogue in the last few years, although some people find the strange, strong, distinctive flavor unpalatable. This is one herb you either love or loathe. Guacamole (see page 303) and seviche (see page 308) are dishes that depend for their flavor on freshly chopped coriander, which is more often sprinkled over food as a seasoning and garnish than cooked in a dish. Chinese and Spanish-American markets always have coriander, but now you find it in some vegetable markets, especially on the West Coast. This is one herb that is always sold with the roots on. Do not remove. To keep, wrap, roots and all, in damp paper towels and store in a plastic bag or a covered glass jar in the refrigerator. Do not wash until ready to use. Coriander is easy to grow, but goes to seed quickly in hot weather. The dried seeds, which have an entirely different flavor, are much used in curries, and are excellent with pork and chicken.

*Dill.* Very popular in Scandinavian, Russian, and Central European cookery. The dill sold in markets is mostly raised in hothouses. The branches are about 8 inches long, extremely feathery, and highly aromatic. Garden dill goes to seed fast, especially in the summer. Dried dill seeds are a standby for pickles—in fact, for most of us, our first acquaintance with dill was the ubiquitous dill pickle. Finely chopped fresh dill leaves are good with fish, veal, chicken, vegetables such as sauerkraut, cabbage, and boiled new potatoes, in cucumber salad (see page 293), sour-cream sauces, and soups. A whole bunch of dill is part of the curing ingredients for the Scandinavian *gravlax* (see page 309). In most cases, dried dill weed, although not as flavorful as fresh dill, is an acceptable substitute.

*Mint.* Popularized by the English in the form of mint sauce (see page 63) with roast lamb, which to my mind smothers the good flavor of the meat, mint, both fresh and dried, is used with great imagination in Middle Eastern dishes such as *tabbouleh* (see page 302) and cucumber and yogurt soup (see page 305). Mint is chopped and added as a flavoring and a garnish, rather than cooked. Use it in some salads, with cooked dandelion greens, on new potatoes and peas—and don't forget one of its most important roles, crushed in a mint julep. Can be bought in markets across the country and is an easily grown perennial—beware, it spreads like mad.

*Parsley.* Probably the most widely used of all fresh herbs—and the most easily available. There are 2 kinds, the familiar curly parsley that garnishes practically every platter, and the Italian flat-leaf parsley, not as useful as a garnish (it wilts easily) but infinitely better for cooking, with a subtler, more refined flavor. Curly parsley is delicious fried in hot fat (see page 202) as a garnish for fish. Parsley belongs in a bouquet garni, in stocks, soups, stews, almost everything from salads to a chicken sauté. Parsley butter, like other herb or flavored butters (see page 104), can be made in quantity, frozen, and put on cooked vegetables, a broiled steak, or broiled fish. Parsley keeps well in a plastic bag in the vegetable compartment of the refrigerator. A sturdy biennial, it will flourish in the garden for 2 years, then disappear.

*Rosemary.* A marvelously fragrant perennial that grows wild in great bushes in Europe, especially the south of France. Quite easy to grow and very ornamental, but best potted in cold climates as it cannot survive an icy winter. The sweet-and-bitter pungency of rosemary does marvels for roast lamb (see page 61), beef, chicken, and turkey, but it is a powerful herb and must be handled with caution and never overused. The needlelike leaves are as good dried as fresh (or even better), but must be crushed before using.

*Sage.* This may well have been the herb that traveled the covered-wagon trail in the days when pork and game were the mainstay of our diet and usually seasoned with sage. Nowadays dried sage is most often used in sausage and in poultry stuffings, but a little can enhance pork, duck, goose, and some beef dishes. Use sage with discretion; it can be unpleasant if overdone.

*Tarragon.* One of the most highly prized members of the family of herbs; French tarragon being considered the choicest. The pungent but light anise flavor of the long pointed leaves is highly complementary to sautéed chicken (see page 164) or rabbit (see page 170), roast chicken, veal, fish, poultry stuffings, and egg dishes. A lovely salad herb, and the essential flavoring for Béarnaise sauce (see page 280). Always cut, rather than chop, the leaves.

Tarragon is a perennial, usually grown from plants rather than seeds. After a few years, it will lose its flavor and have to be replaced.

*Thyme*. Next to parsley, the most useful of the kitchen herbs for stocks, soups, stews, marinades, bouquet garni, poultry stuffings, brown sauce, braised dishes such as shoulder of veal (see page 131), or a roast loin of pork (see page 68). There are very few savory dishes that can't benefit from a touch of thyme, including beefsteak and kidney pudding (see page 27). There are various kinds of thyme, all easily grown as perennials in the garden or in pots. English and French thyme, very similar in flavor, are preferred for cooking. Lemon thyme has a distinct and pleasant lemony tang.

HOMINY. Corn kernels treated with lye and steamed until the skins come off and the kernels are puffed and look like white popcorn. Whole hominy is a much neglected vegetable, excellent cooked in butter and combined with sour cream and green chilies, or served with bacon and gravy. Available both dried and canned. Hominy grits is a cereal made from ground dried hominy. As served in the South, on the breakfast plate, it pleases me not. I prefer, after cooking it, to combine it with butter, garlic, and grated cheese and bake it as an accompaniment to entrees or to mold the hominy, then slice, and sauté it until crisp in butter or bacon fat, to be served with game birds or chicken.

HORSERADISH. A pungent root that carries a tremendously hot message. Freshly grated and combined with vinegar, or with sour cream or whipped cream, it is one of the greatest accompaniments for hot or cold roast or boiled beef. Also good with steak, ham, oysters, smoked trout. Excellent combined with applesauce and served with roast pork. Widely available ready-prepared in jars, but best if you buy the root and grate it fresh. Country markets and stores in Jewish neighborhoods often carry horseradish root.

JERUSALEM ARTICHOKES. Now sometimes marketed as "sun chokes," these are no relation to globe artichokes but are another vegetable entirely, kin to the sunflower. They look like small, knobby new potatoes. Scrubbed, they may be boiled in their jackets in salted water to cover for 8 to 10 minutes or until just tender, peeled, sliced, and dressed with butter, or puréed. Also good as a soup, or pickled. Sliced raw and used in salads they add an excellent, crisp texture.

KOHLRABI. A small pale-green, slightly knobby, turnip-shaped root vegetable. Sometimes called cabbage turnip but with the virtues of neither. Not one of my favorites. Both tops and bulbous root may be eaten. The root is the better part. Buy small or medium kohlrabi. Remove tops, peel bulb, and slice thin. Put in a pan with a small quantity of salted water, cover, and steam gently until tender, about 25 minutes. Drain, dress with butter, and season with salt and pepper to taste.

LARD. Lard, the rendered fat of the pig, has fallen from favor since we have become so accustomed to using vegetable shortening. However, good lard, especially the pure and delicate leaf lard rendered from kidney fat, is excellent for baking, frying, and sautéing. Pastry made with leaf lard is even shorter than pastry made with butter. An interesting fat for the kitchen. If you have never used it, I would advise you to experiment a little bit.

LEMONS. Brilliant yellow citrus fruit, irreplaceable in cooking. Fresh lemons, available all year, easily outdistance the artificial lemon juice and flavorings. The juice is an essential flavoring for hollandaise (see page 279), mayonnaise (see page 281), egg-lemon soup (see page 286), for pies, soufflés, cakes, ice cream, and sherbet (see page 334). A squeeze of lemon in the butter for vegetables gives a zesty tang. In marinades for meat, game, or fish, the acidity of lemon juice is a tenderizer. Lemon juice or a cut lemon rubbed in the cavity of poultry or game birds freshens the meat and improves the taste. Lemon is used widely as a garnish and condiment for caviar, fish, all shellfish, veal, and beef. The lemon zest, the yellow part of the rind, is added to many dishes, from frozen lemon mousse (see page 319) to Viennese goulash (see page 141), and it is an important part of the Italian garnish called *gremolata* (see page 146). To remove zest without pith, use a special tool called a zester, or a grater, or strip it off with a potato peeler and shred fine with a knife.

LIMES. Like the lemon, the green-skinned, green-fleshed lime is immensely valuable in cooking, for baking, marinades, as a flavoring for chicken, duck, or fish. Lime juice "cooks" raw fish for seviche (see page 308). Tough of skin, the lime is best juiced with a small metal hand squeezer of the type used in bars.

MANDARINS. The mandarin, which originated in China, is a type of small orange with a soft, loose skin that peels easily. Tangerines belong to this family, as do satsumas, the type of mandarin orange found in cans, and hybrids such as the tangelo (a grapefruit-tangerine cross) and the temple orange (an orange-tangerine cross). Mandarin oranges and tangerines have a bouquet and flavor slightly different from a true orange and are excellent eating fruits. Mandarins make delicious sherbet. Tangerines can be made into preserves and chutneys, and the sections are often used in salads. As with other citrus fruit, pick tangerines and mandarins that are heavy in the hand, which means they are full of juice.

MEAT
We have two categories of markets where we buy meats. One is the rapidly vanishing small private butcher, who cuts meats to order, and the other is the supermarket, which deals primarily with packaged, ready-cut meats, although many do have a butcher on the premises who will, on request, cut meat for you and order special cuts and variety meats.

To buy packaged meats requires a working knowledge of the cuts most suitable for the various cooking processes and the difference between the more expensive and less expensive cuts (for instance, if you are making braised beef, you have a choice between the very lean top or bottom round and the fatter but less costly chuck). Once you know your cuts, you can start experimenting and use parts of the animal you never thought of before.

When buying meat cuts with a good deal of bone, estimate 1 pound per person. For cuts with a small amount of bone, ½ to ¾ pound. And for boneless beef, 8 ounces is a generous serving, 5 to 6 ounces normal.

I personally feel that uncooked meat should be kept in the refrigerator no longer than 4 or 5 days. It should not be wrapped airtight, but have an opening at the end so the meat can breathe. Ground meat is best cooked the day of purchase because bacteria grow easily. Certainly it should never be kept in the refrigerator for more than 24 hours. Wrap like other meat. The freezer can be a great boon. When there are specials on meat, you can stock up on various cuts and refer to them as you would a library of books, knowing there is always something to cook in an emergency. I find the commercially flash-frozen meats to be equally as good as fresh, but on the other hand I have eaten a good deal of meat that has lost its savor and texture because it was carelessly wrapped and tossed into the freezer. If you freeze meat, wrap it well and tightly and store at a temperature of 0° or below.

## BEEF

Certainly more beef is consumed in the United States than any other meat and, because of the diversity of cuts and names, it is the most difficult and tricky to shop for. Beef is sold by U.S. Department of Agriculture grades, of which the finest is Prime. Prime beef is grain-fed, well marbled with little flecks of fat that break down in the cooking and lubricate the flesh, and therefore very tender. While most Prime beef goes to restaurants, a certain amount can be found in markets. Choice, the most generally available grade, has less marbling of fat in the meat. A recent change in grading has allowed a higher percentage of grass-feeding. Grass-fed beef has less fat content, is more chewy, and requires longer cooking to become tender, so one must be doubly careful these days when buying and cooking Choice beef. Examine it carefully. Grain-fed beef will have a little more fat on it and more marbling in the lean. Unfortunately, there is no chart that gives you cooking times for grass-fed vs. grain-fed beef—it's something you have to find out by experiment. Some people prefer the chewier texture of grass-fed beef, claiming it has a better flavor, but this is a matter of palate, and palate is a very personal thing. Decide for yourself. The other, lesser grades are Good, less tender and with less fat; and Commercial, used almost entirely for sausage-making and for adding to other products. You seldom come across these grades, but if you do, this is meat to use only for soup or stock.

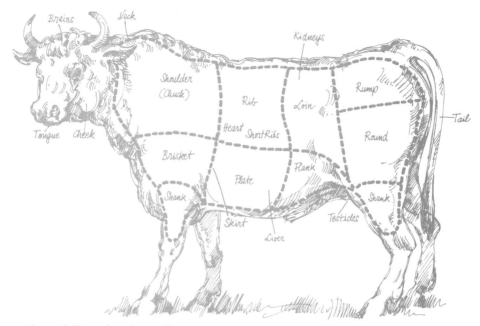

If you follow the chart above, you will learn a great deal about beef cuts and how to cook them. We will start at the head, wherein lies the *tongue*, excellent boiled and served hot with a sauce, cold in a salad, or thinly sliced for sandwiches. Then we go to the *shoulder or chuck* section. The individual chuck cuts are blade cut, arm cut, and cross cut. They may be bought bone in or boned and are braised (see page 125), stewed, pot roasted, and ground for hamburger. Cuts with a lot of bone can be used for stock and the boiled meat saved for hash. The rack of the *rib* section, from which we get rib roasts, usually contains 7 ribs. The 3 closest to the chuck are the least desirable because of excess fat. The next 4 ribs are the choicest and usually sell for a premium price. Most roasts for home use are cut short and the cut-off rib ends, known as *short ribs*, are sold separately for braising, or to be marinated and barbecued. A rib steak or boneless rib eye steak cut from the ribs can be broiled or sautéed—pick one that is not too fatty. Under the rib cage is the *heart*, which can be stuffed and braised, or cut up and stewed. Stuffed heart is pretty good eating, but I prefer to use the smaller, tenderer veal or pork hearts.

Next to the rib is the *loin*, first the short loin, which furnishes the most expensive steaks, and then the sirloin. Lining the bone is the tenderloin or fillet, a boneless, fat-covered strip of meat that rates as the most expensive of all cuts but has practically no waste when trimmed. With the tiny tip removed it becomes a luxury roast that needs to be barded with fat or marinated before roasting (see page 66). Beef fillet is exceedingly tender but, for my taste, greatly in need of flavor enhancing. The fillet is also cut into steaks for sautéing or broiling. A châteaubriand is cut on the diagonal from the thickest part.

Smaller steaks cut an inch or more thick are known as fillet steaks or tourne-dos. The most misunderstood term of all, filet mignon, rightly refers only to the tip of the fillet, a part that is usually sliced fairly thin, pounded and flattened, or cut into cubes and broiled *en brochette*. Steaks cut from the smaller end of the loin, nearest the ribs, are first the club steak, which has none of the tenderloin; then the T-bone, which has a small amount of tenderloin. The porterhouse, a real luxury steak with a T-shaped bone, cut from the large end of the loin next to the sirloin, is the best cut. If the entire top loin section is boned out, with the fillet removed, it is sold as a shell roast, or cut into steaks known variously as shell steaks, top loin or strip steaks, club steaks, sirloin strip, *faux filet*, New York or Kansas City cut, according to the part of the country you are in. This is the best cut for a sautéed steak *au poivre* (see page 159). Supermarkets often offer whole or half shells as specials.

The sirloin, which lies between the porterhouse and the rump, is not quite as tender because it includes the hip, a working part of the animal, but it is still excellent eating. Sirloin steaks contain different sizes and shapes of marrow-bone and are known as pinbone (nearest the porterhouse), flat-bone, round-bone, and wedge-bone sirloin steaks. They are good buys and should be broiled. Top sirloin steaks are cut from the largest part of the sirloin, a continuation of the top loin. The sirloin tip, a triangular, boneless piece trimmed from the base of the sirloin (technically, it is the part of the round nearest the sirloin), is usually sold as a roast or cut into steaks for sautéing or cubes for shashlik (see page 112) and kebabs. It costs less than the better-known cuts though, naturally, it isn't as tender.

Next comes the *rump*, sold as a roast or as steaks. Many people prefer the chewier but good-flavored rump to the tenderer cuts. The *round*, the meat from the hind leg, is divided into the top round, bottom round, and eye of the round, the top being the choicest quality. Though less tender than loin or rump, top round may be roasted if barded with fat, cooked quickly to the rare stage—this is the cut sold as roast beef in delicatessens—but it is more often braised (see page 140). Ground round, especially top round, makes good, lean hamburger (see page 161).

The leg bone contains a great deal of marrow. Sometimes it is sold with the knuckle for soup bones, or it may be sawed into pieces and used for marrow-bones and pot-au-feu (see page 23). *Oxtail*, a very bony cut that yields a thick, gelatinous, flavorful broth, is excellent braised (see page 142).

Below the loin and the ribs are two pieces of rather flat, long-grained meat. The one closest to the loin is the *flank*. Flank steak, formerly considered only worthy of braising, makes perfect London broil (see page 101), especially if marinated first, then cooked very fast and close to the heat; a teriyaki marinade (see page 103) is particularly good. Next to the flank is the *plate*, a less tender cut often used for boiling in conjunction with other cuts. Then comes *brisket*, much favored for boiled beef. There is a fairly heavy coating of fat on either side, but the meat itself is juicy and full of flavor. Brisket is good braised (see page 138) and is considered the best cut for corned beef (see page 16). When you are shopping, look for "corned beef brisket" on the package. "Corned beef rump" is less good but acceptable, but do not buy "corned beef spiced," which is highly spiced and has liquid in the bag. Kosher corned beef is always a good buy. Now we come to the *shank* or shin of beef, the lower part of the fore or hind legs, cut in crosswise pieces. It has a great deal of gelatinous fiber and is an excellent cut for soup or stock (see page 22). Less tender than brisket for boiled beef, but very flavorful.

The other variety meats and lesser-known cuts that are found in certain markets should not be ignored. They are usually a good buy. *Skirt steak*, for instance, similar in texture to flank, is very often rolled up and braised or, if you care to try, marinate and broil it like flank. Butcher's tenderloin is a small tender piece of beef from below the tenderloin, by the kidneys, also known as hang tenderloin. It's unlikely that you'll find it, as there's only one to an animal, but if you do, it is tender and can be broiled or sautéed. Butt is a triangular piece of meat found between the sirloin and the short loin. One end is very tender and can be broiled; the other is much less so and should be braised or boiled. If it isn't labeled, ask your butcher to identify it. *Beef kidneys* are larger and less tender than veal or lamb kidneys. Never try to broil or sauté them, only braise. I always soak them in milk for 2 hours before using them, to draw out some of their strong flavor. *Beef liver* used to be extremely coarse and heavy and was shunned by most people. Now, with smaller cattle and shorter grazing and fattening time, beef liver is much more acceptable. Best braised or simmered in wine, but may be sautéed if it is sliced very thin and cooked very quickly (see page 162). Tripe, the lining of the stomach, varies in textures from that of a Turkish towel to a large honeycomb. Honeycomb tripe is considered the best. Although tripe is partially cooked before being sold, it still needs quite a lot of simmering to make it tender. Braise, stew, or precook and broil. *Testicles* have a rich, heavy flavor and are regarded by some people as a great delicacy. They must be peeled and sliced before being broiled or sautéed.

## LAMB

Good lamb with pinkish-red flesh and rather flaky, creamy-colored fat is available in markets throughout the country, especially on the East and West coasts, where most of the lamb is eaten. Yearling lamb, approximately 1 year old, is what one generally finds. Younger, smaller lamb, known as spring lamb, is available at certain times of year. A very small number of butcher shops, mostly those with a clientele of European origin, will have for about 2 weeks of the year baby lamb so tiny that a whole lamb may serve only 3 or 4 people. This, naturally, is a great delicacy and expensive. Mostly we must content ourselves with yearling.

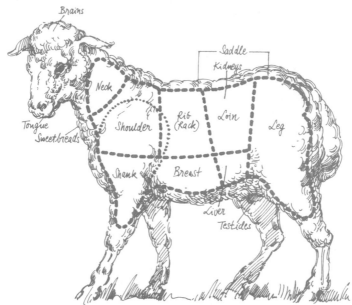

In some areas and markets you may be able to buy the head, which should be split and either roasted or braised. *Lamb's brains*, while less well known than calf's brains, are equally good and may be prepared in the same ways, as may the very small *tongues*, which, if properly seasoned, make tasty and inexpensive morsels. Pickled lambs' tongues, sold in jars, are very popular in America.

*Neck* is a good cut for stews and similar dishes. Sometimes it is included with the *shoulder*, a cut usually boned, rolled, and tied for roasting, braising (see page 145), or poaching. Many people consider roast shoulder of spring lamb to have an even more delicious flavor than the leg. Shoulder chops are extremely bony, but well flavored. Don't try to sauté them; broil or braise. The *rib* section is used in a variety of ways. The whole rack of ribs is a popular roast (sometimes 2 racks are tied together to make a crown roast). The ribs are cut into thick chops—when the rib bones are scraped to look fancy, they are known as Frenched chops. Rib chops can be broiled (see page 106) or braised (see page 145). For a special dinner, the eye section may be removed from the rack, cut into thick slices, known as medallions, and sautéed. Next to the ribs is the *loin*, the choicest part of the lamb. Here, as in beef, the bone becomes a T-bone, with meat on both sides of the bone: the tiny tenderloin, which is hardly ever removed, and the top loin. This part of the lamb is sometimes cut as a double loin, known as a saddle, and sometimes tied with the kidneys in. A whole saddle and the 2 legs as one piece is called a baron and is sometimes roasted for a large dinner party. Loin chops are broiled or braised, like rib chops. I find the flavor of lamb *kidneys* is better if they are soaked in milk for an hour or so before being broiled, braised, or used in beefsteak and kidney pudding (see page 27).

The most commonly used cut of lamb is the *leg*, which can weigh anywhere from 4½ to 9 pounds, according to the size of the animal. In many markets you can buy half a leg, either the shank (leg) end or the sirloin or butt end, the part that is next to the loin. For roasting, I prefer not to have the shank bone cracked or the little sirloin chops removed, as is so often done. A good butcher will remove the fell, the thin papery covering, from the leg. If he doesn't, remove it yourself (see page 61). A leg may be roasted (see page 61), braised, poached, or boned, butterflied, and broiled (see page 106) or sliced for lamb steaks. Boned and cubed leg of lamb is the standard cut for shish kebab (see page 111), and the ground meat (or ground shoulder) makes the Middle Eastern dish *kibbeh* (see page 306).

Lamb's *liver*, while as delicate as calf's liver, is less appreciated and therefore less expensive. Cook in the same ways—sauté, broil, or roast whole. The humblest of the cuts is the breast. If not too fatty, it may be broiled to crispness over charcoal or under the broiler and makes delicious eating, almost like spare ribs. In some markets, the breast is cut into 1- or 1½ inch strips and sold as lamb riblets. Broil in the same way. The breast may also be braised, stewed, or poached and deviled (see page 176). The front legs of the lamb are usually cut short and sold as *shanks*. When braised, the meat is chewy and moist. Lambs' *sweetbreads* from the neck, near the shank, are less common than calves' sweetbreads, and lend themselves to the same styles of cooking. Tiny, tender lamb hearts may be cubed and broiled like kebabs, or braised. Lastly, let us not forget the *testicles*, which are highly prized by some people, especially the Basque sheepherders, who sauté or fry them.

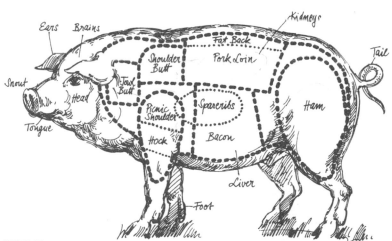

## PORK

The pig is by far my favorite meat-yielding animal, for he is edible from snout to tail and provides an enormous variety of eating. Unfortunately, like many humans, the pig has been put on a diet within the last 10 years—and we have suffered because of it. The meat is less streaked with fat and less juicy and tender than before. Let's hope that the streamlined porker will not last forever.

We start with the *head*, the basis of headcheese, a highly gelatinous mixture of bits and pieces of meat from that area, which is one of our more popular cold cuts. The *tongue* is of medium size, and 1 person could eat 1 or possibly 2 at a sitting. Tongue is often braised, sometimes boiled with sauerkraut. The *brains*, less often seen than calf's brains, may be prepared in the same way. *Pig's ears* have a chewy, gelatinous texture for which one has to develop a taste. I like them parboiled, crumbed, and either sautéed or fried, or stuffed and braised.

Behind the head comes the *shoulder* and *fatback*, the plain white fat sold for larding meat, for barding (see page 66), and for lining molds for pâtés. Below the fatback and before the loin comes the *shoulder butt*, used fresh for braising, roasting, and boiling, and also one of the choicest smoked cuts. Adjoining it is a very fatty square piece at the end of the head known as a *jowl butt* or pig's jowl, mostly smoked like bacon and extensively used in southern cooking, in boiled dishes, boiled with greens, or occasionally sliced and fried.

The *loin* is one of the choicest cuts. It extends from the shoulder to the ham and includes the rib and loin sections and the tenderloin. Rib chops are smaller and less choice than the loin chops, which contain a good piece of the tenderloin and are broiled, sautéed (see page 175), and braised. *Loin chops* cut extra thick are often split and stuffed before braising. In certain parts of the country or in pork stores, the succulent little tenderloin is removed and sold separately for sautéing, braising, or broiling. The loin is the most popular roast (see page 68), and the best for roasting is the *center cut*, which contains part of the rib and part of the loin. It is also the most costly. The two end cuts of the loin are the blade end or rib end (sometimes cut into pieces and sold as thick, meaty country-style ribs) and the sirloin end, the part next to the ham. The loin cuts may be roasted with the bone, or boned, rolled, and tied. For a crown roast, 2 loin roasts are tied together. Boned loin is also good for braising. Below the loin, more or less in the center of the pig but extending right through, is the side pork or siding, which is boned from the rib cage and smoked for *bacon* or salted for salt pork. Some is put down in a brine, or pickle, and sold as pickled pork. The *spareribs* themselves are roasted (see page 72), braised, or broiled. The heart is mostly stuffed and braised. The *tail* is a much neglected little delicacy that is sometimes cut deep into the animal, poached, and barbecued, or cut short with only a small bit of bone and boiled with sauerkraut, collards, or other greens.

The hind legs of the pig are sold as fresh hams or smoked hams, either whole or separated into the butt end, that closest to the loin, and the shank end, closest to the foot. I prefer the shank end; it slices better. Fresh ham takes to roasting (see page 69) or to braising. Steaks from ½ inch to 2 inches thick may be cut from the leg and boiled, sautéed, or braised. *Pork kidneys*, though rather hard to find, are tender and sweet and, to my taste, quite as good as other kidneys. Soak in milk for an hour before cooking. *Pork liver* can be sautéed, but is more often ground for pâtés and terrines because of its high fat content and excellent flavor. The front section of the pig includes the *shoulder* and *butt*. The small *picnic shoulder*, which is cut deep into the shoulder, around and down to the front foot, in the shape of a ham, is often smoked and sold as a picnic ham. It is also excellent fresh, braised, boiled, or roasted. You often see picnic shoulder and picnic ham in supermarket ads. While they have a different bone structure from ham and are less simple to carve, the meat is well flavored and they are good, economical buys. If the picnic shoulder is short cut, a piece of the leg about 2 or 3 inches long is removed. This is the *hock*, which contains some very edible meat covered by a thin layer of fat and skin. When boiled or braised (see page 146), hocks make a delectable dish, and the gelatin in the skin helps to thicken the liquid. Pork hocks are often lightly smoked and may be treated like smoked ham and served hot or cold. In some markets you will find *pig's feet*, cut long or short. Italian and Chinese markets cut them deep enough to include the hock; others cut them short, about 4 to 6 inches. Around holiday time you might see in Italian markets a specialty called *zampone*, which is the entire picnic shoulder, hock, and foot boned and stuffed with sausage meat. It is excellent poached. Pork meat and other bits of the pig are, of course, fumed into various kinds of sausage. Even the blood goes into the making of blood sausage.

HAM. There was a time when there were as many different country hams as there are states in the Union, but things have changed. Now the majority of hams we find in the market are what are known as ready-to-eat hams, very lightly cured and bland in taste. Although they are labeled ready to eat, this merely means that they have been heated during the curing and smoking process to a high enough internal temperature to make them safe for consumption. But they still need the benefit of cooking. I usually bake these hams for 10 to 15 minutes a pound in a 350° oven, basting them with a little red or white wine, cider, or ginger ale to add flavor. (I would avoid, if I were you, that famous southern recipe that calls for basting ham with Coca-Cola.) Country hams are still available by mail from smokehouses in certain states such as Kentucky, Vermont, Virginia, and New York. These are more heavily cured and smoked, and far more delicious. Basically, the difference between these hams and the supermarket hams is that they often need soaking and are then boiled or baked slowly in a covered pan (see page 69) and sometimes glazed before serving. They should be cooked according to the directions that come with them. You can often buy slices of country ham from these mail-order smokehouses. Broil, like ham steaks (see page 109), or cook in a heavy skillet and eat for breakfast with eggs, fried potatoes, and red-eye gravy made from the pan drippings. A good ham will keep for several weeks in the refrigerator. Eat it cold or use in casseroles, soufflés, quiches, and ham mousse (see page 320).

One of the world's greatest hams is Smithfield ham, a Virginia ham with a special cure that may be made only in the county of the same name. Heavily cured and quite salty, it is usually eaten cold, in paper-thin slices. The taste is quite similar to that of Chinese ham, and practically all Chinese restaurants use Smithfield ham in their dishes. Canned hams are, to me, the least interesting in flavor of all the hams, but some people find them extremely practical to have on hand. Be sure to prepare according to the directions given on the can.

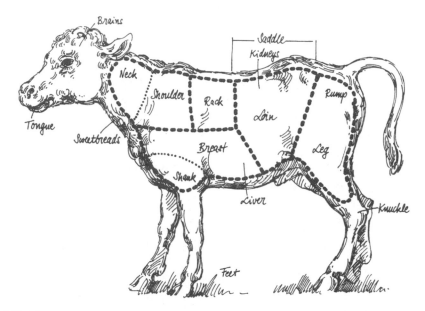

## VEAL

The best veal, which exists in this country in exceedingly small quantities, is pinkish-white, an indication that it is very young. Most of the veal sold in supermarkets is a reddish-pink and is really baby beef. In the last 10 years, better meat markets have been carrying milk-fed veal from calves up to 6 months of age. It is tender and pale, admittedly costly but worth the money. Because of its youth, veal has very little fat and needs some moisture in cooking. Usually it is better braised than roasted or broiled. This is also one of the most gelatinous of the meat animals, and the bones and bony cuts are ideal for stocks, aspics, and meat jellies.

The head, while difficult to get in this country, is a great delicacy; in France it is boiled and served as *tête de veau vinaigrette*. The small and extremely tender *tongue* is delectable braised, especially in the Italian manner, with tomato sauce, and is often incorporated into terrines and pâtés. *Calf's brains*, by far the best of the animal brains, are usually blanched about 15 minutes in slightly acidulated water, then sautéed, but they are also extremely good poached, sliced, and served cold with vinaigrette sauce.

Bony veal *neck* is used extensively for stock (see page 22). The pieces of meat from the bones make lovely jellied veal (see page 22). Veal *shoulder* is generally boned and braised (see page 131). Eat hot or press under a heavy weight and serve cold, with the natural jelly around it. Use boned, cubed shoulder meat for stews and braised dishes. Shoulder chops, while not the most desirable, braise successfully. I don't recommend sautéing them. Veal *loin* and *saddle* (the saddle comprises the 2 loins and part of the legs) is the tenderest part of the animal. A rolled and tied saddle, boned or bone in, sometimes with the kidneys included, is a luxurious and spectacular roast for a special dinner party. A roast of rib chops is called a rack. A loin may be roasted whole, with or without the bone, or cut into thick chops for sautéing or braising (see page 136). If the chops are broiled, baste well with butter or oil to prevent the meat from drying out. The *kidneys* are very delicate and lend themselves to broiling (see page 110), braising, and sautéing (see page 173). Never overcook or they will toughen. Kidneys should still be slightly pink in the center. Certain butchers will prepare *rump* of veal as a roast. While not all markets carry this cut, it is worth a try.

The *leg* is prepared in many different ways. It may be roasted (usually after being boned and tied), or braised, or sliced into veal cutlets. Steaks may be cut across the leg, either bone out or with the tiny round bone left in. Smaller, thinner pieces of veal leg, cut as scaloppine or veal scallops and pounded thin, are usually sautéed (see page 173) or braised as veal birds (see page 137), although they are occasionally deep-fried, as Wiener schnitzel (see page 204). The *breast*, boned or bone in, is an excellent cut for stuffing and braising (see page 134) and for stews. There's a famous Italian dish, *cima di vitello*, for which the stuffed breast is wrapped in a cloth and poached, then braised and eaten cold. The breast meat has a rather long grain and an interesting texture. The bones from both the leg and the breast are much valued for stocks, as is the highly gelatinous *knuckle*. The *shank*, which adjoins the breast, is commonly braised for such dishes as the Italian *osso buco*, or it may be used, like the neck, for jellied veal, once a very popular American summer dish. Although *calf's feet* are pretty hard to come by these days, if you find them they make a delicious dish when poached and served with a sauce poulette, hollandaise, or Béarnaise. Highly gelatinous, the feet are much sought after for stock.

*Calf's liver* and *sweetbreads* are the most delicious and prized of all. Veal sweetbreads may be blanched in boiling water for 12 minutes. They are then plunged into ice water and, when cool enough to handle, excess fatty pieces are removed. Sweetbreads are often placed in between 2 plates and weighed down before cooking. The liver may be sliced thick and broiled rare (see page 109); sliced thin and sautéed quickly; rolled, tied, barded with bacon, and roasted rare, to be served with mustard sauce; or cut into pieces and deep-fried, along with kidneys, brains, and thin pieces of veal, for an Italian *fritto misto* (see page 198). Veal hearts, which weigh about a pound, lend themselves to braising. Ground veal goes into certain sausages, such as bockwurst and bratwurst, and is important in the making of pâtés and terrines. Because of its lack of fat, it makes a very dry meat loaf unless combined with fattier meats such as pork and beef.

## MELONS

Some of the members of this large family are seasonal. Others, like cantaloupes, are widely grown and can be found in the markets throughout the year. Melons are one of the hardest fruits to pick out. If you have a trustworthy fruit dealer, ask him to select a melon for you; he should know more about judging ripeness than you. If the melon you buy is less than ripe, leave it at room temperature until it ripens. A ripe melon will keep for a week in the refrigerator, 2 to 4 days if cut and tightly covered with plastic wrap. Leave the seeds in a cut piece; it helps to keep the flesh moist.

*Cantaloupes.* Small melons with webbed skin and orange flesh. Extremely sweet and pungent at their best, tasteless at their worst. While not as desirable as other melons, cantaloupes are the most easily found. Halve and eat for breakfast, as a dessert, or cut into balls for a fruit compote.

*Casabas.* White-fleshed melons, extremely sweet when ripe, undistinguished when not. Serve like cantaloupes, or as a first course, with prosciutto or Virginia ham and a little pepper.

*Cranshaws or Crenshaws.* Yellow-skinned with pinky-orange flesh, these are probably the most delicious of all melons when fully ripe, with an intoxicating bouquet. Enjoy them as they come, unsullied by sugar or liqueurs, or eat as a first course with prosciutto or Virginia ham.

*Hand melons.* Named for the man who created this strain, Hand melons have a beautiful perfume, even before they are cut, and a superb flavor. Raised in relatively few parts of the country, so one must search them out. Do not chill. Eat at the peak, as soon as possible. Fine for breakfast, dessert, or as a first course with ham.

*Honeydews.* White-skinned, green-fleshed melons that 9 times out of 10 are quite dull. The tenth time they can come right out and surprise you. Good used in combination with other varieties in a melon-ball compote.

*Persian melons.* Large russet-colored, orange-fleshed melons with a breathtaking flavor and bouquet when fully ripe. In the market in the fall, all too briefly. Serve cool, not chilled, with a tiny touch of sugar if you wish, nothing more.

*Spanish melons.* Between a Cranshaw and a casaba. Extraordinarily sweet and pungent melons that come late in the fall and last into the winter.

*Watermelons.* Round or oblong in shape, brilliant green on the outside and pure watermelon pink on the inside, these are the quintessential American melons, with a luscious, liquid sweetness that is positively addictive. Pick one up and thump it with your knuckles. If it sounds hollow and resounding, it is probably full of juice. Best eaten very cold on a hot day. Good for sherbet. The leftover rind makes highly prized watermelon pickles. To gild the lily (or watermelon), fill it with liquor for drunken watermelon (see page 314).

MUSHROOMS. Cultivated mushrooms with firm, snowy-white caps are available year round. They need no peeling and usually no washing—just a wipe with a damp cloth. Should mushrooms look dusty or dirty, toss under running water in a colander and dry well before cooking. Sauté sliced or whole mushrooms quickly over fairly high heat in butter, or butter and oil, seasoning them with salt and pepper. Use alone, or combine with other vegetables, such as green beans or turnips (see page 187). Cook mushrooms soon after buying; they discolor and shrivel if stored more than a few days. Discolored mushrooms (often sold off at a lower price in markets) may be made into duxelles, a delicious mushroom paste. Chop very fine, stems and all, squeeze dry in a towel, and sauté slowly in butter (½ pound for 2 pounds mushrooms) with a finely chopped shallot or garlic clove, stirring occasionally, until dry and dark in color. Season with salt and pepper. Duxelles will keep for a week or two in the refrigerator or may be frozen in small quantities. Add some to scrambled eggs, omelets, vegetables, sauces, stuffings, or spread on toast as an appetizer with drinks. Use raw firm white mushroom caps for salads (see page 293), broil (see page 117), or cook à la Grecque (see page 53).

*Dried mushrooms*, imported from Europe and the Orient, are wild, not cultivated, varieties, with a totally different taste. Soak in warm water, or in wine, to rehydrate, then drain, and chop or slice. They don't have the texture of fresh mushrooms but bring delicious flavor to stews, soups, and certain meat dishes.

MUSTARD. A universal and widely used spice of varying degrees of hotness and pungency. Available in two forms: dry mustard or mustard powder and prepared mustard of different types, strengths, and flavors. Most of the good prepared mustards, like the Dijon mustards, come from France. Some contain coarsely ground mustard seeds; others are perfumed with herbs such as tarragon, dill, or thyme, spiced with green peppercorns, or mixed with wine. These mustards are delicious with meats, in certain sauces, and for dishes where mustard is the main flavoring, like the classic French *lapin à la moutarde*. Sometimes kidneys or liver are coated with mustard before being broiled. German mustards mostly ally a little sweetness to their bite and are excellent with pork, ham, and sausage dishes. American mustards are the mildest, with a sweet-sour flavor, and are good mainly for hot dogs, hence the popular name, "ball-park mustard." Use dry or prepared mustards to flavor sauces, dressings, mayonnaise.

NECTARINES. Fruits that look like fuzzless peaches, with golden flesh and a lovely aroma that sometimes belies their flavor and ripeness. Look for well-fleshed fruits, not too hard, or they will take a long time to ripen. Best eaten as a dessert fruit, with no accompaniments.

## NUTS

Today, most nuts sold for cooking purposes, such as baking, stuffings, and garnishing, are already shelled. They come either whole and blanched (with the skins removed) or unblanched, sliced, chopped, or broken into pieces. In supermarkets, nuts are sold in glassine or cellophane bags or vacuum cans, but if you use a lot of nuts and can locate a store where they are sold in bulk, you can save an amazing amount of money. Why pay for packaging? Bulk nuts (or any nuts apart from those in the shell or in sealed vacuum tins) keep better if put in plastic bags and stored in the freezer. Exposure to heat turns the oil in nuts rancid. Distributors of nuts always keep them at freezing temperatures because they hold better, so unless you are using them right away I strongly recommend that you store them in the freezer. Thaw at room temperature before using. You can chop whole nuts by hand with a chef's knife, but it is infinitely faster and easier to chop or grind them in a food processor or blender, if you own one.

*Almonds.* The nuts we use most in cooking and as a garnish for sautéed fish (see page 178) and vegetables—either the long Jordan almonds or the California almonds, which are interchangeable. You can buy almonds unblanched or blanched and whole, thinly sliced, slivered, or chopped, and toasted. To blanch almonds in the skin, plunge them into boiling water, remove after 30 seconds, and when cool, rub the skins off between thumb and forefinger. Unless a recipe requires pure white, blanched almonds, I think a little toasting for 10 minutes or so in a 350° oven, either before or after cutting, improves the flavor of almonds—and most other nuts. Should a dish require a strong almond flavor, intensify it with 1 or 2 drops of almond extract.

*Brazil nuts.* These very large nuts are sold whole or sliced, and semi-blanched (with part of the brown skin on). Blanch if you wish. To slice them yourself, soak whole nuts in boiling water for 30 minutes to soften them up. Also improved by toasting at 350° for 15 to 20 minutes.

*Filberts or hazelnuts* (two names, but the same nut). These have heavy skins, and I strongly advise blanching them, or rubbing them vigorously between Turkish towels—it is amazing how much skin will come off. Available whole, sliced, or chopped, and also improved by a slight toasting.

*Peanuts.* Need no blanching since the skins rub off easily. Unless you buy raw peanuts, they are already roasted and need no further toasting. Be careful when chopping them in a blender or food processor not to overdo it, or they will turn into peanut butter. If that should happen, add a little salt and oil and enjoy your own good homemade product.

*Pecans*. Sold halved or chopped. They do not blanch well because of their crinkly contours. A strong-flavored nut, seldom in need of toasting. Excellent for pies, cakes, cookies, or in dishes such as celery and pecan ring (see page 264).

*Pine nuts*. The tiny kernels of certain pine cones, they are probably the least known of all nuts. There are two varieties. The thin, tapering pignolia nut is sold shelled and blanched. A very oily, delicately flavored nut, it is improved by toasting for 10 minutes at 350°. The harder-to-find Indian pine nuts of the Southwest are more the shape of a coffee bean and have to be shelled. They have a slightly more piny flavor, but may be used in the same ways, in stuffings for poultry (see page 78) and vegetables (see page 263), and in casseroles and various other dishes.

*Pistachio nuts*. The most distinctive because instead of being white-meated, like other nuts, they are pale to medium green in their natural state (avoid those that have been dyed red). More often used for decoration, because of their lovely color, than as an ingredient, although there are several cakes and a pistachio bread that include them in the batter. When bought shelled, they are usually salted, but the small amount of salt can usually be rubbed off and what remains is hardly noticeable. Pistachios are fairly easy to shell, because the nuts crack on one side during the roasting process. Extremely expensive but cheaper bought in bulk.

*Walnuts*. There are two varieties. The glorious American black walnut is practically unobtainable. If you are fortunate enough to find any, use them for black-walnut cake or to dress sautéed fish (see page 178), for they are as delicious as they are precious. The English walnut, grown extensively in California, is the common type. Usually bought shelled, in halves or broken into pieces. Like pecans, the contours of walnuts make them hard to blanch, but it can be done. Toasting at 350° for 15 to 20 minutes gives walnuts a different and better flavor. Next to almonds, the most popular nut for pastries, breads, cakes, cookies, and as a garnish for vegetables (see page 190) and fish. Salted and toasted they are a popular and addictive snack or cocktail nibble.

OIL. A kitchen staple that varies enormously in quality, taste, and price. The finest oil, to my mind, is olive oil. One finds 8 or 10 different qualities, from the very rich first pressing, called "virgin olive oil," down to the low-quality oil made from the final pressing of fruit and cracked pits. The best and most flavorful, fruity olive oil comes from Provence, in the south of France. After this I would rate the better Italian and Greek oils and then the Spanish and North African. Buy the best you can afford and store it carefully. Olive oil should not be kept in the refrigerator (when refrigerated it turns thick and cloudy); if the weather is warm or the oil is left open for a long time, it can turn rancid, so buy in small quantities unless you are a liberal user. The vegetable oils (corn, cottonseed, soybean, peanut) are mostly flavorless and odorless—to my mind too tasteless for salads, but practical, inexpensive, and highly efficient for deep-frying, sautéing, mayonnaise, marinades, and general cooking. Peanut oil is my preference. Two other oils which have come into great favor in the last few years are safflower and sunflower oil. Both are very light, flavorless, and acceptable for frying, sautéing, baking, and certain pastries.

## ONIONS

The members of this family see more service in the kitchen than any other vegetable. They range from the dry yellow, white, and red onions to small brown shallots, green onions, leeks, garlic, and chives. When bought, dry onions, garlic, and shallots should be hard and firm, with no soft spots or green sprouting tops. Buy as needed and store in a cool, dry place. Refrigerate green onions, leeks, and chives.

*Yellow globe onions.* Sometimes called Spanish onions. General-purpose onions with brownish-yellow skin, either large or medium size. Excellent raw, baked, boiled, braised (see page 154), French fried (see page 199), or in soup (see page 34). Used in many dishes, chopped or sliced.

*Large white onions.* Sometimes called Bermuda onions, though they no longer come from that island. Mild and sweet, excellent French fried or for salads. Sweet white onions, namely Walla-Walla sweets and Maui sweets, are superb in salads, or sandwiches, or sliced in vinaigrette sauce.

*Small white onions.* About 1½ to 2 inches in diameter. Fairly mild. Excellent whole in stews and braised dishes, such as *coq au vin* (see page 147) and *boeuf à la mode* (see page 138). Smaller ones may be prepared à la Grecque (see page 53). If dropped in boiling water for 3 to 4 minutes, the skins will peel off easily. Canned white onions are acceptable, if not overcooked.

*Pearl onions or pickling onions.* Very tiny white onions, usually pickled but also good for garnishing dishes.

*Red or Italian onions.* Exceptionally sweet and decorative onions, delicious raw in sandwiches and salads (see avocado, onion, and grapefruit salad, page 301).

*Green onions.* Also called *scallions* and, in some parts of the country, *shallots*, which they are not. Fresh young onions with a white bulb and leafy green top, harvested while immature. Those with thin white bulbs are to be preferred to the rounder, thicker ones. Trim off the root end, all but an inch or two of the green tops, and the outer layer of skin before using. Cook quickly in boiling salted water to cover, like asparagus, and serve with hollandaise, or cook à la Grecque (see page 53). Chop and sauté for use in various dishes. May be used in place of shallots. Eat raw in vegetable hors d'oeuvres and salads.

*Leeks.* Somewhat similar in appearance to green onions, but much larger, with darker, coarser green tops. Known in France as "poor man's asparagus," but expensive here and often hard to find. Trim off root end and all but about an inch of the green top, wash thoroughly, running water between the leaves (slit the top, if necessary) to remove the gritty sand lurking between them.

Widely used as a flavoring, an aromatic vegetable in soups, stews, and braised dishes, traditional in pot-au-feu (see page 23). Good poached à la Grecque (see page 53), braised, or boiled and served with vinaigrette sauce.

*Shallots.* Sometimes called the aristocrat of the onion family, these small bulbs of cloves covered with papery brown skin have a subtle flavor, more pungent than onion, more delicate than garlic. A little goes quite a long way. Chopped and sautéed, they are an important flavoring for many dishes, from sauces such as Béarnaise, Bordelaise, and diable (see Thickeners and Liaisons chapter) to sautéed chicken (see page 166). Much used in French cooking. Hard to find in stores, but available by mail order. Packaged freeze-dried shallots are more easily found, although not as desirable.

*Garlic.* The most pungent member of the family. Widely used in soups, sauces, salads, braised dishes, sautés, and as a seasoning for roasts, such as leg of lamb (see page 61) or pork loin (see page 68). Always use cloves of garlic, never garlic powder or garlic salt, which have an ersatz flavor. Look for full, firm, heavy heads and buy garlic loose, not packaged in the cardboard boxes sold in supermarkets—the packaged kind is frequently old and stale. Buy only as much as needed and use quickly. To peel, either drop in boiling water for 5 seconds to loosen the skin, or bruise the clove slightly with the flat of a large knife blade, which splits the skin. Chopping garlic with a touch of salt prevents it from sticking to the knife blade. In sautéing, do not let garlic brown or burn or it will turn bitter. Garlic cloves cooked whole in their husks, either in liquid or in a sauté, add flavor but lose their strong pungency and become delicate, mild, and buttery-soft. Squeeze the garlic out of the husk after cooking.

*Chives.* Herbs that are also members of the onion family, with a delicate onion flavor. Sold cut or in pots. The more you cut chives, the better they grow. The blue chive flowers have an intense onion flavor and can be tossed in salads. Chop chives and use in fines herbes mixtures for omelets (see page 184), in scrambled eggs, cold soups, salads, herbed mayonnaise, and dressings, on sliced tomatoes, or anywhere their bright color and zippy flavor are appropriate.

ORANGES. Smooth-skinned Florida oranges, the Spanish or Valencia type, are most favored for juice. The temple orange, which has a more textured skin, is preferable for eating or slicing. California oranges, mostly navel oranges, have a more brilliant color than the Valencias and usually a thicker, pithier skin. They are better for slicing, sectioning, and general cooking, extremely good for candying and glazing, or for eating out of hand. Try to find oranges that are not waxed. Pick those that are not overripe or scarred or have soft spots. They should be firm and heavy in the hand, which means that they are full of juice (this applies to all citrus fruits). Team oranges with onions for a salad. Use the juice and/or grated rind as a flavoring for soufflés (see page 225), sauces, glazes, frozen desserts, Bavarian cream (see page 322), the fruit for open-face tarts. Section or slice oranges for fruit salads, compotes.

PAPAYAS. A tropical fruit with brilliant orange flesh, round black seeds, and an extremely delicate, unusual flavor and texture. Known as pawpaw in the West Indies, where it is also cooked, when green and unripe, as a vegetable. Fully ripened, soft-skinned papayas are the best buy. Serve chilled, halved, and seeded, with a wedge of lime, or as a first course with prosciutto, like melon. Delicious in fruit salads or, puréed in a blender or food processor, for ice cream and sherbet.

PAPRIKA. Paprika can easily fool you—it looks like red pepper, but it's not. Nor was it created to garnish food and look pretty, as some people think. Paprika is a spice in its own right. The finest comes from Hungary, where it is much used in dishes such as paprikash and goulash (see Viennese goulash, a slightly different version, on page 141), in sauces, and in salad dressings. There is also a paprika from Spain, coarser in texture and flavor, that I favor a great deal for Spanish recipes. The spice is ground from a variety of capsicum peppers, some of which are sweet, others hot—in some cases, almost as hot as cayenne pepper, from another capsicum variety. A very perishable, heat-sensitive spice, paprika should be kept in a tin, never a glass bottle or shaker, preferably in the refrigerator. If you are purchasing paprika in bulk from a specialty food shop, you may be asked if you want the sweet or the hot variety—sweet paprika is what is called for in most recipes, unless otherwise specified.

PARSNIPS. A much maligned creamy-colored root vegetable, long and tapering in shape. Sweetish in flavor and extremely good boiled, puréed, and mixed with plenty of butter and a little Madeira (see page 52) Can be used, sparingly, in soups, stews, and boiled dinners, or in the mirepoix for braised meats (see page 132). Look for firm, good-sized roots. In season all winter long.

PASTA. Pasta is one of the 3 or 4 most popular foods in existence, and as versatile as any single food can be. The Chinese had noodles; the Italians perfected pasta. In one form or another it has gone the rounds of most of the major Eastern and Western countries. Nothing takes more readily to seasonings and flavorings, and it can be anything from a first course or main dish, with a sauce, to a salad, a soup, or a dessert. Nowadays, with the aid of an electric or hand-operated pasta machine, it's easy to make your own pasta fresh, dry it briefly, and cook it right away—fresh pasta takes only a few minutes to cook, much less than the commercial, dried type. You can also, in some cities, buy pasta from shops that make it fresh. There are many, many brands of dried pasta, and you should shop around until you find one to your liking—the imported Italian pasta is usually the best, and of the American brands I prefer Buitoni.

In dried pastas, we have the various round, straight ones, starting with the very small spaghettini, usually listed on the package as spaghettini #2, which can be used generally with any of the spaghetti sauces, from the simplest of all, which is just melted butter and grated cheese (see page 38). Then you have a larger spaghetti and macaroni of various sizes and shapes, from the small elbow macaroni to larger, straight macaroni to the huge ziti. Pasta comes in dozens of other shapes; some are like little seashells (conchiglie) or butterflies (farfalle). The cooking time for dried pastas varies according to shape and size. Naturally, the thin spaghettini cooks faster than the large macaroni and the small seashells faster than the large ones. This is something you gauge from the package directions and your own experience and preference—whether you like your pasta cooked to the traditional Italian *al dente* stage, still firm to the bite, or cooked to a mushy paste. Pasta should always be cooked in a large pot in ample amounts of salted water kept at a rolling boil throughout the cooking period (see page 37). After 6 minutes, taste often until it reaches the degree of doneness you prefer. Drain at once. If you wish, you may rinse the pasta with hot or cold water and then with hot water again. If you are going to serve the pasta on individual plates, toss it with a spoonful or two of oil first so it doesn't stick together, then add the sauce. However, I have come to like the modern Italian way of saucing pasta (see page 38), in which the cooked pasta is marinated in the hot sauce for 2 or 3 minutes and tossed well with 2 forks so that it becomes imbued with the flavors. Pasta is usually served with grated Parmesan, Romano, or asiago cheese, save for seafood pastas and one or two others that are best without it—though that, too, is a matter of personal taste.

PEACHES. The sweet, tender, and perishable peaches that used to abound in our markets have been almost ruined by modern growing and shipping practices. Now peaches may look beautiful, but they are hard-hearted under the skin. Naturally, try to find soft-fleshed ones. Take advantage of the 2 to 3 weeks when local tree-ripened peaches may be found. Early white peaches, if you can find them, are pure nectar. Simply chill and slice; eat with sugar and cream. The later, golden-fleshed peaches are good this way, too, or with a raspberry purée (see page 311). They are superb in ice cream (see page 333), and for preserves or pies. Peaches may be broiled (see page 120), baked, or poached (see page 54) with the addition of a little lemon, vanilla, or bourbon for flavoring, and make a great dessert. Poaching is a good way to treat hard peaches. For certain cooked dishes, such as roast duck with peaches (see page 84), a firm canned variety may replace the fresh.

PEARS. Like peaches, pears for the market are picked too green and are artificially ripened. They never approach the lusciousness of tree-ripened fruit. If you find pears that are soft and ripe to the touch, rush them home and eat them at once. The Bartlett or Williams pear, bell-shaped and yellow, is the earliest, on the market from July to November. At its best, it has an indescribable perfume and wonderful flavor and texture and is delicious eaten raw or poached. The small sweet brown Seckel, good for eating, pickling, and cooking, arrives in September. The later, winter pears are the chunky green or greenish-yellow Anjou; the Bosc, brown or russet color with a tapering neck; the large Comice, yellow or greeny-yellow, splashed with red; and the brown Winter Nelis, all artificially ripened. However, all these pears poach extremely well (see page 55), and most of them bake well. Baked pears are usually not peeled, just halved, cored, and baked with brown sugar and a clove or two for about an hour in a 325° oven. The result, when cloaked in heavy cream, is pretty spectacular. Pears make interesting tarts and fritters (see page 200), and are good sautéed (see page 192). They are very friendly to cheese—Roquefort, Brie, Camembert—and practically all of the fine cheeses are good companions for pears.

### PEAS
*Green peas.* When buying fresh green peas in the market, break open a pod. The pods should be juicy, crisp, and bright green, and the peas inside small, green, and tender. Avoid peas that are large, pale, and starchy, with old, dry-looking pods. To cook, shell and boil briefly in salted water to cover, just until tender (time depends on size and age), then toss with butter. Or braise with lettuce leaves (see page 153). This is one vegetable that freezes well. Often frozen peas are better than fresh. Choose the tiny frozen peas and never follow the package directions or you will have stewed peas. Merely heat them through with butter to keep that nice crisp freshness.

*Snow peas.* Once a delicacy confined to Chinese restaurants, these edible-pod peas are becoming more generally available. Buy very young, when the pods are flat and the peas undeveloped. Test by breaking one. It should snap easily and have no strings down the sides. To cook, trim the ends and boil in salted water to cover for just a minute, until merely blanched, so they stay crisp. Drain and toss with butter. Or sauté sliced mushroom caps in butter, cut snow peas into julienne strips, and toss with the mushrooms for less than a minute, until they turn bright green. Add more butter, season with salt and pepper, and serve. They may also be cut into julienne, tossed quickly in butter, and added to lamb or beef stew at the last minute, as a garnish. Frozen snow peas are passable, but they lack the delicious crispness of the fresh.

### PEPPER
Pepper is a funny spice, really three spices in one, each with a different flavor. Peppercorns are the berries of the tropical *Piper nigrum* vine and no relation to the vegetable, capsicum pepper.

*Black peppercorns.* The dried berries—the ones we use most generally. They are sold whole, to be ground in a pepper mill, or cracked or ground by spice companies. As with other spices, best ground fresh.

*White peppercorns.* The black peppercorns minus the wrinkled black outer layer—and minus much of the flavor. Some people feel it is more refined to use white pepper in a white sauce or dish so that you don't have black specks. To me white pepper is unpleasant, acrid, and lacking in flavor. Forget niceties—who cares if there are a few flecks of black in a white sauce? It's the taste that counts.

*Green peppercorns.* The fresh immature berries, imported preserved in brine or frozen, are soft in texture, with an extremely pungent and exciting flavor, totally different from dried peppercorns. They have been on the market less than 15 years and are our newest flavor. Very perishable, they should be used quickly, made into green-pepper butter and frozen, or put into a small jar, covered with water, and frozen. Use crushed green peppercorns in sauces and butter to serve with meat, poultry, and fish, as a replacement for crushed black peppercorns in such dishes as broiled peppered duckling (see page 105) or steak au poivre (see page 159). *Cayenne pepper* is not ground from peppercorns but from the capsicum pepper (see below).

## PEPPERS

*Sweet or bell peppers.* Members of the capsicum family, come in green, red, and yellow. The red and yellow peppers are ripe versions of the green. Look for firm, shapely peppers without soft or discolored spots or wrinkled skins. Remove stem end, seeds, and white ribs, and slice into strips or rings, or chop, for salads, sautés, cooked dishes. Personally, I feel that if peppers are to be served cooked, they should be broiled until the thin, indigestible skin chars and can be scraped off (see page 119). Broiled peppers make a magnificent vegetable dish if cut into wide strips and sautéed lightly in olive oil with garlic and a drop or two of vinegar. Peppers lend themselves admirably to stuffing. Remove stem end and seeds and parboil for 10 minutes to soften the skin, then stuff and bake.

*Pimientos.* Another type of sweet red capsicum pepper, available skinned, cored, processed, and packed in jars or cans. Very mild in flavor. Use for color in salads and as a garnish.

*Hot chili peppers.* There are many different varieties with varying degrees of heat. These are also members of the capsicum family. When preparing chilies for cooking, remove all the tiny seeds that hold the heat. Wash hands well after handling; the juice from chilies is highly irritating to the skin and eyes. *Tabasco* is a hot, pungent liquid pepper sauce made from small, fiery red Tabasco chilies packed into barrels, sealed with salt, aged 3 years, then mixed with vinegar and bottled. A most valuable product for cooking. Use as a substitute for cayenne pepper, in sauces such as hollandaise (see page 279), and in egg dishes. I always add a dash of Tabasco to scrambled eggs (see page 181).

PHEASANT. One of our finest game birds. Raised extensively on game farms and always available. There was a time when pheasant and other game were not considered to be edible until they had hung in the barn or a tree long enough to become quite green and odoriferous. They were then referred to as "high," which they certainly were. We have, thank heavens, graduated from this barbaric custom. Pheasant must be cooked in such a way that the breast meat is kept moist, otherwise it becomes dry and unpalatable. For roast pheasant (see page 86), bacon or barding fat is usually draped over the breast as protection and lubrication. Young tender pheasant may be sautéed like chicken (see page 164). Older birds are best braised (see page 149).

PINEAPPLES. One of the Western Hemisphere's great food gifts to the world and long a symbol of hospitality. There are several varieties, from the very small sugar pineapples, about 4 to 6 inches long, to the conical Brazilian pineapples (said to be the original fruit) that run 12 to 14 inches. Pineapples are in the market all year, brought in from Hawaii, Mexico, Honduras, the Dominican Republic, and Costa Rica. To test for ripeness, lift the fruit to see if it is heavy with juice, press the skin at the bottom to see if it is soft, and smell it—there should be a full, fruity fragrance. Some say that if a center frond pulls out easily the fruit is ripe. Avoid fruit that looks old or dry or has brown leaves. Large pineapples are a better buy, as there is more edible flesh. To peel a pineapple, slice off the bottom and leafy top and cut away the rind with a sharp knife, removing the little eyes with the knife point. Cut into fingers or crosswise slices and remove the core. There is a special cutter, resembling a wheel, that simultaneously cores pineapple and cuts it into fingers. Unless you are fortunate enough to get a fully ripened, sweet fruit, it will usually need sugaring to taste. Pineapple may be broiled (see page 120) and sautéed (see page 192), but to my mind it is best served raw and very cold, with some added flavor, such as a sprinkling of rum, kirsch, or framboise (white alcohol made from raspberries). For buffet presentation, cut off the top, remove the flesh with a small ball cutter, sugar it, and return to the shell, either alone or with other fruits, and chill before serving. Canned pineapple is one of the more successful canned fruits.

PLUMS. In the summer, plums are in season through July, August, and September in at least 10 to 12 different colors, shapes, and flavors. The most common are the tender-skinned, yellow-fleshed red plums that must be eaten very ripe, or they are sour to the tongue. They are followed by the Japanese plum or greengage, with greeny-yellow skin and yellow flesh, excellent for tarts, pies, stewed plums, and preserves. Then come the large yellow plums, good for eating raw, for baking, or for poaching, like pears and peaches, in a red-wine syrup or a plain syrup flavored with liqueur. Greengage and yellow plums have a delicious sweetness. The last plum of the season is the small blue-black Italian prune plum. Rich in flavor and high in natural sugar, with a pit that separates easily from the firm flesh, this is the kind dried for prunes. It is also a perfect cooking plum for tarts and kuchen, preserves, puddings, baking, and poaching. Extremely good if flavored with a little cinnamon or a little plum brandy or cognac. All plums should be soft to the touch; prune plums will be a little firmer than others. If hard when bought, they can be ripened in a plastic bag in a dark place.

## POTATOES

It was once possible to have a pretty good working knowledge of the different varieties of potato and to choose the best for each cooking purpose. Now, with the standardization of agricultural produce, potatoes have become anonymous. We get simply—potatoes. All we can determine about them is that they come from Idaho, or Maine, or Oregon, or California. There are 2 basic types, mealy and waxy. Waxy potatoes hold together better when boiled and sliced and are preferable for potato salad, sautéed potatoes (see page 188), and hash browns. Mealy potatoes are best for baking (see page 212) and roasting (see page 92), and are also good for boiling. Either type may be French fried (see page 205).

The *brown-skinned Idaho* is our most dependable potato. Grown in lava soil, it is extremely mealy and bakes perfectly. May also be boiled, French fried, or used for potatoes Anna (see page 213). The *russet* potato, very like the Idaho, and the round white Oregon potato can be used in the same ways. *Maine* potatoes, available in the early part of the year, are semiwaxy and best boiled. The widely available *California Long White* I find variable in quality. Carefully boiled in its skin, it remains firm and waxy, excellent for potato salad and sautéed potatoes. It may also be baked or French fried. The small round so-called *"new" potato* (not really new, but dug before it reaches maturity) is a waxy type available almost all year, ideal for boiling or steaming whole. Do not peel. Scrub well, then cut a little belly band of skin from around the center to keep it from bursting. Slightly undercook; it should be firm and crisp. Use for hot potato salad, as one of the accompanying vegetables for corned beef and cabbage (see page 16) and pot-au-feu (see page 23). Or cut into chunks, unpeeled, and deep-fry (see page 205). When buying potatoes, reject those that are soft, have wrinkled, scarred, or green-tinged skins (caused by exposure to the light), and sprouting eyes. Store in a cool, dry, well-ventilated cellar or cabinet, away from the light.

To bake potatoes (see page 212), just scrub well and leave in their jackets. I like the skins crisp, so I don't rub them with fat, and I never, ever bake them in foil, which makes the skins soggy. To boil, either peel or leave the skins on (they hold together better for slicing), put into a deep saucepan with salted water to cover, put on the lid, and boil until tender when pierced with a knife, about 20 to 25 minutes, according to size and whether they are left whole or cut into pieces. After boiling, drain, return to the pan, and let dry out over low heat, covered, shaking the pan so they don't stick. To steam, put into an adjustable vegetable steamer in a deep pan with just enough water to come to the bottom of the steamer. Bring to a boil, cover, and steam until tender—slightly longer than for boiling.

QUAIL. These delicate little game birds are expensive luxuries, except in parts of the country where quail-shooting is a major sport. Quail are raised on game farms, and may be bought fresh or frozen. Frozen quail are quite plentiful. Quail lend themselves to roasting, broiling like squab, and sautéing. My favorite method is to remove the breasts and sauté them quickly (see page 172), using the less meaty legs and carcass for broth and soups. Whole roasted or broiled quail should be eaten with the fingers and, to my mind, they are not for company but for the family.

RABBIT. I'm always astounded by the number of people who say they don't like or have never eaten rabbit. They are to be pitied. I find this delicate, flavorful meat to be almost as useful as chicken. Commercially raised rabbits are available throughout the country, fresh and frozen. Fresh rabbits are usually sold skinned and cut up, if you so require. Or you may buy them whole and disjoint them yourself (see page 170). Frozen rabbits have been cut up and packaged. Wild rabbits, spoils of the hunter, must, of course, be skinned and cleaned. Young tender rabbits may be sautéed like chicken (see page 170). Older rabbits and wild rabbits are better braised or stewed.

RASPBERRIES. Perhaps the most luscious and, in some ways, the most glamorous of all the fruits. These brilliant red, thimble-shaped berries are in the market for 8 to 10 months—at staggering prices. No other berry comes close to them in flavor, and raspberry jam is probably the most popular of all preserves. Apart from jam-making, it would be a crime to cook raspberries. Eat them raw, with or without sugar, with cream or *crème fraîche*, flavored with a little liqueur, if you like. Use them whole in little raspberry tarts. Purée them for raspberry fool (see page 312) or to spoon as a sauce over other fruits, such as strawberries, peaches, and pineapples.

RHUBARB. Long before supermarkets existed, rhubarb was the first fruit of the spring season, and a tonic, too, in the form of the rhubarb and soda given to children as a blood purifier. Nowadays the light-pink hothouse rhubarb appears on the market in January and lasts through most of the year. It is milder in flavor than the later, dark-red field-grown or garden rhubarb, with its coarse leaves and tart taste. Botanically a vegetable, but always used as a fruit, rhubarb is fragile and needs very little cooking, but a good deal of sweetening. Only the red stalks are used; the leaves contain oxalic acid and should not be eaten. Buy crisp, firm, tender stalks, wash, trim off leaves and base, and cut them into 3-inch lengths. Blanch in boiling water for 1 minute, then drop into a simple syrup and poach until just tender. Or place in a casserole or baking dish with sugar to taste and perhaps a little grated orange rind, cover, and bake in a 350° oven for 12 to 15 minutes. The fault with most rhubarb is that, overcooked to a stringy pulp, it is not the firm, interesting fruit it can and should be. Rhubarb makes excellent pies (in the old days, it was known as pie plant). Poached, puréed, and mixed with heavy cream, it becomes a delicious rhubarb fool.

RICE

Probably the most universally used of all the starches, yielding only to the potato in this country. Rice comes in two versions, long grain and short grain, and various types, and may be bought both loose and packaged. I like to use *long-grain rice* for boiling (see page 41), pilafs, and most recipes where rice is needed, such as stuffings, salads (see page 43), casseroles (see page 266), the Spanish paella and arroz con pollo, and for egg-lemon soup (see page 286). *Short-grain rice* is better for puddings. *Converted or parboiled rice* works well steamed (see page 41), according to the directions on the package. *Precooked or instant rice* needs no cooking; it is just mixed with boiling water and left to stand, covered, for 5 minutes, until it swells. *Brown rice*, unpolished rice with merely the husk removed, is treated like long-grain rice but will take longer to cook—40 to 50 minutes. *Arborio or Italian short-grain rice* with a plump starchy grain is the classic rice for risotto (see page 42), although I find long-grain rice works almost as well, if carefully cooked. One of the very few rices that still needs washing and soaking is the Indian *Basmati rice*, used in Indian cooking and also for Middle Eastern dishes such as *chello*. Rice expands considerably in cooking—1 cup of raw rice makes 3 cups cooked (converted rice somewhat less).

ROCK CORNISH HENS. Small birds, weighing about 1 pound, a cross between a chicken and a game hen. Until recently, available mostly frozen, either stuffed or unstuffed, and while not too flavorful, popular because they were inexpensive, quick cooking, and the right size for an individual serving. Now available fresh, in larger sizes, and fattened properly, they are one of the more rewarding birds on the market, with delicate meat. Cook like squab chicken: roast, stuffed or unstuffed, at 400° for 35 to 40 minutes, or split and broil. Good hot or cold. If you don't find fresh Rock Cornish hens in your market, request them.

SALT

Salt, which comes from salt flats formed by evaporated sea water and from land deposits of rock or crystalline salt, has always been considered to be the most basic and necessary of all seasonings. Salt is one of the oldest known methods of preserving or curing meats and fish, especially beef, ham, and cod. Salt is used to "cook" the Scandinavian cured salmon called *gravlax* (see page 309). There are several kinds of salt on the market, of different strengths and types.

*Ordinary table salt.* Often mixed with magnesium or sodium carbonate to make it flow more easily, table salt is fine and quite intense in flavor. Use it with care.

*Kosher salt.* Coarser in texture and less salty in flavor, I consider this preferable for both cooking and the table. It is pure salt, with no additives.

*Malden salt.* This salt from England and other sea salts have large crystals and must be ground in a salt mill. They are expensive and are mostly used as table salt.

*Ice-cream salt or rock salt.* Used in ice-cream freezers or as a bed on which clams or oysters on the half shell are broiled or roasted (see page 121), has the coarsest crystals.

## SAUSAGES

A favorite subject of mine. I adore them, especially with sauerkraut (see page 29). There are hundreds of varieties of sausage, but the following are some you find most often in supermarkets, pork butchers', and sausage shops. If you can shop around in ethnic markets, you'll find many more.

*Blood sausages.* There are two kinds. One, known in French as *boudin noir* or in German as *blutwurst*, is made with pig's blood, meal, and coarse pieces of pork. Traditionally broiled and served with potatoes and applesauce. The other, known as blood-and-tongue sausage, is a dried, ready-to-eat blood sausage inlaid with pieces of tongue and fat, usually sliced and served cold.

*Bockwurst.* A German veal sausage, flavored with chives. Generally available in the spring. Poach (see page 29) or broil (see page 109). Serve with mashed potatoes or sauerkraut, or for breakfast with scrambled eggs.

*Bologna.* The most common of the ready-to-eat sausages, served cold and thinly sliced. The American version of this Italian sausage is made with pork and beef, and is very bland.

*Bratwurst.* A veal and pork or pork sausage, rather bland, with an herby flavor, popular in German and Swiss cuisine. Readily available and delicious broiled and served with sauerkraut or sautéed onions. Weisswurst is very similar.

*Chorizo.* A sausage of coarsely cut pork colored with paprika, slightly piquant, and much used in Spanish dishes, such as paella, and in Mexican cooking. Can be bought fresh or dried. May be poached, sautéed, or broiled. Available in some supermarkets, in Spanish-American markets, and imported, canned in lard, from Spain.

*Cotechino.* A large Italian sausage that should be poached before using.

*Frankfurters.* Our beloved hot dogs. The best are made from beef, the lesser quality from a variety of meats and innards. Their flavor ranges from very bland to very spicy. Look for all-beef kosher frankfurters and those known as "specials," which cost more but are better flavored and better eating. Heat through in water, or broil. *Knockwurst* are similar but thicker and heavier—4 to the pound as against 7 or 8 to the pound for frankfurters. Again, the all-beef are best.

*Italian link sausages.* Coarsely ground fresh pork sausages, either sweet or hot—the latter are spicily seasoned with very hot pepper. Much used in Italian cooking, with pasta, cooked with green peppers, or served with polenta.

Good with eggs, or in a casserole with lentils (see page 264). Parboil sausages first to draw out excess fat. Place in a skillet with cold water to cover, bring to a boil for 1 minute, drain, then sauté or broil (seepage 109).

*Kielbasa.* A large, highly seasoned Polish sausage, widely available. Sold as long sausages or as rings. Some are fresh and should be poached or broiled; other types are dried and can be eaten cold, or heated.

*Mortadella.* An enormous dried sausage, similar to bologna but larded with fat pork. Should be sliced very thin. Sometimes served wrapped around a breadstick, as an hors d'oeuvre.

*Pork sausages.* The familiar link sausages or sausage meat we buy or make. May be finely or coarsely chopped with varied seasonings, mostly sage, but also thyme, garlic, coriander, chives, and anise. Treat link sausages like Italian link sausages. Form sausage meat into flat cakes and sauté gently until cooked through and crisp on the outside.

*Salami.* There are a dozen different varieties of salami, from the very dry Italian Genoa salami containing peppercorns and garlic to salamis seasoned with paprika and other spices. Taste and decide which of the many are for you. May be bought sliced, but I prefer to buy a piece and slice my own.

SHELLFISH

*Clams.* Found in great variety along our shores. The two East Coast species are the soft-shelled or long-necked clams, usually steamed, and the hard shelled, known in New England as quahogs, that come in three sizes: the largest used for chowder, the smaller littlenecks and cherrystones eaten raw on the half shell, broiled (see pages 121 and 122), baked, or added to seafood stews and similar dishes. On the West Coast one finds both hardshelled clams and the soft-shelled razor clams of Oregon and Washington. The long, meaty razor clams are sautéed, deep-fried, scalloped, made into chowder and fritters. All clams need to be scrubbed well and washed in cold water to remove the sand inside the shells. Raw clams—one of my dislikes—are best served very cold, on the half shell like oysters, with nothing but lemon juice and freshly ground pepper. Red cocktail sauce ruins the flavor. Steam clams in a half inch of water or wine from 5 to 10 minutes, until the shells open. Discard any with closed shells. The resulting broth may be sipped with the clams or used as the liquid for a seafood sauce. If you live near the shore, gather your own clams if possible—a sport I loved to indulge in as a child. Clams can be minced and used for fritters, quiches, or clam sauce for pasta (see page 39). Canned minced clams are extremely good and may be substituted for fresh.

*Crabs.* We have wonderful crabs in this country. From the West Coast comes the enormous *Alaska king crab*, shipped frozen. Carefully thawed, the coarse but flavorful meat is good for cooked dishes such as crab soufflé and deviled crab, but is not as successful in salads. The huge, meaty legs may be split and broiled. *Dungeness crab*, caught from California to Alaska, is to me the most distinctive of all. The legs are meaty, the lump crabmeat deliciously sweet. On its native coast, it is usually sold precooked and served cracked with mayonnaise, in salads, deviled crab, and other dishes. It is sheer, unadulterated crab heaven. Available flash-frozen in other parts of the country.

Next to Dungeness, my favorite is *Florida backfin lump crabmeat* (backfin meat is the choicest), sold cleaned, shelled, and chilled, in pound cans. It is extremely meaty and well-flavored and perfect for salads, sautéed (see page 180), or in cooked dishes. The *stone crab* of Florida, unique because only the large claw is sold (the crab is returned to the water to grow another claw), has a coarser texture, but is considered a great delicacy, hot with melted butter or cold with mayonnaise. *Virginia, Carolina, and Maryland backfin lump crabmeat* is equal to Florida, though in short supply and therefore expensive. It may be used in the same ways or made into such regional specialties as crab cakes and crab Imperial. Also sold refrigerated, in cans. Recently some eastern markets have been receiving refrigerated *Maine crabmeat* of excellent quality. The legs are small, the meat delicate and sweet, perfect for crab salad or cocktail. When buying crabmeat, estimate 1 pound for 3 to 4 servings. Occasionally you will find *live blue crabs* in eastern markets. They may be boiled (allow 8 minutes a pound), cleaned, and eaten from the shell. The delicious little *soft-shelled crabs*, found in the markets at certain times of the year, are merely blue crabs that have molted and are growing a new shell. The small tiny ones are best; larger ones develop a coarse shell. Two or three of these babies make a serving. Soft-shelled crabs are best sautéed (see page 180), but can also be broiled or deep-fried. They are eaten in their entirety, shell and all, and rate as one of the great American delicacies. If you buy them live and uncleaned, either have the fish market kill and clean them for you or follow the directions on page 180.

*Crayfish.* After having almost disappeared from our waters, crayfish have now become an industry. California, Minnesota, Wisconsin, and Louisiana are producing excellent crayfish in quantity and shipping them around the country. Cook crayfish in a highly seasoned, spicy court bouillon or *à la nage* (see page 33)—nothing is more fun than a feast of beer and freshly boiled crayfish, eaten from the shell with your fingers. Or shell them and use for salads or in various seafood dishes, like other shellfish.

*Lobsters.* The Atlantic lobster, mostly found off Long Island, Massachusetts, Maine, and on up into Canada, is one of our great delicacies. Store-bought lobsters, kept on beds of seaweed or in salt-water tanks, lack the quality of those taken fresh from the ocean, on their native shore, but that is what most of us must settle for. You can also have live lobsters shipped by air from Maine lobster farms—at a price. Lobsters are sold both live and cooked, and vary in size from babies of 1 pound or less, known as chicken lobsters, up to giants of 25 to 30 pounds. Smaller lobsters are better eating. The average 1- to 2-pounder, boiled or broiled, is considered a serving for 1. For cooking, buy only lively lobsters. Have the fish merchant lift one so you can see how active it is. There are dozens of ways to prepare lobster but, to me, the simplest and by far the best is boiling (see page 33). Serve hot with melted butter or cold with mayonnaise. Fresh or frozen lobster meat, though horrendously expensive, goes quite a long way in salads, seafood combinations, lobster *au gratin* (see page 123), and other cooked dishes. Canned lobster is not bad, but the taste is not the same as the fresh.

In the South and on the West Coast one gets *small rock lobsters*, sometimes live but more often cooked. These are really members of the crayfish family, without the big claws of the true lobster. They have good flavor and may be used for salads and cooked dishes. Then we have *frozen rock lobster tails* from various parts of the world, such as Spain, South Africa, and India. They vary in size from ¼ or ½ pound up to 3 or 4 pounds. Some of the larger ones can be quite tough, so check the weight before buying. Thaw and boil or broil, following directions on the package, and use like lobster in salads and main dishes.

*Mussels.* A delicious bivalve with a tapering bluish-black shell. Although mussels abound in our waters, they are much neglected, possibly because they are at times subject to a disease called "red tide" and, therefore, particularly on the West Coast, are unavailable at times. Consult your local fisheries before gathering them; those you buy in the markets are perfectly safe. Mussels must be carefully cleaned (see directions on page 36). They are usually sold by the quart (a quart will serve 2) and range in size from about 1½ inches to almost 6 inches long. Small ones are the choicest. May be eaten raw, like clams, but are more usually steamed in water or white wine until the shells open and served in their lovely broth, or used in seafood stews and paella. Eat from the shell or remove and use in soup (see page 36), salads, and as a cold hors d'oeuvre with rémoulade sauce. They're a tremendously addictive delicacy.

*Oysters.* There are three species of American oysters: the eastern, the large Pacific or Japanese oyster, and the tiny coppery Olympia. The Olympia, native to the Northwest and seldom seen in the East, is to me the most distinguished. We get oysters from Canada, from Cape Cod, Long Island, Chesapeake Bay, the Gulf of Mexico, and the waters off Oregon and Washington. According to the locale, they differ in size, flavor, and texture and carry a local name, such as the Blue Point of Long Island or the Chincoteague of Chesapeake Bay. Sold in the shell or on the half shell by the dozen, freshly shucked (shelled) by the pint or quart, and in jars especially treated so they will keep under refrigeration. Fresh raw oysters are very perishable and should be eaten right away. To serve raw, open the shells with an oyster knife (or have the fish dealer do it for you), loosen the oyster from its lower shell, and serve it that way—resting on the half shell. Count on at least half a dozen raw oysters per person, or about ½ pint shucked oysters, if they are to be cooked. Oysters may be broiled (see page 121), baked or scalloped (see page 262), fried, added to beefsteak and kidney pie (see page 242), or simmered in soups and stews just until the edges curl—they must never be overcooked.

*Scallops.* Scallops are so pretty in their shells with the little white round muscle and the red comma of roe, the way they are sold in Europe, that it's a pity we can't buy them that way. Here only the shelled white muscle is marketed. The large, rather coarse sea scallops, sometimes as much as an inch thick and 2 inches in diameter, are shucked and frozen at sea. The tiny sweet and delicate bay scallops caught in coastal waters are by far the greater delicacy. Though sometimes frozen, they can usually be bought fresh. Bay scallops are delicious marinated in lime juice for seviche (see page 308) or even eaten raw. All scallops, whether broiled (see page 116), sautéed, poached, or deep-fried, should be cooked very quickly, otherwise they toughen and become tasteless. One pound of scallops will serve 2 or 3.

*Shrimp.* Shrimp come in all sizes, from the tiny Pacific, Alaskan, and Maine shrimp, perfect for salads, shrimp cocktail, or potted shrimp, to the medium-sized pink-shelled Florida shrimp and the very large gray-green Gulf shrimp. Occasionally you see enormous shrimp from the Indian Ocean, weighing as much as a quarter of a pound apiece. I find the medium size best for most general cooking, such as sautéing and frying (see page 197), for shrimp casseroles and other dishes, and for eating cold as appetizers or in salads. The very large ones are fine for broiling (see page 116) or for butterflied shrimp. One pound of shrimp serves 2 as a main course. You can buy raw shrimp in the shell, cooked shrimp in the shell or shelled, and quick-frozen shrimp both raw and cooked. Most ready-cooked shrimp are so overdone they are mushy and tasteless (and canned shrimp are not worth buying). If possible, buy fresh raw shrimp and cook them yourself. There's no need to remove the black vein from raw or cooked shrimp, except for aesthetic reasons. To do so, cut the shell along the back with sharp-pointed scissors, and remove the vein. The shrimp are then easier to shell, before or after cooking. I don't think it makes one whit of difference whether you cook shrimp in or out of the shell. The important thing is to cook them in well-salted water or court bouillon or *à la nage* (see page 33), to give them flavor. Bring the liquid to a boil, add the shrimp, and, timing from the moment the water returns to a boil, cook from 3 to 4 minutes, according to size, never more. Drain at once; they overcook if left in the water. Serve cold shrimp as an appetizer with lemon, mayonnaise, or rémoulade sauce, but never, please, with that overpowering red menace known as cocktail sauce if you value their sweet and delicate flavor.

SHORTENING. Hydrogenated vegetable fats used for baking and deep-frying, but not something I use very often. Whenever you find the term shortening in a recipe, it simply means any cooking fat. Butter can always be substituted.

SPICES

There are two important things to remember about spices. 1. Buy in small quantities only as needed and don't buy every spice you see. 2. Don't keep spices too long. The principal spices you need for general cooking, apart from peppercorns, which are discussed on pages 382 and 383, are *cloves, cinnamon, ginger* (see page 356), and *nutmeg*. Also useful to have on hand are *anise seed, allspice, caraway seed,* and *mace*. Commercially ground spices deteriorate very quickly and lose their brightness, bouquet, and pungency. I grind most of my spices as I need them, using a small electric coffee mill that I keep just for that purpose. It even grinds cinnamon bark. Spices may be ground in a mortar and pestle, but it is an arduous job and the results are never as even and fine. If you don't want to grind spices, buy them ground, in small amounts, from a spice store (many sell by mail) and discard them when they lose their freshness. Nutmeg should always be bought whole and freshly grated; the little tin nutmeg grater of classic design costs only a dollar or so. Spices are for use, not for show. Keep them away from heat and light, in the dark of a kitchen cabinet, not in pretty jars on open shelves.

SQUAB. Young domesticated pigeons, weighing about ¾ to 1 pound. Usually bought cleaned and ready for the oven. The meat is darkish and flavorful. Squab may be roasted like squab chickens (see page 77). I like to stuff them with fresh herbs, garlic, and a tiny onion and roast them in a baking dish with bacon over the breasts for 40 to 45 minutes at 400°. Or they may be split down the back, flattened with a blow of the fist, and broiled on both sides, like chicken. Squab, like quail, should be regarded as finger food. They are ideal birds for picnics if roasted or broiled the day before.

SQUASH

Despite the fact that many squash are in the market all year round, they are commonly referred to as summer squash and winter squash. Summer squash are the soft-shelled types which are eaten at an immature stage: zucchini, yellow straightneck and crookneck, the round, scalloped-edge pattypans or cymling squash. Winter squash, the large mature types with hard shells, are acorn, buttercup or turban, butternut, banana, and Hubbard.

*Summer squash.* At their best when very young and small. Unfortunately, too often they are allowed to grow until they are oversized and watery, with hard, inedible seeds. Look for small, firm, unblemished squash. Never boil until mushy or they'll taste as interesting as old dishrags. Steam them quickly in a very small amount of salted water or, preferably, in butter, until tender-crisp. Summer squash need no peeling or seeding. Leave them whole if really tiny, otherwise quarter, or slice, or cut into strips, toss in butter in a skillet or sauté pan, sprinkle with salt, cover, and steam over low heat until just tender. If the squash are rather large, you can eliminate some of their water by first blanching them briefly in boiling water.

*Zucchini* particularly are good sliced or shredded, salted to draw out the liquid, drained, and sautéed (see page 190). They may also be French fried (see page 196), cooked à la Grecque (see page 53), or eaten raw in salads or as a vegetable hors d'oeuvre. Large zucchini may be hollowed out, stuffed, and baked like eggplant (see page 263).

*Winter squash.* Once one of our standard cold-weather vegetables. We used to store the huge Hubbards in the barn, chop them into pieces with a hatchet, then seed them and bake them in the shell with butter or bacon fat. Or we might steam them, scrape out the pulp, and whip it up with butter and a little nutmeg or cinnamon. In some parts of the country you can sometimes find Hubbard and banana squash in the markets in the fall, chopped up and ready to cook. Mostly it is the small, round, green-skinned acorn and turban squash and the pale-skinned cylindrical butternut, available most of the year, that appear in the markets. When buying winter squash, gauge ¾ to 1 pound per serving. Choose squash with firm, hard shells and no mildewed or decayed parts. To bake hard-shelled squash, halve small types like acorn, turban, and butternut. Large ones should be cut into big pieces. Remove seeds and strings. Butter well or add bacon fat or bacon. Bake in a 350° oven until tender, 50 minutes to 1 hour for smaller squash. Hubbards will take from 1 to 1¼ hours. Serve small squash in the shell with salt, pepper, and other seasonings, such as nutmeg and ginger. Acorn squash can also be spread with butter and sprinkled with brown sugar before baking, or stuffed with well-seasoned sausage meat, or baked with bacon, maple syrup, nutmeg, and cinnamon. Winter squash may also be steamed in the shell, scooped out, and mashed. Butternut, often sold peeled, cut into long pieces, and packaged, can be cut up, steamed, and mashed. Puréed cooked squash makes a delicious soufflé and, like pumpkin, a damned good pie.

*Pumpkin*, incidentally, is not just for jack-o'-lanterns on Halloween, and for Thanksgiving pumpkin pie. Halved, seeded, and baked like Hubbard squash from 45 minutes to 2 hours, according to size, it makes an excellent vegetable. Puréed, it can be turned into one of the world's most luscious and creamy soups.

SQUID. Squid belong to the family of mollusks, but have no outer shell, only a thin bladelike bone inside the tubular body. With their greyish skin, beady eyes, and long tentacles, squid look like smaller, elongated octopuses, which may be the reason they are unfairly shunned. Most people don't like the look of them, don't know how to prepare them, and seem to be afraid to try them—a great pity, for the flesh is delicious if not overcooked. Squid need careful cleaning and should be skinned before cooking. Remove the head and pull out the pulpy intestines. Remove the thin, transparent, bladelike bone, leaving the tubular body in one piece. If the recipe calls for the tentacles, which are just below the eyes, cut them off and reserve them. Also reserve the sac of inky fluid if this is needed; otherwise discard it. Peel off the thin greyish skin covering the outside of the body. The cleaned body may be stuffed and braised, sliced and sautéed, cooked in rice with its own black ink, cut into rings, floured, and deep-fried, along with the tentacles, or used in a fish stew or paella. Squid are plentiful and inexpensive and should be used more often than they are.

STRAWBERRIES. Strawberries were once a great seasonal delight, heralded in summer with strawberry socials. Now we have them the year round, but unfortunately some are bred more for beauty than for taste. One has to be careful about buying, especially in the winter. Don't let your eyes fool your palate. Snitching and tasting one is kind of hard to do in today's markets, but you *can* feel and smell the berries. They should feel ripe but not mushy, and have a good fragrance. Be sure to check the box to make sure there are no rotten ones hidden on the bottom. Strawberries vary in shape and size from plump and rounded to long and pointed to enormous bulbous berries cut and sold with the long stem intact, perfect for dipping into sugar and eating by hand. Wild strawberries, tiny and deliciously sweet, may be picked in the summer all over the country, but are seldom seen in markets. Eaten with cream, with raspberry purée (see page 311), or in strawberries Romanov (see page 310), a pint of strawberries will serve 2. Or stretch them in a tart (see page 235), shortcake, *sorbet* (see page 334), or ice cream (see page 333).

SUET. Suet, or beef kidney fat, was once quite common in this country for cooking, especially for the traditional steamed puddings, most of which are English or early American in origin. Finely chopped suet makes an interesting and different pastry for meat pies and turnovers, and it is a necessity for beefsteak and kidney pudding (see page 27). If rendered until melted in a heavy skillet on top of the stove, it adds great flavor to a steak sautéed in the French manner. Rendered suet or rendered beef fat trimmed from steak are marvelous for French fried or home fried potatoes.

SWEET POTATOES. An elongated tuber with an orange or reddish skin, resembling a potato, but not as thick. There are two types, the moist-fleshed orange sweet potato, often called a yam (although the true yam belongs to another family entirely), and the dry and mealy sweet potato, which is smaller and has yellowish flesh. Bake (about 1 hour) or boil (30 to 40 minutes until tender) in the jacket, like potatoes. May be mashed or puréed and used in casseroles, as a pie filling, sliced and sautéed, or peeled, cut into strips, and deep-fried like French fries.

TOMATOES. One of the most versatile and popular of all our fruits, but seldom as good as they might be. We find in our markets the small, round, generally unripe "cannon-ball" tomatoes, sold in plastic containers, which for my money are not worth buying; the very large beefsteaks, best sliced as a salad; the firm red, vine-ripened tomatoes that come in summer and have a superior texture and flavor; and the tiny cherry tomatoes, once laudable, but now grown more for shelf life than for flavor. In country districts you may find seasonal yellow tomatoes, less acid than the red, and delicious for salads. Pale hard tomatoes can be ripened by keeping them in a dark place in a brown paper or plastic bag. Use only firm, ripe tomatoes for broiling (see page 118), sautéing, or tomato salads. For cooking, tomatoes should be peeled and seeded. Drop in boiling water for half a minute to loosen the skin. Cut out core at stem end, peel, cut in half crosswise, and squeeze in your fist to force out the seeds. Or quarter and scoop out the seeds with your finger. Unless tomatoes are fully ripe, canned peeled Italian plum tomatoes or solid-pack tomatoes are a better buy for cooking. Other canned forms of tomato are tomato purée, often used as part of the liquid in braised dishes, and concentrated tomato paste, used to intensify tomato flavor in dishes such as tomato sauce (see page 39).

TURKEY. What used to be the great Thanksgiving treat is now one of our more common and inexpensive foods, plentiful throughout the year. Turkeys nowadays are bred to grow firmer, larger breasts, much to the dismay of those who prefer the dark meat. Fortunately, one may buy turkey in parts, fresh or frozen, so dark-meat lovers can feast on legs and thighs. Turkey breasts of varying sizes are an excellent buy, as they are practically solid meat. Roast them or use for a variety of dishes such as turkey salad, turkey tonnato, and escalopes of turkey (sliced thin, like veal scaloppine). It has become increasingly difficult, although not impossible, to find fresh-killed, hand-plucked turkeys. While they are more expensive, I happen to feel that they are superior enough to the frozen birds to warrant the higher price. What we mostly see in the markets are frozen turkeys of various types, chiefly what are called "self-basting" turkeys. This means that the breast has been injected with fat, either butter, vegetable oil, or vegetable fat, to lubricate the breast meat during roasting and keep it moist. You can, of course, also buy frozen turkeys that are not self-basting. Don't go by the packer's directions for roasting or you will get overcooked white meat. Frozen, stuffed self-basting turkeys need to be roasted with great care and attention. While whole turkeys are most often roasted (see page 78), they may also be braised or poached. They vary in size from very small, around 5 pounds, up to 30 and 35 pounds. Buy according to how much you and your family like turkey, for there are bound to be leftovers and it's silly to buy more than you can use. An 8-pound turkey will serve 4, with ample leftovers; a 10-pounder will serve 6, with leftovers; and a 12- to 14-pounder will serve 8 to 10.

While the chances of getting a tough, scrawny bird are almost nil these days, I find that, despite the so-called improvements, these perfect-looking birds have less of the real turkey flavor. *Wild turkeys* or domesticated wild turkeys, available from specialty markets in some cities, while not as beautifully structured, have a remarkably good flavor, reminiscent of the old-time turkeys.

TURNIPS. There are two types of turnips in our markets, the small purple-topped white ones and the huge yellow rutabagas, available all winter. White turnips are at their best when young and very small, about egg size. Peel, slice, and cook in boiling salted water to cover until just tender. Combine with carrots or celery, or purée and mix with puréed carrot. Also good braised, or parboiled and sautéed (see page 189). Use turnips as an accompanying vegetable for boiled corned beef and cabbage (see page 16), in oxtail ragout (see page 142), or in the mirepoix for braised meats. When buying rutabagas, look for the small or medium size. Large ones are often pithy and spongy. Rutabagas, like many vegetables, are coated with wax. Peel carefully. Cut into pieces, steam, or boil in salted water to cover until tender. Mash with plenty of butter and freshly ground pepper. Mashed rutabagas are extremely good with mushroom duxelles (see page 375) swirled into them, excellent baked in a casserole with eggs, crumbs, and onions. I also like to cut white turnips and rutabagas into julienne strips, blanch them, and sauté with julienne strips of broccoli stalks (see three-vegetable sauté, page 191).

VANILLA. Probably the most popular and widely used flavoring for cakes, cookies, puddings, custards, and creams such as crème anglaise (see page 277), ice cream (see pages 331 and 332), poached peaches (see page 54), and other desserts. Use only vanilla bean or pure vanilla extract, made from vanilla beans soaked in alcohol. Artificial vanilla, known as vanillin, has only the smell and not the rich taste of the real thing. The thin, long, dark-brown vanilla bean, though expensive, will give you a lot of mileage. Put into a jar of sugar, vanilla beans aromatize the sugar and give it a permanent delicate flavor. For a fine homemade vanilla extract, slit 4 or 5 beans, put into a pint bottle of cognac or vodka, and after 2 weeks, it's ready to use. Or slit an inch of vanilla bean and scrape the tiny, flavorful black seeds into custard, an ice-cream mixture, or a cake or pudding batter. Single vanilla beans packaged in glass tubes can be found in supermarkets, but the finest, moist and almost overpowering in flavor, are sold in bulk by bakers' supply houses. Also check your local spice stores.

VINEGAR. In salad-making, remember the old adage, "A spendthrift for oil, a miser for vinegar." Vinegar should never overpower. The recent vogue in French cooking for chicken, rabbit, and game birds with a vinegar sauce is, to my palate, more fashionable than delicious. Traditionally, in many Western and Asian countries, vinegar and sugar are combined in sweet-and-sour dishes, such as sauerbraten and sweet-and-sour pork. And, of course, vinegar and sugar go together in pickling. Vinegar alone is for vinaigrette sauce and salad dressings, marinades, and court bouillon, and a touch is essential in mayonnaise (see page 281). If you can beg or borrow a "mother," the natural yeast culture that, put into leftover wine, turns it into vinegar, it is easy to make your own. Otherwise, buy the best wine vinegar you can, either white or red. Should you want a tarragon or basil flavor, steep fresh herbs in the vinegar for a week or two. For general cooking purposes, use wine or cider vinegar. For salads, use wine vinegar, rice wine vinegar, sherry vinegar, fruit vinegars, herb-flavored vinegars. For pickling and preserving, use cider vinegar or distilled white vinegar.

YAMS. Often confused with the orange-fleshed sweet potato, commonly known as the Louisiana yam. The true yam belongs to another family, and is an entirely different tuber most often seen in West Indian markets. The flesh is white or yellow and the texture rather like a potato. Boil or bake in the jacket, like potatoes. Peel, slice, and dress with butter, or purée.

YEAST. Sold commercially in two forms: granular yeast in packages and jars and fresh yeast in cakes. Both are standardized for our baking convenience and are equally efficient. Granular yeast is stocked by every supermarket, but in many communities fresh yeast is hard to find. One may have to beg a 1-pound brick of it from a friendly baker. A pound of yeast will keep for several months if you cut it into small pieces (enough for one batch of bread at a time), wrap it tightly in foil or plastic wrap, and store it in the freezer. Just remove as needed and place in warm water to proof (the foaming and swelling that proves the yeast is still active). Granular yeast dissolves best in lukewarm water (110° to 115°) with the addition of a tiny bit of sugar to make it proof faster. Fresh yeast, on the other hand, must not be put in water over 95°, or the delicate organism that causes fermentation and makes the bread rise will be killed. The best way to make sure the water is the right temperature is to test it with a very sensitive meat thermometer, the kind that registers from 0° to 220°, but soon you will get the feel for the appropriate temperature when you simply test it on your wrist.

# Carving

## CARVING A STANDING RIB ROAST

*With small sharp knife cut along rib bones, holding roast steady with fork.*

*Slice with sharp slicing knife toward the ribs. Slice thin for English cut, thick for American.*

*Transfer slices with knife and fork to serving plate or platter.*

# CARVING A TURKEY

With fork to balance, remove leg and thigh at joint.

Slice section from the drumstick and the thigh on separate board or platter.

With sharp, pointed knife remove wing at joint.

*Continued*

With fork to balance and
sharp carving knife, cut
medium-thin, long slices
of meat.

When meat has
been sliced away,
turn bird and
proceed with
other side in the
same manner.

# CARVING A LEG OF LAMB

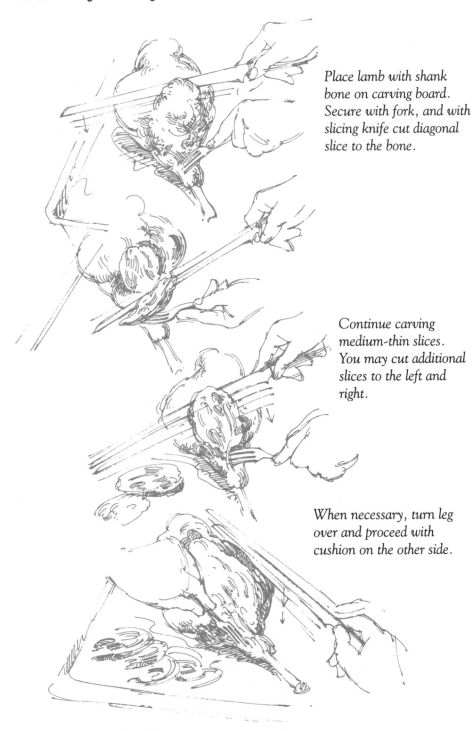

Place lamb with shank bone on carving board. Secure with fork, and with slicing knife cut diagonal slice to the bone.

Continue carving medium-thin slices. You may cut additional slices to the left and right.

When necessary, turn leg over and proceed with cushion on the other side.

# CARVING A GOOSE

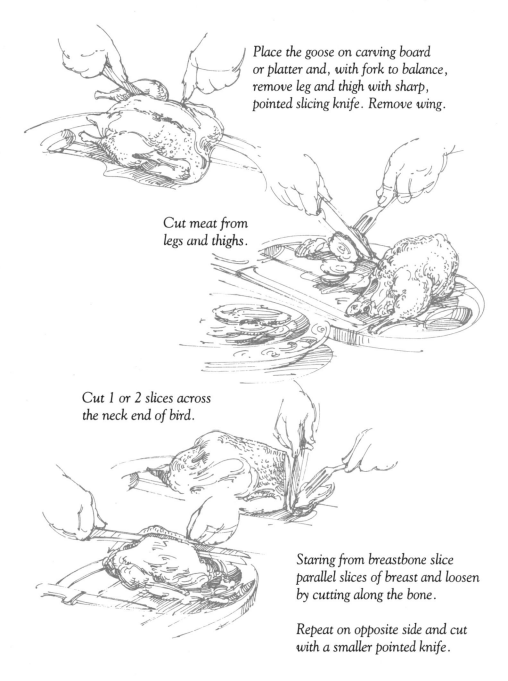

Place the goose on carving board or platter and, with fork to balance, remove leg and thigh with sharp, pointed slicing knife. Remove wing.

Cut meat from legs and thighs.

Cut 1 or 2 slices across the neck end of bird.

Staring from breastbone slice parallel slices of breast and loosen by cutting along the bone.

Repeat on opposite side and cut with a smaller pointed knife.

# Index

clarified, 177, 344–345
cream frosting, 257, 258
herb or flavored, 99, 104, 361
salt, 344
unsalted (sweet), 344
buttermilk and avocado soup, cold, 306
butternut squash, *see* squash, winter

## C

cabbage, 345
blanched, 15
boiled, 345
coleslaw, 296–297, 345; spicy, 297; sweet-
and-sour, 297
red, 345; braised, with apples, 345;
braised with chestnuts, 153; shredded,
vinaigrette, 295
in salad, 291, 345
with sautéed pheasant, 171
savoy, 345
stuffed, 25–26, 345
vinaigrette, 295
*see also* sauerkraut
cakes, 250–252; doneness, testing for, 2;
mixing by hand, 2, 252–255; pans and
equipment, 9–10, 250–252
crumbs, as thickener, 285
flour, 252, 355; to sift, 251–252, 253
génoise: with butter cream, 257–258;
with orange Bavarian-cream, 322–332;
with trifle, 323
1-2-3-4, 252–255
savarin with apricot glaze, 255–256
California gazpacho, 304
calf's brains, 372–373
*fritto misto*, 198–199
calf's feet, 126, 373
calf's liver, 373
*fritto misto*, 198–199

steaks, broiled, 109
calf's sweetbreads, *see* sweetbreads
cannellini (white beans), *see* dried beans
cannelloni, quick, 218
with port, 313
caper sauce, 275
caramel coloring, 24, 275–276
caraway seed, 393
*carpaccio*, 289, 308
carrots, 186, 345
boiled, 186, 345
and cucumber ring, with
crabmeat, 325–326
poached, à la Grecque, 53–54
puréed, 52
roasted, 92
sautéed, 185; three-vegetable, 191; Vichy,
186
vinaigrette, 295
carving, 61
beef: flank steak, 101; rib roast, 64, 399
(illustrated); sirloin steak, 99
duck, 85
goose, 403 (illustrated)
knife, 4
lamb, leg of, 402 (illustrated)
pork, roast loin of, 68
turkey, 400–401 (illustrated)
casseroles, 210, 211
cassis ice cream, 332
with crème de cassis: and peaches, 332,
and raspberry purée, 332
catfish: fried, 202
cauliflower, 345–346; to buy, 345
baked, with béchamel sauce and cheese,
345
boiled, 345
flowerets: boiled, 345; poached, à la
Grecque, 53–54

squab chickens, 348; roast, cold, 77, 78;
    roast, stuffed, 77–78
  stock or broth, 19, 20; double, 19, 20
chicory (curly endive), 357
  salad, 291, 357
chicory, witloof, *see* endive
chili con carne, Jeanne Owen's, 142
chili peppers, hot, 303, 383
chilling, 315–316
Chinese parsley, *see* coriander
chives, 360, 379
  butter, 104
chocolate, 349; to keep, 349; to melt, 349
  roll, 227, 228–229
  sauce, 244–245; custard, 278
  soufflé, 227
chorizo, 388
Choron, sauce, 280
*choux* pastry, *see* pastry, *choux*
cilantro, *see* coriander
*cima di vitello*, 373
cinnamon, 393
clams, 389; to clean, 122, 389
  bisque, cold, 324
  Casino, 121
  quiche, 238
  sauce, 39
  steamed, 389
  stuffed, 122
clarifying:
  broth, 21, 23
  butter, 177, 344–345
  oil, 195
cloves, 393
cod, 353, 355
  baked, 266
  fillets, broiled, 112–114
  salt cod, 353
  steak, sauté Provençale, 179

*coeur à la crème*, 314
coffee custard sauce, 278
coffee *granité*, 335
coleslaw, 345
  favorite, 296–297
  spicy, 297
  sweet-and-sour, 297
collards, 358
cookies, 259; kinds, 259
  meringue kisses, 261
  sand tarts, 260
  Scotch shortbread, 259–260
*coq au vin*, 147–148
Corbitt, Helen: Roquefort mousse with
    seafood salad, 317–319
coriander (Chinese parsley; cilantro), 360
corn, 349; to buy, 349
  on the cob, boiled, 50, 349
  sautéed, 185
  succotash, 342
  vinaigrette, 295
corn bread, 250
corned beef, 367; to buy, 367
  boiled, and cabbage, 16–18
  hash ring, 265
cornmeal, 349
  as breading, 349
  corn bread, 250
  mush, 44–45; fried, 45; sautéed, with
    game, 86, 87
  as thickening, 349
corn oil, 195, 377–378
  teriyaki marinade, 103
corn salad, *see* field salad
cornstarch: as thickener, 270–271, 278, 315
cos lettuce, *see* romaine
*cotechino*, 29, 388
  poached, with sauerkraut, 29
cottage cheese, 346

custard, 212
    crème brûlée, 95, 123–124
    sauce (crème anglaise), 277–278;
        Bavarian cream, orange, 322–323;
        chocolate, 278; coffee, 278; génoise,
        257–258; liqueur or spirits, 200, 278;
        trifle, 323
cutting, 3

## D

dandelion greens:
    salad, 291, 357
    sautéed, with bacon, 358
deviled beef bones, 102
deviled breast of lamb, 176
deviled kidneys, 110
diable, sauce, 277
dicing, 5
dill, 360–361
    in salad, 291, 293; mushroom, 293
    sauce, 275
doughnuts, 195
    raised, 208
duck, 84, 351; doneness, testing for, 85;
    frozen, 84, 351
    braised, with beans, 149
    broiled, 105–106; duckling, 105;
        peppered, 106
    roast, 84; and lentil casserole, 264; with
        peaches, 84–85
    wild, 351; broiled, teriyaki marinade, 97;
        roast, 87–88
dumplings, 45
    and old-fashioned chicken, 45–46
duxelles, 375

## E

eggplant, 351–352; to remove excess water,
    351

broiled, 117, 118; with Parmesan cheese,
    118
    French fried, 204–205
    poached, à la Grecque, 53–54
    ratatouille, 145
    stuffed, 263
eggs, 352; to freeze or store, 352; to separate,
    2, 221–222, 352; whites, 2, 352; yolks,
    352
    hard-boiled, 16
    lemon soup, 286–287
    mollet, 16, 48
    omelet, perfect, 182–184; fillings, 169,
        184
    poached, 47
    sauce, 275
    scrambled, perfect, 181–182; additions to,
        182; in spinach roll, 224–225
    soft-boiled, 16
    as thickener, 271, 315
electrical appliances, 7–8, 12
endive (Belgian or French; witloof chicory),
    357
    braised, 189
    salad, 291, 357
    sautéed, with brown butter, 189
endive, curly, *see* chicory
equipment, cooking, 1–12
escarole, 357
    salad, 291, 357
*estouffat de Noël*, 140

## F

fat:
    barding, 66, 69, 86, 88, 370
    frying, 195
    goose, 82
    lard and pig fat, 66, 67, 86, 88, 195, 363,
        370

in salad, 291

sauces: Greek, 284–285; Greek, variations, 318; and oil, 38–39; oil and anchovies, 39

sautéing with, 379

vinaigrette sauce, 291

gazpacho, California, 304

génoise:

with butter cream, 257–258

with orange Bavarian cream, 322–323

with trifle, 323

ginger, 356, 393

ice cream, 332

*glacé de viande*, 15, 24

gnocchi, 45

potato and semolina, 46

goose, 81–82, 356; to carve, 403; doneness, testing for, 83; frozen, 81; to truss, 73–74

fat, 82

roast, with prune and apple stuffing, 82–83

goulash, Viennese, 141

Grand Marnier soufflé, 225–226

*granité*, 334

coffee, 335

lemon, 335

grapefruit: to peel segments, 301

broiled, 120

salad, with avocado and onion, 301

and sherry jelly, 328

gratin of greens, 262

*gravlax*, 289, 309–310

Greek garlic sauce, 284–285

variations, 285

greens (for cooking), 358–359

boiled, 50

gratin, 262

greens (for salads), 291–292, 356–358

mixing with hands, 2, 292

*gremolata*, 146

grilling, *see* broiling and grilling

Gruyère cheese, 347

quiche, Swiss onion, 239

salad, 301

guacamole, 303–304

variations, 304

## H

haddock, 353–354

baked, 266

fillets, 353; broiled, 112–114

smoked, 353–354

halibut, 354

steaks: broiled, 114; sautéed, 178; sauté Provençale, 179

ham, 371–372; to remove excess salt by blanching, 15; to remove excess salt by soaking, 70

baked, 70, 371; glazed, 70–71; glazed, cold, 71

broiled steaks, 109

canned, 372

country, 70, 371

crêpes, 218

fresh, 371; kebabs, 111; marbelized, 69–70

mousse, cold, 320

omelet, 184

picnic, 371

quiche Lorraine, 237

ready-to eat, 70, 371

sautéed, 158

in scrambled eggs, 182

Smithfield, 372

in spinach roll, 224–225

and veal pâté, 329–330

Virginia, 371, 372

hamburger, 366
    broiled, 101
    sautéed, 161–162
hash:
    chicken, in omelet, 184
    corned beef ring, 265
hazelnuts (filberts), 376
headcheese, 370
    mock, *see* jellied veal
health salad, 300
hearts:
    beef, 365
    chicken, broiled, 95
    lamb, 369
    pork, 370
    veal, 374
herbs, 359–362; to buy, 359; to keep, 359;
        ratio of dried to fresh, 359; steeping, 16
    bouquet garni, 360
    butter, 99, 104
    marinade, 97
    omelet, 184
    rice, 41
    scrambled eggs, 182
    vinaigrette sauce, 291
hollandaise sauce, 95, 271–272, 279–281
    with anchovies, 281
    with mint, 108
    with mustard, 280
    with tomato paste (sauce Choron), 280
    variations, 280–281
hominy, 362
    grits, sautéed, 86, 88, 362
horseradish, 362
    sauce, 274
huckleberries, 343

## I

ice cream, 316, 331

apricot, ice-tray, 333
banana, 332
cassis, 332
ginger, 332
lemon, 333
peach, 333
strawberry, 333
vanilla: basic, 331; French, 332
ices, see *granité*; sherbert
Iranian cucumber and yogurt soup, 305
Irish stew, 127, 144
Italian link sausages, 388–389
    broiled, 109
    and lentil casserole, 264–265

## J

jellied veal, 22, 326–327
jelly:
    currant, glaze, 235
    sherry and grapefruit, 328
Jerusalem artichokes, 362
"julienne," how to, 4

## K

kale, 359
kebabs, 95, 110–111
    beef shashlik, 112
    marinades, 97, 101, 103
    shish kebab, 111–112
*kibbeh nayé*, 289, 306–307
kidney beans, *see* beans, kidney
kidneys:
    broiled, 95
    lamb, 374; beefsteak and kidney pudding,
        27–28; sautéed, in omelet, 184
    pork, 370–371
    sautéed, 156
    veal, 368; beefsteak and kidney pie,
        242–243; beefsteak and kidney

pudding, 27–28; broiled, 110; to clean,
243; deviled, 110; flambe, 173; *fritto
misto*, 198–199
kielbasa, 29, 389
poached, with sauerkraut, 29
KitchenAid electric mixer, 7, 12
knives, 2–6, 8
care of, 2
to sharpen, 6
knockwurst, 388
and lentil casserole, 265
kohlrabi, 362

## L

lamb, 367–369; cuts, 368–369; doneness,
testing for, 107, 108
brains, 368
braised, 144; shanks, and lentil casserole,
264; shoulder, with ratatouille, 145
breast, 369; deviled, 176
broiled or grilled, 94, butterflied leg, 95,
97, 108; marinades, 97
chops, 368, broiled, 97, 106–107
eggplant stuffed with, 293
hearts, 369
*kibbeh nayé*, 289, 306–307
kidneys, 368; beefsteak and kidney
pudding, 27–28; sautéed, in omelet,
184
leg, 369; butterflied, broiled or grilled, 95,
97, 100; to carve, 402; roast, 61–63;
roast, baker's style, 63
liver, 369
roast, 59; leg, 61–63; leg, baker's style, 63
shish kebab, 111–112
stew, Irish, 144
sweetbreads, *see* sweetbreads
testicles, broiled or sautéed, 369
tongues, 368

lard, 195, 363
larding, 69, 370
leeks, 378–379; to clean, 378
poached, à la Grecque, 53–54
lemons, 363
*granité*, 335
ice cream, 333
mousse, frozen, 319
lentil casserole, 264–265
lettuce: kinds, 356–358
blanched, 15
braised, 152
in salad, 291–292, 356–358
in stuffing, 357
*see also* endive
lima beans, *see* beans, lima
limes, 363
liqueur custard sauce, 278
liver:
beef, 367; *bourguignon*, 162–163
broiled, 95
calf's, 373–374; *fritto misto*, 198–199;
steaks, broiled, 109
chicken: broiled, 95; sautéed, 169
lamb, 369
pork, 371
sautéed, 156
lobster, 390–391; to buy, 33
*à la nage*, 33
*au gratin*, 123
boiled, 33
creamed, in celery and pecan ring, 264
in cucumber and carrot ring, 325–326
spinach and seafood soup, cold, 287
London broil, 96, 101
Lyonnaise potatoes, 188

## M

mace, 393

soup, cream of, 286
in tomato sauce, 40
mussels, 391; to clean, 36
soup, 36
mustard, 375
hollandaise, 280
mayonnaise, 283
sauce, 274; sweet, 309–310
vinaigrette sauce, 291
mustard greens: boiled, 50
sautéed, 359

## N

nectarines, 376
New England boiled dinner, 16–18
nutmeg, 393
nuts, 376–377; to buy, 376; to keep, 376
roll, 228
as thickener, 271, 286

## O

ocean perch fillets, 355
oils, 195, 377–378; to clarify and purify, 195; to keep, 290
vinaigrette sauce, 290
olive oil, 377; to keep, 290, 377
marinades, 114; red wine, 89, 112; teriyaki, 103; vermouth and herbs, 97; white wine, 116
vinaigrette sauce, 290
omelet, perfect, 182–184
fillings, 169, 184
1-2-3-4 cake, 252–255
onions, 378–379; to keep, 378
French fried rings, 158, 199
green (scallions), 378; poached, à la Grecque, 53–54; in scrambled eggs, 182
omelet, 184

pearl or pickling, 378
quiche, Swiss, 239
red or Italian, 378; avocado and grapefruit (or orange) salad, 301; avocado and tomato salad, 299
in salad, 292; with oranges, 88, 158
sautéed, 158, 185; with cheese, 158; with wine, 158
soup, *au gratin*, 34
stuffed, 263
vinaigrette, 295
white, large (Bermuda), 378
white, small, 378; to peel, 68, 378; poached, à la Grecque, 53–54
yellow globe (Spanish), 378; braised, 154; French fried, 199
*see also* chives; garlic; leeks; shallots
oranges, 379; to buy, 379; to peel segments, 301
Bavarian cream, 322–323; génoise, 257–258
frosting and filling for 1-2-3-4 cake, 253, 255
mandarins, 363
marmalade soufflé, 229
salad: with onion, 88, 379; with onion and avocado, 301
sauce, for duck, 277
sugared, 313
temple, 363, 379
Owen, Jeanne:
chicken sautés, 158–159
chili con carne, 142
oxtail, 366
braised, 142–143
broth, 142–143
ragout, 142–143
oysters, 391
Casino, 121

black walnuts, 178; with herbs, 178

tuna:

  mayonnaise, for cold roast veal, 284

  and white bean salad, 302; with
    anchovies, 302

turkey, 78, 396; to carve, 400–401;
    doneness, testing for, 80, 81; to truss,
    73–74

  casserole, with rice, 266

  crêpes, with mushrooms, 218

  frozen, 396

  quiche, 237

  roast, 59, 396; without stuffing, 81; with
    two stuffings, 78–80

  wild, 396

Turkish cucumber and yogurt soup, 305

turnips, 397

  blanched, 15

  glazed, 189

  greens: boiled, 50; sautéed, 359

  and mushrooms, sautéed, 187

  sautéed, 185; three–vegetable, 191

  see also rutabagas

V

vanilla, 397

  extract, homemade, 397

  ice cream: basic, 331; basic, variations,
    332; French, 332; French, variations,
    333

veal, 372–374; cuts, 372–373

  aspic, 22

  birds western style, 137–138

  braised, 131; breast, stuffed, 134–135;
    breast, stuffed, cold, 135; shoulder or
    leg, 131–133

  broth, see stock or broth below

  chops, 373; Niçoise, 136

  and ham pâté, 329–330

hearts, 374

jellied, 22, 326–327

kebabs, 111

kidneys, 374; beefsteak and kidney pie,
    242–243; beefsteak and kidney
    pudding, 27–28; broiled, 110; to clean,
    243; deviled, 110; flambe, 173; fritto
    misto, 198–199

knuckle, 373; in braising liquid, 126

roast, 58–59; cold, with smoked salmon
    mayonnaise, 284; cold, with tuna
    mayonnaise, 284

sausage, 374, 388

sautéed, 172

scallops (scaloppine), 156, 373; fines
    herbes, 173; fritto misto, 198–199

stock or broth, 18, 19, 22, 131–132

tongue, 372

vitello tonnato, short-cut, 284

Wiener schnitzel, 204; with egg and
    anchovies, 204

vegetables: pressure cooker, 18

  blanched, 14, 15–16

  boiled, 14, 50–51

  braised, 128

  fritto misto, 194; with meat, 198–199

  kebabs, 95, 110, 111, 112

  mirepoix, 126–127

  omelet, 184

  poached, à la Grecque, 53–54

  purée, basic, 51

  roasted, 92

  sautéed, 158, 185; three-vegetable, 191

  soup, four-day, 35

  stock, 19

  stuffed, 263

  vinaigrette, 293–295

  see also salads

velouté sauce, 274
　with chicken broth, 87
venison, 89
　marinade, 89
　roast, 89; haunch, 91; rack, 90
verte, sauce, 283
Viennese goulash, 141
vinaigrette sauce: basic, 290–292
　garlic, 291
　herbs, 291
　mustard, 291
　vegetables, 293–295
vinegar, 397
　wine vinegar, 290, 397, 398
*vitello tonnato*, short-cut, 284

## W

walnuts, 377
　black, 377; sauce, 178
　eggplant, stuffed, 263
　zucchini, sautéed, 190
watercress, 358
　omelet, 184
　puréed, with spinach, 359
　salad, 291–292, 358
watemelon, drunken, 314
wax beans, *see* beans, wax
waxed paper, 12, 250–251
weisswurst, 388
wheat, cracked, *see* bulghur
whitefish: baked, 266
white sauce, basic, 269, 272–273
　to thicken or thin, 273
　variations, 274–275
white wine:
　court bouillon: for fish, 30–31; for
　　shellfish, 33
　marinade, 116
　quail sautéed in, 172

sauce, for fish, 32, 274
　vinegar, 295, 397–398
whiting:
　broiled fillets, 112–114
　fried, 202–203
Wiener schnitzel, 204
　with egg and anchovies, 204
wine:
　in braising liquid, 126
　marinades, 89, 112, 116–117
　vinegar, 295, 397–398
　*see also* red wine; white wine
witloof chicory, *see* endive

## Y

yams, 398
yeast, 210–211, 398; fresh, to keep, 398
　to proof, 246, 398
　bread, 246, 247
yogurt:
　and cucumber soup Iranian, 305; Turkish,
　　305
　and lemon juice dressing, 294
Yorkshire pudding, 65

## Z

*zampone*, 371
zrazys Nelson, 163
zucchini, 394
　blanched, 15
　fried, 194, 196–197
　*fritto misto*, 198–199
　gratin of greens, 262
　poached, à la Grecque, 53–54
　ratatouille, 145
　sautéed, 185, 190–191; three-vegetable,
　　191; with walnuts, 190
　stuffed, 263

# A Note About the Author

Born in Portland, Oregon, in 1903, James Beard was destined to find his calling in the food profession. He acquired a sophisticated palate while still a boy, thanks to the good example of his mother, who had run a small residence hotel with a fine kitchen, but he first aspired to be a singer and then an actor. He failed to make his mark as either, and in the late 1930s joined two friends in a catering service in New York. It was called Hors d'Oeuvre, Inc. and led to the publication in 1940 of his first book, *Hors d'Oeuvre and Canapés*, which remained in print for nearly sixty years and has become a classic. More than twenty cookbooks followed, including the best-selling *James Beard Cookbook*, *James Beard's American Cookery*, *James Beard's Theory and Practice of Good Cooking*, and *Beard on Bread*. In 1946 Beard appeared on television's first cooking program, and in the 1950s he started the classes that grew into his renowned cooking school. Throughout his career he was sought after as a consultant by restaurants and food producers. On behalf of the latter he toured the country continuously, giving lectures and food demonstrations. He was an exponent of simple, honest cooking, using the best ingredients, and an early believer in the existence of genuine American cuisine. By the time he died, in 1985, he was generally acknowledged to be the country's most influential food authority.